PM: A New Deal in Journalism

PM: A New Deal in Journalism 1940–1948

Paul Milkman

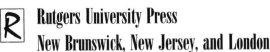
Rutgers University Press
New Brunswick, New Jersey, and London

Library of Congress Cataloging-in-Publication Data

Milkman, Paul.
    PM : a new deal in journalism / Paul Milkman.
      p. cm.
    Includes bibliographical references and index.
    ISBN 0-8135-2434-2 (alk. paper)
    1. PM (New York, N.Y. : Daily)   2. PM (New York, N.Y. : Weekly)
   3. Press and politics—United States.   4. New Deal, 1933–1945.   5. United
States—Politics and government—1933–1945. I. Title.
PN4899.N42P485 1997
071'.471'09044—dc21   97-5675
                                                    CIP

British Cataloguing-in-Publication information available

Manufactured in the United States of America

*Dedicated to Judith Milkman, 1925–1972.
Like* PM, *she was against people who push other people around.*

CONTENTS

Illustrations follow page 84

ACKNOWLEDGMENTS

T he idea for this study originated in conversations with my former graduate adviser, the late Warren Susman. His warm encouragement in the
early phases of my work was vital to my undertaking the effort. Professor
Norman Markowitz has been a friendly and responsive graduate chairman. He has read several versions of what appears here, and his valuable
contributions have enriched the text. Professors Dee Garrison, John Leggett, and
David Oshinsky have made careful and acute observations.

Librarians and research staff at the Forty-second Street branch of the New
York Public Library, Mugar Memorial Library at Boston University, the Nieman
Journalism Center at Harvard, and the Manuscripts and Archives Division of
Sterling Memorial Library at Yale were generous with time and information.
Yale's Judy Schiff takes a friendly interest in the work of scholars. She knew that
PM's long-withheld official papers were finally available at the Nieman Center.
Those papers are integral to this work.

Without vital support from two families (my own and *PM*'s), this study could
never have been undertaken or completed. Though the *New York Times* receives
some unfavorable attention herein, its unchallenged stature as the "newspaper
of record" proved to be essential. A single one-line author's query below a book
review brought dozens of responses from *PM* veterans. The interviews that resulted have greatly enriched this work. Mary Morris Lawrence and Rae Weimer read and commented on early versions of the first two chapters. Penn
Kimball read most of the original manuscript; his support for this effort has
transformed it.

The remarkably supportive and competent staff at Rutgers University Press—
Managing Editor Marilyn Campbell, Production Coordinator Trish Politi, Copy
Editor Diane Grobman, whose meticulous work is awe inspiring, and Editor in
Chief Leslie Mitchner, whose loving encouragement and belief in this book have
been vital in sustaining my effort—is the best possible team for a first-time
author.

The opportunity to complete this long-deferred study arose when I took a
sabbatical from my teaching job in order to spend the second year of my daughter

Caitlyn's life as her principal child-care provider. When my wife, Catherine, returned from work, we "played tag," enabling me to carry on this effort. My long study days pouring over *PM* microfilm were made possible by the generous time and caring provided by Esther Kaczmarek for her granddaughter. Emily and Norman Milkman, Marilyn Milkman, Catherine Kaczmarek Milkman, and Rebecca Alson-Milkman have all read and improved sections of the manuscript. Like them, Jesse Alson-Milkman had to make do with a part-time family member whose obsessive interest in a fifty-year-old newspaper often blotted the present from his mind.

Like *communist* and even *liberal*, the word *comrade* has a forbidden aura today, conjuring up visions of alien conspiracies. It is nonetheless the best word to describe thirty years of friendship with Steve Fraser. Together we fought now-ancient political battles. Today we continue to struggle to understand and define the world and our place in it. Steve has read and made substantial criticisms of this work which have led me to recast much of what follows.

Although I was born months after the final issue of *PM* was sold, the newspaper remains alive for me. The interpretations and presentations of fact herein are my responsibility alone.

PM: A New Deal in Journalism

INTRODUCTION

On Tuesday, 18 June 1940, hundreds of small burnt-orange trucks left industrial Brooklyn, bound for the suburbs of New York. Inside were bundles of the first day's edition of a new tabloid, pledged to revolutionize journalism. After several months of an enormous publicity campaign containing grandiose claims, the paper's editors had printed over 400,000 copies. The trucks for the suburbs and separate newspaper racks for the city's newsstands had been made necessary by the vigorous opposition of the powerful *New York Daily News*, which despite its mammoth circulation of over two million copies a day, feared the potential of the entering upstart. As the trucks pulled away from the loading docks, they were surrounded by hordes of eager customers. Few of the trucks made it to their destinations. Most of the drivers gave up, selling the papers in some cases at ten times the decidedly upscale printed price of five cents to the near hysterical crowds preventing their movement. All of the newspapers except those kept for souvenirs by hopeful staff members were gone in a few hours.

Almost precisely eight years later, on 22 June 1948, the last edition of *PM* was sold in New York. Having achieved a modest, steady daily circulation of slightly over 150,000 copies, the paper had proved to be an enormous financial failure. Its principal publisher estimated he had lost about $7 million in the first six years of publication.

Nonetheless, during its brief history, *PM* was responsible for scores of innovations in newspaper publishing. It leaped decades ahead of any of its competition in its masterly use of photography, presenting clearer and more vivid pictures to its daily audience than ever before or since. It pioneered the use of color, aesthetically pleasing layouts, and creative use of drawn art and graphics. It championed consumer news long before anyone understood the meaning of the term. The paper's sophisticated arts critiques matched those found in any mass-circulation periodical. It brought daily news of radio programming to newspaper readers, breaking a boycott unanimously practiced by the competition. It did all of this through most of its history while refusing paid advertising for fear of jeopardizing its independence.

Moreover, *PM*'s revolution in journalism was political. The paper was conceived of as a fighting liberal crusader. Tilting against the prevailing conservatism of the established press, the tabloid championed U.S. intervention to defeat fascism and trumpeted the rights of unionists, Jews, and blacks while exposing those who would oppress them. Coming to creation as the 1940 presidential campaign progressed, *PM* joined the *New York Post* as the only New York papers boosting the reelection of President Roosevelt.

PM's writers believed in the New Deal. They defined it as a continuation of the revolutionary democracy of the United States, bringing justice to millions previously unrepresented in the nation's ruling parties. The editors and writers of the feisty tabloid were archetypical of the shift in American intellectuals, moving toward a committed political stance after decades of disgusted distance from American political life.

That revulsion began in the first years after the Civil War, when rapid economic growth in the United States ran parallel with the development of crass materialism. The era of the robber barons was dissected in the work of Frank Norris. The withdrawal of American authors was symbolized by Henry James's deliberate self-exile to Europe. By the 1920s' "era of good feeling," when American political leaders endorsed isolation from international politics while ignoring (or supporting) growing inequities in class and race relations at home, an entire expatriate generation fled: Hemingway, Fitzgerald, and Stein made plain their abhorrence of dominant American values by abandoning native shores for the romance of old Europe. Sinclair Lewis, who stayed, satirically dissected the triumph of bourgeois materialism in his brilliant Zenith novels. The Sacco and Vanzetti case cast those who did not abandon politics as radical opponents of a regime which tacitly condoned political murder.

The onset of the depression brought an end to disengagement. As the dominant Republican political coalition shook, intellectuals sensed possibilities for fundamental transformation of American society. Crusading liberals, radicals, socialists, or communists appealed to disenfranchised masses; thinkers now wanted to make history instead of being repelled by it. Solutions to society's woes, once seen as hopelessly unavailable by the few willing to recognize problems, appeared in bunches on the horizon.

The growth of the labor movement throughout the 1930s provided evidence that old power relations were being transformed. As General Motors and U.S. Steel acceded to CIO representation, the absolute power of the industrial giants to determine the lives of the average American was successfully amended. The apparent sympathy of President Roosevelt toward union recognition in the workplace and within the New Deal hierarchy turned many intellectuals' early distrust into veneration.

The president was aided by intangibles: an enormous smile, a bevy of brilliant speech writers, a magnificent speaking voice. Not the least important was his quick appreciation of the technological explosion in communications during the early twentieth century. Radio became his instrument for undercutting political enemies and building coalitions even before he became president. He released a documentary sound movie in 1930 as an aid to his reelection as New York governor. He used his considerable charm to entrance journalists even when their editors hated him.

Roosevelt was a master at obscuring differences. Capable of militant rhetoric (he promised during his second inauguration to chase moneylenders from the temple), he was as skillful in maintaining alliances with the old-style political bosses in Democratic urban and southern power bases. When Roosevelt ran for reelection the last time, in 1944, he was supported by racist demagogue Theodore Bilbo and by NAACP founder W.E.B. Du Bois; Ronald Reagan and Woody Guthrie both campaigned for him.

The actual and apparent changes of the New Deal attracted the innovators who founded *PM*. The president himself worked to support the paper; its writers pictured him at their side in exposing injustice and righting the wrongs they detailed. Frequently they presented a mythologized version of President Roosevelt; occasionally such a version required self-hypnosis or at least willful forgetting of inconvenient facts. For years the paper's staff seemed unable to believe that State Department functionaries served the president who appointed them; less frequently Justice and War Department personnel seemed independent of presidential leadership as well.

Paradoxically the mythology proved empowering. From the first, *PM*ers presumed with breezy impertinence that it was being studied in Washington as assiduously as the *New York Times*. While the *Times*'s arrogance was (and is) reflected in the on-high detachment of its editorial voice, *PM*, particularly in its early days, frenetically rallied its readers to rout Roosevelt's "enemies" in Congress and even within the administration, "knowing" that they stood for what Franklin Roosevelt stood for, or should have stood for. Indeed, *PM* was read daily by at least three Supreme Court justices, by several cabinet officers, by the vice president, and by the first lady, who plugged it in her newspaper column in the Scripps-Howard press. She was a personal friend of the paper's onetime labor and national editor and of its lawyer; the Supreme Court justices were all friends of the paper's leading editorialist after 1943.

The heady sense of appreciation where it mattered helped to sustain the lively editorial independence and self-confident bravado which was *PM*'s style. When writers exposed fascist conspiracies, antiunion activity, or racist vigilantes, they did it from the perspective of absolute confidence in their outlook and a deep belief that their values were shared by the chief executive.

Ironically, *PM* made its entry into the world at precisely the moment when Roosevelt was abandoning New Deal politics to create an interventionist coalition. Many of those he welcomed into his administration—like Republican stalwarts Henry Stimson and Frank Knox—were interventionists not because they were antifascists, but because they saw the need to protect the United States from a victory by the German Reich. While the new paper touted him as the great leader of a liberal alternative to fascist rule, the president built bridges to the industrial giants he had once denounced in order to win them to his prowar stance. *PM* celebrated institutional changes which were largely over. It continued to presume a left-liberal alliance when the president had widened the door to include what some might have called the class enemy.

PM's writers were hardly alone. The president held the left's affections even while distancing himself from its positions. He was aided by the liberal views advanced by his wife, several administration officials, and above all by Vice President Wallace, whose rhetoric exactly matched *PM*'s beliefs about the world at war and the one at peace to follow.

Roosevelt's death and the rapid advance of violently anti–New Deal politics brought the paper to crisis. Its writers now faced a difficult divide. To remain constant to its most cherished beliefs meant to be treated as irrelevant or worse in the new America. Those who had grown used to the heady feeling of being listened to found their own politics altered by the new political climate. Those who insisted on the essential correctness of the past vision found themselves alone. Though there are many particular reasons for the demise of *PM*, perhaps the most important was the cerebral hemorrhage suffered by Franklin Roosevelt in April 1945. The newspaper needed not only his life but the illusion of influencing power he allowed his supporters.

FDR's passing came just weeks before the surrender of Nazi Germany and signaled the expiration of a broad political culture which perhaps found its clearest expression in the pages of *PM*. Antifascism was a political credo, but it was more: It represented an emotional and cultural commitment to change in the United States as much as in Europe and Asia. The depression decade seemed to present two clear alternatives for the future of the world: the violent xenophobia and military hatred of threatening fascism or the romanticized version of eliminating class oppression, racial intolerance, and economic royalty allegedly to be found in trade union solidarity in the United States, popular-front governments in France and Spain, and in the much beleaguered Soviet Union. One need not be a communist or even be sympathetic to the USSR to embrace the wider ethos of antifascism.

In New York in 1940 the symbols of antifascism were everywhere: in the combative persona of the city's multiethnic mayor Fiorello La Guardia, in the mammoth heroic representation of workers painted and sculpted not only in the lobbies and forecourts of post offices but in frescoes at (of all places) Rockefeller Center, in Paul Robeson's singing the popular-front patriotism of "Ballad for Americans" on NBC Radio, or available at the neighborhood movie theater. There Tom Joad struggled against planter violence in John Ford's reverent filming of John Steinbeck's *Grapes of Wrath*, and Jefferson Smith and a year later John Doe defeated cynical and conspiratorial political bosses who plotted to crush the common citizen and democracy. The ultimate Everyman—the Little Tramp—finally accepted the sound revolution long enough to overthrow a comic Hitler in Charlie Chaplin's *Great Dictator*.

PM expressed this commitment on each of its thirty-two pages. Every battle for trade union rights, every crusade against racial and religious discrimination in New York, every exposé of a crooked merchant was perceived as a missile aimed at Hitlerism. Tom Meany and Joe Cummiskey initiated sports-page battles to integrate baseball; Robeson's concerts at City College's Lewishown Stadium were featured on the arts pages; comic-page hero Vic Jordan managed to conduct a soap-opera life while aiding the French underground. Even the cheesecake layouts had a plebeian tone.

By the time *PM* ceased publication, antifascism was becoming an extinct political culture. The immediate movement from World War II to cold war made attention to class inequality not only extraneous, but unpatriotic as well. Those who retained allegiance to the old culture reproduced it in increasingly irrelevant venues. Soon, to advance such notions was to invite government persecution.

Yet the antifascist culture was the apex of American intellectual social involvement. It marked an optimistic commitment to the democratic transformation of the United States.

PM came into existence at the culmination of a process which did in fact change, though not revolutionize, power correlations in the United States. The paper assumed those changes were immutable. Its writers defined a new connection between dissenting intellectuals and liberal politics. One of the consequences was the creation of a mythology—a Rooseveltian paradigm—from which political thinkers have never recovered. Each generation finds a paler Roosevelt, a politician ever less committed to social change and economic justice: from Stevenson to Kennedy to Clinton (a right-to-work governor as liberal champion). In *PM* we see the roots of intellectual attraction to enlightened power at the moment it offered the most hope.

1 | The Roots of *PM*

Young Penn Kimball disembarked from the blue-ribbon French liner *Normandie* in New York on 31 August 1939 prepared to begin his lifelong career as a journalist. He was returning from a two-year Rhodes Scholarship, which had considerably broadened the education begun at Lawrenceville Preparatory School and Princeton University. Kimball had proven himself to be an unusual Princetonian even before going abroad, though not in his background. Descended from an old-line New England Protestant family, Kimball traced his ancestry back to Salem "witch" Rebecca Nurse, immortalized in Arthur Miller's *Crucible*. His father manufactured electrical appliances; his mother had attended the 1920 Republican convention, which nominated Warren Gamaliel Harding for president. His parents were not typical Republicans, however. When the depression began, there was no governmental agency in New Britain, Connecticut, to aid the unemployed. Kimball's father helped form a manufacturers' group to provide relief. His mother's convention experience made her loathe most politicians; she told Penn she once voted for Socialist party candidate Norman Thomas for president. During the depression, she served on the local board of education and battled any attempts to cut teachers' salaries.

Some of his parents' more liberal mores seeped into Kimball. He traveled through New York City on trips between his New Jersey schools and Connecticut home; the breadlines and apple venders had a profound impact on him. Fascinated by politics and having made an early decision to be a newspaperman, Kimball attended political events at Princeton. He heard Secretary of Agriculture Henry Wallace speak on government policy to battle the depression and attended a discussion about the "Scottsboro boys," the black youths victimized in a hysterical southern rape trial. As a senior in 1936–1937, Kimball was chairman (editor-in-chief) of the *Daily Princetonian*. Appearing on a campus which backed Republican nominee Alfred M. Landon by about three-to-one, Kimball's editorials supported President Roosevelt for reelection. Most of the campus did not seem to notice. Politics was not a serious avocation for many Princetonians. He was noticed at home, however. When he registered as a Democrat in 1936, the *Bridgeport Herald* found his apostasy worthy of comment.

At Oxford, Kimball was surrounded by a charged atmosphere. His classmates included Edward Heath, Dennis Healey, and Roy Jenkins, all future leading British politicians. Many at Oxford were disgusted with British appeasement of Hitler's Germany and revolted by Great Britain's advocacy and enforcement of the League of Nations neutrality decisions, which helped Franco's fascist forces crush Republican Spain. Students sympathetic to the Labour Party and trade union rights were the leading antifascists. Kimball spent vacation time traveling though Europe. He "was in Austria during *Anschluss* and in Rome when the Italians invaded Albania and had just driven through the Sudetenland and Prague at the time of the Munich crisis in the late summer of 1938." A wide-eyed observer, Kimball recorded the dramatic times in passionate letters to his parents. He encountered a Nazi storm trooper and friend on the way to Vienna on the eve of *Anschluss*:

> The Brown Shirt looked on America as nothing better than a Jewish-controlled refugee station for Jews driven out of Germany, and the way he would say "Juden" was enough to make you shudder. Deutschland, he said, was now strong enough to defy the world if it had to, and if the world tried to prevent the rightful unity of Germany—especially with Sudeten-Czechoslovakia—Germany was ready to fight. . . . During all this speech both the Storm Trooper and his friend got more and more violent, shaking their fists, shouting louder and louder and beaming with more pride at every mention of "Deutschland." They sounded more and more like fanatics who had been sold on an ideal for which they were ready to fight the world—regardless of the consequences. . . . It certainly brought home to me what a tremendous emotional force lies at the back of Fascism, a force which can be whipped up to white heat at a moment's notice.

The following week in Vienna Kimball watched "the most perfectly staged affair," the ceremonial creation of "Greater Germany":

> Saturday I stood in the square before the Rathous to hear Goebbels proclaim the New Germany. As he finished, sirens and bells began sounding everywhere. 10,000 pigeons were released (supposedly carrying the good news to the homeland) and almost blocked out the sky, planes roared overhead and at the climax Der Fuehrer appeared on the balcony to receive the adulation of the masses. He said nothing, saluted only twice, but stood straight and firm with his eyes towards heaven with the screams of the people in his ears. [After journeying from Vienna to Budapest] . . . Now I shall listen to Gypsy music in the hopes that it may drown out the strains of Prussian marches—marches to which the Army of Fascism is goose stepping over the fragile body of a city whose cultural and artistic fame will long outlive the words of the "Horst Wessel."

Back in the United States, Kimball went to work in Washington. He first found work as a researcher for the Washington correspondent for *Reader's Digest*, but moved quickly to the infant *U.S. News*, owned and edited by Princeton alumnus David Lawrence. Kimball's successor as chairman of the *Daily Princetonian* was already working for Lawrence and recommended his former chief. Penn enjoyed his new job. Paid relatively well at twenty-five dollars a week, he became an active member of the fledgling American Newspaper Guild. He disagreed with his periodical's editorial policy, but found the heady atmosphere of Washington politics fascinating. He attended presidential news conferences in the Oval Office, watching the press corps "belly-up" to Roosevelt's desk, and was riveted by FDR's "performance." As the journalists hurried out to meet their deadlines, Kimball observed the president "deflate" after the strain of charming and sparring with the press was ended. One evening while dining with his father, he saw FDR carried off an elevator and placed in his wheelchair. He was impressed that Roosevelt never exposed his "helplessness" at the press conferences or at any official function.

Lawrence's opinions were conservative for reasons of principle and profit. He claimed he had "once said a friendly word about the New Deal and lost 25 advertising clients." In the face of nascent organizing by the Newspaper Guild, which successfully enrolled Penn Kimball (British Labour had made him a firm trade unionist), Lawrence held firm. He would not agree to paying time and a half for overtime until the Supreme Court ruled on its constitutionality.

Perusing the newspaper-business journal *Editor and Publisher*, Kimball chanced on an article describing the creation of a new newspaper in New York. Founded by Ralph Ingersoll, whose magic touch had reinvigorated the *New Yorker, Fortune,* and *Time,* and who had helped to create Henry Luce's newest success—*Life*—the new paper promised to revolutionize journalism. Journalists would be free to write their own ideas in their own styles, even writing their own headlines and captions on accompanying photographs. The paper was to operate democratically and would be free of advertising pressure. It was to be a liberal newspaper, almost unique in breaking with the conservative Republicanism dominating the American press. Kimball hurriedly sent in an application. Arriving in New York, he found himself interviewed by Duncan Aikman, who had been an anonymous ally in a political argument among journalists several months before at Washington's National Press Club. At the time Aikman had been working for Nelson Rockefeller at the Inter-American Affairs Department. Now he had been hired away to help establish the new paper. Aikman was delighted to be introduced to his onetime political debate partner—and to give him a job as a reporter on the national desk of *PM*. It was May 1940 and the newspaper was scheduled to make its first appearance by mid-June.[1]

Climactic times in the nation, the world, and the newspaper business mark the arrival of *PM*. Founder Ralph Ingersoll's first musings about the paper began in 1937; organizing efforts started almost immediately and were intensified during 1938 and 1939. In the United States, President Roosevelt had begun his second term, identifying "one-third of a nation ill-housed, ill-clad, ill-nourished." Promising a further extension of the New Deal, FDR suddenly lost political clout, finding his top-heavy Democratic majorities in Congress opposed to his Supreme

Court–packing plan and resistant to expensive social welfare programs. The second term accomplished little for that "one-third."

On the other hand, the victorious sit-down movement unionized most of the automotive industry, and U.S. Steel agreed to allow its workers collective bargaining. Roosevelt's refusal to bring the armed forces in to evict strikers—a policy also followed by Michigan governor Frank Murphy—made him a hero to most workers, though as William E. Leuchtenburg notes, "Essentially a 'patron' of labor, Roosevelt had far more interest in developing social legislation to help the worker than in seeing these gains secured in unions."[2] He had been late to support the Wagner Act, which legalized collective bargaining. Only after it passed the Senate did he announce it as "must" legislation, thus identifying himself with the most important labor law in the history of the United States. Following the sit-downs, the Congress of Industrial Organizations rapidly expanded into dozens of industrial fields. Attacks by businessmen and Republican politicians on the New Deal only made FDR more popular among unionists and the unorganized poor. The ever-deepening recession of 1938–1939 pushed the reluctant president back to the government public works spending which had begun recovery in 1933–1934. The passage of the Fair Labor Standards Act (which standardized the forty-hour workweek, eliminated child labor, and introduced the minimum hourly wage) was the single New Deal congressional achievement of the second term. A public posture of identification with the concerns of the common man outweighed a record of limited legislative accomplishment.[3]

Unionization spread to the fourth estate. Under the leadership of the celebrated columnist Heywood Broun, the Newspaper Guild began organizing editorial employees in 1933. Affiliating with the American Federation of Labor in 1936, the guild shifted to the CIO in 1937, after the General Motors sit-down strike had kept the new industrial labor federation on the front pages for months. More than a bread-and-butter union, the Newspaper Guild took committed stands in favor of New Deal social legislation and militant antifascism. It vigorously supported the Spanish Republic during the Spanish civil war.[4]

As Penn Kimball observed firsthand, Hitler's imperial designs became manifest in 1938 when he added Austria and the Sudetenland of Czechoslovakia to his expanded Germany. Soviet calls for collective security against his plans were spurned by British and French administrations determined to appease Hitler and turn him eastward. Already the British and French governments (with the compliance of Roosevelt and Congress) had helped the Fascist revolt in Spain by denying the Republican government aid when German and Italian men, planes, and guns were providing Franco with critical support. The year 1939 saw the rest of Czechoslovakia destroyed. The German invasion of Poland on 1 September 1939 finally forced France and Great Britain to declare war. Kenneth S. Davis speculates that the Non-Aggression Pact of 22 August 1939 between Nazi Germany and the Soviet Union discouraged the appeasers from their ultimate hope that Germany would destroy the USSR.[5] *PM* was being organized in the early spring of 1940 as the "Phony War" period of no fighting on the Western Front dominated, but Nazi forces overran Denmark and Norway in April 1940. By May, Hitler turned west, driving through the Netherlands and Belgium in days and rapidly advancing through France.

The technological explosion of the twentieth century enabled people interested in these dramatic events to have new means of communicating them. Radio became pervasive in the United States during the depression decade; listeners could be entertained and informed. Speeches by Mussolini, Hitler, Chamberlain, and Churchill were broadcast from abroad. President Roosevelt, who crafted his speeches to Congress and his inaugural addresses with the national radio audience in mind, was a master of the medium. FDR appealed to the people directly with his "Fireside Chats"; his warm voice and confident manner fostered a comforting illusion that the president was speaking directly to each individual family that huddled by the home receiver.

After the sound revolution, movie companies began including narrated newsreels of national and international events as part of the entertainment packages they sold to theaters. The intimacy of the movie theater made the figuratively larger than life (Nazi rallies at Nuremberg, for example) literally larger than life.

The publishing world was in turmoil. Newspapers were in trouble. In New York the *Globe* and the *Advertiser* had both folded in the 1920s, while the first merger had saved some jobs at the *New York Herald* and the *New York Tribune*. The *New York World*, Joseph Pulitzer's great success (and the major Democratic newspaper of the 1920s), floundered; by 1931 Roy Howard had merged it with the *New York Telegram*, another struggling paper, as the flagship of the Scripps-Howard chain. The *Daily Graphic* expired after a decade's sensationalist struggle with the *Daily News* and the *Daily Mirror* to grab the tabloid audience. The publishing empire of William Randolph Hearst began to contract. While maintaining the circulation of the *Mirror*, Hearst combined his morning *Journal* and afternoon *American*. The *Sun* and the *Post* teetered on the edge of extinction. Depression meant loss of advertising revenue; unemployed or marginally employed New Yorkers could not be expected to frequent department stores. With the exception of the *Post*, purchased in the 1930s by the liberal David Stern, all of the New York papers were voices of conservatism. The *News* and Hearst publications were jingoist, xenophobic, and hysterical. The *Times* and *World-Telegram* began FDR's term of office with pro-Roosevelt editorials; by 1937 both papers were frequently in opposition. The *World-Telegram* was distinguished as the home of the viciously antilabor and anti–New Deal columnist, Westbrook Pegler. The *Herald Tribune* remained a consistent voice of traditional pro-business Republicanism. The papers, even the tabloid press, were technologically antiquated. They offered few photographs, and no wonder: most of the photographs were muddy reproductions which did little to convey information or ideas.

The tabloids were stuffed with comics and a relatively new phenomenon—gossip columns originating in Los Angeles or New York. They were most rewarding when filled with tidbits of the lives of Hollywood or Broadway stars. Several of these columnists had developed star power of their own, exerting journalistic control far out of proportion to their talents. Hedda Hopper and Louella Parsons from California and Walter Winchell, Leonard Lyons, and Ed Sullivan were among the columnists who were extensively read. Several of them parlayed their connections into variety shows or news commentaries on radio.

Opinion columns were the innovation in the standard press. Anne O'Hare McCormick and Arthur Krock for the *New York Times*, the aforementioned Pegler in the *World-Telegram*, and Victor Riesel in the *New York Post* impressed readers with vigorously expressed right-of-center politics (Riesel was a "labor" columnist, but his ferocious anticommunism induced a hatred of the CIO that sabotaged his credibility). On the liberal side, Walter Lippmann and Dorothy Thompson wrote for the *Herald Tribune*, and Roy Howard syndicated the most famous columnist in America in all of his papers (including the *World-Telegram*) when Eleanor Roosevelt's "My Day" began appearing there in the mid 1930s. Liberal champion Heywood Broun, who made his reputation at the defunct *World*, watched in fury as Pegler's copy, including ferocious attacks on the Newspaper Guild, was considered sacrosanct, while Broun's was regularly cut or suppressed at the *World-Telegram*.[6]

It was in magazine journalism that important innovations were taking place. At the center of two experiments—one of little and the other of great significance—was Ralph McAllister Ingersoll, descendant of two distinguished American families. The Ingersolls arrived in the United States before the Revolution and produced several successful nineteenth-century politicians associated with the Whig and Republican parties. Robert Ingersoll, the crusading atheist and Republican orator, was distantly related to Ralph. Ralph's father was a staid and dignified engineer who wanted nothing more than to have his son follow in his professional footsteps. Teresa McAllister was descended from a Scottish family which also arrived in the eighteenth century. Ralph's most famous relative on his mother's side was Ward McAllister, who succeeded in living and celebrating a life of aristocratic leisure. Marrying wealth when his own ran out, McAllister had a great success with the publication of *Society as I Have Found It* (now out of print), in which he toasted the special qualities of the effete social grouping to which he belonged. He coined the phrase "the Four Hundred" to describe the richest and most desirable families in New York City. The short story master O. Henry responded by calling his book of stories set in New York *The Four Million*.

Ingersoll was torn between the two heritages. Possessed of enormous initiative, energy, and creativity, he was powerfully driven to be a "success." He also found New York society magnetic. His college years and early professional career show a tension between his father's conservative desires for him (his mother died when he was ten) and his own need to make something entirely his own. Hotchkiss Preparatory School led inexorably to Yale, where he was chiefly interested in the fortunes of the football team. After graduating in 1920 he made an attempt to become an engineer; even in this field he was drawn to the exotic, and he traveled to a Mexican mine. His encounters were professionally important, not because he learned to be an engineer, but because his already acute abilities as a careful observer led him to write a book about his experiences. The publication of *In and Under Mexico* cinched his determination to write.[7] He cast about for jobs on publications. Briefly a reporter for Hearst's *New York American*, he quit after a personal encounter with his boss convinced him that Hearst was a lying charlatan. He landed a job on the struggling new publication the *New Yorker* as all-purpose assistant to the famously irascible Harold Ross. As Ingersoll himself tells the story, Ross was desperate to gain acceptance from the elite social set in order to establish the magazine's stability. He did not think much of his prospective employee and was casting about for ways to get rid of him.

> Ross had rallied to explain that there simply wasn't such a person as the kind of reporter he had in mind. He would have to be a Richard Harding Davis and a Ward McAllister rolled into one.
> "Well," I was able to interject, "I've been a reporter and Ward was my mother's uncle."
> "Jee-sus," Ross snarled, as if completely disgusted with himself for having given me this opening.
> Then a sigh escaped him and he looked me sadly in the eye. "Okay, you're on," he said. "Hell, I hire *anybody!*"[8]

Ingersoll did have society connections, and he knew how to write about them in a light, entertaining style. He also had an eye for talent. Working with Ross, he developed the Talk of the Town department with its air of supercilious detachment. By the time Ross's notorious abuse of all of his employees led Ingersoll to leave in 1929, the *New Yorker* was a growing, stable magazine, its look, tone, and audience securely established.

He was hired away by fellow Yale alumnus Henry Luce, whose success in founding *Time* made him the most important innovator in contemporary journalism. *Time* divided the week's news into departments. Readers responded well to the convenient indexing of the troublesome world, the picturesque and almost fictional language of its reporting style, and its snappy editorial arrogance. Luce's conservative stance after the second Roosevelt election makes it easy to forget that *Time* was considered on the cusp of a revolution in journalism. Nonetheless, the early issues of the magazine still appear to have all the weaknesses of the contemporary product. Although contemptuous of the Republican mediocrity dominant in the nation at the time of the journal's founding, it was snarlingly anticommunist while frequently enamored of Mussolini's Italy throughout the 1920s. Many of its judgments seem unsupported. Its revolution in syntax— chiefly changing the order of words in sentences to heighten dramatic effect— was often stilted. This particular quality led to easy spoofing. The "News on the March" newsreel which opens *Citizen Kane* is a parody of the March of Time newsreels Time, Inc., successfully circulated, but the best satire appeared in the *New Yorker*. A 1936 profile of Henry Luce was written by *New Yorker* writer Wolcott Gibbs with virtually every sentence done in *Time*-ese. "Backward ran sentences until reeled the mind. . . . Where it will all end, knows God!"[9] Despite the mockery, *Time* was a huge success. Even the established "newspaper of record," *New York Times*, was driven to create a Sunday News of the Week in Review in response to the impact of Luce's magazine, as Review editor Lester Markel confided to Ken Stewart.[10] Luce was determined to expand his influence by founding the quintessential business magazine, *Fortune*.

After a year of publication *Fortune* was foundering under the editorship of Wilton Lloyd-Smith. Luce brought Ingersoll in to revitalize the magazine; Ingersoll wrote extensive memos in which he described all that was wrong with it. Lloyd-Smith agreed to share in the reshaping of the monthly, but his suicide shortly thereafter led to Ingersoll's sole control. Ingersoll's whirlwind energy caught the staff up in revitalizing the periodical. He insisted on many more photographs, dynamic drawings, and other graphics. He encouraged investigative reporting and in-depth treatment of individual firms, regardless of whether that led to a friendly or unfriendly analysis. *Fortune* was not to be filled with pro-business puff pieces. The talented crew that worked under Ingersoll's direction included Dwight Macdonald, Archibald MacLeish, James Agee, and Margaret Bourke-White. Writers were given extensive time to prepare their treatments; even if they missed the deadline for one issue, their better-prepared articles would make the next. He kept more stories in progress than could be used. *Fortune* emerged as the second Luce success.

The experience of working on this magazine brought Ingersoll into contact with intellectual political dissent. Macdonald and MacLeish had socialist sympathies; the business exposés they wrote included stories of labor exploitation. Macdonald's attack on U.S. Steel's labor policies led to Luce's objections, Macdonald's resignation, and Ingersoll's meeting with U.S. Steel president Myron Taylor. Ingersoll told his biographer that he thought the *Fortune* piece induced Taylor to recognize the Steel Workers Organizing Committee.

Whether *Fortune* changed Taylor's politics, it changed those of Ingersoll, who had little interest in politics before working there. MacLeish's sympathy for the labor movement was infectious; his interest in socialism led Ingersoll to investigate the splintered strands of American socialism. Writing an article about Roosevelt after the Hundred Days, MacLeish was introduced to the president. "What a man!" he enthusiastically reported. Ingersoll did not need to be convinced. He had interviewed FDR in Albany when Governor Roosevelt was running for president. The nominee's reply of "Balls!" to his being characterized as a "country millionaire" charmed Ingersoll, as it was no doubt intended to. He became an instant admirer.

The success of *Fortune* made Ingersoll the second most important executive at Time, Inc. He put great pressure on Luce to begin a weekly picture magazine. Luce allowed Ingersoll to plan the magazine and create its first issue. *Life* was a sensation. Its dynamic use of quality photographs enchanted the public and stirred journalists everywhere. Luce was so impressed that he decided to place himself in immediate charge of developing *Life*, moving Ingersoll over to *Time*, a magazine Ingersoll had begun to detest. Luce's politics were reflected in *Time*. By 1937 these politics were anti-Roosevelt, antilabor, in favor of appeasing the fascists in general, and particularly supportive of Franco's putsch in Spain. Ralph Ingersoll was moving in a different direction. Even his romantic liaisons were moving him to the left.

Ingersoll's charismatic qualities made him attractive to women. During the 1930s he had had many affairs, two with high powered intellectuals. Laura Hobson was in awe of him, but Lillian Hellman introduced him to additional left-wing ideas and people. Plunging into New York's political crowd, Ingersoll briefly attended a Communist party study group. He soon gave it up. By this time he was soliciting financial help for his new paper, and exposure could ruin his plans. He was also too independent and inconsistent in his thought to be held by anyone's discipline.[11]

Ingersoll's disappointment at being bumped off of *Life* led him to explore a new alternative. Confident in his ability to run a publication, he began to consider starting a daily newspaper which would incorporate many of the journalistic principles he had introduced or been introduced to at the *New Yorker, Fortune, Life*, and *Time*. At this newspaper he would be his own boss. The paper would combine the photographic and artistic beauty of *Life* and *Fortune* with the stylishness of the *New Yorker* and the developing political commitments of Ralph Ingersoll to Roosevelt, labor, antifascism, and journalistic excellence.

Setting in motion a vast campaign to recruit journalists, Ingersoll hired Ed Stanley of the Associated Press as his front in Publications Research, Inc., which enabled the process of staff selection to go on while Ingersoll maintained his job with Henry Luce. Stanley began with the editorial staff; those editors, like Duncan Aikman at national affairs, interviewed and selected the journalists who would work under them. Ingersoll's contacts with Luce Publications and Stanley's at the Associated Press brought in the first crew. Among them were foreign affairs editor Robert Neville and critics Louis Kronenberger and John T. Mc-Manus of *Time*, William McCleery of the Associated Press Features Department, and George Lyon, a Scripps-Howard executive who had won his newspaper a Pulitzer Prize for public-interest crusading while running the *World-Telegram* in the early 1930s. Lyon was to be managing editor. He brought with him a large group of "green eyeshades," defined by Penn Kimball as the "veterans of the editing and copy desks who wore green visors to protect their eyes from the light and metal armbands around their shirtsleeves to prevent ink from staining them."

Lyon's last job for Scripps-Howard had been heading a drive to save the dying *Buffalo Times*; the news chain had brought in two other able veterans—John P. Lewis from Colorado and Rae Weimer from Akron, Ohio—to help reorganize the paper. When it failed, Lyon took Lewis and Weimer with him to *PM*. Weimer was attracted to the liberal slant of the proposed newspaper. While at Akron, he "saw unfairness to an awful lot of people who were in trouble. . . . I used to take a bag of groceries out to people in the street." He liked the idea of an adless paper which would fight "for the minorities."

According to Kimball, Lewis, on the other hand, was the ultimate "green eyeshade," a veteran newspaperman with no apparent political beliefs. "I never heard him utter a word or express an opinion about any political question." His job was simply "to get the paper out." Lewis would replace Lyon when the latter went to work for the Office of War Information in the spring of 1941; he was to be educated in liberal politics by the intellectual ferment around him.[12]

The future staff members responding to the promotional campaign tended to be younger and more idealistic than the green eyeshades. Four of the new recruits were Nieman fellows, young veterans of five years' newspaper experience selected by Harvard for a year's stay in Cambridge to take advantage of any facility or educational experience available at the great school and to meet with leading journalists from around the nation in seminars and lectures organized by the Nieman Foundation. When Ingersoll came to talk to the fellows in the fall of 1939, nine of the twelve were interested in working at his newspaper. When the staff was organized Weldon James of the United Press, Volta Torrey of the Associated Press, Hodding Carter, who had his own paper in Mississippi, and William P. Vogel of the *Herald Tribune* were the Nieman fellows who joined the new experiment. Mayor La Guardia had recommended Vogel to Ingersoll as a fine City Hall reporter. Within a year, Ken Stewart took leave of *PM* for a stay at the Nieman Center. Later, writers Herbert Yahraes and Ben Yablonsky would be Nieman fellows.[13]

Many future *PM*ers had traveled their own paths to prolabor and antifascist principles, though few had so much direct experience with so many of the great storms and politicians of the 1930s as Penn Kimball: depression, Roosevelt, New Deal, trade unionism, fascism, and war. Nonetheless, the tumult had profound impact on them all.

Snowden Herrick, like Kimball, was a scion of an old American Protestant lineage. His grandfather was a Unitarian minister; his mother inherited her political proclivities from active abolitionists of earlier generations. A friend and sponsor of Senator Robert Wagner, she was the first New York regional director of the National Labor Relations Board, where she became friendly with New York union leaders Sidney Hillman and David Dubinsky. She helped found the American Labor party in 1936 to give Roosevelt a non–Tammany Hall line to run on in New York City; young Snowden at seventeen was addressing ALP envelopes. Snowden went off to Yale determined to be a journalist. He spent summers working as a cub reporter at the *New York Times* and *Herald Tribune*. While at Yale, Herrick joined the American Student Union to condemn the Soviet invasion of Finland in late 1939; ironically his membership in the ASU would lead to an FBI file documenting his "communist sympathies." Herrick characterized himself as a "Menshevik": sympathetic to socialism but disgusted by Stalin's dictatorial practices. Because of his mother's friendship with *PM* investor Chester Bowles, Snowden was able to read Ingersoll's prepublication memos. Excited by Ingersoll's reputation in the publishing world, Herrick anticipated that the new paper would have the same impact as *Life*. Further impressed by the paper's commitment to trade unionism and racial tolerance, Herrick applied for a job with Bowles as a patron. He was assigned to the city desk, working under City Hall reporter William P. Vogel, who knew him from his past summer job at the *Herald Tribune*.[14]

Hannah Baker had been working for the McClure Newspaper Syndicate for five years when she applied for a job on the new paper. She was revolted by her boss, "a fan of Europe's Fascists and an America Firster." Her uncle, an Associated Press and *Herald Tribune* foreign correspondent, recommended her to Duncan Aikman. Filling out her application, she was delighted to experience "the first time 'religion' did not appear on the application and where I felt comfortable being Jewish and happy to see some Jewish faces here and there." Radicalized by her early contact with the Newspaper Guild and her awareness of Nazi anti-Semitism, Baker believed that at *PM* she would be able to "work in a political atmosphere compatible with my own beliefs and principles." She worked first on the national desk, then switched over to editing comic features and threw herself into Newspaper Guild activities, serving on the grievance committee.[15]

Baker was one of scores of Jewish journalists attracted to *PM*'s liberalism. Many of them were nominal Jews: not religious, but aware that they were descended from victims of European oppression, at that moment raised to its ultimate murderous expression in Nazi Germany. Many were first- and second-generation descendants of immigrants who fled the pogroms of czarist Russia; the antiautocracy sentiments of the socialist movement appealed to them. The overthrow of czarism was universally acclaimed, but the Jewish socialist movement in America was divided in its response to the Bolshevik victory in November 1917. By the 1930s dozens of fissures in Jewish socialism reflected the fractures in American socialism nationally. Many of the writers coming to work for *PM* had experience in several separate strands of American socialism. Others followed the political path of most Jews, converted by Franklin Roosevelt's New Deal to Democratic politics.[16]

James A. Wechsler came from two generations of ambitious achievers. His grandfather was a rabbi who wrote for the first Jewish daily in the United States and eventually founded his own. Wechsler characterizes him as an "editorial writer and an orator, a Talmudic scholar and a crusader." His father taught by day while putting himself through law school. Wechsler entered Columbia University in 1932 at the precocious age of sixteen. Revolted by the smug complacency of President Hoover in the face of national disaster, he was not sympathetic to his Democratic rival, who seemed to be mouthing platitudes instead of making concrete suggestions. Like many on the Columbia campus, poles apart from Princeton's undeterred Republicanism, Wechsler campaigned for Socialist Norman Thomas. Wechsler forged into politics and journalism at Columbia. Before he graduated he was editor in chief of the *Columbia Spectator* and a member of the Young Communist League, to which he was recruited in part by his future wife, Nancy. The militant antifascism of the Communist party appealed to him, particularly in light of Franco's revolt in Spain. Before long he tired of what he considered the intellectual dishonesty of international communism; he had particular trouble swallowing the contention of the 1936–1937 purge trials in Moscow, wherein most of the original Bolshevik party leaders were accused, found guilty, and executed as agents of Nazi Germany. Though propelled into leadership of the American Student Union by his Communist allies, Wechsler and his wife resigned from the YCL after a trip through Europe to the Soviet Union. Wechsler continued to see himself as a radical supporter of trade unionism and antifascism. While working at the *Nation*, he participated in study and discussion with many members of the staff. When Leo Huberman, an editor at the *Nation*, was hired to be the labor editor of Ingersoll's newspaper, he took Wechsler along as his assistant.[17]

The journey of Wechsler's future antagonist I. F. Stone was not remarkably different. Isadore Feinstein was intended by his immigrant father to be heir to the family dry goods store. The young Feinstein, a voracious reader, was far more sympathetic to the intellectual influence of his educated uncle. Having devoured the works of Jack London, Isadore discovered in the independent radicalism of the *Nation* and *New Republic* passionate dissent from the Republican complacency of the 1920s. As a youth, he printed his own commentaries on national politics, many of which expressed fury at the "frame-up" of Sacco and Vanzetti and their subsequent execution in 1927. In spite of poor eyesight, the young man carefully studied all written documents before him in his search for facts and truth. He sought jobs as a stringer for local newspapers in the Philadelphia area, eventually leaving school to pursue his journalism career. Finally he dropped an editorial on the desk of the editor of the *Philadelphia Record*, to which he had contributed local news pieces. The new publisher, David Stern, was attempting to transform that paper into a liberal standard. He hired Stone (whose new name he thought would be less subject to anti-Semitic defamation) to write editorials and eventually took him to New York after Stern purchased the *New York Post*. That paper's allegiance to Franklin Roosevelt's New Deal was not fully endorsed by Stone, who shared Wechsler's skepticism about FDR's commitment to meaningful reform. Stone, like Wechsler, explored official Socialist and Communist party alternatives through the mid-1930s, though he never joined any party. He came to find Roosevelt more sympathetic in his second term, in part because of the attacks of FDR's enemies, and contributed many pieces to the *New Republic* and *Nation* through the late 1930s. Breaking with the *Post*, which was moving right as he moved left, Stone began writing editorials for the *Nation* attacking fascism, appeasement, and Soviet policy after the Nazi-Soviet pact. He was delighted to supplement his *Nation* writings with contributions to *PM*, where his careful research created some of the newspaper's finest journalism.[18]

Sally Winograd's dominant intellectual influence was her father, a Menshevik immigrant. His socialism was ended by the victory of Franklin Roosevelt's New Deal. After 1932 and the subsequent legalization of trade unionism, first through the National Recovery Act and then the Wagner Act, "Roosevelt was it." Her first job was doing secretarial work for an obscure trade journal named *P.M.*

When Ingersoll bought the name, Winograd was protected from losing her job by being guaranteed one at the new paper. She began as a secretary, but when the staff was decimated by armed forces enlistments, she became a reporter on the city desk.[19]

Even those who were recruited for their newspaper expertise were sympathetic to the paper's "idealism." William McCleery graduated from the University of Nebraska at nineteen; a brief stint with the Hearst press in New York killed his enthusiasm for a journalistic career. He went back home and stayed until fellow Nebraskan Ed Stanley convinced him to come to Washington for a job with the Associated Press working on features. It was the fall of 1932; by the following spring the new president was having press conferences in the Oval Office. Years before Penn Kimball was impressed by FDR's "performance," young McCleery was awed by the president. A reader of the *New Republic*, McCleery found his liberalism buttressed by favorable reaction to the Roosevelt administration ("this was the depression and I was impressed by Roosevelt's real efforts to do something about it"), and to an exclusive phone interview with his hero Harold Ickes ("I loved the guy"), which launched McCleery's rapid rise in the AP hierarchy.

Young and personable, McCleery charmed Interior Department secretaries to learn that Nebraska was about to be awarded a $2 million Public Works Administration project. As this was big news back home, McCleery's exclusive was picked up by all the Nebraska papers carrying AP dispatches. Governor Charles Bryan (younger brother of William Jennings Bryan) was conducting a private war with New Dealers in the state. After McCleery's story was printed, Bryan asserted that no project would be allowed in Nebraska until a state committee within his domain approved the project. A hurried phone call to the secretary of the interior provoked this threat: "You tell Governor Bryan that if he doesn't approve that allotment in three days, it's canceled." McCleery's new dispatch containing Ickes's threat was disputed by veteran United Press reporters in the state. McCleery got Ickes to repeat it in person; the PWA project was approved, and the UP hired a reporter to follow McCleery around in Washington.

McCleery was not there long, however. His reputation made, he was dispatched to several cities to set up feature bureaus, finally arriving in New York to run the Associated Press Feature Department nationally. He was twenty-five. Features meant far more use of photography than standard news stories. He developed an excellent eye for the design of news stories, learning how to make effective use of photographs and drawings. The job was rewarding, but he was still frustrated in his desire to write. He left.

Before long he was recruited to *Life*, but he found himself "miserable" surrounded by the elitism of the "Ivy League crowd" there. When George Lyon recruited him to be picture editor at *PM* a couple of months before the start of publication, he jumped at the chance. "It was an idealistic young man's dream. It was against anti-Semitism and the bad treatment of blacks. It was prolabor and against the influence of ads. . . . Also, it was going to be experimental and use pictures in a different way." Even before publication began, McCleery's job was shifted to what Ingersoll called "dominion status": He was given total control of producing the Sunday Magazine, which made use of his features background— and enabled him to write.[20]

Lyon was encouraged to pursue McCleery by feisty Mary Morris, who had already made feminist history by becoming the first woman photographer for the Associated Press or any daily newspaper. Morris was the daughter of a Republican banker in Illinois; her mother first called her "impudent" when she rebelled at the enforced propriety of an exclusive boarding school outside Washington, D.C. Her parents allowed her to attend experimental Sarah Lawrence College; the school's interdisciplinary humanities program intrigued her. Her charismatic, intellectual professor, Max Lerner, introduced her to radical political ideas which meshed with the broad humanitarian ethos current on the college campuses of the New Deal era. Morris's independent streak was fortified by the "jazzy" crowd she ran with. Determined to become a photographer, she gamely enrolled in the Charence H. White School of Photography in New York; a classmate from Sarah Lawrence bound for Broadway became her roommate. McCleery, then with the Associated Press, began dating the actress. Impressed with Morris's skills, education, and spirit, McCleery hired her. Morris was teamed with writer Charles Norman doing feature stories; she often surprised him by asking penetrating questions of her own. She frequently suggested assignments to him. Her portraits of Aldous Huxley, André Malraux, Al Smith, and Edna St. Vincent Millay exposed hitherto unrevealed facets of the characters of those famous people. In these still-early days of photojournalism, Morris was an innovator, developing new techniques to give depth to flash photography, using two lights angles or bounced where ordinary newsmen used one light stuck right on the camera, which gave a standardized flat look to all news photos. Gypsy Rose Lee was so impressed with her work that she returned to Morris often for publicity stills. Ed Stanley was impressed, too; Morris was one of his earliest recruits. She eagerly signed on to a newspaper committed to photographic excellence.[21]

"For as far back as I could remember, I had wanted to be a newspaperman," wrote Ken Stewart. While in high school he "pestered" the editor of his hometown (Eureka, California) newspaper for a job. By the time he graduated he had landed a full-time position there. He spent the 1920s and 1930s collecting experience on newspapers while moving from West Coast to East; in the early 1930s he married journalist Evelyn Seeley. Stewart and Seeley moved from the political indifference and cynicism prevalent among writers of the "lost generation" to concerned liberalism and radicalism during the depression. Like Wechsler and Stone, their attitude in the 1932 election was one of anger at Hoover but distrust for Roosevelt; they liked FDR more as time went on. The cynical political distortion practiced by newspaper owners Hearst and Howard outraged their sense of fair play. Seeley lost her job on the *World-Telegram* because of her union activism and her liberal column. Stewart worked for the *Times*'s News of the

Week in Review during the late 1930s. Though impressed with his newspaper's unmatched resources, he was distrustful of its "objectivity." He could not abide the paper's neutrality in the Spanish civil war. Enamored of guild founder Heywood Broun, Stewart was ready to join *Broun's Nutmeg*, a small journal of crusading liberalism. When Broun died suddenly of pneumonia, Stewart and Seeley eagerly moved to *PM*, which they felt would carry on the best of Broun's tradition.[22] They were one of several married couples working at the paper; Carl Randau and Leanne Zugsmith were another. While at *PM*, Tom O'Connor married Ann Henry of the News for Living section. It would amuse several at the paper when rocket expert Willy Ley married Olga, the exercise model for the Sunday Magazine.[23]

Many of the new staff members were most attracted by the notion of an ad-free paper. Cecilia Weimreich, who had been working for the racing newspapers, thought that working for *PM* would be freer because, without pressures from advertisers, "people could write what they wished to write." Coming over as secretary to the city circulation manager, Weimreich eventually ran the paper's syndication department.[24] John A. Sullivan, a former junior editor at *Time*, jumped at the offer of former *Time* foreign editor Robert Neville to work at *PM*, because "we were blazing a new trail—no advertising pressures."[25]

Others were taken with the promise of writing in their own styles. "It was every journalist's dream," said John Kobler. The whole idea of a liberal tabloid was enormously attractive." Kobler's father had been a publisher of Hearst's *Daily Mirror*. "I was a rich man's son," not a political radical. The promise of the paper was in being "given complete freedom of expression."[26]

In 1949, after *PM* and its successor, the *New York Star,* had both folded, Ken Stewart surveyed staff members about their reasons for joining *PM*. Ninety-one editorial staffers responded. Many of the responses echoed these selections:

> *I had always dreamed of a paper like the one Ingersoll promised.*
> *"Save the world" dept.*
> *Because it promised to fill a great need.*
> *Hope.*
> *It looked as though it might become THE NEWSPAPER.*
> *Major interest: writing. Enthusiastic about plan for really intelligent liberal paper.*
> *Sounded like big event in journalism.*
> *Excitement.*
> *Chance to do photographically what you couldn't do elsewhere.*
> *Eyes shining.*

Few of the responses were confined to "Money" or "out of work."[27]

Ralph Ingersoll dreamed of a beautiful, modern newspaper controlled by its staff. Thousands found the vision appealing. Some were politically aware liberals or radicals. Some were nonpolitical. Those with conventional or nominal politics found the daring premise of Ingersoll's proposed paper challenging; in that sense they were making a "political" commitment to a new journalism. Some were veterans of traditional newspapers; the majority were at the beginning of their careers. They came together after dramatic years of political and journalistic change to join Ingersoll's experiment. Many would find that their time at *PM* was a period which defined the rest of their lives. "Here . . . might be a newspaper-man's newspaper," Stewart wrote, "as well as a newspaper that spoke the language of the people."[28]

2 | The Creation and Early Days of *PM*

"Chicken Ghouls Grow Rich"
—Front-page headline, 4 September 1940

Having decided to create a newspaper, Ralph Ingersoll threw his prodigious energy and persuasiveness into the effort. Four months after being shifted from *Life*, Ingersoll had given enough thought to creating an independent newspaper to write a long *Discursive Outline of a Proposition to Create a Daily Newspaper*. The basic ideas of his later *Proposition to Create a Newspaper* and the series of memoranda he wrote to his new staff through 1940 are articulated in this *Discursive Outline*. In many ways the basic principles are more fully developed in the early draft than they are in later documents.

Asserting that "the American newspaper had undergone no important change in design in 50 years," Ingersoll condemned the condition of the fourth estate.

The inefficiency of the contemporary press was first demonstrated . . . when a [1925] pressmen's strike shut down all the newspapers in New York City. In this emergency, the editorial staffs of all New York's papers joined together to write and publish a strange little sheet which appeared under the combined mastheads of all metropolitan dailies, both morning and evening . . . It was about the size of a tabloid, a single sheet which, folded, made four pages . . . the paper was printed better than the usual papers and was produced by a concentration of the best journalistic writing talent in the biggest city in the world—with neither time nor space to waste on endless words . . . it was far better than average written and the pleasure of getting all the news literally in half an hour is something I recall after 12 or more years.

Here is the genesis of *PM*'s page 1 boast that "*PM* Gives You More News in Less Time."

Ingersoll was more positive about the newspapers of the late nineteenth century created by James Gordon Bennett and Joseph Pulitzer. Their papers, he insisted,

had principles. I would say at least two. One was that the public was entitled to the truth on all subjects and that the paper had an obligation to get the truth and tell it. The other was that, editorially, the paper should stand for the publisher's conception of a better world. Newspapers emphatically believed in the existence of Right and Wrong and campaigned for their principles—largely against political corruption, since political corruption was the issue of the day.

Despite the great technological advances of the twentieth century, there had been no advance in newspapers. In fact, they were worse. "The great press services have broadened news coverage and made it less imaginative." The new feature column was "no more than the editorial page which has walked out of the grave. . . . No one is moved by—few even read—the dry words still printed under the title 'Editorial.' " Another negative development

was the dreadful influence of William Randolph Hearst. Unimaginatively retaining all the trappings of creative journalism—the picture-stealing and the invented-storying—he killed the spirit in his own conception of a group of great newspapers without any conscience but his own. His wealth and the prosperity of his papers made it possible to suck into his organization the cream of journalistic ability. . . . He removed its conscience, insisting that men who worked for him change their opinions when he changed his.

Finally, the "terrible tide of inertia" kept the newspapers from advancing to progressive modernism.

Part of this inertia is—or is supported by—that kind of capitalist inertia which is based on respect for plant equipment and going concern values. Mr. Ochs would certainly not be interested in a new format for the *New York Times* to achieve which would mean scrapping his organization and perhaps most of his press equipment.

The one new development was the arrival of the tabloids. They, however, were only "a minor modification" in a "more convenient size" utilizing more photographs. But the photography was a major disappointment because "the pictures bear practically no relation to the text [and] are certainly not used in any intelligent scheme of imparting information." Furthermore, the tabloids were misusing photography.

The sensationalism inherent in picture journalism, the natural tendency of pictures to operate in their own areas of increasing returns—sex and gore—ran tabloids off the track into sensationalism, [and] gave the whole movement the unpleasant connotation implied in the new epithet: tabloid journalism.[1]

An examination of the daily press in New York at the time Ingersoll's newspaper burst onto the scene in June 1940 reveals that his assessment of his future competition was accurate. Eight daily mass-circulation papers were printed in Manhattan and distributed throughout the city. A ninth paper was printed and distributed in New York's largest borough, Brooklyn. Seven of the nine were broadsheets, wider than today's *Times*, with eight columns instead of today's six. The

Times, Herald-Tribune, News, Mirror, and *Sun* were morning papers, available to commuters at newsstands before they left for work. The *Journal-American, World-Telegram,* and *Post* competed for the afternoon market. A subway rider could conceivably read one paper on the way to work and another on the way home.

Nor were readers restricted to those eight (or nine in Brooklyn). Daily newspapers in Yiddish, Italian, and Spanish circulated in large enough numbers to be considered mass dailies; the Communist party's *Daily Worker* was available throughout the city. Other foreign-language and neighborhood papers were printed weekly. Except for the two tabloids—the *News* and *Mirror*—which cost their daily readers two cents, the newspapers demanded three copper pennies during the week.

Still, except for the *Times* and *Herald Tribune*, New York's English-language daily press was thin in news, repetitive in advertising, and astonishingly ugly to read.

After the death of the *World* in 1931, the *Times* became recognized in the city and throughout the nation as the unchallenged number one news source, with unparelleled resources for collection and presentation of national and international news; the sheer size of the newspaper, both daily and on Sunday, dwarfed the competition in both editorial and advertising content. Throughout 1939 its daily circulation averaged 475,000 copies; on Sunday, nearly 800,000 copies were sold.[2]

Times readers usually found international news on the opening pages. Even after war broke out in Europe, several of the paper's own correspondents remained there; their accounts were buttressed by Associated Press wire stories. A daily Text of War Communiqués usually appeared on the second page. By the time the paper's coverage moved to national news (by the sixth page on Saturday or the tenth page during the week), advertising consumed much more than half of each page; just as today, a single column of news would adorn a massive department store ad; several pages featured only full-page ads. Many of the regular "news" departments seemed to be excuses to procure advertising; already the *Times* and the competition devoted copious numbers of pages to promoting real estate sales; then as now the Sunday real estate section in all the newspapers featured puff pieces to entice the advertising, which overwhelmed the "news."

In 1940, a daily page was reserved for activities at the New York World's Fair; as in so many other areas, the *Herald Tribune* seemed to be supplying flattery by imitation. Religion was covered copiously, with over a hundred Manhattan Christian churches providing small summaries of the following day's sermons on Saturdays; on Mondays the paper rewarded several of these institutions with one-paragraph accounts of their proceedings. Society news was extensively covered; paid wedding announcements were yet another way to secure revenue. The obituary page provided the paper of record another source of funds; at least two full columns of paid death notices were a daily feature. The familiar arrangement of several pages of business news (with scarcely a mention of labor despite the contentious class warfare of the period) and stock listings preceding the classifieds was already located at the back of the paper, which came in two sections six days of the week.

The editorial page was densely packaged in minute type. The paper had two columnists. Arthur Krock's "In the Nation" and Anne O' Hare McCormick's "Europe" alternated several days a week. Their opinions and letters took up less than half the page. The unsigned editorials took up the rest. The *Times* editorialized on six or seven subjects a day. McCormick's columns were devoted to the war in Europe; clearly a partisan of the Allies, she attempted to analyze military and political fronts of the war. Krock's domestic pieces were, like his employer's, liberal Republican. He thought bitterly that labor had too much power in the Roosevelt administration; he often caustically referred to the New Deal as a "Labor Government." The principal editorial perspectives in 1940 called for curbs on labor's power and increasing aid to Great Britain. The day before *PM* began publication the *Times* warned the nation, "This is the most critical hour in the world's history that Americans have ever known. We now know that there is no such thing as isolation. . . . We have no possible alternative but to use every available moment to strengthen the bulwarks of democracy with every ounce of strength at our command." [3]

The Sunday paper was already a weight lifter's tool. Costing a dime, the paper included nine sections. The news section, normally at forty-eight pages or more, was a department-store advertising jubilee. (These advertisers were the backbone of all the city's newspapers; only the juggernaut *Daily News* had such a diversity of advertisers that it might have replaced these establishments with little difficulty had they all gone out of business at once. Still, Macys, Gimbels, Sterns, Bloomingdales, McCreerys, Lord and Taylor, Altmans, Arnold Constable, Franklin Simon, and the rest dominated the large advertising sections in all the city's papers; as might be expected downtown Brooklyn's Abraham and Straus was the principal advertiser in the *Eagle*.) The second section was small and devoted to society and fashion. One jarring note: The *Times*'s Paris fashion correspondent was still writing trendy costuming accounts from the French capital as late as 2 June 1940, while Nazi troops approached the city. Separate financial and sports sections, and the eight-page News of the Week in Review—the *Times*'s response to the success of *Time Magazine*—are close representations of what appear today. The paper's Sunday magazine already closed with pages of school and camp ads (but there was no crossword in the *Times* on Sundays or weekdays). The magazine was much smaller (only twenty-eight pages), and articles tended to be restricted to a single page; the Book Review had smaller dimensions and only twenty-four pages. A section for photographs, the Rotogravure Picture section, was eight pages, but three were ads and only the first two pages included pictures of world or important news; the rest were society photographs. Section 9 was reserved for the arts; each one (stage, screen, music, etc.) being given one page. Radio programs on twelve stations were given partial and sketchy treatment in the Sunday paper only.

Photographs were scattered lightly throughout the newspaper; most were undistinguished head shots. A three-column-by-three-inch war map often appeared on the front page during a major European battle.

Readers of the *Times* discovered little about their city. The newspaper occasionally weighed in with heavy words of advice for Mayor La Guardia; as we shall see, like the rest of the city's press, the editors loathed the city's Transport Workers Union. But no neighborhoods or local issues were regularly described; no sense of the city's multiethnic population emerged from its pages. The *Times* clearly belonged to the city's well-off Manhattan establishment; what was of particular interest to ethnic or working-class populations did not appear to be newsworthy.

By 1940, the *Herald Tribune* had shaken off the effect of the death of each of its single progenitors to have a recognizable face and place of its own. Unfortunately, that place seemed to be "almost as good as the *New York Times.*" Its 1939 circulation averaged almost 350,00 daily readers and about 525,000 on Sundays, but both advertising and circulation numbers were rising impressively from mid-depression levels.[4] Headlines used stylistic lowercase letters in contrast to the *Times*'s use of bold capitalized type. Like its rival, the *Herald Tribune* concentrated on international and national news; it relied somewhat more on the wire services for its news accounts, though it did have a small collection of international and national correspondents. Dorothy Thompson's liberal internationalism was reflected in her "On the Record" column; within two years the business-oriented Republicanism of her host paper no longer found her welcome, and she switched her column to the *Post.* She alternated with Walter Lippmann, whose "Today and Tomorrow" column frequently expressed impatience at congressional dallying over aid to the Allies. The *Herald Tribune* was experimenting with features. It already had a daily crossword and bridge and nature columns to accompany its book reviews. One comic strip appeared daily, but *Mr and Mrs* was buried at the back of the classifieds. Although more classically business oriented editorially than the *Times*, the *Herald Tribune* had at least heard of the city outside of Manhattan; the paper occasionally ran a Brooklyn neighborhood news section; the *Times* covered Brooklyn regularly only during the baseball season, when it faithfully covered the Dodgers (as well as the Yankees and Giants).

Sunday's paper featured ten sections. The extra section was eight pages of comics. Not one of the strips is remembered today. On Sundays the *Herald Tribune* listed only four radio stations' program notices, and they all paid for the privilege. Conspicuously absent were WNYC (then owned by the city) and WQXR (owned and operated by the *New York Times*).

Herald Tribune editorial policy was openly probusiness and Republican. Throughout June 1940 it attacked President Roosevelt for failing to prepare the United States for war and strongly supported Wendell Willkie's bid for the Republican nomination. It too advocated strong support for the Allies. "The Nazi war machine brings only a message of sterility and death to the world which it is overrunning."[5] It was shriller than the *Times* in its attacks on labor and labor's friends in government, charging that "the Wagner Act . . . has sapped the spirit" which made America the richest country in the world.[6]

The remaining "respectable" morning daily—the *Sun*—competed for a less affluent and vanishing Republican political constituency, the small business man. Its circulation of under 300,000 readers gave it the second fewest number of daily readers of the eight papers; its incredibly skimpy news coverage promised to erode its reading base still further. Virtually all the news, which was covered in the first six pages of the paper, was culled from Associated Press or United Press stories. A typical day found "Bathing Suits and Fashions" covered on page 5; after that the paper was a hodgepodge of disorganized news and feature items. The *Sun* seldom was longer than thirty-two pages; since it did not have a Sunday edition, its Saturday paper tended to be longer. The *Sun* had a suburbanite's interests at heart before there were suburbs: it gave gardening, dogs, antiques, astronomy, and arts and crafts regular coverage while short-changing international, national, and local news. All of these areas, of course, came accompanied by specialty advertising. Of its five comic strips, none has survived or been remembered.

If the *Herald Tribune* was shriller than the *Times* when it came to labor, that subject drove *Sun* editorialists into a frenzy on a nearly daily basis. It demanded that the nation "Cut the Shackles," by which it meant the Wagner and Wages and Hours acts. "The misuse of power which remains in the hands of those who will block production if they can" would use defense to foist a labor agenda on us all.[7] Editorials frequently accused the labor movement of being dominated by communists.[8]

FDR, the paper claimed, was beholden to labor:

We have not had economy because the New Deal, pretending to prime the pump, was buying votes with relief money. We have not had a balanced budget because the New Deal dared not impose more taxes on the mass. We have had injustice to employers, with no decrease in unemployment, because the New Deal took its orders from John L. Lewis.[9]

The *Sun* differed from the *Times* and *Herald Tribune* in its resolute isolationism. Though attacking Nazi world domination plans, the paper consistently condemned as dictatorial attempts to involve America by aiding the Allies. After the fall of France, editorialists insisted, "The US will not get into the European War unless it is maneuvered in it to serve some personal ambitions."[10]

Moreover, headline writers tried to "prove" that aid was not necessary by consistently missing the point about what was happening overseas. Here are the front-page lead headlines as the Wehrmacht swept toward Paris:

FRENCH SMASH NAZI TANKS; *Report Hundreds Destroyed* [6 June 1940]
NAZI DRIVE IS STALLED; ALLIED PLANES BLAST TANKS [7 June]
AIR RAID ON BERLIN [8 June]
NAZI CENTER HURLED BACK; PARIS IS MADE OPEN CITY [13 June]
NAZIS TAKE PARIS AND SWEEP SOUTH [14 June]

Even this last headline did not convince the editorialists, who insisted that "the fall of Paris is not the fall of France." [11]

The *Sun*'s intractable isolationism and bitter antilabor invective, together with its lack of interest in covering the news, seemed to reflect a readership of hounded middle-class reactionaries, vainly trying to protect their position from the demands of a world at war and of a frighteningly empowered "mass."

The two other morning papers, though equally reactionary editorially, competed vociferously for the interest of the masses. The two morning tabloids, the *Daily News* and the *Daily Mirror*, sold for two cents each and seemed designed for the interests of the "common man." Both papers had emerged from the great struggle to dominate the tabloid audience. The *News*, born after World War I, had created a new shape. A newspaper could be five columns across, taller that it was wide, and could be read easily by holding the entire paper in one hand; this was a great innovation for riders of subways, buses, elevated trains, and trolleys. The *Mirror* was publisher William Randolph Hearst's response to the success of the *News*, which threatened the core readership among the city's poor and working classes of his *Morning Journal*. For a time in the 1920s, the two papers were joined by a third tabloid—the *Daily Graphic*—but that paper was long dead by the time Ingersoll was writing. The three papers had engaged in a wild game of competitive hysteria to cement their hold on the tabloid audience; the *Graphic* had actually paid someone to shoot up its own editorial office in order that the newspaper could report it had been threatened by violence. [12]

By 1939, the *Daily News* was the reigning champion, averaging almost 1.9 million for its daily edition and selling nearly 3.4 million copies on Sundays. A typical front-page headline contained two or three bold headlines of two or three words per line, with a single photograph underneath. Throughout June 1940, the battle of France was front-page news; inside the news stories about it were AP or UP dispatches. But the paper could not bother with international news for long. Page 2 would have four or five stories, some UP or AP dispatches from Europe, some news from Washington (the paper did have its own capital correspondents), and some gossip. On June 7, with the French events clearly the lead news story, the lead on page 3 was hearsay about the Windsors; on page 4 the lead story was headlined "Spurned Husband Shoots Horses, Attacks Bride." The same page also found room for a one-panel comic, "The Neighbors." The following page was mostly an ad for Bloomingdales. By page 5 or 6 almost all pages were represented by a single three- or four-paragraph story surrounded by ads; as previously mentioned, the *News* represented every kind of retail store in New York, relying less heavily on the department stores than its competitors.

In fact, the *News* made advertisers king. By not laying out the paper in any coherent way, *News* ownership seemed to invite advertising throughout. Since readers would scan the whole paper looking for items that interested them, an advertiser would be happy with a location anywhere. The paper ran ten daily comic strips, but no comics page. Instead, its strips would each run atop a page otherwise devoted entirely to advertising. Among the strips appearing daily were "Little Orphan Annie," "Winnie Winkle," "The Gumps," "Moon Mullins,"

"Terry and the Pirates," "Dick Tracy," and "Gasoline Alley." Broadway gossip by Ed Sullivan, John Chapman, and Danton Walker dominated their pages.

The paper's editorial policy was isolationist and anti-Roosevelt, though it was considerably milder about FDR than its frenetic older brother, the *Chicago Tribune*. The editorial column did not take long to write, probably employing no more than 150 words on any given day, but it could summarize views in a pithy, memorable way. Thus the paper warned that, under the New Deal, "we are drifting toward socialism," [13] and decided that the cause of the war abroad was that "there are too many people in Europe." [14]

The paper's more lavish Sunday edition cost five cents and consisted of about forty main pages, sixteen comics pages, and ten "coloroto" pages. The picture section actually contained far more advertisements than photographs.

Like its rival, the *New York Daily Mirror* was strikingly disorganized and ugly. In both tabloids, ink seemed to bleed all over the reader's hands, even more than with most newspapers. Headlines appeared to be most of the stories. Somehow, the *Mirror* looked even uglier, although the differences are minor. Though a loser to the *News* in circulation (and therefore advertising) revenue, the *Mirror* was no slouch: in 1939 it boasted a daily circulation of nearly 800,000 and almost 1.5 million Sunday readers. There was little doubt the *Mirror* was a Hearst newspaper; though it did not include the publisher's own column, which appeared only in the *Journal-American*, the paper clearly demonstrated its owner's obsessions. A crusade in both newspapers threatened the patriotism of CBS Radio after the latter broadcast Communist party presidential candidate Earl Browder's address. The *Mirror* made use of Hearst's INS wire service for the sketchy news it printed. Like the *News*, it had little patience for war stories, except if there was a celebrity angle; the lead on page 5 one day told how Laurence Olivier and Vivien Leigh were returning to England to aid the war effort. [15]

A typical daily paper contained only twenty-eight pages. Walter Winchell's Broadway hearsay was featured on page 10; other gossip columnists found their work just beyond the pictures in the centerfold. Winchell was an anomaly in the *Mirror* because he was enamored of the president. He could not spell out FDR's politics in his own paper, but he did not have to hide his personal enthusiasm, either. After one presidential address, Winchell gushed, "They may trounce FDR at the polls, but he'll never be licked on the air waves." [16]

The comics were spread throughout the paper. Among the regulars were "Li'l Abner," "Joe Palooka," and "Henry."

Hearst was much more strident than the *News* in his isolationism. His morning tabloid reflected his views with a boxed message that warned "Congress: No War; We Want Peace," [17] and another which cautioned readers to "Remember that wars are chronic to Europe . . . and Remember that Peace is the tradition, not the exception in America." [18]

Hearst's afternoon paper—the *Journal-American*—a hybrid born when the publisher found it prudent to leave the morning audience to the *Mirror*, was more of a soapbox for his ideas, though it was equally inadequate as a source of information. It was the clear winner in the afternoon circulation wars, boasting a daily circulation of over 600,000 in 1939 and with almost one million Sunday readers. The chief editorial message was the danger of communist subversion. Editorials in the *Journal-American* actually appeared in two places: on the editorial page, where the editorial was even shorter than the one found in the *News*, and on page 1, where the publisher's syndicated "In the News" column could be found seven days a week (though he sometimes turned it over to others). The news was dispensed within the first five or six pages; virtually all articles were written by the INS (Hearst) wire service. The *Journal-American* ran a metropolitan section, but this did not mean it had a functioning city desk. Instead this segment featured large photographs of pretty women and gossip columns written by Dorothy Kilgallen and others. Features included an elementary school crossword ("1 across: 3-letter insect"), [19] Paul Mallon's pithy political sayings (one-liners of reactionary ideas), and two comics pages that included "The Phantom," "Bringing Up Father," "The Lone Ranger," "Mandrake the Magician," "Popeye," "Blondie," "Barney Google," and "Donald Duck." On Sundays, these were supplemented with "Flash Gordon," "Prince Valiant," "Mickey Mouse," "The Little King," and "The Katzenjammer Kids."

The Sunday paper featured Smart Set Magazine, which included three pages of Cholly Knickerbocker gossip. The March of Events managed to summarize the week's news in two pages before yielding to yet another gossip column, this one written by Mark Hellinger. Another magazine section, *The American Weekly*, went out of its way to be spurious. One article centered on the apparently amazing "fact" that 95 percent of the world's bathtub bathing was done in the United States; another insisted, "Life on Mars! Plants Certain—Much Intelligent Creatures as Well." A third article was pulp fiction.

Hearst's and his paper's editorial obsession with communism included frequent reminders that it was the communist objective to "DESTROY THIS FREE REPUBLIC and to establish upon its ruins A COMMUNIST SLAVE STATE—a 'Soviet America.'"[20] An editorial warned that new defense appropriations would turn the United States into a "totalitarian nation. . . . The people are not willing that Americans go into Europe's war."[21] Meanwhile Hearst called for defense of the American West Coast against Japan and Soviet Russia.[22]

The *New York World-Telegram* wanted to appeal to both the establishment audience of the *Times* and *Herald Tribune* and the less elite following of the *Sun*, which it would eventually swallow. With a daily circulation of 410,000, dipping on Saturdays to 320,000 (it had no Sunday edition), the hybrid journal was far down on the list of New York's influential newspapers. It was thin; it tended to be thirty-two pages. It relied more on United Press wire stories than on the Associated Press; like most of the New York press, it had few byline correspondents of its own. News could essentially end by the fourth or fifth page; its News Index looked more like the tabloid than the broadsheet competition. The gossip and Broadway columnists took over by the fifth page; a restaurant review might often be found by page 6.

The *World-Telegram*'s second section began with four columnists daily. Featured first was the rabid Westbrook Pegler; some comic must have suggested that the title for his column should be "Fair Enough." Pegler was a virulent hater. He hated Roosevelt, the New Deal, and unions, especially the CIO, which he considered to be controlled by the Communist party. Unionism was the subject for at least half of his commentary, and invariably he attacked labor organizing as a conspiracy to prevent individual employees freedom of choice. He was followed down the page by Raymond Clapper, who tended to give lukewarm support to the administration; Hugh Johnson, the former general and NRA administrator marching steadily rightward; and Eleanor Roosevelt, whose column was entitled "My Day," aptly conveying its material.

The page directly following the columnists featured the official editorials of the newspaper. The rest of the paper was filled with features, including a Saturday column, "Eminent Laymen," which was surrounded by church-service ads, and six comic strips, among them "Alley Oop." As with the *Sun* and the *Post*, the *World-Telegram* seemed to be over before it was begun. It was a few lines of Pegler's diatribe, the same old ads, and little more. Pegler's invective could be memorable. He hated the Newspaper Guild, which he refused to join, but in the factional fight he sided with

the American members of the Newspaper Guild, as distinguished from the Communists and fellow travelers who now control the organization. . . . The Communist control, centered in New York, is exercised by conspirators who either never have been newspapermen and women in the common understandings of the terms or who were mediocrities and became embittered by their own failure.[23]

Pegler demanded the abrogation of First Amendment rights for communists, since "the American constitution is not now and never was intended to stand guard over those who conspire against the freedom which it guarantees."[24]

As with the *Sun*, *World-Telegram* headline writers seemed to rely too heavily on optimistic United Press reports from France; but the afternoon paper would balance the bold optimistic headline with a smaller, more realistic one:

PARIS DRIVE BLOCKED, FRENCH SAY
Nazis Claim Advance at Channel [5 June]
GERMAN TANKS SMASHED
Somme Crossed Again, Nazis Say [6 June]
GERMAN TANKS WRECKED
    AS PLANE CARAVAN CHECK DRIVE [7 June]
BERLIN BOMBED [8 June]

Editorialists were torn between support for the Allies and dislike for Roosevelt. During June, they followed the lead of their intense columnist and pushed for strong restraints on the National Labor Relations Board, which the paper insisted was coddling labor. Editorials attacked Labor Secretary Perkins and approvingly cited Pegler's communist charges against the CIO.[25]

Struggling to stay afloat was the lone Democratic and liberal newspaper, the *Post*. Still a broadsheet in 1940, the *Post* had the lowest circulation of the eight metropolitan dailies, averaging 235,000 during the week and 180,000 on Saturdays. It had just been redesigned by Norman Bel Geddes, who had chosen the bold, black, diagonal headline style which would be retained after it became a tabloid and which helped to make it the ugliest broadsheet on sale in 1940.[26] This daily seemed to have no reporters on its payroll. Virtually all bylined stories were by the AP or UPI; already it was becoming a newspaper of liberal columnists and not much else. As June 1940 began, ads were trumpeting the syndication of five columnists of the *St. Louis Post-Dispatch*. The page 1 headline was followed by the line scores of that afternoon's baseball games as the *Post* went to press. The reader is struck by the utter chaos of the newspaper's design. Ten stories, all small, often appear on one page; there is often no connection among any of them. All the news the *Post* cared to distill from the wire services was found in the first three or four pages, but single-panel cartoon strips could be found as early as page 2. Stage and screen news started on page 5; gossip columnists Leonard Lyons and Sidney Skolsky appeared on page 9. The editorial section was original; it hosted an American Forum section on Saturdays which featured a debate by prominent Americans. In early June two Texas congressmen—red-hunter Martin Dies and radical Maury Maverick—debated the merits of Dies's House Un-American Activities Committee; readers were encouraged to send in their opinions about the issue.[27]

The *Post*, with almost no resources, did try to cover labor. The paper ran brief three- and four-paragraph accounts on CIO and AFL union elections and organizing campaigns if the wire services covered these stories.

There was a newspaper on sale every day which covered the labor movement. The *Daily Worker* was distributed throughout the country, but its weather box on page 1 described New York conditions. The paper was openly a propaganda sheet, declaring under its banner that it was the "People's Champion of Liberty, Progress, Peace and Prosperity." During the week its eight pages were available for the same three pennies that the other broadsheets sold for; on Sundays the paper expanded to fourteen pages and sold for five cents. In June 1940 the paper was covering the Communist party convention, then nominating Earl Browder for president. Its chief concern during this period was not touting labor's rights, which of course it did, but attacking the Roosevelt administration's desire to extend aid to the Allies. In stories that would later embarrass Communists for years after, the party standard insisted that the war in Europe was simply a fight between competing imperialistic powers. Reading the *Worker*, one had only to read the headlines. The "line" said it all:

No Money, Wall Street Said, for People's Welfare
Now Ready to Spend $20 Billion a Year for Mass Murder [1 June 1940, page 1]
The Nation's Demand for Peace Grows [1 June, page 2]
Anti-war Pamphlet Sold by CP Hits 3½ Millions [1 June, page 4]
Youth, Labor Roused as Bills Speeded to Clear Way for War [2 June, page 4]
People Will Rise against War Butchery [2 June, page 5]
Oklahoma Farmers Hold Fast to Anti-War Tradition of 1917 [2 June, section 2, page 2]

Of course, the threat of war would not be found in the Soviet Union. Alan Max assured the readers of his column, "Point of Order," "Over there [in the USSR], they don't shout hysterically that they are bound to get into this war."[28]

In June of 1940 the Communist party newspaper found that it did not fear fascism much more than other forms of capitalism. In fighting for peace, it sounded very much like the *Journal-American.*

The surprise for today's reader of the old *Daily Worker* is seeing that it, too, had some traditional advertising. Classified items including want ads and apartments for rent took up a quarter of a page. Ads for the left-wing resorts Camp Unity and Camp Beacon appeared, as did ads for seven eateries, including four Chinese restaurants.[29]

New York's largest borough had a plebeian identity of its own, and the *Brooklyn Eagle* tried to address this audience, but it could not quite tell what it was trying to accomplish. Its Sunday circulation of 88,000 was a small dip from the nearly 96,000 it sold during the week. Using the broadsheet format, the *Eagle* tried hard to cover the world, the nation, the city, and Brooklyn in eighteen confused pages. It was not unusual to have fourteen stories on one page; it gives the reader a headache to just look at the newspaper. All of the news outside the borough was culled from United Press and Associated Press wires. All nonlocal news was finished by the third page. Society news and wedding announcements began on page 4.

The paper was slightly more successful in covering local stories. It had a Neighborhood Notes section with news from several Brooklyn areas. A regular feature was news from the police precincts which repeated informational items exactly as the police transmissions gave them. This was called Ears to the Ground. If religious, civic, or other local organizations let the *Eagle* know what they were doing, the paper gladly reported on their activities. Thus, the sports section included a running record of the Brooklyn bowling leagues. It did not have a staff bravely interested in getting to the real conflicts between people, so that the result of reading the *Eagle* was that the reader was no more informed about Brooklyn than about the wider world.

It was little wonder that Ralph Ingersoll looked at the daily press and found it wanting.

Measured against this stagnation in the newspaper industry was the advance made by *Time.* "Easy digestion" of the news was mixed with "provocative writing—a provocative whole attitude toward life, in fact." Ingersoll theorized that the advances had come in magazines rather than newspapers because the latter required extensive investment capital. Luce had begun on a "shoestring." Ingersoll was convinced that he could demonstrate to investors that a revolutionary new paper would justify the enormous expenditures necessary to begin publication. "The success of a pseudo-invention, the *New York Daily News*, is all the evidence that needs to be presented to prove the availability of profits for a new medium successfully invading an established market."

The new paper would assimilate the best of his past journalism experience. As in *Fortune*, the paper would make extensive use of the photograph, the drawing, and the diagram based on "a conception of the story clearly in mind." It would have as complete a guide to goings on about town as did the *New Yorker*. Despite his aversion to advertising, Ingersoll thought "the advertising profession is a generation ahead of the journalistic. Almost all advertising is put together after an analytical consideration of the power of words, photographs, and drawings to convey ideas." The new paper would use similar criteria to determine "page size, format, paper stock, printing processes, editorial organization." The creation of the paper would be "so clean a break from tradition that when our paper is assembled we will know that every decision has been conscious and for reasons which have been articulated and discussed and agreed upon as the most practical possible."

Ingersoll turned to broader principles. "Journalists serve two things larger than themselves. The first is the truth as it exists. The second is the idea of a better mankind." Truth was difficult to ascertain, but the search for it was the first condition for useful journalism. Ingersoll described what the struggle for a "better mankind" meant. "No one will disagree with the conception that human beings change for the better when they are better fed, clothed, and housed. . . . Fear and insecurity are bad things for them." To alter the world for the better seemed to mean adopting a radical approach:

> I have been forced to use the word "radical" to clarify my conception. Here it is almost too comprehensive a word to be practical. . . . Mankind seems to move in this cycle: first it is carried away with the conception of what it might be—freed of the drudgery of labor simply to exist and freed of each other's persecutions. And it lifts itself up with a great faith—to revolutions, to material and scientific achievements. Then its plans do not work out and in despair it turns back, resigning itself to the fact that the strong can support themselves on the labor of the weak. . . . And then that doesn't work out so well. And then something else in man moves him to new faith in himself as a whole. . . . I am a Radical in believing that people can improve their lot and that they—I—get some satisfaction out of doing it. . . . I would be willing to subscribe to journalistic inquiry admittedly and openly more interested in and more sympathetic to all Left movements—Liberalism, New Dealism, Socialism, Communism, Anarchy. . . .
>
> What we have of course, would be an organ of the United Front. Not an organ dedicated to putting over the United Front, or any part of it. But an organ that believed in the destiny of the people and that therefore all those conflicting elements of the United Front were, with greater or lesser efficiency, moving in the right direction. And we would have our charter assigned us to criticize the efficiency of these movements. But at the same time we would stand firm and openly against the Reaction. We would fight hard and ceaselessly against all attempts at stratifying society. . . . We would be against racial and religious discrimination. Admitting the fact that our problems of social reform are still unsolved, we would be excited by, and interested in, and constructively critical of, and open-minded about attempts to solve the problem.

The same brash confidence Ingersoll brought to creating a journal is evident in his faith in the future. As he wrote, United Front governments in Spain and

France were enunciating hopes for the future while fighting desperately against fascist attack. France would fall to Hitler during the very week *PM* arrived on the newsstands; by then the Spanish Republic was a painful memory. But the commitment to a United Front would linger in Ingersoll and in *PM* as a testament to open-minded opposition to reaction.

Ingersoll's ability to generate ideas, whether the myriad flashes of journalistic insight and political experimentation that erupted from his energetic mind or his own half-formulated version of the theoretical analyses of his friends in New York leftist circles, was the center of his charismatic appeal.

His *Discursive Outline* now turned to more specific needs. The new paper demanded new journalists, true experts in the many fields the paper would cover. The overriding expert would have to be Ingersoll himself, the editor.

> I still hold to the early Rossian premise of the editor printing what he likes. If other people like it he is a success. . . . There is no magic by which he can conjure up an average reader and talk with him as he would talk to an individual.

But a great editor would succeed, and Ingersoll was convinced his paper would.

> I would not consider the idea worth a tinker's damn if it could not get an honest million circulation in New York. And just because I feel the opposition is so soft, I would expect real success to double the Daily News circulation, i.e., get four or five million a day.

This optimism was not deterred by his belief that the paper should cost five cents when each of the other New York dailies sold for two or three cents. This would enable the paper "to be as nearly free as possible from dependence on advertising revenue."

To justify the price, Ingersoll was determined to use a rotogravure press which would make possible fine photographic reproduction. He wanted to use much better quality paper and inks.

He wanted to broaden what was considered news to (these are just a few of his notions) the latest discoveries in medicine, discussions of American history, and extensive coverage of radio and movies. Ideas poured out of his head and ran over the *Outline*. He turned again to the paper's perspective, endorsing "crusades for decent living in this city. . . . Does Mrs. Schmaltz care if she pays more than she should for inferior meat?" This was tied to his conception of a "woman's page" which would treat "women's issues": health, education, clothing, food, shelter. "I have long thought that a newspaper ought to be able to do a woman's housekeeping for her."

He endorsed Archibald MacLeish's conception of objectivity as "keeping the object in view," which meant being able to make informed judgments. It did not mean being neutral.[30]

The sweep and scope of the *Discursive Outline* is breathtaking. It contains a perceptive analysis of the state of journalism, an optimistic and committed political creed, and scores of ideas—most of them original—about every aspect of creating a vibrant new journal. Like the newspaper that would emerge, it was full of ideas and not shy about articulating them. Addressed to a small coterie of collaborators, it was more than enough to begin the process of creation. The *Discursive Outline* might just as well have been called *The Ingersoll Manifesto*.

It was not long before Ingersoll turned from theory to action. While still editing *Time*, he began searching for financial backers for his newspaper. To Ed Stanley, just beginning the process of recruiting staff, he cautioned, "My name will not be used without my specific instructions." By 1939 he was churning out an endless stream of memos to describe the plans for his paper to the staff and to sell it as an investment to the well-heeled. The second objective was given an immediate boost when he called on an influential American named Franklin Roosevelt.[31]

The president had his own reasons for cultivating Ingersoll. Although his biographers differ about how seriously he was affected by his political setbacks during the second term, they all agree that nothing incensed him more than "unfair treatment" in the press. Always able to charm the Washington press corps, Roosevelt could not control the editorial pages of the newspapers which were first arrayed against him in 1932 and became increasingly hostile as the 1930s wore on. Fewer papers (about 25 percent of the press) backed him in 1936; by 1937 such influential papers as those in the Scripps-Howard chain, the *New York Times*, and Luce publications were also in opposition. Despite scurrilous attack in the editorial pages during his first term, Roosevelt had won a 1936 endorsement from a *New York Daily News* undoubtedly protecting itself from widespread reader revolt; now Joseph Patterson's editorials were sounding more like his cousin Colonel McCormick's *Chicago Tribune*. That paper was perhaps the most violently anti-Roosevelt in the country (it was a toss-up between the *Tribune* and the Hearst press). During the 1936 campaign, phones at the Tribune were answered "Only _____ more days to save your country. What are you doing to save it?" Betty Winfield notes, "After the President spoke in Chicago, the *Tribune* staged a picture of a man sweeping up discarded Roosevelt buttons from Chicago streets. *The Chicago Times* discovered that McCormick had paid the sweeper and donated the buttons."[32]

Roosevelt's biographers stress that FDR had not determined whether he would run for a third term in 1940; certainly he was disclosing his future to no one. The option of retaining his office was open, at least as a political threat to his opponents. Even if the president chose not to run he did not want to see an election which would overturn the political direction of the New Deal. He listened attentively as Ingersoll sketched his plans for a crusading liberal tabloid in New York; a fighting vehicle to counter the shrill attacks of the Hearst papers and the *Daily News* undoubtedly appealed to him. Hoopes reports that Roosevelt "chatted on for an hour—while his secretary held his phone calls—making suggestions about what ought to be in the paper."

Shortly after this session Ingersoll was summoned to a meeting with White House "brain truster" Thomas Corcoran. Corcoran had miraculously "solved" the entire financing problem, inducing assistant secretary of commerce and Life-savers manufacturer Edward J. Noble and his brother to put up the entire $1.5 million, which Ingersoll determined was the bare minimum necessary to get the project going. A written agreement was drawn up finalizing details. At that moment World War II began in Europe and the Nobles decided the world was too uncertain a place to begin new financial ventures.[33]

Determined to have his new paper come out quickly, Ingersoll frantically courted potential backers. He drew up the first of several documents for investors. The first, called *A Financial Proposal: A New Type of Newspaper*, briefly sketched Ingersoll's successes. It announced:

> The purpose of this newspaper is twofold:
>   1) To make money for its owners through
>   2) Keeping its readers more intelligently, entertainingly and truthfully informed, each day, on what has happened in the world in the previous twenty-four hours. . . .
>   The editorial policy of this paper calls for a return to crusading journalism in the old sense, but with numerous innovations both editorial and technical.

The first part of the proposal stressed Ingersoll's technological innovations at his old publications and the innovations he wanted for his newspaper, discussing photography, color on the front page, larger type, and better writing. Several successful recent magazines had proven an expensive new product could be sold to the public and to advertisers (at this stage Ingersoll was advocating limited advertising). This was a brand-new paper; people would buy it. Certainly the 200,000 readers necessary to break even would be quickly forthcoming. The features of the anticipated newspaper were described.

Ingersoll headed the next section "The Profit Opportunity," showing profits of half a million dollars for each increase of 50,000 readers over the break-even point of 200,000. He would sell common stock to raise $1.5 million. He would make money for his investors, but he made sure it was clear that "the editorial policies of the paper will be controlled by Mr. Ingersoll."

A longer reminder of Ingersoll's track record followed, including an endorsement from Henry Luce. Only on the nineteenth page did Ingersoll turn to the analysis and politics which had dominated his *Discursive Outline*. Blaming the "men of property" who controlled newspapers and who were "not journalists," Ingersoll traced the lack of newspaper innovation to publishers' desires to protect their antiquated plants. Since the new paper would not own its presses, no such obstacle would present itself. News would be gathered by better journalists excelling in a situation which maximized their talents. Only in the last three pages did Ingersoll approach editorial policy; he discussed it as vaguely as possible: "We cannot here, in a few paragraphs, do justice to such a complicated conception as an editorial policy and a journalistic credo." Nonetheless the paper would believe in truth, democracy, and "great crusades" and would be "without political affiliations . . . (political affiliations circumscribe crusades for truth)." Finally it endorsed the credo Ingersoll had coined for his staff: "We are against people who push other people around." He promised to begin publishing "ninety days after the completion of our financing." [34]

The proposal was designed to make the paper financially appealing without being specific enough about a political orientation to frighten anyone. Additional documents aimed at investors stressed the same themes. [35]

The $1.5 million Ingersoll needed he divided into fifteen units of $100,000 each. Even before he met Noble, he had had his first success landing Marian Stern, family heir to Sears. He appealed to his attorney, John Wharton, who had already incorporated Publications Research, for aid. Wharton lined up John (Jock) Whitney as the purchaser of the second unit. Whitney was enamored of the "against people who push other people around" phrase. A beginning had been made, but the going was slow. Once again the long arm of the Roosevelt administration reached out to cradle the infant publication.

Louis Weiss was John Wharton's partner. He was also attorney to Marshall Field III, recommended to Field by Field's—and Ingersoll's—psychiatrist, Gregory Zilboorg. Field, the designated inheritor of the fortune amassed by Marshall Field I in the dry goods (later department store) business, had emerged from a miserable marriage and idle life determined to do something meaningful. Zilboorg, a former Menshevik activist in Russia, counseled political and social involvement; Weiss was a socially conscious lawyer who could make connections for him. The name seemed familiar to Field. "You mean that Jewish lawyer who represented my wife in the divorce?" The discovery did not deter Field from seeking Weiss's help. It turned out to be fortunate. Field was about to inherit the bulk of his grandfather's estate; under the new inheritance taxes he stood to lose as much as $50 million of his astonishing wealth (when the first Field died in 1906 he left $120 million, most of which was placed in trust for his grandson). Weiss's able representation enabled Field to pay only a small fraction of the estimated taxes.

Weiss received a telephone call from Ingersoll's former mentor, Archibald MacLeish, then librarian of Congress and a friend of Eleanor Roosevelt. Mac-Leish told Weiss, "You have in your office what is potentially one of the greatest sources for liberalism in America, and it's just dying." Weiss went to Wharton's desk and read Ingersoll's *Financial Proposal*. He quickly arranged for Field to meet Ingersoll. As the latter spoke, Weiss asked questions. Field remained silent. As he was leaving, he apologetically informed Ingersoll he could take "only" two units. Richard Green, who would become secretary of *PM*'s board of directors, insisted that Ingersoll "would not have been able to put together the money without Louis Weiss."

The $1.5 million was finally raised from financial angels from across the political spectrum. While Field's interest was tied to his determined liberal activism, most of the investors were purchasing Ingersoll's reputation as a publishing genius. They expected to more than recoup their investment. Another "socially aware" investor was Chester Bowles. Having made a fabulous fortune in advertising, Bowles and his partner, William Benton, were devoting their lives to public service. Only Bowles invested in *PM*, but Benton was asked to work on publicity. Perhaps the most unusual investor was A&P heir Huntington Hartford III, whose life had already begun to unravel. His mother invested the money to subsidize a journalism career; to give stability to his life, Huntington was to be a cub reporter.

Weiss's contacts brought in Lincoln Schuster (of Simon and Schuster). Richard Green insists that others invested because of Weiss's influence, but he does not remember which ones. Field, of course, was the biggest fish. Ultimately, he would be the only one. The final group of investors were Marian Stern, Howard Bonbright (Ladenburg Thalmann investment banking), John Loeb (Loeb, Rhoades investment banking), Deering Howe (Deering tractors), Garrett Winston (corporate attorney), Elinor S. Gimbel (Gimbel's), who was a backer of many left and liberal causes, Marshall Field, Huntington Hartford, Harry Scherman (Book-of-the-Month Club), Dwight Deere Wiman (John Deere heir, a theatrical producer, and friend of Wharton's wife), Chester Bowles, Ira Williams, William and Lessing Rosenwald (Stern's brothers-in-law), Philip Wrigley (Wrigley's gum), and John Whitney. Stern and Field were each in for $200,000; Wrigley, Williams, Bowles, and Schuster for $50,000 each. The others invested $100,000 each. Dorothy Thompson originally planned to invest $50,000. Unlike the others, she was taking a considerable personal risk. Ingersoll returned her money.[36]

Making full use of his reputation as the man behind the revitalization of *Fortune* and the inventor of *Life*, Ingersoll's first *PM* crusade was to recruit future readers and the writing and production staff of the newspaper. William Benton was made a member of the executive committee of the board of directors to organize a massive publicity effort. Ingersoll later called it a "Blitzkrieg . . . stak[ing] our [financial] reserves and our reputation on a single campaign." Placards aimed at recruiting readers and staff members were placed in the subways. Harry Scherman's success at Book-of-the-Month Club led him to manage a publicity barrage to generate a list of home subscribers, which cost at least $100,000. *Editor and Publisher* was prevailed upon to carry articles and advertisements heralding the new venture.[37] The struggle was certainly effective. More than ten thousand journalists applied for fewer than two hundred positions. The campaign succeeded in selling over one hundred thousand subscriptions of varying lengths: one month, three months, or a year.[38]

Ingersoll promised his future employees a total break with the traditional practices of newspapers, including a hitherto unknown empowerment of all of *PM*'s writers. His spring 1939 *Proposition to Create a New Newspaper*, which ran through several drafts, again began with a diagnosis of the state of the press.[39] The best writers were not making careers in journalism, he argued, because the press had become rigid and conservative. Writers could make far better money in advertising, pulp-fiction production, or in trade journals. Newspapers further handicapped writers by forcing them to write "the torturous 'tell-all' lead sentence from which facts dribble away to fill space." Furthermore, they were forced to write from a fraudulently "objective" point of view in order to better represent the reactionary political perspectives of the "men of property" who owned newspapers.

Newspaper publishers had become a conservative caste for several reasons. In the narrowest sense their views reflected their investments in what had become archaic plants. Their old presses were not capable of printing on high quality paper, could not accommodate color, and made quality photographic reproduction impossible. Because they owned these presses, publishers were forced to use them and had recently decided to use cheaper (and lower quality) paper. (The argument is fascinating in light of the New York City newspaper wars of the 1980s and 1990s. Faced with a declining readership and advertising market, the *Daily News* and the *New York Post* were forced to try some of the innovations that Ingersoll claimed the papers of his time would not experiment with. Both introduced color and better photographic reproduction to fend off the challenge of Long Island–based *Newsday*. Even the aloof *New York Times* responded to the challenge. It revamped photographic coverage of sports events and then added color to several Sunday sections.)

Ingersoll found a ready analogy in transportation. The railroad companies were ignoring the new diesel technology because of their heavy investment in coal-burning locomotives. Imagine how backward airplane transportation would have been if that industry had followed railroad (and newspaper publishing) policy. We would still be flying Wright Brothers–type planes.

A second source of conservatism was to be found in the pernicious effects of advertising dependence. Because newspapers needed advertisers to remain in existence, they were afraid to offend their sponsors. This not only meant that the products of individual advertisers could not be critically appraised, but also that a contagious don't-rock-the-boat approach became the dominant attitude in creating newspaper policy.

Ingersoll proposed to remedy the problem by guaranteeing editorial independence from financial pressures. He insisted that the editorial staff would decide all questions of content and that a separate board of directors would deal with financial concerns. Left unsaid was the central notion that only Ralph Ingersoll would function in both groups. Furthermore *PM* would not buy its own presses— not as a matter of financial necessity, but as a matter of principle. In order that the new paper always be ready for the latest in production techniques, it would always rent the most up-to-date production plant and equipment. The implication of the *Proposition* (it had been explicit in the *Discursive Outline*) was that if in a year or two some better form of production became available *PM* would move its operation to the site and machinery which could produce the best newspaper. (When *PM* did move, it was to its own production facility in Manhattan. Ingersoll was in the army, Marshall Field was sole publisher, and managing editor John P. Lewis cheered the "permanent" home of the paper. No one worried then that the publication would be dangerously wedded to its own equipment.)

Advertising would not be a problem. The *Discursive Outline*'s musing about a five-cent cost was now policy. Ingersoll retained his confidence that his paper would sell despite its high price. The *Saturday Evening Post*, a periodical he thought should be extinct, was having trouble selling for five cents, but *Life* could not print enough copies to satisfy demand despite its ten-cent cost. Since *PM* would be worth buying, it would have no trouble selling enough copies to pay its way without advertising.

Nonetheless, Ingersoll did not rule out advertising in the *Proposition*. Having established financial independence of advertisers, the newspaper would be pleased to accept the right kind of advertising. There would not be much of it, because space was too precious, but there would be some, provided it made no fraudulent claims, did not stoop to debasing sales techniques, and provided a genuine service to the readers. Here Ingersoll seemed to be reflecting the attitudes of Harold Ross, his employer at the *New Yorker*, who had bitterly complained to Ingersoll about having to accept degrading advertising in his journal. Ingersoll's help in creating the detached air of that magazine had enabled it to accept only the tony advertisements which had become part of its fame.[40]

The paper would be innovative in its use of photographs. Not only would its presses print the highest quality reproductions, but the photographs would be used differently. Unlike existing newspapers, which used a photograph "solely as an illustration, an ornament, a supernumerary," Ingersoll promised a paper which could use pictures as "a *primary* means of conveying information." He envisioned a high-quality, tabloid-size paper, "very slightly larger than the most successful paper in the U.S., the *New York Daily News*." He expected a circulation of 250,000 at the end of the first year and with typical confidence repeated the *Discursive Outline*'s extravagant claim "that its ultimate circulation may reach 5,000,000."

Most important to the would-be journalists reading this declaration of principles, Ingersoll insisted that reporters would have the opportunity to write in their own styles what they themselves considered important news. He envisioned a democratic group process in which the entire editorial staff would collectively decide the newspaper's contents, while the individual stylistic talents of the writers would tell the stories. Furthermore, the objective of the paper would be to communicate the "truth," not "objectivity." Ingersoll rejected the notion that impartiality could be achieved. Such a view did not exist. Although his own vantage point is much less explicit than in the *Discursive Outline*, the generally liberal slant is obvious:

> We are against people who push other people around, just for the fun of pushing, whether they flourish in this country or abroad. We are against fraud and deceit and greed and cruelty and we seek to expose their practitioners. We are for people who are kindly and courageous and honest. We respect intelligence, and accomplishment, open-mindedness, religious tolerance. We do not believe all mankind's problems are soluble in any existing social order, certainly not our own, and we propose to applaud those who seek constructively to improve the way men live together. We are American and we prefer democracy to any other form of government.

"*PM* is against people who push other people around" became the cornerstone slogan of the newspaper. It was printed several times a week until Ingersoll resigned as editor in November 1946. As a political credo it appears banal, but compared to the deeply conservative, Republican, stridently anti-Roosevelt editorial policy dominating the newspaper world, it had great appeal.

The future staff of the paper was expected "until it makes its first profit . . . to make personal sacrifices, in time and money, to insure its success." Afterward, the staff would "be well paid and shall share in its profits." This was to happen once—in 1945—when John P. Lewis told the readers that *PM*'s staff had received its first dividend. It was a modest amount, as the more than four hundred editorial and production employees shared a total of $22,064.98 put aside for "employee share of profits."[41] Arthur Leipzig's share brought him $44; obviously it had little financial impact on his life.[42] George Lyon would later estimate that with a handful of exceptions, including City Hall reporter William P. Vogel and sports columnist Tom Meany, most *PM* writers who left other journals did so at a financial loss.[43] Given the great expectations that the new paper's promotional campaign had created, journalists were flocking to the paper, not for an anticipated profit, but for a place in the revolutionary experiment to reinvent journalism and empower its writers and photographers.

As a further inducement to both investors and journalists, Ingersoll put together a crew of friends to print a sample. Called simply *Newspaper*, the sample anticipated *PM* in many ways, though the issue—dated 26 April 1939—was fourteen months ahead of the first day of mass publication. It featured burnt orange in addition to black and white on the front page, decorating a map inside, and on sketches of a governmental hearing inside. Several photographs were done in shades of blue rather than black. The most spectacular effort was a husband-and-wife report on the Midwest. Erskine Caldwell described the life of wheat farmers. Margaret Bourke-White illustrated with a stunning, full-page photograph looking up at a farmer standing in his wheat field, which Bourke-White took from ground level. A one-column story on a coal strike was made arresting by Walker Evans–type photos from the Farm Security Administration; captions created a poetic essay on the lives of miners and their children. A story on tuberculosis in New York featured Mary Morris's uncredited stark photograph of a Harlem sufferer.[44] Dorothy Parker and Alan Campbell reviewed the opening of *No Time for Comedy*, Dashiell Hammett discussed *Finnegan's Wake*, Oscar Levant reported on a concert at Carnegie Hall, and Lillian Hellman critiqued the movie *Juarez*. Ingersoll's friends were having fun; the letters page was done entirely in Latin. The dummy issue proved how beautiful and impressive Ingersoll's ideas were.[45]

By 22 April 1940, Ingersoll's *Confidential Memorandum to the Staff of "PM"*[46] was able to forecast accurately much of the look and contents of the paper. It was to be thirty-two pages daily, except for sixty-four pages on Sunday. It would be slightly bigger than eleven by fourteen inches. The promise of high-quality photographic reproduction, paper stock, and clear, large print had been fulfilled by locating the necessary equipment in a plant owned by the publishers of the *Brooklyn Eagle*. Stories were "to be printed in full, in one place (no 'continued on page ____')." An additional color for the front page besides black was promised, and the color was to change daily. In practice, the colors were most often green, red, and burnt orange, which was the signature color. All of the small delivery trucks were burnt orange.[47] To keep the tabloid together, the paper was to be stapled.

Despite Ingersoll's somewhat exaggerated claims, *PM* was strikingly attractive, even after rationing shortened it and eliminated its second color. Ingersoll recruited the artist Thomas Clelland from Luce publications to design it. Clelland created the wide four columns, chose its large Caledonia type, and created its eye-pleasing front page. A quarter-inch border of color boxed the top, bottom, and left sides of the paper. In the top left corner, the color extended to create a nearly three-inch-square box, where ꝑꝳ *Daily* FIVE CENTS was printed in white. Underneath the box the volume number, date, and weather had its own box, and below this some of the news inside was highlighted. The remaining 70 percent of the front page was turned over to one or two stories—most often just one. Many styles of headline (from the preferred bold to script or italics) would usually fill this space, but occasionally important editorials would begin there. Impressive photographs or drawings might supplement a headline. Clelland's work was well recognized. During the first four years, *PM* annually won the N. W. Ayer Award for typography and makeup.[48]

Although the place for this section was changed, six to eight pages were generally reserved for *PM*'s Daily Picture Magazine. The photographs, whether reproduced from wire services or taken by *PM*'s own photographers, are sharper than photographs in newspapers of fifty years later. Photographs of cops beating striking workers, miners smeared with coal dust, the *Normandie* lying on its side in New York Harbor, or a full-page photograph of Franklin Roosevelt smiling through the rain in his New York campaign appearance of 1944 indeed "conveyed information." *PM* anticipated television in its stunning pictorial news reporting. (Whether the name *PM* stood for P.M.—it was supposed to be an afternoon paper, though its first editions came out in the morning—or "Picture Magazine," or something else entirely is unclear. Ingersoll's biographer thinks miscommunication between Lillian Hellman and Broadway gossip columnist Leonard Lyons may have named the paper. Reporter Charles Michie gave columnist Walter Winchell naming honors, for continuing to call Ingersoll's proposed daily "the new P.M. newspaper." In a letter to readers in 1943, John P. Lewis wrote, "A lot of people have speculated that it means Post Mortem, Post Meridian, Pell Mell, Pock Marked, Prime Minister, and a dozen others, but actually it wasn't intended to mean any of these things. It was picked out, frankly, with one eye on the fact that readers would speculate about it.")[49]

A legend in the making, freelance news photographer Arthur Fellig sold his photographs to *PM* and to the other daily papers. Known to everyone as "Weegee," he "lived in a little hovel with a police radio." His careful monitoring of the police band allowed him to be first at many crime scenes. His graphic work of the seamy side of New York, highlighted by *PM*'s brilliant reproduction capabilities, turned him into an "urban reporter with a camera." His specialty was photographs of prostitutes and victims of gangland murders. Too reclusive to be a full-time staff member, Weegee sold his work to *PM* as a freelance artist. Even as independent and creative a photographer as Mary Morris found him "exotic."[50] The 1992 film *The Public Eye* presented a fictionalized Weegee type.

Photographers were liberated from existing shibboleths. Arthur Leipzig recalls his first shoot. He arrived at the scene to find several press photographers framing the subject from the same angle. He shot a picture with them. Then, as the other photographers began to leave, he decided to approach the subject from a different location. The other photographers, annoyed, returned to take a picture from the second vantage point. Back at the office, a *PM* colleague explained to Leipzig that photographic editors insisted that their photographers have the same picture as the competition. But Leipzig and his colleagues at *PM* were encouraged not only to find a better angle, but to find a better subject. If a picture assignment had "Must" written on the assignment sheet, a photographer was required to return with the photograph; if not, the photographer's discretion was welcomed. No other New York City paper so empowered its photojournalists. The results were rewarding. Leipzig was once asked to go to the Waldorf-Astoria Hotel to cover a blood drive. He could not imagine a more boring assignment, but he soon forgot all about the tedium. Also at the hotel was a group of absurdly costumed dowagers, who turned out to be the national leadership of the Daughters of the American Revolution. Grabbing the opportunity, Leipzig took several portraits, capturing the haughty "dignity" of the elderly xenophobes better than any words could. His editors were delighted. A two-page spread displayed the DAR in all of its would-be aristocratic grandeur. It was as eloquent as any angry denunciation of the group's racism could be.[51] No wonder Leipzig continues to believe that working for *PM* was unique, because "anything was possible."[52]

Ingersoll thought it was. In the *Memorandum* he confidently predicted no one would have to read the rest of the press to find the day's news—something his newspaper never made possible. He explained that gossip and other trivial information would be summarized in a feature called "File and Forget." A similar column of straight news that would elicit no comment would be summarized under the headline "For the Record." Both columns did appear throughout the first year or so of *PM*'s existence. He outlined the three departments that would be unique to his newspaper: the labor, press, and radio sections. Chapter 4 below examines *PM*'s treatment of labor. The press column lasted only as long as Hodding Carter, who wrote it, stayed with the paper. Ingersoll, disappointed in his work, fired him during the first economy cutbacks of August 1940. Carter was not particularly sorry. Despairing both of *PM*'s journalistic soundness and his own adjustment to life in New York City, he returned to Mississippi.[53]

The radio page was a great innovation. It was a constant at the paper even after *PM* reduced its size to twenty-four shorter pages. On occasions when the whole paper would be given over to a major event like D-Day or to a major crusade, the radio page would be all that survived of the paper's regular features. Ingersoll envisioned it as "two pages of tables to help the reader find his way through the ether, a daily column called the Listener's Digest which prints excerpts from the most interesting scripts of the last twenty-four hours, news of the commercial success of programs, etc., etc."

The radio section was all that and more. Developed by *Time* veteran John T. McManus, the schedule took a full page. A separate page carried radio news, including program recommendations. Today's newspapers all perform this function for television, but before *PM* no newspaper had carried such a guide. Whatever radio news appeared in newspapers was paid advertising or an open effort to procure advertising revenue. The new paper was consciously providing a public service no one had thought of before. Complete movie listings were similarly provided, also a *PM* first.[54]

Ingersoll recognized that radio was a medium in which news could be made or dramatically reported. He assigned John A. Sullivan the task of following international cables from CBS and deciding which ones made good reporting. Sullivan selected many dispatches for transcription in the newspaper. Another source of news and commentary was the daily CBS file of international shortwave broadcasts. Several CBS reporters returned to the United States and summarized their experiences in *PM*, no doubt remembering their past representation in the paper.[55] Radio commentary was often summarized beside a drawn lightning bolt representing radio waves. Whenever a *PM* writer appeared on radio, as Max Lerner did regularly, news of his broadcast would be reported on the radio page.

What Ingersoll does not disclose in his *Memorandum* is the social meaning implicit in carrying radio and film listings. By doing so, the paper was addressing its middle- and working-class audience as consumers. Recognizing the leisure habits of most New Yorkers, *PM* undertook to meet their concerns in a way no other newspaper had treated as important before. The tabloid considered the cultural choices its readership made a legitimate avenue to explore and to comment on. McManus frequently reviewed radio programs and movies. Cecelia Ager, formerly of *Variety*, also reviewed film, Louis Kronenberger, wrote about theater, and Henry Simon criticized music. The reviews are shorter and snappier than are currently fashionable, but the film reviews still read as apt commentaries on their subjects. Kronenberger had been hired away from *Time*, which found that it could not bring in a replacement so astute. He then wrote reviews for both publications, but signed his own name only to the ones appearing in *PM*. Members of the staff maintain that, in Green's words, "No other paper—not even the *Times*—could come close to our 'back of the book' section."[56]

Approaching ordinary people as consumers was not limited to the arts. The longest section in Ingersoll's *Memorandum* is his description of the News for Living section, which was developed by Elizabeth Hawes, whose book *Fashion Is Spinach* had been a best-seller.[57]

News for Living meant regular discussions of housing, educational, and health issues, which the newspaper faithfully covered throughout its existence. In a series which is eerily applicable today, *PM* ran Morris Engel's graphic photographs demonstrating that one-third of New York City's schools were "unfit for habitation," including a picture of an outdoor toilet at one school. The paper was pleased to proclaim "*PM* Gets a Victory" when the board of education announced it would replace the schools the paper had photographed.[58] Albert Deutsch, health and science editor, exposed the appalling state of the mental hospitals in the city thirty years before Geraldo Rivera used the scandal at Staten Island's Willowbrook State Hospital to climb his ladder to fame.[59]

News for Living was to contain summaries of advertising in the other newspapers, so that what was newsworthy—the actual facts of the sale—could be presented to *PM*'s readers without any hype. Ingersoll claimed, "Thus *PM* could have its cake—give its readers the news in the ads—without getting indigestion from eating it." The paper would search out real bargains and report them to its readers. It would report on good values available in food and clothing daily and in other areas occasionally.

None of this sounds exciting today, but before the expansion of the *New York Times* into four sections during the 1970s, *PM* was the lone pioneer. It regularly treated these "women's issues" as the basic needs of all citizens, and tried to meet those needs as a disinterested observer. When the *Times* entered this field thirty years later, and was closely followed by the rest of the press, attracting new advertising dollars was the transparent motive (anyone who clips food coupons on Wednesdays or searches for computer bargains on Tuesdays can attest to this). *PM* writers thought that designing a meal for a working-class family of six was more important than describing a banquet attended by the Windsors. They thought that recommending a skirt on sale at Orbach's for $2.29 was necessary and that describing the outfits worn by European royalty or Hollywood stars was not. Their models were attractive children and women wearing bargain clothes. Until rationing eliminated these pages from the paper, it was not unusual to have clothing bargains, sales, and information fill pages 28 and 29.

Charlotte Adams, Hawes's sister, covered food on page 27. Often a low-cost menu for a full day was represented on the left, while a medium-cost menu was represented on the right. Recipes, shopping lists, and costs were provided. Costs included "left-over value" for a readership whose consciousness was formed by the depression. Low-cost meals were created for families with annual incomes of $1,750. Medium-cost meals were for families whose annual incomes began at $3,000. One day's recipes included sauteed potato balls, lemon meringue pie (both low cost), and leftover lamb and mushroom casserole (medium cost).[60] Ironically, *PM* was explicating the nineteenth-century middle-class value of thrift, while its competition encouraged a twentieth-century extravagant consumerism which made advertisers content.

Ingersoll's *Memorandum* again endorsed vivid photography as a news principle and added his insistence on gathering an excellent stable of graphic artists to draw. Margaret Bourke-White, whose reputation as an artist had already been made at *Life*, was an original photographer. She would stay at *PM* for less than a year because she could not get used to newspaper deadlines. She was famous in the office for going out to poor neighborhoods, where workers would react to her use of the hair rinse fashionable among the well-to-do by staring at the "lady with the poiple hair," and returning "with a freight car full of negatives an hour before deadline."[61] The group that remained—Gene Badger, Wilbert Blanche, John DeBiase, Steven Derry, Morris Engel, Alan Fischer, Morris Gordon, Irving Haberman, Martin Harris, Arthur Leipzig, Mary Morris, and Ray Platnick—

produced memorable work regularly. Platnick's use of zoom lenses to capture runners sliding across home plate at Ebbetts Field, the Polo Grounds, and Yankee Stadium was an innovation extensively imitated. Harris's picture of FDR in the rain is perhaps the most renowned.

The graphic artists working under art director Charles Tudor were also to find fame. Dr. Seuss was *PM*'s first regular political cartoonist, leaving, as so many on the staff did, to serve in the war against fascism. Harold Dietje contributed the brilliant maps that dominated war coverage. Reginald Marsh's sketches and Charles Martin's satirical "War Relief" drawings were a regular feature of the Sunday Magazine. John Piorotti began his career at *PM*. He eventually became editorial cartoonist for the *New York Post*. Right-wing congressman Hamilton Fish was the subject of frequent attention in *PM*. Every article was accompanied by a drawing of a dead fish on a plate.

By the time of the *Memorandum* it was clear that *PM* would carry no advertising. Ingersoll had been convinced by Nelson Poynter, briefly appointed as business manager, whose experience as editor of the *St. Petersburg* (Florida) *Times* indicated that for small newspapers, advertising was not cost-effective. Ingersoll wrote that "this way, people will be convinced from the very beginning that we are getting out a paper entirely in their interest—instead of in the interest of merchants trying to sell them something." Richard Green asserted the decision had nothing to do with principle. Without advertising, which would have been difficult to acquire to meet Ingersoll's specifications, the paper did not have to hire an advertising staff or handle its claim on the limited size of the anticipated newspaper. Green said the decision was purely an economic one.[62] Two untitled and undated memos in the Ingersoll papers obviously written between the *Proposition* and the *Memorandum* contain the first "Announcement: We are going in business without advertising." In these memos, Ingersoll makes clear his intention to gather the advertising news from other papers and to pass on the material to *PM*'s readers; he also notes that supervising advertising to make sure it was worthy of printing would have been a burdensome job and that ads had only been considered to begin with as a public service to the readers. That public service could now be accomplished without actually accepting ads and without the necessary advertising staff and additional printing-equipment expenses. Both principle and cost seem to have been factors; Ingersoll decided to trumpet the decision as one of principle. Anti-advertising rhetoric quickly became the gospel. Jonathan King, who worked as a cub reporter for *PM*, wrote, "I thought adlessness was next to godliness."[63]

Only at the end of his *Memorandum* did Ingersoll directly address the "editorial purpose" of his new paper. He defined its liberalism as including "a philosophy of optimism—that we who live in it can make the world a better place than it is today; that we should not resign ourselves to injustice and inequality of opportunity, to fraud and corruption, to the cruelty of man to man—any more than the scientist of yesterday should have resigned himself to the fact that yellow fever was thought to be incurable." The only specifics Ingersoll offered his staff were that "*PM* believes in the institution of the trade union. . . . The cause of racial tolerance will be championed without fear." The belief in trade union-ism was translated into a "model" Newspaper Guild contract covering all edito-rial employees, including the copyboys. It was generous: the average salary and benefit package at *PM* was better than at any other newspaper in New York. The second guild contract made *PM* the first newspaper to offer severance pay for workers who resigned. Among those who served on the guild's *PM* grievance committee were Penn Kimball and Hannah Baker. Carl Randau and John T. McManus, outgoing and incoming presidents of the New York guild, gave *PM*'s chapter experienced leadership. Kenneth Crawford, hired away from the *New York Post* to organize *PM*'s Washington bureau, served as interim national presi-dent of the guild after Broun's death. His April 1940 loss in the guild elections to a candidate backed by McManus and Randau brought union factionalism to the paper before it had printed a single issue.[64]

Was the retreat from the United Front motivated by a desire to mollify his investors, who could read not only Ingersoll's memoranda to them, but also the voluminous material he was sending out to the staff? Perhaps in part. John Kob-ler remembers Ingersoll at a social gathering of the staff making sneering refer-ences to his investors and expressing the hope he would soon be financially able to be rid of them.[65] More relevant, perhaps, was the changed state of the world. The Spanish Republic was gone, and the Soviet Union, which had championed the "United Front against Fascism," was at that moment sworn to nonaggression toward Nazi Germany. The "Radical" of the *Discursive Outline* might have been reevaluating. Even before the nonaggression Pact, Ingersoll's *Notes on Where We Stand Politically*,[66] written in May 1939, indicated a far more agnostic political stance than the United Front endorsement of the *Discursive Outline*.

"It must be obvious by now, " Ingersoll began, "that we are doing everything we can to sidestep direct questions on contemporary politics. We do that princi-pally to be sure our words cannot be twisted to say things we don't mean them to say." Nonetheless, certain principles could be articulated.

> The Fascist philosophy [represents] a live threat to everything we believe in, be-ginning with a democratic way of life. . . . We do not believe either the study of the works of Karl Marx or membership in the Communist Party in America is anti-social . . . and its practitioners ducked or burned alive for no further cause. But the Russian Communists have, in our opinion, only their good intentions to justify their present government by dictatorship because we do not believe in any permanent dic-tatorship. (Their good intentions: to educate their 160,000,000 people to a point where they can govern themselves democratically.)

The forthright condemnation of fascism was certainly not likely to cost Inger-soll the investors, readers, or potential staff members he would want, but the explicit refusal to engage in anticommunism was potentially troublesome with all three groups. The commendable civil libertarian sentiment might offend many people's prejudices. An endorsement of the "good intentions" of Stalin's government reads like blind naïveté today.

The rest of the document is expressly agnostic. "We do not know the answer to . . ." began paragraphs on "the Negro question . . . the Unemployment question . . . Centralized Government vs States Rights . . . the Farm problem."

Though most of us voted for Roosevelt in the last election, not one of us will admit [that] . . . means unqualified approval of The New Deal. . . . We are in business to tell people what's going on in this world so that they may do whatever pleases them about it. Not to bully them, or to preach to them or to hold up to them anything but the image of themselves and the world they have created.

No reader of *PM* would recognize the paper to come from that last injunction.

Ingersoll mentioned in the *Memorandum* that the paper would cover sports. Tom Meany and Heywood Hale Broun began distinguished careers in sports journalism writing for *PM*, though the younger Broun was soon lost to the armed forces. Tom O'Reilly and Joe Cummiskey, the sports editor, completed the staff. The newspaper's overall emphasis on personal writing styles was most compatible with sports. Most of the articles combined news reporting with column-style features. Meany was able to develop friendships with many of New York's baseball players. His amicable interviews set the standard for the kinds of sports profiles that appeared in the 1950s and 1960s, before the search for dollars and scandal often made sports writers and athletes antagonistic. Meany's success eventually led him to a career as a publicist for the Brooklyn Dodgers. While still with *PM*, he accompanied Joe DiMaggio to visit troops overseas. Before war rationing, sports took up all of pages 30 and 31, and often a photograph page in the Daily Picture Magazine. After rationing, sports coverage shrank, on rare occasions disappearing altogether.

The one feature not anticipated by Ingersoll was the development of the paper's own comic strips and their subsequent syndication. The first strip, appearing in August 1941, was "Patoruzu," a broad comedy serial drawn by Quinterno featuring a stereotypical American Indian. Today, it would probably be considered racist or at least in bad taste. "Vic Jordan," a soap opera featuring an antifascist working underground in occupied France, followed in December 1941. It most resembles Milton Caniff's "Terry and the Pirates" with overt antifascist politics. Crockett Johnson's "Barnaby," which began in the spring of 1942, gained the most fame. The title character was a baby-faced child who thought with more common sense than his imaginary, winged friend, Mr. O'Malley. That peculiar figure spoke in opaque English and frequently made poor decisions, needing Barnaby to straighten him out. The humor was surreal; Dorothy Thompson wrote that she could not start her day without reading the strip. The cult that developed around the comic ensured that "Barnaby" would outlive *PM*.

Ingersoll made no mention of cheesecake, but pictures of pretty young women were a staple, particularly in the early years. In the beginning, photographic editors scrambled to announce excuses. Once the paper announced it would feature "*PM*'s Birthday Girl of the Week"; a week later the idea was changed to "Bathing Girl of the Week." Bathing suits on Coney Island made many summer days' "swimsuit issues," and *PM* also photographed union beauty contests, other kinds of beauty contests, stewardesses, chorus girls, and female defense workers. When it could not find a particular theme the paper proved that "New York is a City of Beautiful Women." Photographers were partial to what headline writers called "leg art."[67]

The war cut down the cheesecake in the daily paper, but regularized it in the Sunday Magazine, which became Picture News in 1941. There, a full-page photograph called "Okay, Joe?" offered GIs and any other males reading the paper full-page pinups of the famous and would-be famous. Jane Russell's sultry stills from the unreleased *Outlaw* made the most appearances. Earlier Picture News had combined cheesecake with *PM*'s plebeian orientation. It ran a weekly feature about "*PM*'s Average Girl," following the adventures of a pretty young working-class woman around town. When one married, the paper ran a contest: "Want to be *PM*'s average girl?" The contestants were told they should be pretty, but not beautiful. Ultimately the second "average girl" left the paper and the feature ceased. Even when exposing the constraints of chauvinism, the magazine could not help indulging it. Elizabeth Hawes's attack of uplift bras as being unnatural torture was accompanied by a full-page photograph of a model wearing one.[68] A regular feature of exercise on the beach provided still more ogling material.

Although *PM*'s flashiest posture on sexual roles was all too traditional, it championed the rights of women to enter the workplace and advocated child-care services for women defense workers.[69] The women staffers insist that no sexism restricted their roles on the paper. Margaret Bourke-White and Mary Morris were the first women press photographers on a daily paper; Sally Winograd Berger believes that she was the first woman reporter assigned to a newspaper's city desk. Cecilia Youngdahl was given responsibility for handling all syndication matters, including comic strips and columns—one of the few ways *PM* found to make money. John P. Lewis was cast from an older mold. When financial pressures forced him to reduce the staff, he wrote to Mary Morris, trying to break the news gently. She reports, "Lewis told me that it hurt him to do it *but after all I had a husband who could support me!*" (Morris's emphasis).[70]

Picture News was run with total control by William McCleery. He had established his credentials by directing the Associated Press features unit. Though Ingersoll tried to keep up with all aspects of the paper, he gave McCleery free rein. John P. Lewis, a careful, hands-on editor, continued to give McCleery complete independence. He designed a beautiful magazine that reflected the overall political posture and concerns of the parent newspaper. His features tended to be longer. For its first two years, *PM* celebrated its growth by charting the progress of "Baby Lois," who came into the world when the paper did. McCleery's pediatrician was the anonymous source for Lois and provided the information which accompanied her photographs. The pediatrician ceased writing about Lois around the time his book on child care was published. The doctor's name was Benjamin Spock.

McCleery wrote a weekly letter to GIs called "Dear Joe," in which he wrote genially about problems back home and abroad from a liberal perspective. Issues that had been raised in the paper might be treated at greater length in Picture News, which spent three weeks telling the story of College of William and Mary students who demanded that their school desegregate. Reviews of new books by Roi Ottley, Max Werner, and Max Lerner marked the first appearances by these men in the pages of *PM*. Movies were highlighted with a series of stills. McCleery's magazine was successful enough to induce Marshall Field to use it for the Sunday supplement of his new *Chicago Sun*. The increased Sunday circulation of *PM* and the *Sun* convinced Field to syndicate the weekly supplement. It is *PM*'s most lasting success. Today the syndicated version is called *Parade*, and appears in hundreds of newspapers around the country, including the *New York Sunday News*. McCleery insists that its impact was immediate. Within a year of the appearance of Picture News, both the *New York Times* and the *New York Herald Tribune* transformed their Sunday magazines, adding more features and photographs and cleaning up their printing processes. As with *PM*, the *Herald Tribune* is survived by its Sunday magazine, which now sells independently as *New York*.[71]

While not following the *Proposition* and the *Memorandum* in every detail, *PM* looked much like the paper Ingersoll described. It was beautiful; its News for Living and radio and movie guides addressed working people's consumer needs; and its photographs easily excelled those which appeared in the competition. Its sophisticated treatment of the arts rivaled any contemporary publication. Photographs from the war in Europe were powerfully evocative (see Chapter 3 below). The sympathetic and fulsome treatment of labor was unprecedented (see Chapter 4 below). That all of this was accomplished from the initial issues is impressive; given the utter chaos of the opening days it is nearly unbelievable.

Before publication began, a major threat to *PM*'s existence was created by the *Daily News*. Newsdealers were refusing to carry *PM*. The stands the papers rested on were donated by the *News*; that paper was invoking a clause that said if the stands were full, no new paper would be able to take the space of an existing one. But *PM* was an afternoon paper; there was plenty of room. Well, no. *News* management had insisted that the other afternoon papers be placed *horizontally* on the stands to take up all the room. The dealers were sympathetic but the *Daily News*, with an average daily circulation of 2.25 million, was their bread and butter. *News* management had been explicit: It was to be either *PM* or the *Daily News*.

Ingersoll went to see Joseph Patterson. He was amiable but made it clear the *News* was going to test the new paper every way it could. At midnight an exhausted but irate Ingersoll was pounding at the door of Gracie Mansion. "Who runs this city," he demanded of Mayor La Guardia, "You, or the *Daily News*?"

Attorney and board secretary Richard Green was dispatched to see the assistant attorney general for antitrust prosecution, Thurman Arnold. While Green watched, Arnold placed a call to the *News* lawyers and threatened them with an antitrust suit. By the next week a compromise had been arranged: *PM* would provide the dealers with a separate rack for the new paper. There would be no further interference with its sales.[72]

For over a week before publication day, dummy issues were printed for the staff's review.[73] Ingersoll was eager to get a paper out as soon as the presses in Brooklyn were ready to roll; his staff was already being paid, and he badly needed to generate income from the sale of the paper to avoid totally depleting his funds.[74] He would later estimate that half of his $1.5 million seed money was spent on the initial promotion efforts.[75] The rotogravure production presses had never attempted a daily paper before; clearly the presses would take more time to print *PM* than the traditional newspapers needed. There was a technical problem that arose with mass production. After about 200,000 copies, the rotogravure plates would lose sharpness. This would mean new plates would have to be made, which would inexorably further slow production.

Finally 18 June arrived. Editorial staff joined with production staff to get the paper out and loaded onto trucks: *PM*'s own trucks because the Mail Deliverers Union, working with *Daily News* management, was refusing to deliver the newspaper to New York's newsstands. Suddenly fire broke out in the newsroom; firemen arrived to extinguish it. No one had time to notice the distraction because everyone was working frantically to produce and deliver 400,000 papers.

Ingersoll had decided on that number because of the phenomenal success of Benton's campaign. The whole city was waiting to see what the new experiment would yield. Few trucks even got to the newsstands. Deliverers were surrounded by crowds who demanded to buy the paper. Most of the drivers surrendered; they sold their stocks of newspapers to the crowds encircling them. Ingersoll had decided people would pay a nickel for the new paper; on the first day "scalpers" were selling copies secondhand for fifty cents. Not since Charles Dickens had serialized *The Old Curiosity Shop* and Little Nell had been left at death's door had a periodical been so eagerly awaited. At least Dickens's work made it to the newsstands.

Amid the commotion of circulating the first day's paper, all but a few hundred copies left the plant. Exhausted, Ingersoll and company retired to the newsroom. Suddenly, someone remembered the subscribers. Had home delivery been successful? Aghast, the staff realized that home delivery had not even been attempted. It was too late for 18 June, but surely the mistake would be remedied for the next day. But where was the subscribers' list? No one could find it. Weeks later, a mass of dumped file cards containing some of the list was found near a wastebasket. No one knew how many cards had been lost or why they had been lost. Gone was at least $100,000 of Ingersoll's desperately needed seed money. The goodwill of those who had committed themselves to subscriptions was dissipated as well. It would take months to record what remained of the list and determine the length of each subscription.[76]

The chaos of opening day was only partially diminished during the next couple of weeks. One problem was caused by Ingersoll's promise of editorial independence for the reporters. To guarantee that what the reporters wrote would be what was printed, *PM* began publication without a functioning copy desk. Reporters submitted their copy; typographers had to make it fit on the page assigned for that story. No copy desk meant no last minute reporting from the scene; it meant minimal technical supervision. It meant more delays in the production room. It was ridiculous, particularly since, as Ingersoll confided to Ken Stewart, "I'll admit that we need both screwballs and competent technicians. So far I've been concentrating pretty heavily on the screwballs." Stewart noticed one "technician" working with a group of "screwballs":

> John P. Lewis, one of the hardest working and most patient of men . . . was driven nearly to distraction by the "school of journalism" he was forced to conduct in the News for Living department, composed largely of young people who knew about education, consumer service and the like, but who had scarcely seen a typewriter, let alone a linotype. Technical newspaper experience had not been a requisite at *PM*, and in fact Ingersoll sometimes regarded it as a handicap . . . [but] some orthodox practices couldn't be summarily scrapped if you wanted the paper to get to press on time.[77]

This was a consequence of Ingersoll's unusual hiring procedures. According to Stewart,

> The original staff was largely recruited from three main sources: The field of experts and writers on special subjects who had little or no technical newspaper background, and who might be called the non-professional intellectuals; the field of orthodox technicians from such training schools as the Associated Press and the Scripps-Howard chain, and who might be called the non-intellectual professionals; the men trained in Henry Luce's "new journalism" or fresh from a year at Harvard as Nieman Fellows, who might be called the professional intellectuals.[78]

To correct the chaos, "green eyeshade" Rae Weimer was assigned to the copy desk. For the next eight years, "all the copy that went into the paper went through me." After Weimer's initial editing, Dashiell Hammett was prevailed upon to proof articles anonymously for last minute improvements in writing style prior to publication. Weimer enjoyed Hammett's quiet wit, but he thinks that assigning the writer to improve prose style after it had been through the copy desk was foolish.[79] William McCleery remembers him as every bit the "thin man": tall, tweedy, silent, puffing at his pipe.[80] By mid-July the thin man had disappeared, replaced by greenshades and, according to Ken Stewart's account, banished by Ingersoll's grandiloquent response to the first attack of red-baiting made on *PM*.

The issue of communism and anticommunism as *PM* treated it in its own pages and as it affected the internal workings of the newspaper will be discussed later. The first appearance is relevant here because of how it contributed to the air of frenzy in the already harried newsroom. A friendly reporter on another paper brought in a leaflet being distributed to the other newsrooms in town. It charged that *PM* was being dominated by a group of communists; thirty were identified by name as either party members or sympathizers. The inaccuracy of the list is immediately apparent: James Wechsler is named as a sympathizer. Befuddled Huntington Hartford is accused of being a "parlor pink." Ingersoll decided the best way to confront the leaflet was to print it under the title "Volunteer Gestapo." Surrounding his copy with photographs of his named journalists, he announced, "We are sending this slanderous document to the FBI, asking that as soon as they have hunted down all the Fifth Columnists and have some time, they come and investigate us. Or if they wish, they could do it right away." Writing before the Freedom of Information Act, Ingersoll had no way of knowing what the FBI would do with such a document. *PM* would generate quite a large file, almost all of it filled with the kind of scurrilous material represented by the leaflet. In his haste to appear the beleaguered hero, Ingersoll never asked his named staff what they thought of being publicly identified as either reds or the red-baited in their own newspaper.[81] Stewart, at least, found it difficult to be amused. He noted that Hammett had attempted to talk Ingersoll out of printing the list (Hammett himself was not named). The editor had agreed, but in the middle of the night he had a change of heart. He called Hammett to inform his "friend" that he was going to publish the list and to ask Hammett to help cool the red-baiters by staying away from the paper for a time. He was not seen in the newsroom again.[82]

As young veterans of the newspaper business, Penn Kimball (national affairs) and William Walton (foreign affairs), were prevailed upon to help edit copy. Weimer needed the help, since Ingersoll had a habit of taking carbons of the articles back to his apartment, returning at 8 P.M. with changes of his own—after Weimer had already proofed them. The "green eyeshades" had fortunately been able to disabuse Ingersoll of another of his pet notions before publication. He had wanted to paste each page of the newspaper on the wall and fill in articles as they were written. Lyon and his crew convinced their boss that, though such an approach might work for *Fortune* or *Life*, unless the idea was abandoned they would never get a daily newspaper out on time.[83]

Ingersoll was now a whirling dervish, operating on all fronts. He was trying to stabilize circulation, break in copy editors, instruct his editorial staff, and placate his investors. During the first week newsstands were mobbed by frenzied anticipation. *PM* continued to sell in excess of 350,000 copies daily, but no pattern of circulation had been established. Many newsstands still were not getting the paper; the truck drivers delivering to the suburbs were still learning their routes. The subscription list was still not found.

For much of the first week most buyers were merely the curious. After they read the paper many wondered what the fuss was all about. Others, who had a more realistic understanding of what the paper was trying to accomplish, could not find it. By the second week circulation was way down, and soon it was in free-fall. Ingersoll later estimated that through July the paper was losing 5,000 readers a day in New York City. At the bottom of the curve—by the middle of August—total circulation was down below 40,000. Between 18 June and 31 August 1940, the operating loss was $398,081.91, or $40,000 a week. The investors were restive. At the rate the paper was going, *PM* would be bankrupt at the end of August 1940, after just two and a half months in print.[84]

Ingersoll's backers were divided into camps. Those who had bought in for the usual reason—to make money—were angry that they had not. Some wanted to be bought out; others wanted more editorial control. Whitney, Hartford, and Field were more sympathetic. Field's continuing calm support for the paper forestalled angrier action. Louis Weiss was kept busy writing up Field's commitments to increase his support for the paper; Hartford and Whitney also offered more funds. By late September many of the directors were in open revolt. At a dramatic stockholders meeting Field quietly proposed to buy out all of the stockholders for twenty cents on the dollar. Some were furious, but none saw any alternative. After three and a half months, fifteen investors had been replaced by one. Ralph Ingersoll was no longer a "publisher." He would continue to control the editorial content of his paper, but the owner was Marshall Field, who told the outgoing stockholders he was committed, not to money, but to "an idea." [85]

The financial crisis had taken its toll on the staff. Despite its model Newspaper Guild contract, the paper could not keep everyone on. Scores were fired in August. Guild grievances were filed, but there was no arguing with the paper's dismal fiscal state. Among those let go was Snowden Herrick. His postgraduate journalism career had been shorter than his summer newspaper experiences while he was at college.[86] It was sobering, but the Field commitment was welcomed as auguring more stability.

The shake-up at the board of directors cost *PM* its most unusual cub reporter. Hartford, interested in covering crime, had been assigned to work with John Kobler. He had decided to pick up Kobler on the way to work—in his chauffeur-driven Rolls-Royce. Once the scenic drive was over, Kobler had tried vainly to instruct his protégé. Now Kobler could work without his willing, if not able, disciple. This ended a perplexing mystery. A bookkeeper handling accounts payable had complained to Richard Green that "some cub reporter named Hartford Huntington [sic]" had not been cashing his paychecks. After September there were no further checks issued to that name.[87]

There is some evidence that despite his continuous written output, Ingersoll was not fully understood by his staff. In the winter of 1941, Marshall Field commissioned R. A. Lasley, Inc., to survey the newsroom. Reporters were interviewed, assured that their jobs were not at stake, and asked about their work. While almost everyone reported steadfast loyalty to the newspaper and its editors, many were confused about their jobs. Some staff members, originally employed for one purpose, were being used in other positions they knew nothing about. Writers did not understand the difference between editorials and news articles. Most people only saw Ingersoll's coattails as he rushed by; Lasley recommended that he slow down and work with one section of the paper at a time, until each staff member assimilated his principles. Lasley found that Ingersoll did not know how to delegate responsibility and was rushing from one aspect of the newspaper's production to another; Lasley's report reminds *PM*'s leader that "there is already a Managing Editor." [88]

Ingersoll must have been aware of the problem. All through the anxious summer of 1940, he attempted to instruct his staff on what he wanted in his newspaper. Mostly this was through a raft of memoranda. Number 31 is dated

22 June 1940; Number 37, 22 June; Number 46, 17 July. (Ingersoll's tireless ability to write may be partially explained by the ironic fact that he did not "write" at all. Unable to type, Ingersoll dictated all of his output, both the uninterrupted stream of memoranda flowing around the office and the fiery editorials he contributed to the paper. Staff members observed him, dictating to his personal secretary, Virginia Schoales, as he paced in huge strides in his office, ideas pouring out, while Schoales avidly took down every word. As Penn Kimball has speculated, this might explain the "breathless" quality of his style.)[89] The memos attempted to reassure the staff that the paper would make it despite the chaos, explained new deadline procedures and how to work with the new copy editors, and commented on the tone and content of the paper. George Lyon studied the paper and found it humorless and unable to generate scoops. The staff still did not seem to realize that "every person on *PM*'s staff ought to visualize himself as the people's advocate seven days a week. . . . Stories of social injustice can be found that will tear the town wide open and give us a reputation for crusading journalism."[90]

The first crusade was literally just around the corner, in both time and place. Fulfilling a promise from the *Discursive Outline* and the premise of the News For Living section, Ned Armstrong headed a group of investigative reporters who exposed a criminal practice of many of the city's butchers: injecting water into meat in order to increase its weight. Not only was this fraud, but the health of consumers was imperiled because bacteria in the water sometimes poisoned the meat. Not content with attacking the butchers, *PM* accused Health Commissioner Sol Pincus of neglecting his duties, especially since some of the "watered meat" was sold in those city markets the La Guardia administration had established in working-class neighborhoods. The flap soon embroiled New York's feisty mayor, who angrily defended his health commissioner and denounced the new paper. Victory of sorts was achieved when several of the butchers were cited by the Health Department and one went to jail.

A side effect of the meat crusade was to open a confrontational relationship with Mayor La Guardia, which continued throughout the Little Flower's term in office. Like La Guardia, the paper was a champion of the underdog. Like the mayor, the paper was devoted to President Roosevelt. Both parties were prone to self-dramatization. But *PM*'s insistence on exposés and its championing of the trade union rights of city workers turned the mayor into an opponent. It did not help that La Guardia was notoriously thin-skinned. Nonetheless, at election time *PM* preferred the incumbent, both when he ran in 1941 and when he did not in 1945. In 1941 the paper suggested a slogan, "Although he sometimes gets my goat, La Guardia's going to get my vote."[91] Despite the confrontations, La Guardia chose *PM* as the newspaper for which to write a Sunday column after he left Gracie Mansion. He was given all of page 3. He wrote throughout 1946 and into 1947 until his fatal illness ended his career as a journalist. As might have been expected, his major difference with other *PM* writers was about the issue of government workers' union rights.

The meat campaign illustrated the new tabloid at its best and its worst. It was made possible by good investigative reporting. Staffers bought chickens, weighed them before and after water was extracted, took graphic pictures that exposed unhealthy poultry, and uncovered evidence that Pincus had received information about the poor meat a year earlier. Protecting the public against fraud was what being "against people who push other people around" was all about.

Nonetheless there was an intemperate style that bordered on the hysterical. The following are all front-page headlines: "Watered Meat Cost You Millions"; "Watered Meat Dealers: *PM* Tells Who They Are"; "Consumers Demand Health Board Act on Meat"; "Open Letter to Sol Pincus; Tomorrow *PM* Will Expose Rotten Chickens"; "EXCLUSIVE: Chicken Ghouls Unload Rotten Poultry in City"; "Chicken Ghouls Grow Rich; How Does Pincus Explain It?" As in all the crusades to follow, the coverage was extensive.[92] An editorial by Roger Dakin wondered, "Does La Guardia Care about Chickens?" McManus informed his readers that Ingersoll would go on WMCA Radio to detail the chicken charges. By November, the city was prosecuting several offending butchers. *PM* congratulated itself.

The timing of the campaign was unfortunate. Ingersoll's prepublication publicity had made *PM* the subject of intense interest. This newspaper was going to revolutionize journalism. In the middle of the chicken campaign the *Daily Mirror* called its new competitor a "news pamphlet." Louis Kronenberger proudly replied, "Just like *Common Sense*, thank you." A reader might have been hard-pressed to see watered meat as the cause for "times that try men's souls."

Penn Kimball speculated that the meat story was generated by geography. Within offices in industrial Brooklyn—remote from the news capital in midtown Manhattan—city reporters looked around them for news. The meat markets on Atlantic Avenue were just blocks away and provided a convenient locale for the newspaper's first crusade.[93]

More than one condescending study of *PM* remembers the chicken crusade as characteristic of the paper.[94] Comedian Henry Morgan summarized this view when he said that the problem with the new paper was that every article began, "My name is Minnie Moskowitz and I live on Flatbush Avenue, Brooklyn, and I think it's a shame . . . "[95]

Despite patronizing attacks from critics, the brouhaha over watered meat gave the struggling paper the attention it desperately needed. *PM* quickly exposed two more consumer frauds. Leanne Zugsmith ran a ten-day exposé of the exorbitant interest rates charged by installment loan companies, illustrating the usurious rates by documenting how many dollars would be paid out in interest charges on many specific items. One ironic note: 12 percent was considered usurious then, though Zugsmith attacked a firm which charged its customers 36 percent after getting its money from major banks for 1¼ percent.[96] Willard Wiener exposed price gouging by "Sheffield and Borden, the Tweedledee and Tweedledum of the milk industry," which together monopolized the processing of all milk sold in New York. Armstrong detailed Borden's control by the Rockefeller family, a favorite villain because of Standard Oil's cartel ties to IG Farben. The campaign ended when the two firms were indicted by a federal grand jury on charges of price-fixing.[97]

One subject that fascinated *PM* was *PM*. Its first two birthdays were occasions for the printing of congratulatory telegrams over two or three pages. Celebrities ranging from Sidney Hillman to Jack Benny sent best wishes, but the letters that were most eagerly awaited—and solicited[98]—were signed by President Roosevelt. J. Edgar Hoover had to be the least likely to send congratulations.[99] A full-page photograph of Franklin and Eleanor Roosevelt marking Lincoln's Birthday at the Lincoln Memorial showed the first lady carrying *PM*. The paper noted that when the *Daily News* carried the picture, it cropped out her newspaper.[100] Eleanor's "My Day" plugged *PM*. Most of the Scripps-Howard papers printed the endorsement ("I wonder if *PM* is becoming as interesting to you as I find it? There is barely a day when some article in it is not worth reading from beginning to end"), but the *World-Telegram* deleted it. *PM*, of course, crowed about the plug and the *World-Telegram*'s "censorship." Roy Howard informed the first lady she could not expect her employer to praise the opposition, a fact Mrs. Roosevelt passed on to her friend Jimmy Wechsler when he asked her to endorse *PM*'s antiracism campaign.[101]

Attacks on and parodies of *PM* by other journals were given full coverage—and responses. Awards were touted.[102]

The most embarrassing case of *PM*'s self-obsession occurred when Ingersoll received a draft notice. He was forty-one, an unlikely age for a draftee, so there was probably truth to his claim that he was being harassed by a Christian Front–dominated draft board for his antifascist stance. The ensuing ado, including Ingersoll's insistence that he was ready to fight for his country and Marshall Field's claim that Ingersoll would better serve the nation by editing *PM*, were unfortunately given enormous space in the newspaper. The draft board was vilified and Ingersoll's bravery defended against harangues by the other papers, whose editors were still bristling over his loud campaign for U.S. entry into the war a year before. It was a no-win situation, because the more the paper attacked the draft board, the more it looked as though Ingersoll was seeking to avoid service. *PM* would have been better off keeping the matter out of the newspaper altogether, instead of putting it on the front page.[103]

Four hundred staff members signed a letter to President Roosevelt requesting Ingersoll's exemption. FDR was apparently ready to intercede; his correspondence shows the letter was being sent to General Hershey of Selective Service with a recommendation that he personally look into the matter, but Ingersoll wired the president saying he wanted to serve.[104] Ultimately, Ingersoll enlisted before the draft board could act; he was rapidly promoted to captain, and his book *Top Secret*, serialized in *PM* in 1946, revealed that he had fashioned an elaborate phony campaign to help disguise the actual timing and placement of D-Day.

The White House did come to Ingersoll's rescue once he was in the service. By then Ingersoll was involved in a torrid affair with Gerry Morris, wife of theatrical agent William Morris. He had asked her to marry him before he had received his draft notice; she was happy leading a double life: married, yet free to pursue various romantic liaisons. By the time Ingersoll had been in Europe a few months, Morris had filed for divorce and suddenly realized she was madly in love with Ingersoll. She wanted desperately to see him. Cecelia Ager, her close friend and *PM*'s movie critic, appealed to her friend Creekmore Fath, working for the OSS and assigned to the White House. Fath told me, "Gerry Morris got into uniform and came to see me, to go overseas. . . . There was no way to get there unless someone would intervene. Mrs. Roosevelt said we ought to. She'd speak to General George. It was taken care of." Morris was placed on a supply plane and flown for a romantic rendezvous with *PM*'s erstwhile editor.[105]

Ingersoll's enlistment changed the paper for both good and ill. Gone was the egocentric hysteria of the crusades. Rotten chicken would no longer be front-page news. But some of the verve that characterized the crusades was gone as well. Ingersoll, who "governed with loose reins," was replaced by John P. Lewis, "a solid middle of the road citizen, smart enough but limited."[106] A more serious, controlled journalism was the norm. Max Lerner, who took over as chief editorialist (though not for another six months), was pontifical where Ingersoll had been the breathless observer and advocate. Notwithstanding James Wechsler's insistence that a communist cabal was out to capture *PM*, the paper's staff maintained its spirited fellowship. Rae Weimer remembered, "I never worked so hard in my life. We had lots of fun."[107] John A. Sullivan remembers "Weimer giving people a 'hot seat' with flash powder . . . on hot nights men stripping to underwear because clothing got wet with sweat."[108]

On the great issues of the day the paper was remarkably consistent, maintaining an impassioned antifascist, prolabor, left-liberal New Deal outlook. How *PM*'s writers defined these politics is the subject of the next several chapters.

3 | FIGHTING THE WAR AGAINST FASCISM

"Well, What Are We Going to Do about It?"
—*PM* prowar campaign, spring and summer 1941

A reader of Ralph Ingersoll's *Confidential Memorandum* to the staff in April 1940 would have expected the first issues of *PM* to have focused on the struggles of labor. Nowhere in the memorandum is World War II even mentioned, perhaps because it was written during the "phony war" period when hostilities between Nazi Germany and Great Britain and France were more verbal than military. By the time *PM* began publishing, however, the world was a different place. Having stormed through the Low Countries, the Wehrmacht was marching rapidly in France. Paris fell four days before the paper was sold to the public for the first time, on 18 June 1940. Events dictated *PM*'s primary news front.

The dummy issues of 14 to 17 June 1940, written as staff warm-ups for circulation, were dominated by the French events. The first six pages of the 14 June issue, beginning with the front-page headline "French Won't Defend Paris," were devoted to the Western Front. War bulletins from wire services surrounded graphic pictures of bombed Paris; a large map of the Nazi advance dominated page 5. Similar treatment continued through the week. *PM* offered its nonexistent readers the "First Radio Pictures of Nazis in Paris—They Reached New York at Two-Thirty This Morning." A dramatic picture of the swastika flying above the Arc de Triumph illustrated the fear given words on the following page: "Only Hope Is That USSR Will Fight Germany." The paper worried that the American public was fearful and opposed to the war.[1]

The *PM* offices were divided about the war in ways that reflected divisions among liberals and radicals nationwide. Everyone working for *PM* detested fascism, particularly as it was manifested in Nazi Germany. With the conflict in the spring of 1940 limited to the Nazis and the foremost appeasers—the Chamberlain and Daladier governments in Great Britain and France—however, staffers like Ken Stewart found it difficult to advocate U.S. intervention. Maintaining the power of British and French colonial empires was distasteful for many. Richard Green distrusted French and British motives. It was not until the evacuation at Dunkerque signaled French collapse and British resistance that Green took the Allied cause seriously. Those closest to the American Communist party would continue to see the war as an imperialist conflict being foisted on the people by President Roosevelt until the invasion of the Soviet Union in June 1941. The *Daily Worker*'s Adam Lupin claimed, "The Administration is moving swiftly toward curtailing the right of labor to strike by creating a War Labor Board."[2] The *Worker* boasted, "The Communists have stubbornly and resolutely combated the pro-war convoy propaganda in every city of the country."[3]

James Wechsler was among the last on the staff to accede to a prowar stance, finally rejecting the pacifist posture of Socialist party leader Norman Thomas, who insisted that American involvement in the European conflict would mean fascism here.[4]

Ralph Ingersoll and Penn Kimball had no such qualms. For them and those who shared their views, the unparalleled evil that was Nazi Germany made its defeat paramount, no matter who fought it for whatever motives. Kimball's militant stance was in part a reaction to observing the impact of appeasement on the morale of those at Oxford. He had written home shortly after the Munich Pact sold out Czechoslovakia:

> The general attitude is more or less of a resigned but humiliated nature broadening out into utter dejection and disgust in some. Like all young men when their very highest ideals have been betrayed, their disillusionment tends to be fashioned in utter pessimism and despair.
>
> They are like a post-war generation that has lost a war. Ashamed, defeated and robbed even of the consolation of a vain struggle, life for them seems to have lost its fundamental anchor, and their search for readjustment is complicated by an inherent aversion to the very principles upon which their existence is assured.

Kimball wanted no such humiliating peace for the United States.[5]

The first editorial on the war illustrated the division. The paper said it was "(1) against the U.S. going to war; (2) in favor of helping to beat Hitler in any way that does not mean going to war. (3) We are unconditionally in favor of preserving civil liberties." Expanding on this several days later under the front page headline "What Do Americans Think of Our Entering War?" the paper seemed to echo what it took to be the public feeling at the moment: that the U.S. should help Great Britain but not fight. The paper was concerned that pacifism would help the Republicans. Again, it hoped for a break in the Russo-German Nonaggression Pact. Dorothy Thompson, writing as a friend, best expressed the quandary. She wanted to defeat fascism, but had no idea how to do so.[6]

The policy of do-everything-but-just-don't-fight was not tenable. It may have been the best that President Roosevelt could hope for the country, but it was a weak creed. Publicly hoping another nation would do the fighting that many members of the staff earnestly believed had to be done while opting for peace for the United States could only sound like cowardice. Despite continuing differences among the staff, Ingersoll started pushing the paper for an all-out interventionist stance.

He began probing the softness of American resistance to fascism. He noted a growing anti-Semitism, a reactionary drive to lengthen the working day, and what he called a "defeatist" attitude toward Great Britain's prospects. While warning against civil liberties violations as America began its defense buildup, he worried that our army was poorly organized and inefficient. A nation of forty million workers that had mass-produced the automobile and which had the world's richest natural resources must be able to produce an aggressive and efficient army.[7]

Ingersoll pressed presidential candidates Roosevelt and Willkie for an effective antifascist strategy to go beyond the call for a draft. Perhaps he was hoping for a road map to provide a clear path on which to travel. On that same day his newspaper looked schizophrenic as Willard Wiener profiled Representative Vito Marcantonio at an antiwar rally, denouncing J. Edgar Hoover's FBI for wiretapping antiwar activists, all the while attacking profascist "Fifth Columnists (a charge some directed at Communist Party–allied people like Marcantonio during this period of the Soviet-Nazi Pact)." As always when dealing with Marcantonio, the paper could not disguise its admiration for the left-wing congressman, even when in sharp disagreement with his politics. The next page, however, offered support for army war games. The paper devoted its centerfold to illustrating them.[8]

PM transcribed CBS commentator Elmer Davis's review of how appeasement of Hitler helped the Nazis take Europe. He attacked American neutrality as benefiting Franco's fascist revolt against the Spanish Republic. The boxed words "Congratulations to Elmer Davis" underscored the paper's growing impatience.[9] Ingersoll was the leading belligerent. He was sick of euphemisms like "defense" or "rearmament. Call them by their name. . . . Plans to kill our enemies. And more power to them!" He warned, "Let's face the fact that when and as he comes—we know he's coming—we want to kill him. Let's be proud of it." The paper approved of a trend it had discovered: "USA Begins to Act like a Nation at War." The article described an urgent readiness to use the country's wealth for war and to force rearmament. Ingersoll wanted FDR and Willkie to explain their rearmament programs to the nation in order to build political support for them.[10]

As the Blitzkrieg intensified, Ingersoll demanded, "We Must Act to Save Britain," but he was still vague about how that might be accomplished.[11]

PM seems to have believed that one way of arousing the American public was to have it become as frightened of the Nazis as the staff members themselves were. A stark map in August illustrated "How Axis Powers Might Invade USA." The following day Washington columnist Kenneth Crawford found fears of a Nazi invasion in the capital. Duncan Aikman warned "Pacific Coast Open to Jap Attack." Future warnings of Nazi invasions, often containing maps with huge arrows directed at the American heartland (or more pointedly, at New York City), continued both before and after the United States entered the war. The most effective treatment appeared in the Sunday Magazine, where five pages used *Daily News* typeface and headline styles to describe and illustrate an imagined Nazi bombing of New York.[12]

If terror did not work, perhaps reassurance would. Richard Boyer, a reporter just back from Germany, wrote the first of what would prove to be many series describing life there. His first article got front-page billing: "*PM* Exclusive: Despair Sweeps Germany—Secrets of Nation Revealed." Inside, his own headline read, "Victorious Germany . . . Land of Gloom." He explained:

> While the rest of the world regards Russia and Germany as allied, it generally is taken for granted in Nazi circles that Germany will invade Russia in 1941. Responsible Nazi officials declare in off the record but scarcely secret conversations that the Soviet Union will either stand and deliver the Ukraine, the Baku oil regions and the former Baltic States or Germany will seize them if and when she conquers or makes peace with England. . . . The most surprising development in Germany is that a bad listlessness, akin to the disease of the spirit that caused the collapse of France, is spreading through Germany, like a plague, infecting an increasing number of her people with defeatism.[13]

As his series continued, Boyer described a poor diet, numerous shortages, and the omnipresence of the secret police contributing to poor German morale and reminded his readers that the German army, while good, was not made up of supermen. They looked invincible because no one in Western Europe had fought back. "There was more fighting in any three large battles of the American Civil War than there was in the entire Western campaign in Europe." He found the French collapse remarkable, not the Nazi advance.[14]

PM DECLARES WAR

Still, few Americans were awake to the fascist menace. Aikman traveled to Kansas for a series of reports that showed that the farm country was uninterested in the war and vehemently opposed any American involvement.[15] Ingersoll was frustrated. "I am moved to wonder at what terrible things have to happen before the American people, who alone are strong enough and resourceful enough to put an end to these things, are stirred to act without compromise." While Americans slept, all of continental Europe was fascist except Russia. A battle for the future of mankind would happen there while the United States became more isolated and reactionary.[16] He foresaw danger of enslavement to the Nazis arising

> . . . with one of the two major political parties of this country taking a wishy-washy attitude toward Fascism, and the other afraid to move boldly for fear of endangering an already won election, and with a dangerously befuddled and treacherous peace movement in this country, and with a great inland population to whom conceptions of fascism are so strange and foreign that they seem to have great difficulty in taking them as more than fairy tales.[17]

After a trip to England he tried to arouse Americans with this description of Europe:

To the East there are Germans who are starving for the privilege of killing you and beyond them the Poles and the Czechs whose days and nights must never seem to end and then the land where twenty years ago there was a people's revolution and where now six million men may not plow their fields or build their houses or sew together their clothes but must drill and drill and practice the art of killing with no profit to their or anyone else's society because like the rest of the world they are frightened. [The world] is no longer the world I had grown up in. It is unrecognizably changed and irretrievably lost. . . . The world in which your children will grow up you must make for them now with your own blood, sweat, and tears and—Churchill should have added—with your laughter.[18]

By January, Ingersoll was willing to commit himself but not his newspaper to American troops being sent to Britain. Ben Robertson, Jr., thought the British had beaten back the Nazi attempt to subjugate them, but they could not invade Europe. His readers were to infer that *their* country could and must. He reminded them that the British were fighting alone for the survival of all democracy, including ours. Ingersoll warned of an anti–New Deal counterrevolution if Great Britain lost. After Churchill's "Give Us the Tools" speech, Crawford predicted that if Great Britain lost, the United States would be forced to fight. Leonard Engel, who had already adopted the pseudonym "The General" when writing about military strategy,[19] wanted an armed U.S. convoy to Britain to brave Nazi attack, regardless of the consequences. American public opinion had to be aroused.[20]

PM was not alone in sounding the alarm. As voices of the financial establishment, both the *Times* and *Herald Tribune* understood that German expansionism threatened their security. The *Times* warned:

There is a clear alternative to the suicidal risk of choosing to face alone a ring of hostile Powers closing in on us from all directions. That alternative is to take advantage of the fact that we still have a courageous and resourceful ally in the field; to strengthen that ally by every means at our command; to accelerate to its top speed the full force of our war industries, and to rake whatever action may be needed— convoys of ships included—to bring our productive equipment into contact with the battleships.[21]

The *Herald Tribune* made clear war might be necessary to defeat German military expansionism and echoed the *Times*'s call for convoys.[22]

Those who opposed expanded military aid to Great Britain became shriller in their opposition. Hearst angrily attacked the Administration's use of the first person plural pronoun in summoning Americans to aid Great Britain. "We are a divided nation. . . . 'We' positively does not mean the mothers of America. . . . Nor has the Administration even disclosed to what extent it has secretly committed the nation to war."[23] In a front-page editorial entitled "The Crucial Hour—Speak Out for Peace!" the *Daily Worker* claimed that the 1940 election was rigged because "both candidates Roosevelt and Willkie promised peace and both supported war. . . . The *Daily Worker* has warned from the beginning that the 'aid short of war' policy was a fig-leaf for war itself. . . . The American people demand peace." [24]

As President Roosevelt's speeches got tougher, *PM* used them to rally Americans to the war, using fragments of each speech for front-page headlines, and reprinting the speeches in double-size print, often boxing them in elaborate borders. On 28 May, seventeen of the paper's thirty-two pages were devoted to one such speech. *PM*'s page 1 headline was "Our Conclusion: We're in It." The following day Ingersoll gushed, "At exactly the right moment, the President of the United States turned on the light." [25]

The *Times* agreed. Under the title "A Call to Action," the paper editorialized, "President Roosevelt struck a mighty blow last night for freedom. . . . He summoned the American people to resolve their doubts and dedicate themselves to ACTION." Even the steadfastly Republican *Herald Tribune* declared, "The President's address last night was a masterly call to every form of action." But the *Sun* claimed, "The President virtually took into his own hands powers over the national economy that fall little short of dictatorship." Communist analysis was remarkably similar. The *Worker*'s front-page editorial warned its readers to "Guard US from War and Military Dictatorship." [26]

Actually the speech was by no means a declaration of hostilities. Although insisting that Nazi defeat of Great Britain would be a disaster for the United States because Germany's ultimate objective was world domination, Roosevelt proposed only two courses of action: accelerating America's shipbuilding (the Nazis were destroying British ships three times faster than the British could build them) and protecting American ships in the Atlantic. While FDR's hatred for Hitlerism was forthright, there was no blueprint for belligerence in his words. The speech was in part the result of the anxiety in his cabinet that he was not moving the country fast enough. War Secretary Stimson, Navy Secretary Knox, Interior Secretary Ickes, Treasure Secretary Morgenthau, Attorney General Jackson, Justice Frankfurter, and Archibald MacLeish all worried that Roosevelt was sitting on his hands when action was necessary. Stimson despaired of FDR's leadership. The following day the president undercut his own remarks by insisting to reporters at a news conference that America's neutral status was not changed in the least.[27] Ingersoll had declared war, not the president.

For a month before Roosevelt's radio address, the drumbeat for war was sounding loudly in the Brooklyn offices of *PM*. Ingersoll launched a series which demanded, "Well, What Are We Going to Do about It?" On the first day of the campaign, several pages were given over to listing Nazi atrocities, citing the bravery of the Allies, applauding the voluntary involvement of the Canadians, and pointing the finger at suspected fifth columnists. Each article ended with the rhetorical question above. The paper was aiming to mobilize Americans. Ingersoll wrote in double size type, "This is an anti-fascist paper. If this is a call to war, perhaps the facts demand it." A photo-story asked, "Could You Live in a World Dominated by Men Who Did These Things?" The four pages of pictures illustrated such Nazi horrors as book-burning, war atrocities, and attacks on Jews.[28]

Before beginning the campaign. Ingersoll met with the whole staff, announced his intention, and told those who did not agree that they would not be forced to write in the campaign. As Ken Stewart has pointed out, if the communist influence on *PM* was as great as was later claimed, this would have been the moment for opposition. Stewart says simply, "None developed."[29]

A quote from the president was invoked on page 1: "The Fascists Shall Not Win." The paper continued, "But the Fascists Are Still Winning: What Are We Going to Do about It?" Inside the headline exclaimed, "Hitler Rode to Power on Hoodlum Violence. Do We Have the Making of Fascist Violence Here?" Pictures of the Klan, Christian Front, Black Legion, and Henry Ford's labor goons were the answer. Meanwhile, Ben Robertson, Jr., wrote from London that the British wanted to know, "Is It All Talk . . . or Do We Mean Business?"[30]

PM's campaign did not go unnoticed. The *World-Telegram* praised the president for ignoring "the little but loud minority" who wanted war, and Hearst himself attacked "some cyclonic siroccos of hot air [who] are seeking to carry us bodily into foreign wars."[31]

Perhaps the strangest installment attempted to convince Catholics to become militant antifascists, with the front-page headline, "What Are Catholics Going to Do about It?" Amid all the articles was a barefaced attempt to capitalize on Catholic anticommunism: "How the Germans Crushed Catholic Poland . . . and Shared the Spoils of Conquest with Communist Russia." May Day was an ironic date for invoking anticommunism. Nothing like it would be seen in *PM* again.[32]

The Sunday Magazine devoted an entire issue to imagining the United States as a fascist country. Several pages illustrated the ethnic mix of America, predicting vicious race war under fascism. The theater would be bereft of Saroyan, Sherwood, Odets, Hellman, O'Neill, Kaufman, and Ryskind.[33]

If many Americans were afraid of war, *PM* grew afraid of peace in the momentary pause between the Nazi air attack on Britain and the invasion of the Soviet Union. The paper printed a five-page "exclusive" which "exposed" German plans to convert to peace production in order to "annihilate democracies." Ingersoll editorialized that a negotiated peace with Hitler meant an industrial war to the death.[34]

In the remaining months, the staff took every moment to press for war. Dr. Seuss drew a long-necked bird with a hat labeled "U.S.," sitting in a rocking chair. The caption was, "Talk, talk, talk." Crawford expressed irritation with State Department bureaucrats negotiating with the Japanese; clearly there was nothing to talk about. Though *PM* loved the principles of the Atlantic Charter, it passed on these grumbles heard in London: What was this fuss about "peace aims" before the United States was in the war? John P. Lewis approvingly noted that the *New Republic* had called for a declaration of war.

PM itself declared war before the attack on Pearl Harbor. Invoking a phrase from FDR, Lewis editorialized, "Now Is the Time to Stop Hitler. . . . We're in this war to lick them . . . up to and including a shooting war against the forces which have fired upon [U.S. ships]." Crawford announced, "We are now at war, or something like it, on the high seas." He called FDR's "When You See a Rattlesnake Poised to Strike" speech "a declaration of undeclared war at sea on Germany and Italy." There was more credence to the analysis of Roosevelt's remarks this time, as the president announced an active policy of protecting American shipping by launching attacks on German warships which came near his own defined security zone in the Atlantic. Lewis asserted that Hitler had already chosen war between his nation and ours. "The only choice we now have in our hands as free men is the choice of how well we fight." Lewis, Crawford, and I. F. Stone all claimed that the sinking of the *Reuben James* had forced us into the war; Stone wrote that our naval losses in "peacetime" were already as bad as in World War I.[35]

Ingersoll grew impatient with Lend-Lease: "Are we lenders or fighters? To be an American abroad where others are fighting fascism is to feel cheap. . . . Lease and lend are the meanest words I have ever heard. . . . After having visited every front in the World War against Fascism, there's only one question that seems important to me now. That question is, When are we going to get into this war?" He warned that a delay could mean a two-front attack from Germany and Japan. "How would you like to have Japan take a crack at us in the Pacific while Hitler is attacking us in the Atlantic?"

The old pacifist turned warrior, Sergeant York, was quoted demanding a declaration of war on Germany.

While responding to the Japanese attack with fury and resolve, *PM* was nonetheless grateful. Despite all of his newspaper's crusading, Crawford admitted, "Japan united the nation as the nation had not united itself and probably could not have united itself." Ingersoll announced twice in three days that *PM*'s "sole objective" would be "winning the war."[36]

PM's WAR AIMS

PM now has history on its side. Fascism has been demonstrated to be exactly the monster the paper said it was. The war was a battle to defeat evil, so it may seem unremarkable that *PM* was a strong advocate for war before the bombing of Pearl Harbor. But at the time it was remarkable. Americans were not willing to go to war. Hitler's aggression was frequently justified by the largest-circulation dailies in the United States, eager to appease and strengthen the pacifism of their readers or to express the views of publishers like Hearst, who thought, "We can do business with Hitler." That portion of the American left affiliated with or influenced by the Communist party was so taken with defending the Nonaggression Pact between the USSR and Germany that it actively campaigned against aid to Great Britain and conversion to a war footing before 22 June 1941. The Socialist party was also in the pacifist camp. *PM*'s was a lonely position, growing out of a firm belief in antifascism. Defining that antifascism was an important theme in *PM*, a theme it warmed to many months before Pearl Harbor was attacked.

Ingersoll began by asserting that the master-race theory, which created a caste system according to racial origin, was what was both central to fascism and most repugnant about it. This created

> our own irreconcilable conflict with the Axis nations. For the very foundation of our world is that all men of all races and creeds and colors are born with free and equal opportunity, that only those freely and democratically chosen by us should rule us and that we, a people of many races, bow to none.

Furthermore, fascism was based on a militarism which meant foreign aggression. Citing China, Libya, Spain, and Europe since 1938, he attributed losses for democracy as the result of a failure to fight.[37] Nearly three years later, Max Lerner was afraid most Americans did not know what fascism was. His definition was less specific than Ingersoll's: "Reactionary leaders use the forces of social hatred to destroy the machinery and the fabric of democracy."[38]

Ingersoll tried to convince the worker that he knew what fascism was like; he had been fighting it all along:

> In fighting his war he remembers that it is a war against the perpetuation of share-cropping, the unhappiness of migratory labor, the viciousness of the labor spy, the stupidity of mean vermin filled tenement housing and of starvation in the midst of plenty. And he fights both native and foreign Fascism with equal zeal.

Accompanying photographs proved that "U.S. Labor knows that this country is worth fighting for." The broad definition of the word *fascism* to connote anything that *PM* designated as undemocratic expanded the meaning of the war. After the bombing of Pearl Harbor, Ingersoll presented a wartime credo which combined a commitment to war and antifascism with the successful completion of the New Deal:

> For all out production of weapons . . . For intelligent training of our Armed Forces . . . *PM* believes that the War against Fascism must be waged at home as well as abroad. . . . Labor's interests are synonymous with the country's . . . against Democracy's Reported Enemies in the U.S.A.

Herbert Agar began the series "What Are We Fighting For?" on 9 March 1942. It continued for more than a year. In it he presented his views of what the war was about and solicited the views of others. Frequently the attack was on *PM*'s domestic enemies. Agar's first column accused the *Chicago Tribune*, Representative Martin Dies, and Father Coughlin of being isolationists and apologists for fascism.[39]

Vice President Wallace's "Century of the Common Man" speech turned Wallace into the personification of American liberalism at *PM* for the rest of the Ingersoll era. The paper printed the speech the day after it was delivered and then again two weeks later. It devoted several articles in the interim to declarations of support from labor and liberal leaders. Directly replying to *Time* publisher Henry Luce, who saw victory in the war creating an "American Century," Wallace envisioned the defeat of fascism making possible a cooperative world linked together by international trade and a series of international guarantees to eliminate hunger, illiteracy, and poverty. These guarantees most resembled New Deal agricultural ("a world-wide granary") and industrial labor policies but were not antithetical to socialism. Wallace linked U.S., French, Latin American, and Russian revolutions as a "march of freedom" that "spoke for the common man." Despite mistakes, they were part of the process by which "the people groped their way to the light." The Russian revolution was invoked as leading the way for "economic democracy" as the American Revolution was the vanguard in the struggle for "political democracy." The war was about freeing the world from tyranny and making sure it never returned to it by securing for all common men an economic and political bill of rights.[40]

PM's owner was as impressed as the paper's writers. Marshall Field undertook a mammoth mailing project to spread the message. Wallace wrote in thanks, "I am utterly amazed that you sent out 200,000 copies of my speech."[41]

Among its lesser consequences, the Wallace speech created a vocabulary with which *PM* enunciated its goals in World War II and beyond. With Ingersoll in the army after July 1942, managing editor John P. Lewis and chief editorialist Max Lerner invoked the linking of economic and political rights as central to the antifascist struggle time and again.[42] *PM* had found in the Wallace speech a full exposition of the politics of antifascism. Such ideas could not get a hearing in many other journals—the *Nation* and the *New Republic* excepted. Certainly there was no other place in the daily press for such views. While the *Post* might be sympathetic, it offered writers and intellectuals little space to expound their principles. The Wallace speech was far longer than any article the newspaper carried.

Wallace's and *PM*'s version of the nation's war aims, which united the battle for political democracy abroad with demands for economic democracy at home and an expansion of political freedom to all citizens of the U.S. and the world, was not the same as the *Times*'s and *Herald Tribune*'s commitment to the war effort. Those papers, like the Republicans Stimson and Knox in FDR's war bureaucracy, were fighting to maintain the status quo of American capitalism. But it was an attractive credo to a wide range of intellectuals, politicians, and celebrities. Broadway gossip columnist Walter Winchell, whose occupation was naturally housed in the *Daily Mirror*, moved with a smart set of theatrical people; he adopted his New Deal liberalism from them, and when his employer prevented him from spouting those notions, he made ghost appearances in *PM*.[43] Dorothy Thompson printed whatever the *Herald Tribune* blocked in *PM*. Impassioned CBS reporters Edward R. Murrow, William L. Shirer, and Howard K. Smith, who had witnessed fascism abroad, found that *PM*'s fiery anti-Hitler sentiment exactly corresponded to their own. Later, Edwin Newman began his journalism career as a reporter for Ingersoll's experiment. Rising young writers destined for political careers—their aspirations as yet untinged with cynicism—reported for the newspaper. Future Nixon adviser Herbert Stein and Lyndon Johnson's press secretary, George Reedy, both wrote for *PM*. The future Speaker of the House, Tip O' Neill, attacked Mississippi demogogue Theodore Bilbo in a series for the newspaper. Two writers of note who would make their mark outside the political arena nonetheless began their careers as staffers on this crucible of antifascism. Lillian Ross learned how to write features by working for years at *PM*'s Sunday Magazine, and future Henry James biographer Leon Edel was a national reporter. Even those who had cut their teeth as political cynics answered the clarion call of antifascism. Ernest Hemingway and Dorothy Parker accepted guest writing assignments.

THE ENEMY WITHIN: CORPORATE MALFEASANCE

The joining of economic and political freedom was a natural link for *PM*, which saw the New Deal as the latest development in the long march of the nation toward full democracy. Moreover, I. F. Stone and Nathan Robertson spent much of the war demonstrating how labor's most powerful industrial enemies in the United States were reluctant to enroll in the antifascist struggle. Some firms were tied by international cartel agreements to giant Nazi war manufacturers, such as IG Farben and Krupp.

As the nation's defense industry began to boom under Roosevelt's 1940 preparedness policy, *PM* adopted an antimonopoly approach, demanding that industry pay FDR's proposed war profits tax. Writers were furious that new defense plants were given to corporations at taxpayers' expense. Ingersoll suggested sarcastically that the 1790s slogan ("Millions for defense, but not one cent for tribute") be rewritten as "Billions for Defense, but Not Less than 10% for Profit." Weldon James wrote that it was easy for Congress to draft young men, but it could not muster the votes for an excess-profits tax. Industrialists who refused to convert their factories to defense plants because they did not want to sacrifice consumer profits were denounced. ALCOA was particularly hated for using its monopoly control of aluminum to charge the government exorbitant prices. Penn Kimball found zinc producers in the United States selling as much zinc as possible to Japan, creating a shortage here to drive up the domestic price. Leonard Engel exposed the copper industry for similarly gouging the government. The Japanese were getting bargain prices to prepare attacks on the United States; to defend itself the United States had to pay record high prices. A Nathan Robertson exclusive denounced the government for awarding defense contracts to Wagner Act violators (those who violated National Labor Relations Board rules or procedures in order to prevent unionization). He predicted correctly that President Roosevelt would have to restructure the government bureaucracy to prevent these violations from occurring. Robertson found it unsurprising that corporate giants like General Motors and Du Pont were now making record defense profits, inasmuch as their representatives were sitting on government boards. He summarized the problem: "The Defense Commission is too big and too cowardly."[44]

Most distasteful of all, many of the corporations now earning defense contracts had participated in the rearming of Japan and Germany, like General Motors and scrap-iron traders to Japan. As Crawford noted, it was particularly ironic for the president to name William Knudson to the War Production Board, given that "General Motors is in the position of selling the U.S. Army machines which have no other purpose than to defend this country against machines it previously sold the Third Reich." Many American firms had cartel agreements (international understandings to limit competition, set prices, and share industrial secrets, based on reciprocal ownership of stock) with German firms. Kenneth Crawford was the first to sketch these agreements, mentioning ties between Standard Oil of New Jersey and IG Farben, and between Krupp and General Electric.[45]

Pure greed was motivating firms in many areas. Manufacturers of plumbing supplies, oil pipelines, and wallboard were investigated and some indicted for attempting to fix prices charged to the government at absurdly high levels. Colt machine guns were sold to Great Britain at twice their normal cost. I. F. Stone exposed a "dollar-a-year-man (the name for company executives who worked for the government's defense bureaucracy for the token fee of $1)" who nearly doubled the price of gloves his firm sold to the armed forces. Greed extended to trading with the all-but-formal enemy. *PM* dug up a shipping order between Standard Oil of New York (Socony-Mobil, today, Mobil) and Japan during the spring of 1941 which was supposed to be destroyed to hide the sale; Victor Bernstein exposed Texaco sales to Japan during the same period.[46]

As hostility between the United States and the Axis powers increased during the summer and fall of 1941, trade between American firms and Axis warmaking industries continued unabated or increased. Lowell Leake took a rare writing assignment to explain how IG Farben was getting rich from its shares in Standard Oil of New Jersey and Sterling Drug. He disclosed that U.S. companies were shipping steel to Japan despite defense shortages in steel here and exposed California oil bankers lending the Japanese $1.5 million. I. F. Stone confirmed Leake's charges with additional data. Ernest Hemingway cabled from abroad that Japan was using American rubber imports for weapons to conquer the Dutch East Indies.[47]

By late summer Stone had seen enough to indict the entire U.S. defense bureaucracy. In a series titled "Business as Usual," he called for Knudson's ouster because the General Motors executive typified the problem: "The shortage of raw materials, the unwillingness to divert the production capacity of big business to defense, the failure to spread out orders to the little business men, all go back to the domination of defense—as of our economy—to comparatively few big businesses and monopolies." He noticed how Du Pont, favored trading partner of German and Japanese arms manufacturers, got a defense contract a small business man had bid for. It was no accident that big-business failures were down 69 percent, while small-business failures were up 10 percent; these statistics represented the fruits of government policy. "It is the absence of . . . will to make the profits of Bethlehem Steel and Du Pont and General Motors secondary to the efficiency of the defense program that make the history of the defense program such a mangy saga of self-deception." Stone endorsed Senator Truman's committee investigations into the defense industry. He reported and amplified the committee's work. Truman wanted the defense industry "drafted." Stone passionately agreed.[48]

Stone scooped the Truman committee when he reported that American oil being shipped to Spain was "beyond question" getting to the Luftwaffe. He had sources in the Treasury and Interior departments, who blamed State. (The Interior source was probably Harold Ickes himself, who had a mostly friendly but sometimes antagonistic relationship with Stone. Some years later Ickes said, "Mr. Stone probably started to be a crusader when his grandfather was born. . . . There is one, possibly apocryphal, story that Mr. Stone once spent four weeks chasing down the possible Nazi connections of a well-known Washington personage, who had the misfortune to sneeze at a cocktail party and to follow the sneeze with the word, 'Gesundheit.' ")[49]

Stone's story sparked debate in Congress, where Representative John Coffee (Democrat of Washington) demanded a probe of all State Department "dollar-a-year men." State Department officials denied the story, Treasury Department officials affirmed it, and the Economic Defense Board momentarily stopped oil shipments to Spain. Stone took credit in *PM*'s name but State "temporarily" over-ruled the board, claiming that shipping oil to Franco would keep him out of the war, while Loyalists predicted Spain would become a fueling station for Hitler. Sure enough, Stone discovered reports of German submarines refueling on the Spanish Canary Islands, and (on the day Pearl Harbor was attacked) reported that tin and bomb materials were being shipped to Spain.[50]

When Stone renewed his attack on Knudson's defense management, the auto executive replied, "The war is only two weeks old." Stone's riposte was, "Knudson has been in charge of defense for 18 months." As the Truman committee readied its reports, Stone reviewed and updated his charges, focusing on the auto industry's slow pace of conversion to war production despite Walter Reuther's "500 Planes a Day" plan. *PM* printed the committee's findings in full, and Ingersoll crowed. He had a right to; everything Stone charged was confirmed by the Truman report. The auto industry reluctantly began reconverting. Stone promised to wait a few months before exposing its failings again.[51]

PM shifted its focus to the relationship between Standard Oil of New Jersey (then Esso, today Exxon) and its German cartel partner. Crawford had explained the relationship earlier, but it was now examined in detail by Nathan Robertson. Robertson, like Stone, was an indefatigable researcher armed with passionate commitments to liberalism and exposing hidden truths. Already a veteran journalist when Crawford recruited him to the original Washington bureau, Robertson had spent his whole life in the nation's capital. His newspaper career began with Hearst's *Washington Times*. Later he worked for both the United Press and the Associated Press. Frustrated by the superficial treatment of economic affairs in the traditional newspapers, Robertson became a specialist for *PM*, subjecting presidential and congressional tax bills to in-depth analyses unknown in the contemporary press.[52] Turning his attention to the malfeasance of the corporate giants, Robertson detailed their cooperation with the Nazi war manufacturers.

A particular outrage was that Esso and IG Farben owned a synthetic rubber manufacturing process in common; under their cartel agreement IG Farben sold the secret to the German government, which used the process to build weapons, but Esso was bound by the trade agreement to keep the process secret. It was keeping that secret from the United States government even after the United States and Germany were at war. After Robertson's initial articles, Truman promised an investigation, and Ingersoll wrote a letter to Standard Oil stockholders denouncing "treason." Predictably, he demanded, "What Are You Going to Do about It?" Meanwhile, Standard was making a fortune on the price of its secret synthetic rubber being sold to Nazi Germany. Finally Assistant Attorney General Thurman Arnold made a deal with Esso: There would be no antitrust litigation if the company turned over the synthetic rubber process to the government. *PM* was disappointed. "Next time let's make No Deals."

Truman was as dissatisfied as *PM* and decided to go through with the hearings despite the deal. Robertson reported on the hearings, where Standard executives reluctantly admitted their artificially high prices on synthetic rubber and claimed they had been hoodwinked by their IG Farben cartel partners. Robertson broadened his reports to include American producers of aluminum, magnesium, beryllium, tungsten, nitrogen, lenses, and drugs. All ignored new technology in the United States but shipped off their best wares to Germany for high profits. ALCOA was a major villain; it conspired with cartel partners in Germany to cut magnesium production to raise the price. The Germans had all the magnesium they wanted and U.S. defense firms faced a shortage. ALCOA cut its production when Germany agreed to reduce its own exports. Robertson illustrated his contentions with a chart that showed German aluminum production multiplying six times since 1932 while U.S. production grew 2½ times. By 1938, Germany was outproducing the United States. Krupp and General Electric agreed to limit tungsten production so the price could climb from $48 to $453 a pound, though it cost $25 a pound to produce. Germany had all the tungsten it needed; to fill its own needs, the War Department was being bilked. As Robertson noted, "Meanwhile, Hitler's purposes had been served." He disclosed similar deals by Du Pont and IG Farben to limit glass production. Stone disclosed that Remington Arms, a Du Pont subsidiary, bought a patent for new machinegun technology from IG Farben and refused to sell the new guns to the British. Robertson and Stone must have been delighted when FDR seized all patents controlled by the enemy; in large measure their exposés had enabled liberals like Roosevelt and Truman to strike against the corporate giants.[53]

PM was not through with its campaign to influence Standard Oil stockholders. A telling photo layout reproduced the cover of a German Esso road map booklet. The gas attendant in the photograph on the cover was doing the Nazi salute. *PM*'s caption: "If you gag at the notion that you had to salute Hitler to earn your dividends, you can kick out the corporation directors who put you into that false position." Stone went after the most important stockholder of all, addressing a series of open letters to John D. Rockefeller, Jr. He admonished Rockefeller that the Standard

> officers are your creatures; your frown is their death warrant. . . . No excuses can erase their failure to come forward of their own free will after Pearl Harbor and give up Standard Oil's secret ties with the German Chemical Trust and place its precious patents . . . at the service of [U.S.] defense.

Stone reminded Rockefeller that he had acted during the Teapot Dome affair to disassociate himself from the Harding administration scandal. This was worse. Esso had created an Anglo-American oil cartel that hid from its British partners Esso's own ties to IG Farben. The company blocked coal and oil shipments to Great Britain, the Soviet Union, and China.

> Men who continued, though it was for good business reasons, to be the economic allies of the Axis for months after the war began cannot feel as deeply about the menace of fascism as the rest of us. . . . You must decide and decide quickly, Mr. Rockefeller, whether you choose to leave Standard Oil and its vital interests in the hands of Teagle, Farish, and Howard. Your answer will decide whether it is safe to leave these same resources in yours.

Commerce Department figures showed 89 percent of American business withdrew from cooperation with the Nazis after the attack on Pearl Harbor. Not so Standard Oil. Stone finished his rhetorical rout by reviewing Rockefeller Senior's ruthless rise to power in the oil industry, and replaying Junior's most notorious act: the massacre of striking Ludlow coal miners. He demanded Rockefeller prove he was a changed man by firing the Standard directors.[54]

PM continued to expose industrial noncompliance with defense needs and the record profits of war firms throughout the war. Robertson attacked new defense monopolies which profited by stifling new methods and hindering war production. Anaconda was indicted for endangering troops after it sold defective wire; Stone noticed the company's executives sat on the War Production Board oversight committee and uncovered a navy bureaucrat who extolled Anaconda even after its incompetence was known. Robertson reported the "blackest war story *PM* has ever printed": The Truman committee's exposure of the faulty planes manufactured by Wright Aircraft. The company faked data, destroyed records, improperly recorded results, forged inspections, and failed to eliminate faulty material. For Max Lerner, Wright's guilt was evidence of corporate moral blindness. Stone attended Standard stockholders' meetings and watched the board of directors prevent a vote on its cartel ties to Germany. Worse, they were still trying to profit by controlling the synthetic-rubber formula, charging both the government and other firms. As the war ended, Stone and his colleagues kept wary eyes on German, Italian, Japanese, and Spanish industries and their former

American partners to prevent a recurrence of cartel agreements and fascist industrial power. Stone was among the first to warn against the dangerous imperialist consequences of the formation of the Anglo-American Oil monopoly in the Middle East.[55]

When Vice President Wallace accused Secretary of Commerce Jesse Jones of limiting raw materials needed for war production, *PM* jumped into the fray on the vice president's side. Robertson detailed the Wallace charges, while Stone's editorial, headlined on the front page "The Case against Jesse Jones," used these subheads inside: "A banker thinks of money . . . a banker is trained to avoid risks . . . a banker must be conservative . . . a banker must put his money in a well established enterprise . . . a banker must operate at a profit . . . a banker cannot be an idealist; it's risky."[56] Stone might have added: "A banker is the ally of industry. We've already proven to you how industry 'fights' in this war."

The alternative to corporate entanglements which allied American industry to the Nazi war machine was a political coalition of the powerless. Alexander Uhl, whose political consciousness had been shaped when he reported from Madrid during the Spanish civil war, wondered why our leaders did not use the term "popular front" to describe the antifascist coalition. Lerner called for just such alliances, with parties representing labor, peasants, and antifascist intellectuals as the basis for governments in nations liberated from fascism. All ex-fascists would be barred from such governments, which he demanded be founded on principle, not profit, in order to demonstrate why we fought.[57]

THE ENEMY WITHIN: EXPOSING THE "FIFTH COLUMN"

If the Wallace "Common Man" speech represented the total battle cry, the paper was prepared to use any and all reasons to encourage the fight. Not the least of the reasons was the location in America of spies, saboteurs, and other "fifth columnists," a term borrowed from the Spanish civil war, where it had referred to collaborators with Franco within Loyalist-held areas. Ingersoll warned, "The well-heeled turn to fascism as a last chance." *PM* reprinted navy espionage reports written by William J. Donovan and Edwin Moscone which showed how native fifth columnists "softened up" several European nations for eventual Nazi invasion. Agents and apologists for fascism seemed to be everywhere. One need not imagine invasion to see danger. As early as August 1940, the FBI publicized its plan to arrest German and Japanese spies. *PM* followed every indictment, arrest, and trial of accused spies in the New York and Washington areas. It printed the mug shots of the defendants, often in double-page spreads. A spectacular case included the arrest of German nationals as they left a submarine off Coney Island. One of the defendants hinted that he and his fellow prisoners were the forerunners of a Nazi invasion. The men were subsequently found guilty and executed, much to the delight of the paper. Another big story did not work out so well: a major sedition trial in Washington of such rich socialites and fascist propagandists as Gerald L. K. Smith dragged on through the end of the war and sputtered to a stop. Eager to expose the fascist danger here, *PM* lost perspective, churning out an FBI puff piece for the Sunday Magazine and for one short week going so far as to credit the investigative work of the Dies committee. Leo Margolin crowed that every arrested alien "lessens the 5th Column Danger."[58]

Nor did *PM* rely on the FBI and local authorities to catch spies. It went spy hunting itself, exposing the activities of profascist Germans and claiming that a business like the German Tourist Board in New York was a "front for Nazi spying." The merchant marine was riddled with fifth columnists, according to Associated Press veteran Henry Paynter, who devoted enormous energy to attempting to hunt down "Black Tom," a bombing saboteur for Germany during World War I. Aikman thought sabotage and spying were "rife on the West Coast." Ingersoll declared in December 1940 that any German or Italian businessmen still here must be spies. Margolin announced he would follow an Italian profascist editor to Forty-second Street "to find out what he's up to."[59]

A disaster in New York harbor lent credence to the search for saboteurs.

The *Normandie*, seized by the navy under neutrality legislation as the European war began on 1 September 1939 (the day after Penn Kimball had returned aboard it), was intended to be used for transporting U.S. troops abroad. It exploded into fire. Spectacular photos of the ship lying helplessly on its side accompanied articles suggesting sabotage was possible. Tom O'Connor had anticipated the event. The ship was a mammoth sitting duck in New York's wide-open harbor. He had already written several stories which were on file in the news library. When the disaster occurred, Ed Scott rushed O'Connor's information into print—and won press awards for it.[60] *PM* discovered it had no trouble getting access to the boat and to other military factories and ships in the New York area, several times sending reporters into restricted areas for no other reason than to prove they could be penetrated. Margolin found it easy to buy armed forces uniforms. Ingersoll wrote several editorials called "Holler Bloody Murder," adding the inevitable, "What Are You Going to Do about It?" Even when investigations revealed that faulty equipment caused the disaster, Ingersoll and his reporters found that faulty equipment meant lax supervision, which was tantamount to sabotage in a time of war.[61]

Amos Landman reported pro-Nazi workers in a factory providing something (details deliberately withheld) for U.S. warships. Loyal workers gave the FBI affidavits. They were identified by name. Ingersoll's accompanying editorial claimed *PM* had to go public to make sure the government acted, since it had ignored private warnings about the *Normandie*. Anecdotes told of the suspected workers singing the Horst Wessel song and fistfights between pro- and anti-Nazi workers.

One scoop was the locating of a secret printing press where pro-Nazi propaganda was being published by a WPA employee who turned furtive printer by night. *PM* released the address to its readers.

Fascist sympathies were found in Italian-, Russian-, and Polish-language newspapers. Articles in them were translated and condemned. Activities of the Ku Klux Klan, Christian Front, Black Legion, and the German-American Bund were watched. As fascists, they were leading candidates for collaboration with the America First movement or for treason. *PM* kept watchful eyes on Yorkville—Manhattan's German neighborhood and home of an active Bund chapter—for any signs of profascist activity. A rabid anti-Semite, Joe Mc-Williams, used Yorkville as a springboard in attempts to gain elective office. *PM* made sure no one missed the meaning and the danger of his political message. When McWilliams left politics and found a job in a war firm, the paper exposed his presence there and triumphantly reported on his subsequent firing. A more successful politician, Senator Rice Reynolds of North Carolina, was attacked for being openly isolationist and secretly tied to profascist organizations like the Bund.[62]

But the exposés of all of these organizations and individuals were small potatoes compared to the crusades against two popular isolationist and profascist figures: Charles Lindbergh and Charles Coughlin. Lindbergh was both the hero of the first nonstop transatlantic flight and the martyr whose young son had been kidnapped and murdered. *PM* discovered that he was about to become the leading spokesman for America First, the ardently isolationist organization that held "peace" rallies all over the country. Penn Kimball, as fervid an interventionist as anyone in the *PM* office—Ingersoll included—was investigating America First in the summer of 1940. He arranged to meet a young spokesman, an old classmate from Princeton, at the offices of the advertising agency Benton and Bowles. Chester Bowles was at that time still a *PM* investor though a leading member of America First. As Kimball waited for his interview, he saw Lindbergh emerging from Bowles's office. Shamefaced, his young contact admitted the Lindbergh connection, but desperately tried to avoid the flyer's exposure in *PM*. Kimball made it clear he would write the story. The classmate, future Republican National Committee member Bobby Stuart, refused to speak to Kimball for twenty years. Bowles called Ingersoll, but *PM*'s editor defended his young reporter. The story ran with great fanfare.[63]

Debunking Lindbergh's popularity was essential to Ingersoll. He went after his target, all polemical weapons blazing. One day early in August 1940 the entire front page was this headline: "Denouncing Charles A. Lindbergh." Inside, Ingersoll declaimed, "I can say very simply that Colonel Lindbergh in his speech in Chicago Sunday identified himself as Spokesman No. 1 for the Fifth Column. The Fifth Column, in America as in Madrid, is a group who love their counties' enemies and who first argue and then fight for them. . . . I denounce Colonel Charles A. Lindbergh as the spokesman of the Fascist Fifth Column in America." One had to turn to Kenneth Crawford's history of Lindbergh on page 9 to discover that he had praised German "efficiency" and criticized England's policy in World War II.

Radio speeches of Goebbels and Lindbergh were excerpted side by side to illustrate their similarities. Ingersoll demanded his resignation from the army and attacked his "confidence" in the American armed forces as long as they did not fight Hitler: "What in heaven's name is he confident of it being able to do?

Parade . . ? Colonel Lindbergh has got confidence in the U.S. Army and Navy. Bah!" Robert Sherwood and James Thurber made guest appearances to condemn Lindbergh and his wife, Anne Morrow Lindbergh, whose book, *The War of the Future*, failed to oppose fascism. After Lindbergh spoke to a profascist audience at Madison Square Garden, Ingersoll's denunciation was reprinted word for word. Dr. Seuss pictured Lindbergh as an ostrich with his head in the sand; the caption was "In God We Trust."

Lindbergh set off a new furor in *PM* when he made anti-Semitic remarks at an isolationist rally. Don Hollenbeck called it his "dirtiest speech." *PM* directed the storm to the America First movement, demanding it disavow Lindbergh's oration. After several days of delay it did, expressing annoyance at *PM*'s "bull-dozing." The hero was finished in American political life, courtesy of his own mouth and the close attention of *PM*, but the paper wanted to make sure. A new series devoted to uncovering "What Poisoned Lindbergh's Mind" found him a patsy for Nazi and fascist praise. After the bombing of Pearl Harbor, when Lindbergh offered the United States his help, *PM*'s predictable response was to demand he be kept out of the army.[64]

In Father Charles Coughlin—the "radio priest"—the newspaper took on an enemy who could not be defeated by "proving" his anti-Semitism. Anti-Semitism was part of his appeal. With his headquarters in Detroit, Coughlin moved from a vague populism to strident anticommunist, antiunion, anti-Semitic and anti–New Deal polemics over the radio waves and in his nationally circulated magazine, *Social Justice*. Openly supporting Franco and more guardedly sympathetic to fascist governments in Italy and Germany, he attacked Lend-Lease before the war and argued for a negotiated end after it began. To Ingersoll and *PM*, he embodied the fascist menace. When *PM*'s staff named his political allies in New York and Washington, the reporters were indicting them for treason.

After Attorney General Biddle declared that seditious profascist publications would be closed down by the FBI, *PM* declared war on Coughlin and *Social Justice*, insisting that Biddle target Coughlin's magazine as seditious. The first ten pages of the 30 March 1942 issue were devoted to the priest's writings. A ballot to be mailed to the attorney general, demanding that he "do something about it," was included. Readers could check a line demanding government action against Coughlin or choose this preposterous alternative: "Why shouldn't he tell them lies, preach sedition to them, encourage them to armed revolt against the government?" Lincoln's use of sedition law during the Civil War was cited as precedent.

Reprinting the ballot twice in the next few days, *PM* continued the crusade. On one front page, readers were warned, "Justice Department Still Hesitant about Coughlin—Tell 'em What *You* Think." The paper photographed Coughlin-ite material on New York newsstands and demanded its removal. It compared material in *Social Justice* to material in periodicals already silenced as seditious. Crawford reported that the Treasury Department was going to investigate the "religious" exemption from taxation the priest enjoyed. A story about the Justice Department's receiving 25,000 *PM* ballots was paired with a new ballot, this time straightforwardly declaring that Coughlin was guilty of sedition. On 15 April *PM* declared victory with a seven-page spread; Biddle had banned *Social Justice* from the mails. As the paper displayed Goebbels and Coughlin's words side by side, Ingersoll deemed the Biddle action a victory for the United Nations.

It was also a sign of *PM*'s influence in the administration. Attorney General Biddle confided to Assistant Attorney General Norman M. Littell that he had "wanted to go slowly on this sedition work and let the sentiment of the country build up. . . . *PM* finally took up the matter as a national issue. . . . The President gave me a rough time about it in the cabinet meeting." [65] Roosevelt wanted Biddle to make use of *PM*'s Coughlin campaign. He directed that the attorney general keep all of the paper's attacks on the priest in the government's Coughlin file. [66]

The victory would have to be defended. Two days later Ingersoll declared, "Fighting *Social Justice* and those who unwittingly spread its diseased distortion of fact is America's real job of civilian defense. . . . Don't rest." The attacks continued until *Social Justice* announced it would suspend publication. In the immediate aftermath, Luther Conant and Leo Margolin presented a list of fifteen other journals Biddle should close down. When Coughlin moved out of propaganda and founded a school for boys, Conant and Margolin thought they saw a breeding ground for future fascists; they exposed letters he wrote to former subscribers advocating the same poisonous notions. But Coughlin, like Lindbergh, was gone from the political scene. The Catholic church had decided he was too much of an embarrassment as a propagandist. [67]

Examined from the distance of fifty years, *PM*'s zeal to silence the fascist and profascist mouthpieces shows an alarming absence of concern for civil liberties. Spouting fascist propaganda is not the same as spying; sedition is a dangerously vague charge to bring against unpopular ideas. Furthermore, encouraging government intervention to ban offending periodicals aids a climate of repression which much more frequently chills the left than the right. The year before, William P. Vogel had reported extensively on the New York state legislature's Rapp-Coudert committee investigation into City College of New York faculty members. Forty-two teachers had been fired for being communists on the basis of the testimony of one ex-communist. August establishment voices, such as the *New York Times*, had insisted on the firings, deciding that "there is a great difference between permitting a citizen to advocate certain views and paying him out of public funds to do so." [68] The *Times*'s position, echoed by the "liberal" *New York Post*, was relatively mild. The *Herald Tribune*, *World-Telegram*, and *Journal-American* all advocated making the Communist party illegal. [69] Against the established press's unanimity of intolerance, Vogel, Ned Armstrong, Gene DuPoris, and Ingersoll had defended the civil liberties of the dismissed teachers, including their right to teach. [70] Now *PM* wanted Coughlin and Company closed down for "advocating views."

To embrace even one instance of the work of Congressman Martin Dies was to compound the infraction. Most often *PM* identified Dies correctly: a virulent southern racist using charges of "un-Americanism" to vent xenophobic hatred of

America's multiethnic cities and cosmopolitan ideas. Dies would prove to be the forerunner of Joseph McCarthy: "Communism" was the red hammer used to attack the New Deal. That he would occasionally subpoena a Klansman or Bundist did not suddenly make him a defender of liberty.

At the same time that *PM* was applauding FBI arrests of spies, it was conducting a long series exposing a series of firings in the federal government. In June 1942 Ken Crawford, Luther Conant, Leo Margolin, and Victor Bernstein cited dozens of cases of government workers' losing their jobs for having supported the Spanish Republic against Franco, vocalizing opposition to discrimination against blacks, or calling for a second front in Europe. One of those fired, novelist Josephine Herbst, summarized her problem: "The misfortunes of sharecroppers, the struggle of workers to unionize, the deep burden of the Negro, Pennies for China, meetings for loyalist Spain, enthusiasm for Russian victories, all *Verboten.*" Victor Bernstein lamented that government investigators

> do not appear to know that it is not Russia with which we are at war but the Axis and fascism. The only perceptive quality which cannot be denied them is their ability to sniff out a democrat. And him they prosecute with the blind and unrelenting prejudice that is the hallmark of fascism.[71]

Only an extreme naïveté based on faith in the Roosevelt administration would combine justified anger at the government purge of liberals and antifascists with a cheering section for the FBI. Civil libertarian concerns were not high on many *PM*ers' agendas.

If *PM* could claim partial credit for shutting down Lindbergh and Coughlin, it took on much more powerful antagonists in declaring war on the "Press Axis," a title it bestowed on the Hearst Press and the McCormick-Patterson family's three newspapers: the *Chicago Tribune*, the *New York Daily News*, and the *Washington Times-Herald*. These were the largest-circulation dailies in the United States; as we have seen, it was to offset their influence that Roosevelt administration figures had supported the infant *PM*. It is difficult to convey to today's newspaper reader what passed for a political perspective in these newspapers, but a *National Guardian* commentary came close in 1963 when it summed up *Daily News* editorial policy as "folksy fascism." The *News* had evenhandedly welcomed the sinking of both the British *Hood* and the German *Bismarck*, because it weakened both parties, thus keeping us out of the conflict. The *News* thought that World War I

> was fought not because the Germans surprised and violated Belgium, but because Britain did not want Germany to gain a formidable sea power and become the dominant power on the continent. . . . Germany in 1914–1918 came near bringing about a more natural balance of things. . . . We were induced by the British, however, to throw our weight into the fight. . . . [Now] it is the same old fight.[72]

In the period before the bombing of Pearl Harbor the "Press Axis" attacked British involvement in the war as imperialism, saw Hitler's territorial demands in Austria, Czechoslovakia, and Poland as being reasonable and minor, and thought Japan the most civilized of the "Asiatic" countries. They were shrilly opposed to any involvement in the war. When the Vichy government pledged fealty to Hitler's dominance, Hearst's version of European affairs was astounding:

> If the nations of Europe are willing to accept a new European order, and like France, see salvation in it—and if the nations of Asia are willing to accept a new Asian order, and like Japan and Russia, bury long enmities in it . . . why not let all go their various ways in peace and not destroy the wealth and welfare—the health and happiness—of all the world in futile war? [73]

Hearst identified with a

> second line of thought [which] arrives at the conclusion that Germany's desire is to form the nations of continental Europe into a United States of Europe, free from England's interference and fortified by a doctrine like our Monroe Doctrine. . . . Germany has been continually willing to negotiate a peace guaranteeing the integrity of the British Empire, providing that England will keep her fingers out of continental affairs. [74]

After the invasion of the Soviet Union, Hearst openly rooted for Hitler's legions to defeat godless communism. After Pearl Harbor was bombed, the newspapers constantly worried that the Soviet Union, China, or Great Britain would make a separate peace with Hitler (so they advocated we do it first) and attacked the Allies' goal of unconditional surrender by Germany and Japan. Japan was declared the only important enemy, but the papers nonetheless argued for a "soft peace" for that nation as well.

PM's first column on the press was an attack on the Hearst papers. Ben Hecht wrote of William Randolph Hearst, "That he is lucid and trenchant in the causes of Fascism, Isolationism, Anti-Democracy and Parochialism is doubly unfortunate." When federal Office of Facts and Figures director Archibald MacLeish said some papers helped the enemy, his friends at *PM* were not hesitant to conclude that he must have meant the *Daily News* and the *Chicago Tribune*.

PM opened a broad campaign aimed at proving these newspapers were profascist mouthpieces. For the final days of April and most of May 1942 the Hearst and Patterson-McCormick papers were the main source of attention. The principal technique was to compare Goebbels and "Press Axis" editorials; there were some astonishing similarities that seemed to indicate the American writers had used the German minister of propaganda as a guide. Attacks on Great Britain, China, and the USSR, threats that war would bankrupt the United States and end its democracy, and fears of worldwide communism were shown to be worded similarly in German and Press Axis polemics. The appeasement policies of the American newspapers in the 1930s and their support for the fascist revolt in Spain were extensively reviewed. FDR was quoted as saying that the war effort "must not be impeded by a few bogus patriots who use the sacred freedom of the press to echo the sentiments of the propagandists of Tokyo and Berlin." Mac-Leish's pamphlet "Divide and Conquer," exposing the same practices that *PM* decried, was reprinted in full. Hearst's proclamation that "in this truly world war it is of very little actual importance to the Occidental races which one of them [Nazi Germany or the USSR] dominates Europe" drew an acid response from John P. Lewis: "This world war is NOT a war between races. It is a war between freedom and slavery."

As the campaign ended, Hearst's friends in Boston got a city ordinance passed banning Boston newsstands from selling out-of-town papers, an act vengefully aimed at *PM*. A new campaign aimed at Boston's mayor succeeded in overturning the ordinance.

The *Daily News* claimed Biddle's use of sedition law and Roosevelt's not-so-hidden attacks on it made the president a censor and predicted his assassination. Crawford responded, "For sheer editorial ugliness there has been nothing to match this *News* editorial at any point in the bitter anti–New Deal fights of the last ten years, not even in *Social Justice.*" *PM* was moved again to attack the interlocking directorates of the three Patterson-McCormick papers and replay their editorial discords. Despite excellent documentation from *PM* that there was no difference in editorial policy between the fascist papers Biddle had suppressed and these giants, there was no chance Roosevelt would attempt to close them down. They were simply too big and too powerful, and unlike the semiofficial fascist press, they were read for a variety of reasons. While more shrill than most, their editorials were more indicative of press opinion in the United States than were those in the papers supporting the president. The one victory for *PM*'s side came when a *Daily News* copy editor, Heizer Wright, was indicted and tried for being a secret agent for Japan for ten years prior to the bombing of Pearl Harbor.[75]

The Press Axis took a small measure of revenge. At the height of *PM*'s campaign against the McCormick-Patterson papers, the *Washington Times-Herald* ran a cartoon showing a small monument titled "*PM*" being targeted by a passing dog.[76]

POLITICAL LESSONS

While identifying the enemy at home, *PM* kept its eyes trained on the heinous acts of our enemies overseas. It focused on reports of torture by our enemies, as when it serialized Ben Proux's *I Was a Prisoner in a Jap War Camp.*[77] After an exposure of Nazi atrocities in Kharkov, Lerner wrote, "Fascism is all that is inhuman." The paper took pains to prove him right.[78] After they were liberated, concentration camps were usually displayed in double-page photographic spreads as grim reminders of that inhumanity.[79] Lerner differentiated between any means of defeating fascism, including massive aerial bombardment, and the only civil liberties violations he found the United States guilty of: the Smith Act trial of members of the Socialist Workers party and the internment of Japanese Americans.[80]

PM reviewed the history of fascist dictatorial rule.[81] It cheered every sign of unity among Great Britain, the Soviet Union, and the United States as making possible not only the successful conclusion of the war but also the establishment of world peace. "The Ship of State on which the world's hopes hang today is no longer America alone. It is the United Nations [i.e., the Allies] with the leaders of the great anti-fascist powers at the helm," Lerner wrote. Toward this end he and his newspaper embraced the Teheran and Yalta conferences, even before any decisions made there were known.[82]

Near the end of the war *PM* welcomed Darryl F. Zanuck's production of *Wilson*, a film biography which emphasized the late president's commitment to the League of Nations, to drive home the lesson of international cooperation. On opening day eight pages of the paper were turned over to promoting the film, including a full-page reproduction of a telegram from John P. Lewis to Zanuck, congratulating him. Not content with this, the paper serialized the screenplay. A reader of *PM* in August of 1944 might have concluded that Zanuck had opened not a movie but a third front. Despite *PM*'s extensive promotion, the movie was a commercial failure.[83] Earlier, Louis Kronenberger had welcomed Lillian Hellman's antifascist play, *Watch on the Rhine*, calling it the "best play of the season." The premiere of Alfred Hitchcock's *Saboteur* led to a review of fifth column activity in the United States.[84]

As the Allies moved into enemy territory, Richard Yaffe warned American troops not to trust friendly Germans. Uhl reported with approval French complaints that our army was too soft on German prisoners. The paper reprinted an editorial from the GI newspaper *Stars and Stripes*, "Don't Get Chummy with Jerry." But Lerner stressed it was not the biology of Germans or Japanese that was the issue but the poison of fascism.[85]

Even before the paper was fully committed to war, it worried publicly about American readiness for it. As early as July 1940 Ingersoll attacked the inefficiency of the armed forces. Leonard Engel thought a minimum of nine months was required to bring our military forces up to fighting condition. Margaret Bourke-White did a centerfold spread glorifying West Point, at a time when we needed the best graduates.[86]

PM's editorialists enthusiastically supported the call for a draft, though Ingersoll wanted all young people more fully politically educated in New Deal principles: "The side that knows what it's fighting for is the side that's going to win." Nathan Robertson attacked some old heroes of domestic politics who opposed the draft: senators Wheeler and Norris. Robertson protested that draft legislation was being "slowed down by near hysterical debates." As the legislation took shape, Ingersoll complained that drafting one million young people was both numerically insufficient and politically one-sided: we needed to guarantee returning draftees jobs or education.

The day before the law took effect, *PM*'s front page headline was "Where to Register for Draft." The feature in the centerfold told all twenty-one- to thirty-six-year-old men how and where to register. "Hey Adolf!" the front page called out the following day, atop a John Killian photograph of young men registering.

James T. Howard reported "New Yorkers Register Cheerfully," though William McCleery, registering himself, disclosed that many on the line thought war was in their future. Louis Kronenberger took a break from Broadway reviewing duties to parody society types "put out" by the draft. Jokes and anecdotes collected by the male staff while registering were retold; a snapshot was taken of young *PM* sportswriter Heywood Hale Broun on line. The other side was represented, too: Sutherland Denlinger attended a rally by pacifists who had just registered as conscientious objectors. When the first numbers were announced, *PM* made it front-page news, announcing brightly the following day, "New York City High Number Draft Men Accept Draft Status with Good Humor and Bravery." Enlistees were given more support, as with the large photo-story that crowed, "These Men Can't Wait To Get Into It."

THE WAR'S IMPACT ON *PM*

The paper followed the first crew to basic training, where Roger Dakin reported, "Our New Army Is Healthy and Happy at Fort Dix."[87] Nine months later a new column began, "Private Jimmy Cannon Says." Several times a week for a year and a half Cannon honed the anecdotal style that would win him great fame as a sports reporter in the 1950s. This was typical Cannon prose, describing the prototypical draftee: "He would rather be under fire than do KP. . . . He's a Brooklyn Dodger fan. . . . He's a nice kid." He did feature after feature about the different ethnic and regional types who surrounded him, until he was finally shipped out.[88]

Cannon was joined by many original *PM* staffers in the armed forces. Penn Kimball and Weldon James joined the marines, Dr. Seuss the signal corps. William Walton, by then working for *Life*, parachuted into France on D-Day. These young men proved their commitment to the prowar crusade by enlisting as soon as they could. Richard Green waived draft deferment to join the army. Many who left would not come back. "Once the war started," Kimball says, "the bloom was off the rose at *PM*." Fighting fascism was a more direct way to confront the world's villainy.[89] Others left to join the government's propaganda apparatus. George Lyon left *PM* many months before the bombing of Pearl Harbor to serve in the Office of War Information. Within a few months he was joined by John A. Sullivan.[90]

The biggest individual loss to the paper, of course, was Ingersoll's enlistment. *PM* was his baby. He had been the idea man, the energetic crusader, the charismatic leader. As Kimball declared, "Ingersoll was it."[91] Now he was gone. What remained was clearly a continuation of the project he had begun, but changes were inevitable.

Ingersoll had worn many hats; a separate head was assigned for each one. Stolid John P. Lewis was finally a true editor. He selected the other editors, supervised the activities of all, and provided newspaper expertise to the remain-

The clear, crisp look of *PM*, with its reliance on photography and art, can be seen even as it rolls off the press. (Courtesy of William McCleery)

Rae Weimer, Alexander Uhl, John P. Lewis, and Ralph Ingersoll in Lewis's office. (Courtesy of William McCleery)

Alan Fisher's dramatic photograph of the destroyed *Normandie* aptly illustrated *PM*'s fear of sabotage. (*PM*, 2 March 1942)

Mary Morris went to Campobello to snap two of *PM*'s more faithful and influential readers: Eleanor Roosevelt faces the camera; Felix Frankfurter is directly behind her. (Courtesy of Mary Morris)

Photographer Mary Morris, Sunday Magazine editor William McCleery, and his pediatrician—an anonymous Dr. Spock—ran a weekly update on the progress of Baby Lois, born the same week as *PM*. (Courtesy of Mary Morris)

Crockett Johnson's "Barnaby," featuring an imaginative child and his flawed leprachaun friend Mr. O'Malley, became a cult classic. (*PM*, 25 March 1945. Courtesy of William McCleery)

PM Artist Leo Hirshfield captured the imperious and contentious John L. Lewis. (*PM*, 11 March 1945. Courtesy of William McCleery)

Dr. Seuss captures two aspects of *PM*'s wartime zeal, including an all-too-traditional appeal to racism. (*PM*, 2 March and 13 February 1942)

Monday night: an artist sees the Mayor watching over Harlem

While some critics complained this week that Sunday night's riot in Harlem might never have taken place had Mayor La Guardia initiated certain preventative measures six months ago, everybody agreed that he had done a fine job of handling the situation once it had broken. Don (Newsstand) Freeman spent Monday on the Mayor's trail, accompanying him on his inspection trips of the disordered Harlem streets, joining his press conferences. Late in the day he made this sketch of La Guardia, looking tired and sorrowful, in the tiny office—his temporary headquarters—on the fourth floor of the 123rd Street police station. By now the swift explosion of the pre-ceding night had subsided. All day and evening reporters, army officers, Negro leaders and clergy, police officers, had filled and emptied the hot, box-like office in waves. From the street still rose the uneven roar of motorcycles and riot cars reporting in and out of the station. Across the street, tenants of one of Harlem's simmering tenements hung restlessly out of the window watching the crowds below. Police officers, assigned to prevent throwing of missiles from roofs, tramped back and forth peering from time to time on the littered streets, illuminated by brightly glowing lamps (the dimout had been lifted). At 1:25 a.m. the Mayor climbed into a police car and drove home.

During his stint as an artist for the Sunday Magazine, Don Freeman, later to be an acclaimed children's author, captured Mayor La Guardia after the disturbing Harlem riots. (*PM*, 8 August 1943. Courtesy of William McCleery)

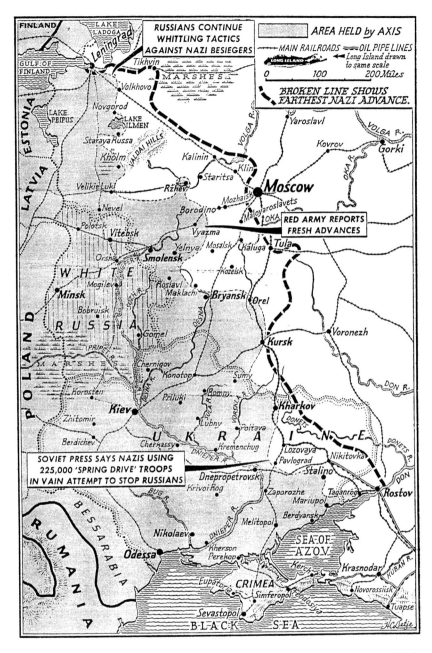

Harold Dietje's detailed and decorative daily war maps were often reworked
at the last minute. (*PM*, 2 March 1942)

Arthur Leipzig demonstrated the independence and
eloquence of *PM*'s photographers when he stumbled on
the convention of the Daughters of the American Revolution, resulting in a centerfold spread. (Courtesy of
Arthur Leipzig)

Morris Gordon captures the joy of VE Day in Times Square. (*PM*, 8 May 1945)

PM ran Mary Morris's photo of Lena Horne several times. She was black, beautiful, progressive, and had just penetrated the Plaza Hotel's racial wall. (Courtesy of Mary Morris)

PM's SUNDAY

PICTURE NEWS

MAGAZINE SECTION   JULY 16, 1944   NEW YORK, N. Y.   Copyright, 1944, by Field Publications   10c

PHOTO BY SKIPPY ADELMAN

The Long Asparagus and the Little Flower

Gen. Charles De Gaulle (known since his school days as the Long Asparagus) and Mayor La Guardia at the welcome for the General at City Hall last week. This picture was taken just as De Gaulle reached City Hall from La Guardia Airport and the Sanitation Dept. Band burst into *La Marseillaise*. (*For the crowd's-eye view of De Gaulle's visit to City Hall, turn this page.*)

Skippy Adelman captures the long and short of the fight against fascism (*PM*, 16 July 1944. Courtesy of William McCleery)

The Champ campaigns in Pennsylvania

This photograph of the President was taken on Friday, October 27, during his 40-mile tour of Philadelphia —in an open car and through rain and sleet. It was snapped as he started to greet somebody along the way.

The Champ. (*PM*, 5 November 1944. Courtesy of William McCleery)

ing amateurs at the paper. By now a committed liberal, he was never a "professional" or "non-professional" intellectual, to use Ken Stewart's terminology. He was a steadying influence who had assimilated *PM*'s unflinching championing of trade union and antidiscrimination politics. His greatest problem was that he was in awe of many of the brighter ideologues around him. He had difficulty confronting them. For some of the younger staff members he was a source of calm, reasonable support. One remembered an incident when Lewis received a complaint from a foreign ambassador about a profile she had written. Lewis asked her what she thought about the objection and changed only what the reporter agreed was fair. "He was exactly what a managing editor should be. He was a decent guy and an honest guy."[92] He developed his own method of communicating with the readers—an informal conversational column on the letters page. This kept the faithful informed of changes in the publication and in its personnel, as well as of the quiet reflections of a gentle mind.[93]

Rae Weimer had become assistant managing editor when Lyon joined the OWI. He "was the only executive who was always on the editorial floor," as Ingersoll and Lewis had private offices. He was a source of much of the newspaper's high spirits; an inveterate prankster, he was once apprehended by a police officer in the act of breaking into Lewis's apartment to leave a live chicken there. He was able to convince the patrolman that *PM*'s editor wanted the bird. Before and after Ingersoll's enlistment, he was always the most accessible of the men running the newspaper. After "putting the paper to bed," he had to wait several hours, sometimes until dawn, for the first issue to come up from the pressroom to make sure any mistakes could be corrected. He organized a staff poker game. It surprised no one that he frequently won. With Ingersoll and Lyon gone, the boisterous, congenial Weimer was now the second-ranking executive.[94]

To defend the paper in its struggle to exist, owner Marshall Field and attorney Louis Weiss took on new responsibilities. Field continued to be the benevolent, unobtrusive, self-effacing publisher of record. When he came to *PM*'s offices, he would meet privately with Lewis while his wife remained in the editorial room, fascinated by Weimer's work changing copy and making it fit. Field continued to supply the financial support. Although he had tried to intercede to prevent Ingersoll's loss to the armed forces, he had reason to be relieved by the latter's absence. There was no one left at the paper quite so ready to spend his money. Once at a board meeting, after a long Ingersoll harangue for additional thousands of dollars for another expensive promotion campaign, Richard Green watched as Field, "in his quiet way, said, 'You know, Ralph, *PM* is not the New York Philharmonic. It is not an eleemosynary institution. I am not an eleemosynary institution.'" (Field was a leading supporter of the philharmonic and frequently made up the deficit after fund-raising drives.)[95]

The veteran journalists at the paper were certainly relieved. "We were more comfortable after [Ingersoll] was in the army," says Rae Weimer. The paper was "more standardized with fewer last-second screwy ideas."[96]

Representing Field's interests, Louis Weiss had become a friend of Eleanor

Roosevelt, as the first lady and Field were the leaders in an organization to settle child refugees from the Nazis in the United States. More than once, Weiss asked Mrs. Roosevelt to protect *PM* from wartime government restrictions. As we shall soon see, he had little luck.[97]

To wear Ingersoll's editorial hat, Lewis selected an entirely new model. The voice was as distinctive as Ingersoll's and about as different as could be from his own in its pitch and tone, even if the song was similar.

Max Lerner, like Ingersoll, was a Yale graduate. But where Ingersoll's distinguished family had been in the United States prior to the Revolution, Lerner had been born in a Jewish *shtetl* in Minsk (then White Russia, today Belarus). Ingersoll paid little attention to his course of study; Lerner was a fervent intellectual who graduated from Yale and continued his studies, emerging with a doctorate in political science from the Brookings Institution. As a graduate student, his attraction to Marxism was tempered by differences on the theoretical issue of the nature of the state. His papers contain an unpublished book on the subject that cites Veblenian and American exceptionalist nuances in Lenin's treatment of state power. Studying at the London School of Economics, he became an admirer of British socialist Harold Laski, with whom he exchanged many worried letters before the United States entered the war. In his correspondence he appears as protégé to Laski and mentor to many. After graduation he combined three careers. He began teaching at the experimental Sarah Lawrence College, where he was able to combine his interest in many branches of the humanities (his influence there on Mary Morris has already been noted). Later, as a professor of political science at Williams College, he penned popular front (although sometimes anti-Stalinist) editorials for the *New Republic* and the *Nation*. Early in the war, he was asked to teach a program for officer candidates in the navy, a job he was glad to abandon for writing at *PM*. He wrote several scholarly books on contemporary ideas. To produce an acclaimed study of Oliver Wendell Holmes, he became a frequent correspondent and finally friend of three of Roosevelt's Supreme Court appointees: Hugo Black, William O. Douglas, and Felix Frankfurter. Paradoxically, his relationship was particularly close with Frankfurter, the least liberal of the three. His political prose tended to be stuffy and sometimes arcane. While both Ingersoll and Lerner were full of themselves, Ingersoll's vanity was in being overwrought, Lerner's in being overwordy. Just before Ingersoll went into the army, he scanned a sample editorial of Lerner's and came to a typical snap judgment. "You'll never be a newspaperman!" he announced, walking briskly away.

Within six months of that conclusion, Max Lerner was writing daily editorials for *PM*. He would be the main editorialist even after Ingersoll returned. To allow Lerner to work fewer hours, which would enable him to work in other fields and take longer vacations than other staffers, Lewis hired him as an "assistant to the publisher." It was an ironic title, as Lewis pointed out, since *PM* had no "publisher" and since the other two with the title were Virginia Schoales, actually executive secretary, and Thomas Clelland, who was doing no work at all for the paper but was being rewarded for having designed it.[98]

Lerner was a novice at newspapers. During his first several months, Rae Weimer held daily conferences with him to suggest topics for editorials. Lerner was also pursuing a busy career as a radio commentator. He and Weimer might meet about an editorial topic in the morning. The columnist would write half of it before his plane landed, cable that half to Weimer over Western Union, speak at Buffalo, be driven (while writing) to Cleveland where he would give another radio address, and cable the conclusion of the column from there.[99]

Several other staff members wrote featured opinion pieces. On weekends and during Lerner's vacations, Stone, Alexander Uhl, and Victor Bernstein contributed page 2 editorials. Lewis wrote in that space occasionally. On matters of great importance, or on matters where Lewis thought the paper needed a pronouncement, Lerner, Stone, Uhl, Bernstein, Wechsler, or O'Connor might write "for the Editors of *PM*." To develop such a piece, the writer would meet with Lewis or Weimer. As Lewis later explained to Kenneth Stewart, he actively sought the aid of others to create editorial policy. The paper's opinion was much more a collective expression than it had been under Ingersoll.[100]

The war changed the paper in other ways. By 1943 it seemed that everything was being rationed. Newsprint and inks were not excepted. For Ingersoll's beautiful experiment, this was a great sacrifice indeed. The paper shrank in both page size and number of pages; the second color on the cover was abandoned; the quality of the paper stock was no longer distinctive. It was no longer stapled. Even the Caledonia typeface was inconsistently used. Louis Weiss made valiant attempts to save the paper; he appealed to presidential press secretary Steve Early only for *PM*, not for Field's *Chicago Sun*, because he was convinced that *PM*'s form was an integral part of its character. Unfortunately there would be no exceptions to the rationing rules.[101]

The paper shrank to twenty-eight pages in 1943; it was twenty-four pages by 1944. The News for Living section was considerably abridged. In a time of war, this was an understandable editorial judgment, but the character of the paper was narrower, more exclusively political than it had been. By 1944 consumer news sometimes vanished entirely; more rarely, sports news suffered the same fate. On some days *PM* printed as few as sixteen pages. That over 100,000 New Yorkers continued to spend their nickels to buy it illustrated the unflinching loyalty of its core readers.

PM'S MILITARY POLICY

The war also suggested new beats.

To break the German war machine, new weapons were needed, more innovative and destructive than the ones the Nazis designed. Ingersoll suggested we harness "native American ingenuity and enthusiasm." He thought that "kids who like to drive at breakneck speed" would be great at designing tanks." Several times *PM* writers attacked American war planes, which they thought slow and poorly armed. The paper declared it scandalous that inadequate planes were being shipped to help the British. Months later, Engel thought our tank production no better than our early planes. This was symptomatic of poor overall mobilization.[102]

Writer Willy Ley, with no expertise in the field, was put to work on a once-a-week feature called "New War Weapons," which explained the mechanics of everything from new bomber planes to new fuses. He turned himself into an expert, studying whatever was not classified at factories and in the library.[103]

I. F. Stone heralded United Auto Workers vice president Walter Reuther's "500 Planes a Day" plan, contained in a letter to CIO president Phil Murray, to convert the automobile industry to war production. Stone reported the automakers were resisting, wanting to turn out cars instead. Reuther—"the red-headed union dynamo"—analyzed plant-by-plant capacity and suggested we could produce much faster by using existing plants than by building new ones from scratch. Reuther claimed there were more skilled tool-and-die workers in Detroit than anywhere else, though many were now unemployed. Stone corralled the Office of Production Management's administrator, William Knudson, who supported the Reuther plan, and sought out dozens of production experts, none of whom had anything negative to say about it. When aircraft officials faulted the proposal, Stone counterattacked; their record profits were at stake if they were forced to compete with the auto industry. Reuther's radio speech explaining his plan was printed in full. Stone's publicity helped to build support for the program and directed attention to Senator Truman's committee hearings on war readiness.[104]

Stone's enthusiasm for the Reuther plan was unique in the press. Sharing Reuther's belief that war production should be overseen by a tripartite planning committee representing labor, management, and government interests (Reuther's trade union militancy had socialist roots), Stone was a natural propagandist for the auto unionist's views. In fact, the journalist had been present at their creation. He revealed to historian Nelson Lichtenstein that he had helped develop the Reuther plan and had produced the final written version of "500 Planes a Day."[105]

The *Times*, consistent in its hostility to labor and reflecting industry's hostility to labor involvement in production planning, tried to kill the plan "technically." The editorial page intoned:

> The main issue is purely a technical one. There is much facile talk of "converting" this or that "facility" to airplane making. This talk overlooks that airplane engines and other essential parts must be made by machine tools which are highly specialized. . . . It is quite obvious that proponents of the Reuther plan think that automobile mass production methods can be easily applied to the military airplane problem; but the two problems, unfortunately, are far different.[106]

Having announced "technical" problems, the *Times* never bothered to document them. It had little to say when many automobile plants were eventually converted to war production, though without the Reuther-Stone labor planning component.

Ingersoll announced his own new plans for planes on the front page; he had liberally borrowed from Walter Reuther ("Ralph Ingersoll Brings His Plan for U.S. Fighting Planes Up-to-Date"). George Reedy wrote that a new riveting process made the Reuther proposal feasible and would end the bottleneck in aluminum production. By July 1941, *PM* approved of our new bomber planes, finding them (finally) equal to or better than the European models. But when Ingersoll returned from visiting Britain, he distinguished between fighter planes, which he thought were both too few and of poor quality, and bomber planes, which he thought the best in the world.[107]

Men and strategy were found wanting, too. Aikman thought our generals were unthinking "yes-men" and, reversing the meaning of Bourke-White's earlier photo-story, blamed this on West Point's factorylike education. The military was condemned for leaving major Eastern cities unprotected from Nazi attack. Willard Wiener was angered that by mid-1943 there was no child-care plan for mothers working in defense.[108]

There were grounds for *PM*'s concern. Both James MacGregor Burns and Kenneth Davis report that Roosevelt's policy of catering to divided public opinion had left him unable to develop U.S. military strength prior to the bombing of Pearl Harbor; the concomitant policy of supplying all possible aid to Great Britain had stripped bare our supplies of ships, planes, and even guns.[109]

Dr. Seuss drew a billboard that asked, "What Have You Done Today to Save Your Country from Them? and pictured Hitler and a stereotypic Japanese." *PM* had many answers. It advised "how to convert your home into a bomb shelter." A photo-story reminded readers, "This Is Total War: Whether You Realize It or Not . . . Ask Yourself How It Has Changed Your Way of Life." Six large photographs of Americans engaged in several war-related activities illustrated the point. "Where Do You Fit in This War?" was answered with a display of New York City area civilian and volunteer war jobs. Young boys collecting scrap rubber were photographed and extolled.[110] President Roosevelt asked Archibald MacLeish to recruit Ingersoll for a project of war propaganda displayed on billboards;[111] while *PM*'s editor declined this role, he editorialized that advertising companies, whose work was spurned in *PM*, must use their skills to push the war effort. He warned that no one would have use for their services after the war if they did not comply.[112]

Early in 1942, Crawford thought we were still losing the war "because idle men and idle factories mean lost battles." The paper located "380 Tons of Idle Scrap Metal in New Jersey . . . While Steel Mills Stay Shut Because of Shortage." The metal was in auto junkyards, whose yield, *PM* suggested, could be used to make howitzers, tanks, and bombs. Amos Landman found an idle plant that could make war chemicals; a Long Island speedboat manufacturer with no work was located. Leo Margolin traveled to Massachusetts to identify a British-owned munitions plant with 15,000 tons of steel. It was closed. As with the Reuther plan, the idle-plants campaign combined two themes: support of the war effort and jobs for workers. "Axis Sinks Ships Faster than We Can Build Them; UN Will Face Defeat at 21,000,000 Tons a Year," warned page 1. Inside Crawford touted union-friendly progressive industrialist Henry Kaiser as just the man to speed up war production and put more Americans to work.[113]

Near the end of the war, *PM* found too few applicants for New York City area war jobs. The paper listed the positions and used photographs and features about the firms involved to urge workers to apply.[114]

COVERING THE BATTLEFRONT

The biggest story, of course, was the actual progress of the war itself. *PM* covered it fully, despite the handicap of having been born with a domestically oriented staff.[115] One problem was getting overseas. Ben Robertson, Jr., could not cut through the red tape needed to allow him access to African and Asian war theaters; the paper sent a wire to the White House. The president ordered the bureaucracy to facilitate his trip.[116] Robertson reported from England, the Soviet Union, and India before he was killed at sea. Frederick Kuh was the London correspondent of Marshall Field's *Chicago Sun*; after that paper was born, Kuh's byline appeared in both newspapers. Later, Ralph Parker reported from Moscow. Ingersoll traveled to England and the Soviet Union for first person reporting (and posturing). While Ingersoll joined many of the *PM* staff in uniform, he contributed little to the paper while in the army, vanishing as a presence from mid-July 1942 until January 1946. Others who were drafted were also drafted as *PM* war correspondents, most notably Roi Ottley, part of a black platoon serving in England and Italy. United Press dispatches from all fronts were used daily; Ilya Ehrenburg was a UP correspondent assigned to the Red Army whose dispatches were regularly featured in *PM*.

Many of the paper's leading editorialists went overseas to view the action for themselves. The paper actually lost Kenneth Crawford that way. He went to North Africa and decided *PM*'s attack on occupation policy was unjustified. In a nasty exchange of letters with John P. Lewis, he accused the paper of doctoring his copy and resigned claiming, "I don't know how to convince you that I'm not a liar."[117] Crawford moved to the foreign desk of *Newsweek*; Wechsler became Washington bureau chief. Max Lerner, Victor Bernstein, Alexander Uhl, Irving Brant, and I. F. Stone made their own trips without defecting.

The most visible aspect of *PM*'s coverage was the war maps, usually spread over the centerfold and illustrated by arrows to show the movement of opposing armies. They were detailed and they benefited from the high-quality paper stock and more expensive ink Ingersoll insisted on, which was not abandoned until war rationing forced the change in 1943. Even after the change, the maps reproduce brilliantly on microfilm. Most often the action showed the movement on the Russian front, but maps of all fronts were updated at least once a week. When battles were raging, they were updated every day. A comparison of *PM*'s daily maps with the war maps in the Sunday *Times*'s News of the Week in Review shows the "paper of record" flattering the upstart tabloid with imitation but failing to capture the nuances and the sharp images Harold Dietje managed routinely. Arthur Leipzig remembers more than one occasion when the presses were halted to remake the maps to conform to the news coming over the wire.[118]

Military analysis was mostly provided by Leonard Engel, in his guise as "the General," and by Max Werner for the last year and a half of the war. The General and his colleagues had impressive records. In August 1940, he observed that the British had achieved a stalemate in the Battle of Britain and predicted Hitler would be impelled to look for action elsewhere. Carl Randau mused that Napoleon gave up on a British invasion and turned east. Would Hitler? Crawford quoted State Department sources as expecting war with Japan by Christmas 1941. The day after the bombing of Pearl Harbor, the General predicted flatly, "Japan has committed hari-kari. The USA and Allies will win the war." In his own name Engel explained his position: Japan had less money and a smaller army with fewer resources, but for a time it could succeed in island battles in the Pacific. Since many islands were undefended, he had thought Japan would win them easily. Randau added that Japan's attack was "the position of a gambler who can be saved only by taking ever greater chances." The General could be unsentimental; while *PM*'s editors were shaken by the British loss of Tobruk and believed they were not aggressive enough, he said the Nazis had a better army and better weapons. On the first anniversary of the attack on Pearl Harbor, despite victories on the Russian and African fronts, the General warned that the battles were just beginning. In April 1943, when the tide had clearly turned, he cautioned that the Nazis still had manpower, oil, and morale. The war would not be over quickly. The Germans would not be bombed into submission any more than the British had. He correctly charted the direction and the greater difficulty of the Italian campaign after the success in North Africa. In May 1943, H. R. Knickerbocker warned that the Nazis were not collapsing; more accurately than he could have known, he predicted two more years of war.[119]

Sometimes the analysts were wrong. Ingersoll decided that if the Nazis were stymied in Yugoslavia, the war might be over; the General thought it augured for more hostility with the Soviet Union, but he thought that war there was still far away. The biggest mistake the General made was in constantly denying that war between Germany and the USSR could happen; he thought the Russians were unprepared, and it seems never to have occurred to him that the Nazis would initiate hostilities. He believed that Hitler had learned to respect the Red Army from the Soviet-Finnish campaign. In the last ten days before the German invasion, the General denied four times that it would happen. On 22 June, all he could say was that he was astonished.[120]

Ingersoll, given to the most grandiloquent pronouncements, decided in November 1941 that a four-power war on Japan by China, the U.S., U.S.S.R., and Great Britain would destroy Japan in six months. He predicted a Japanese invasion of Siberia for spring 1942. The General thought so, too. At the end of the war, guest writer Joachim Josten predicted Nazi leadership would hole up in an "Alpine citadel . . . to carry on guerilla warfare." Max Werner was so taken with the progress of the Red Army after 1943 that he wrote a series of columns suggesting the war would be over in six or eight weeks. The fact that a deadline passed did not deter him from issuing another such prediction; often they overlapped.[121]

The drama of war was a natural for *PM*, which was perfectly capable of turning over the whole paper to any one topic for days at a time. Massive bombing of London in the late summer of 1941 was the sole subject of one thirty-two page issue.[122] With a plentiful supply of its own, the *Chicago Sun*'s, and UP writers in Europe, there were large numbers of written pieces to choose from; the photographic possibilities were even greater. *PM* devoted eleven of twenty-four pages to the liberation of Rome. The long campaigned-for D-Day was greeted with total commitment: a white-on-black front-page headline, page-size photographs of Eisenhower and Montgomery, and twenty-three pages. The renewed Russian offensive took up almost as much space.[123]

Ingersoll had an instinct for drama. His reports from London and Moscow were not always the most perceptive, but they did convey the pulsating rhythms of a nation at war:

> My hotel in London has a black revolving door. I think I shall always remember the sensation of its spinning me out into the dark. One second you are in a cheerful, normal, lighted hotel lobby full of pleasant sounds and talking people. Next—just as if you had fallen through a trapdoor—you are in pitch black. You feel it most in your feet because you don't know where to put them for the next step. Your eyes are unused and see nothing. You put out your hands and you feel—outside most hotel doors— sandbags. Or the coats of unidentified people.

The standing joke was, "Oh, but wasn't it lucky that the bomb missed all those houses and fell in that vacant lot." [124]

Ingersoll's highly publicized reports from London substantially raised the circulation of the struggling paper, bringing it up to the 100,000 level for the first time since the chaotic opening month.[125]

The flair for drama produced elaborate mythmaking. General Douglas MacArthur was profiled lovingly with full-page photographs several times. His departure for Asia was greeted with the front-page headline "Godspeed MacArthur." Only when enemies like the *Daily News* began touting MacArthur as anti-FDR presidential timber did *PM* attack the worshipful stance it had earlier taken. Once selected as European commander, Eisenhower was afforded the same treatment. He was introduced to the readers as a "hard-hitting soldier of the MacArthur school." [126]

PM followed the war in books with back-to-back serializations. Most of them were first-person accounts of aspects of the war, like John Gardner Dowling's *Guadalcanal Diary*, Alan Michie's *Air Offensive against Germany*, Maurice Hindu's *Mother Russia*, an admiring account of Russian resistance to Nazi attack, and Ingersoll's own *The Battle Is the Pay-Off*, which was given great ballyhoo by his home paper. Following his best reporter's instincts, Ingersoll filled the book with careful observations of daily life in the armed forces. His serialization was followed by Robert Goffin's *White Brigade*, a report on the activities of the underground in Belgium. *The Day of Reckoning*, by Max Rotin, imagined war trials of the defeated Nazis.[127] The best journalism in any of the serializations was by CBS reporter Howard K. Smith, whose reports out of Germany were presented in January 1943. Smith portrayed the morale of Germany doomed by losses on the Russian front, which was worsened when the government had to reverse claims of victory. Shortages in food, alcohol, tobacco, clothing, and housing were desperate. Civilian trains had been destroyed by Allied bombing runs. He warned of the extreme indoctrination of the Hitler Youth, whom he saw as "arrogant killers," and described the renewed fury of the attack on Jews, all the more intense now that the war news was bad.[128]

WAR POLITICS ABROAD

To report on the world at war was to comment on the politics of many lands. Unprepared with foreign correspondents at the outset of the war, the paper eagerly sought out the services of experts and sent its correspondents to the furthest battle zones.

Robert Neville went to China to write a series that denounced Chiang Kai-shek for attacking the Chinese Red Army instead of the Japanese and for leading a government dominated by "graft, profiteering, corruption, speculation, hoarding, waste, [and] provincial jealousies." American and Soviet aid to his government was completely wasted. The Chinese Communist army had been "abolished," yet it swore allegiance to the government. Chiang refused to answer questions, but Communist Chou En-lai was accessible, reasonable, and wanted a compromise. Chiang's press censorship was "tighter than Hitler's," especially if the stories were about corruption. Neville spoke with Edgar Snow, who had already achieved fame for interviewing Mao. Snow warned that Chiang's policy would lead to Japanese victory. Neville thought the Red Army's approach of using guerrilla warfare was superior to Chiang's insistence on regular army confrontations with the Japanese.

Ironically, in view of what was to appear in *PM*'s pages two years later, Neville corrected the conception of the Soong sisters popular in the United States; Madame Chiang was committed to luxury and vanity, while Madame Sun was dedicated to the Chinese people.[129]

Months later, Ernest Hemingway went to China to report for *PM*. He wrote that the Soviet Union was still China's leading supplier despite its nonaggression pact with Japan. He was amazed to find Soviet officers continuing to advise Chiang despite the bitter feelings between the government and the Chinese Communists.[130]

Sometimes it appeared that Ralph Ingersoll did not read his own newspaper. As he tried to convince Americans to back war and supply the Allies, he created this "factoid": "The Chinese have the best army in their history in the field— 2,000,000 well-trained, well-uniformed veteran troops who have fought the

Japanese to a standstill. . . . Chiang Kai-shek, who runs China, is scrupulously honest." If we gave them arms and planes, the Chinese would defeat Japan.

PM's amnesia about China was at its worst when Madame Chiang visited Washington and New York in the winter and spring of 1943. Evelyn Seeley reported how her speech "Moved Capitol." The paper was delighted her trip to New York was "not stopped by her cold." As she posed to be photographed by Irving Haberman, Max Lerner paid her "homage." [131] Only sardonic Cecelia Ager failed to parrot the official Roosevelt administration position. She had two interviews with China's first lady. Her repetition of "Madame" to identify her subject and emphasis on "Madame's make-up" and clothing revealed a simmering contempt to those who read carefully. Ager's daughter declared, "Cecelia hated Mrs. Chiang." [132]

PM landed a journalistic coup and erased the bad memory of its Chiang Kai-shek fan club when it printed an exclusive series by Agnes Smedley, who had traveled the Long March with Mao and his army in the 1930s. She ushered in an entirely different fan club. "China's military danger" was due to "the reactionary and corrupt practices of the Koumintang regime." She reported on the practices of the Communists in Yenan, describing land reform, sexual liberation, education, health care, and grass-roots democratic councils. Later she thought that General Joseph Stillwell's removal from China was aimed at making him a scapegoat for the corruption of the Chiang regime and warned that Chiang's reshuffling of his cabinet was a public relations gesture that changed nothing. She got a chance to tweak the nose of Ingersoll's old boss, Henry Luce. He wanted *Life* to use her photographs but cut out her captions, which attacked the Chiang government and extolled Mao's forces. Instead, she turned to *PM*, which was delighted to print both pictures and prose under the headline, "The Regime which *Time*, *Life*, and *Fortune* Have Chosen to Champion Is Crumbling." The newspaper neglected to mention that it had championed the same regime for a while. The following summer the two Maxes—Lerner and Werner—both denounced Chiang for attacking the Chinese Communists and pleaded for unity of the anti-Japanese forces. Despite their ties to Roosevelt administration figures, there is no evidence anyone on *PM* was aware of how fully General Stillwell agreed with their assessment of Chiang's regime. [133]

The fall of France was the trauma *PM* was born with. To explain the collapse, Leon Flechtwanger presented a five-part series, probing a life-style of worshiping comfort which he said led to corruption. He found massive bureaucratic incompetence even in the military; Nazi spies were everywhere. A pervasive xenophobia made the French vulnerable to fascism. The government's censorship was detested. So much resentment existed against the Third Republic that defeatism was rampant. It was no wonder the Wehrmacht had walked through France unmolested. [134]

Ingersoll and his colleagues were itching to fight a year before the United States went to war. Their impatience was not helped by the slow process of mobilization. The paper welcomed the operation in North Africa, but Crawford thought it would have happened sooner if FDR had had more friends in Congress. The ensuing victory brought with it political problems. The staff was furious that a Vichy army man was put in charge of administering the territory; the paper repeatedly called for a government loyal to the French underground and Charles de Gaulle. After D-Day, *PM* pressed for the same sort of government in France and Italy. This led to one of the best pictures in the wonderful photographic output of *PM*: John DeBiase snapped the tall, elegant de Gaulle beside New York's short, squat Mayor La Guardia as they prepared to march in a Fifth Avenue parade honoring France's liberation.[135]

PM VERSUS THE STATE DEPARTMENT

The quarrels between *PM* and government officials responsible for installing Vichy men in North Africa or delaying recognition of de Gaulle were not isolated incidents but illustrations of a fundamental difference about the meaning of the war between the paper and the men running the State Department.[136] That difference was ideological, emotional, and historical, and its traumatic quality was summed up by the word *Spain*. Kenneth Stewart described the impact of the Spanish civil war on one future *PM* writer:

> Robert Neville, bridge columnist of the *Herald Tribune* . . . who had been caught in Granada on vacation when the Fascists invaded from across the Mediterranean, had brought back stories that rang with accusation. Neville, who would later become foreign editor of *Time* and then of *PM*, was never again able to accept the bridge-table approach to life.[137]

For many liberals and radicals the great tragedy of the 1930s was the overthrow of the Spanish Republic by Spanish general Francisco Franco and his fascist political organization, the Falange. Armed and advised by Hitler and Mussolini, Franco was further aided by the League of Nations' "neutrality" and similar U.S. legislation that prevented British, French, or American aid from going to the republic, which received support only from the Soviet Union. American (and French) policy was to follow the lead of Great Britain, hostile to the Spanish experiment. The popular front government in Spain—an alliance of many democratic, agrarian, and workers' parties—had been seen as the antifascist and democratic hope of Europe. Its defeat embittered many toward those who were indifferent to its collapse. *PM* was not alone in seeing a repository for that indifference in the State Department, which had zealously carried out the neutrality policy in the face of the first real use of the Blitzkrieg by Franco and his fascist allies.

When World War II began, many of the staff thought a successful antifascist war would mean the elimination of the Franco regime. John P. Lewis and the paper's mapmakers suggested that Spain would be a fine place from which to launch a second front. Victor Bernstein was sure that "Franco knows, of course, that his life span is measured by Hitler's . . . his only hope for salvation is in a fascist victory." To be sure that Americans everywhere, but particularly in

Washington, understood, the paper ran continuing exposés throughout the war, denouncing Spanish diplomacy in Latin America, which was seen as attempting to retake the old Spanish Empire in a fascist embrace. The continuing commercial and military ties between Franco's Spain and Italy and Germany were loudly condemned. Such activities included the sale of materials imported from the United States to Germany, there to be used in munitions, uniforms, or food, and (most damning of all) the engagement of the Spanish Blue Legion to fight with the Nazis against the Red Army and to fight with Italian fascists against American troops. Spanish shipping and educational representatives to the United States were found to be disseminating Falange (fascist) propaganda. The efforts of Washington State Representative Coffee, Brooklyn Representative Celler, and Interior Secretary Ickes to create a U.S. anti-Franco policy were publicized and applauded.[138]

Yet *PM* never probed the origin of American "neutrality" toward Spain. To have done so would have forced a painful discovery. U.S. policy went beyond its neutrality laws. Because the Spanish conflict was a civil war, and because one of the combatants was an internationally recognized (and democratically chosen) government, existing neutrality legislation did not rule out U.S. aid to the republic during the war. Special legal action was needed to prevent that, and it was President Roosevelt himself who in 1936 had called on the Congress to broaden neutrality legislation to give him the power, *if he so desired*, to extend the ban of arms to a nation involved in civil war. When Congress gave him the authority he wanted, FDR imposed the ban and continued it through the dying days of the Spanish Republic, all the while expressing private distaste for Franco and his Nazi and Italian suppliers. When Ickes confronted him, the president cited the power of the Catholic church, which supported Franco's putsch (the early days of the republic had included both rhetorical and confiscatory attacks on the church's almost feudal power), to influence American Democratic voters against him. Toward the end of the Spanish war, when even steadfast isolationist Gerald Nye readied repeal of the Spanish arms embargo, Roosevelt interceded with the congressional leadership to prevent it. After the republic died, one important liberal "adviser" was unforgiving. Kenneth Davis describes the scene:

> [Eleanor Roosevelt's] cold anger with [Franklin] at this time became evident to Leon Henderson when, one evening after Barcelona fell, he came at her invitation to dine at the White House. Her husband occupied his usual place at the head of the table. She, however, spoke as if he were not there as, turning to her guest, she said, "You and I, Mr. Henderson, will someday learn a lesson from this tragic error over Spain. We were morally right, but too weak. We should have pressed *him* harder." She nodded toward her husband, who made no response. His silence seemed to Henderson an admission that this verbal chastisement was deserved.[139]

After the second front was established, keeping Spain "neutral" no longer had military significance, so *PM* pressed harder for an anti-Franco policy. It avidly followed the revolt that broke out on the Spanish-French border, expecting the liberation of Spain, and watched sadly as the revolt fizzled out, the Loyalist forces beaten by disease, torture, and lack of supplies.[140]

But the State Department was deaf to *PM*'s appeals. Again and again Bernstein, Uhl, Stone, Lerner, Lewis, and Wechsler denounced the State Department policy of granting "neutral" Spain trading ties, ignoring the Spanish republican government-in-exile (even denying visas to ministers of their government), and retaining Ambassador Hayes, who made no secret of his friendship for the Franco regime. More than one headline demanded his recall.[141]

After the war Uhl watched in complete exasperation as the United States referred Spanish policy to the United Nations; the UN studied the problem, recommended breaking diplomatic relations, and did nothing as the Soviet Union vetoed the plan for having no substance. British and American foreign policy spokesmen made plain their desire to keep any UN action punchless. They would rather keep their own tamed fascist in power than risk empowering the left.[142]

Early in its history, *PM* probed the reasons for State Department indifference and worse—aid to fascism in Spain. Tabitha Petran and William Walton wrote an exclusive series in early 1941 that found State Department officials were secretly funneling aid to the Franco government through Argentina. The discovery led to an analysis of the State Department as dominated by social-register types whose guiding principle was the preservation of the old order. Wages were low; to work for the State Department required membership in the leisure class. They concluded:

> There are signs of decay in the brownstone monstrosity on Pennsylvania Avenue where the foreign affairs of the USA are directed. In exploring the minds of men who sit behind executive desks you frequently run into words that reveal a tight-minded refusal to recognize the world of today, a world of swift change and tremendously powerful forces. Too many of them cling to a 19th Century interpretation of events by solely political standards, ignoring economics and other social forces.

While the Roosevelt administration had brought new ideas and people to the rest of the national government, "only the State Department remains a quiet backwater of another era. When the house cleaning comes, dust and reactionaries will fly. . . . Too many rooms in the State Department are fragrant with the ripe odor of reaction and decay."

PM would not wait for the "house cleaning"; its reporters kept trying to start it. Writers steadfastly separated State Department functionaries from the president they served. Petran and Engel were furious with plans to recognize Japan's sovereignty in Asia. It was a "Far East Munich." Crawford denounced a former ambassador to Belgium who had seen the "good" side of Hitler. The Office of War Information refused to make antifascism part of its broadside against the Axis powers, talking only of military aggression. Lerner fulminated about an "abdication." When President Roosevelt attacked fascism, Lerner cheered but longed to see this view reflected in concrete policy actions in Europe. He was impatient with the "19th Century" mind of Secretary of State Hull, whom he felt had no understanding of what fascism was. Uhl tried to enlighten Hull and his colleagues. As Victor Emmanuel attempted to reclaim the throne in Italy and other potential kings made their claims in Greece and Yugoslavia, Uhl hoped that State Department officials knew "that the friendship and trust of the workers and peasants of Europe are going to be a lot more valuable on our side than a tin-pot collection of fascist-tainted ex-kings, petty dictators, and fascist-minded politicians." He quickly decided they did not know at all. Bernstein was outraged that State Department policy was fighting against resistance leaders in France, Greece, and Yugoslavia: "They represent the democratic elements in each land. . . . They have established themselves as their country's most effective wartime leaders." Stone contributed an "imaginary" letter from a German general saying that the Nazis' best weapons for the future were Franco and American fear of communism in China.[143]

When an ill Cordell Hull was replaced by banking scion Edward Stettinius, the president dutifully announced the new secretary's slate of appointments to State in December 1944. *PM* was aghast. Probably the most awful name of the lot was Will Clayton, who had been associated with Jesse Jones in a 1943 faction fight that cost Henry Wallace renomination to the vice presidency. *PM*'s crusade claimed Clayton had cartel ties to German firms; Joseph Grew was an apologist for the Japanese emperor; James Dunn had befriended Franco; Nelson Rockefeller was attacked for his family ties to Standard Oil, cartel partner of IG Farben. It was a nightmare. *PM* tried to rally liberal senators to fight the appointments; when some did, Roosevelt himself interceded on behalf of his new State appointees. Wechsler and Stone led the fight against them, which featured Stone's exposing monopolistic practices by Clayton to control the price of cotton. Stone maintained that the new group

> leaves the department to a greater degree than ever the one branch of our government which is the private preserve of the upper crust of society, the relatives, retainers, and spokesmen of America's wealthiest and most powerful families. We decline to fool ourselves into believing that a Department so constituted can provide us with a democratic foreign policy.

When it was over, Stone said he was glad *PM* had fought the battle, and Wechsler thought it hopeful that only President Roosevelt's intercession forced the names through. No *PM* writer aimed broadsides at the president for making the appointments. But when FDR vetoed an old New Dealer for a State Department post, claiming there were already enough New Dealers at State, Wechsler could not help but see the irony.[144]

If *PM* never condemned President Roosevelt himself, the attacks on government policy in North Africa nonetheless infuriated him. In November 1942, he tried to win *PM* over by directing Press Secretary Early to send the paper advance information about French African appointments. By the following spring he scribbled an angry note to Early: "I want all the releases in *PM* in the last three weeks about DeGaulle, Giraud, Peyrouten, etc. I want to see Max Lerner or whoever the editor of *PM* is." Early wrote back that John P. Lewis was the editor; FDR never arranged a meeting.[145]

No matter what State Department officials or their boss thought of them, underground resistance movements in Europe were honored repeatedly in *PM*. The most successful underground was in Yugoslavia. Tito was interviewed and extolled several times. The presence of ex-*PM* and United Press staffers in uniform in neighboring Italy provided photographs and interviews with partisans. Tito's united front forces were compared favorably to the British-backed King Michael, who had appeased the Nazis; Lerner demanded the Allies (and the recalcitrant State Department) recognize Tito as the leader of Yugoslavia.[146]

THE RUSSIAN WAR

Although *PM* defined Japan as fascist and dutifully reported on the Pacific war, the European war and the defeat of German Nazism was its primary interest. Germany's system was the most tyrannical, its enforcement of racism the most monstrous, and its power the most terrifying. To defeat this menace, the combined effort of all belligerents was necessary. No belligerent was so enthusiastically watched or its victories so celebrated as the Soviet Union, which, the paper repeatedly informed its readers, was doing the lion's share of fighting the Reich.

During the year between the start of publication of *PM* and the Nazi invasion of the Soviet Union, the paper watched every development in the relationship between the Nonaggression Pact signers, eager to discover hints of discord. Moves by the Soviet Union to its west were viewed as defensive acts against future Nazi attack. Nonetheless, as we have seen, when the actual break came the paper had spent a week denying it would occur.

The early German military victories were viewed as not decisive. The General pointed out repeatedly that to win the Nazis had to destroy the Red Army, which the Wehrmacht had been unable to do. Taking territory in the vastness of the USSR would not be enough, and the scorched-earth policy of the Soviets meant the Germans would be sitting on barren land, which would not sustain them. The huge casualties the Germans absorbed in their advance meant these were no victories. As Leonard Engel, he rejoiced that the Nazis had finally met their match in an "up-to-date Red Army." *PM* placed a box on the front page reading, "In Memorium [*sic*]: The Legend of Nazi Invulnerability," long before the Red Army stopped the German advance.[147]

Ralph Ingersoll flew off to Moscow and cabled back his enthusiasm. "I am enormously encouraged, not to say elated, by the obvious evidence of both the heart and ability in the war effort here. It is literally unthinkable that the Germans can conquer this vast, immeasurably powerful, united and heads-up country." He sent a similar cable to President Roosevelt via Marshall Field. FDR wrote Field, "Ever so much thanks for sending me that cable from Ralph. I do hope he's right. I think the next 30 days will tell." Ingersoll had wanted to see the president before his flight to Moscow, to discover, in Steve Early's words, "if he can do anything for you." Roosevelt declined this offer.[148]

Interviewed by Winston Burdett on CBS Radio, Ingersoll found the Russian defense "astonishing." He thought the antiaircraft defense of Moscow the "best in the world." Stalin was a "straight" talker who avoided rhetoric; he was "keen and realistic" and in good health. *PM*'s itinerant editor was seconded by Erskine Caldwell, who, luckily for the newspaper (which turned him into its first Russian correspondent), happened to be in Moscow in June 1941. After Caldwell interviewed soldiers in the Red Army, he found their morale so high that "there can never be any doubt of the war's final outcome." Alexander Uhl, remembering the siege of Madrid, was encouraged because "Madrid had one group of people that Moscow won't have, Fifth Columnists."

Even when the paper announced the dreaded news that the Nazis were just fifty miles west of Moscow, the General reminded his readers that the Red Army was intact, the retreat had been "astonishingly" well organized, and the main fighting had not even begun.[149]

Ingersoll returned to America to report on the front page "Russia Can Hold Out." Inside, expanded over seven pages in double-size print, was his breathless prose:

> The News that I bring back—and I hope it's no longer news to you—is that the Russians will stick. I have seen the men and women on whose fighting qualities, on whose staying power so much depends. They will not let you down. They are making sacrifices that you or I wouldn't even dream of a few years ago. I found them wholly prepared to see the war through, no matter how long it takes, no matter how much it costs.

The power lines were intact, the railroads were running, machinery had been moved east ahead of the Nazi advance, morale was high, the antiaircraft batteries succeeded in protecting Moscow from Nazi raids, and the capital was over-crowded with "cheerful" people. He found the scorched-earth policy working well, though the Nazis did get Ukrainian wheat. The war propaganda was not always true as it sometimes "substituted the wish for the deed," but the battle reports were reasonably accurate. He found the people committed to building their system and saw no wish to impose it on the United States. The "classless" society was not egalitarian: the Communists were privileged. The people knew the revolution's accomplishments in literacy, health, and industrialization were on the line, and they would defend them. He admitted the purges killed innocents but also the "Pétains and lords."

Ingersoll loved his hour with Joseph Stalin, but his report is all atmospherics. Ingersoll thought they understood each other (only an ego like Ingersoll's could have produced such a judgment). He liked Stalin's straightforward answers, which he gave "rapidly with intelligent perception." He reported that the Soviets thought American and Soviet industrialization would be the key to beating Hitler, and they wanted to shatter German morale with a military victory. Already they were calling on Great Britain to launch a diversionary front in Italy. They believed that "Japan is another Italy with a dagger up its sleeve waiting to stab

Russia or America." Ingersoll was surprised by the extent of the "caste" system of Communist party bureaucrats in all parts of Soviet life, but he admired the resources of the Red Army, which "has its own schools and universities, its hotels and apartment houses, and even its own theater."[150]

The first winter counteroffensive was celebrated. "The Russians have already won the greatest single battle in the history of war," Ingersoll exulted. He thought they were winning on "morale and morale alone. . . . It was if in this country, hostile armies had crossed the Alleghenies, taken Pittsburgh and Cleveland, and were coming up to the suburbs of Chicago." Though poor, they had no illiterate among them, but he thought the Russians too doctrinaire to succeed with their next generation. One bizarre hint that Ingersoll himself often "substituted the wish for the deed" was in comparing Russian greatness to their neighbors to the southeast. They were just like the Chinese.

PM reluctantly gave the edge back to the Nazis in the summer of 1942, seeing Russian victories in May even as the Wehrmacht seized back most of the territory it had ceded during the winter. With the announcement of "Kharkov Battle on Verdun Scale," the paper conceded that the Nazis were winning once more, though the General reminded his readers again that the Red Army had not been broken. He drew a circle on Dietje's map of a region that included Stalingrad and wrote that this was "where the main battle of northern Caucasia probably will be fought." Several days later the paper quoted Stalin's pronouncement that the Nazis would proceed "not one step further," but Frederick Kuh pointed out that in losing 600,000 square miles, the Soviets had lost the equivalent of Germany, France, and Great Britain combined. *PM*'s mapmakers aimed the blow closer to home, showing the Nazi gain in the USSR as equivalent to the taking of all of New England, the mid-Atlantic states, half of Ohio, and half of Arkansas.

The day-by-day resistance of the Red Army at Stalingrad was watched anxiously in the *PM* offices. By late September, the General thought the city would fall, but even then made much of the "monster" price the Wehrmacht was paying. By early October the paper celebrated the Nazis' admission that they could not take the city.[151]

The history of the Russian war has again proven *PM* accurate. Before the Red Army held its own, no European force had successfully withstood the savage assault of the Wehrmacht; when the Soviets began ceding territory, many expected the kind of collapse that had occurred in country after country during 1939 and 1940. Young Engel was one of the few who noticed the difference between the Russian retreat and the previous European debacles. Only the Red Army had inflicted enormous casualties on the German army, though absorbing huge losses itself. Engel's prescience about Stalingrad came out of an excellent strategic analysis of the Red Army's continued cohesion.

Later many would charge *PM* with communism and point to its war coverage as justification. In its defense, *PM* might have claimed that the prophets of doom on the Eastern Front were blinded by their anticommunism. Still, Ingersoll's "personal" reflections on Stalin read like foolish romance today. But Ingersoll and his whole staff were charmed by Roosevelt; it was easy to be swayed by the staged attractiveness of leaders of the antifascist struggle. To place the romance of Stalin in perspective, one must remember that so valiant an anticommunist as Henry Luce was celebrating the Russian leader in his publications, and that the Roosevelt administration itself had urged Warner Brothers to make the cartoonishly apologistic *Mission to Moscow*. As we have seen, among the other valiant antifascists that *PM* held up as heroes were Chiang Kai-shek and Douglas MacArthur.

The following year news coverage was dominated by the great Russian drive. The General repeatedly stressed the quick advance through thousands of miles of territory. As winter turned to spring and then summer, the whole paper rejoiced when, instead of retreating before a new Nazi attack, the Russians held on to everything they had recaptured and began a summer offensive, taking back more territory. The great battle of Stalingrad had turned the tide of the war. Lerner profusely thanked the Red Army for saving the world from "doom." He praised it for imbibing the spirit of "social engineering." On 22 June 1944, the third anniversary of the Nazi invasion, *PM* reprinted the reactions of dozens of world leaders at the time; most had seen the Nazis winning with the same ease they had conquered Western Europe. Only George Bernard Shaw had sounded a different note. He had said, "Germany hasn't got a dog's chance." [152]

FORCING A SECOND FRONT

If he were not in the army, Ingersoll might have asked, "What are we going to do about it?" For *PM* writers there were three answers: massive American aid, the creation of political friendship, and above all, establishment of a second battlefront on the European continent. The three themes were thoroughly sounded from the moment Germany invaded.

As early as November 1941, the General predicted the Nazis could only be defeated with the establishment of a second front. Ingersoll thought an invasion should come as early as the spring of 1942. That spring, the Sunday Magazine provided a map which showed four possible invasion sites: from the Middle East, Norway, Italy, and France. Former ambassador Joseph Davies was quoted backing a second front immediately. When it did not happen in the spring, the paper confidently predicted one in the fall, once more showing several projected routes on the centerfold maps. Reporting from overseas, Frederick Kuh noticed British politicians shying away from a second front, while Ben Robertson, Jr., insisted it was necessary for Soviet morale. Later that month, both the General and Robertson were actively campaigning for the front as the only way to save the Red Army. As his parting thought before joining the army, Ingersoll declared that the U.S. military was "moving heaven and earth ever since Pearl Harbor to make the offensive in Europe a reality." His staff was not so sure. Ben Robertson found people too complacent in the United States during the summer of 1942; what about helping the Soviets fight Hitler? Kuh echoed his sense of urgency. Robertson quoted Wendell Willkie demanding the new front while he visited Moscow. The following day Robertson reported that it was humiliating to be an American in Moscow. All "feel that they have failed, and that America has failed." When Willkie returned to the United States, his radio speech calling for a second front was printed in full in *PM*.

The new spring brought new expectations and renewed demands. Max Werner coined a slogan: "Attack Can Win in '43." Commenting on the replacement of the famous Maksim Litvinov with the then unknown Andrei Gromyko as Soviet ambassador to the United States, Victor Bernstein thought an impatient Stalin was rebuking American inaction, while I. F. Stone commented, "It's possible that the Russians have begun to think we envisage the Anglo-Soviet-American coalition as one in which they do the bulk of the fighting, while we issue press releases calling for unconditional surrender." To spur the second front Stone warned of a separate Soviet-Nazi peace that would allow 250 Wehrmacht divisions to face west and south. Stone's sources told him that FDR wanted a second front immediately but that Churchill and the American generals wanted a delay until the spring of 1944, which they would probably get. *PM* kept pushing nonetheless. The General thought the Nazis had deliberately bogged us down in Italy to prevent a Channel crossing.[153]

Stone accused Standard Oil of refusing to share its chemical war secrets (the ones it got from IG Farben) with the Soviet Union. Two days later he credited "*PM*'s" exposé for breaking the logjam of aid to Russia; an oil refinery would be shipped there. He was probably right. The Roosevelt papers contain a churlish note from Harold Ickes to War Production Board chief Donald Nelson, saying that he "did not need a copy of *PM* to tell him that the Russians wanted an aviation plant." Ickes reminded Nelson that he had urged the plant back in April. The secretary was furious that Stone was taking credit, but it was not until Stone's exposé appeared that the factory was sent overseas. Stone warned his readers they must push the State Department to make sure Russia got aid, since the department was "much more interested in keeping the good graces of such mighty potentates as Franco and Pétain than in maintaining friendly relations with Stalin. . . . The War Power Board, the third source of delay, is more securely in the hands of reactionary business than ever before." He accused the "rubber czar" of delaying a rubber factory for the USSR; as in oil, his exposé resulted in the cutting of red tape.[154]

Such forthright calls to aid our Soviet ally made *PM* a likely target for red-baiters. The paper anticipated this reaction. It asked on the front page, "Does Aiding Russia Make America Red?" Ingersoll answered inside, condemning timid liberals who would soft-pedal aid to the USSR for fear of being called communists. He thought the Soviet Union was here to stay, and there was much good there: the Russians believed in universal education, racial harmony, the four freedoms, and the Atlantic Charter. Most important, they were beating Hitler, freedom's number one enemy, and that was what mattered.[155] He was echoing the sentiments of many Roosevelt administration liberals, most notably Vice President Wallace.

The future of American-Soviet relations was a frequent concern for *PM* editorialists during and after the war. The paper surveyed leading liberal politicians and journalists about the topic. Willkie and John Gunther advocated peaceful and friendly relations. When Hitler warned the West about communism, Lerner said the attempt to divide us would not work. The U.S. and the USSR, he said, were "the two creative and powerful nations of the future." There was fear we would pull apart, but the United Nations needed us together. He was annoyed with Churchill's "riddle wrapped in a mystery inside an enigma" remark, declaring, "The Russians are no more a mystery than we are. Actually it's anyone's guess whether we're going to put the fascist collaborationists into power permanently in North Africa, France, Spain, and Italy, or whether that is just a temporary policy which will yield to the setting up of democracies." Who could know whether the United States would be imperialist, isolationist, or interventionist? Stalin was no international revolutionary but had consistently struggled for Soviet security in the world. Only when the West failed to join Soviet attempts to contain Hitler had he authorized attacks on Finland and Poland to get that security. There were two fears about Russia: that they would sign a separate peace with Germany after driving the Nazis out of their territory and that they would keep fighting and "Bolshevize" all Europe. The fears were mutually contradictory and endangered the world's future.[156]

Lerner was revolted by two American ambassadors. Carlton Hayes in Spain praised Franco, while William Standley attacked the USSR for seeking too much Lend-Lease aid. "The fact is that Russia has carried the major part of the war against the Nazis; and that as Lend-Lease Administrator Stettinius several times publicly has stated, the overwhelming proportion of Russian war material has come from Russian and not American factories. . . . Ambassador Standley must be recalled." Time and again Lerner and Alexander Uhl cautioned that, though dealing with the Soviet Union would be difficult, it was the only choice Americans had to achieve peace in the postwar world.[157]

Lerner exchanged charges with Daniel Bell of the *New Leader* and Max Eastman, both of whom hated book and movie versions of *Mission to Moscow*, the memoirs of former ambassador Joseph Davies. Bell and Eastman attacked *Mission to Moscow* as being cynically naive about Stalinism and linked Davies to Willkie and Vice President Wallace, fools for talking about peaceful harmony with Russia. Lerner replied it was foolish to think of anything but peace with Russia. What other sane choice did the world have? One can be sympathetic with Lerner's objective while still maintaining that the defense of the Moscow purge trials in *Mission to Moscow* is ingenuous to the point of incredulity. It is embarrassing to read critic John T. McManus's gushing over the movie, calling it "the most significant film to come out of Hollywood in 25 years" and endorsing its preposterous purge trial conclusions.[158]

ELIMINATING FASCISM

For as long as the war waged and well past its conclusion, eliminating Nazi Germany was the most pressing foreign policy goal at *PM*. As the Soviet Union was the most important partner contributing to that goal, it was treated with friendly understanding by the staff.

In early 1943, *PM* asked leading intellectuals what should be done about Germany after the war. Dorothy Thompson wanted Germany broken up into several states and suggested half seriously that Allied forces stay in Germany long enough to marry the Germans and breed belligerence out of them. Albert Einstein proposed the destruction of German industrial power. Sidney Hillman called for permanent German disarmament, a view echoed by John P. Lewis days later. Thomas Mann foresaw an extended period of German atonement. Jan Masaryk of Czechoslovakia, interviewed by *PM* writer Karl Pretshold, demanded the destruction of Germany's war-making capacity. When the Soviets suggested postwar conscripted German labor battalions, Lerner argued that either German military production should be totally scrapped or the Russian plan should be enforced. Ralph Parker reported the Soviet insistence on the total destruction of Germany, not for revenge, but to prevent a recurrence of German war-making capacity forever. Max Werner echoed this idea.

PM approved of the harsh measures taken in Soviet-held German areas; Lerner accused non-Nazi Germans of having complied with Nazi brutality. Lerner and Victor Bernstein exposed Nazis who were being used in administrative posts by American military occupiers. The American military and the State Department came in for harsh criticism for failing to institute antifascist education among German prisoners during the war and in American-controlled Germany after it. Lerner and other writers worried about the future of Germany when officials in State associated with pro-Vichy politics were placed in charge of policy there. Stone charged that we were sabotaging demilitarization to use Germany in future conflicts with the Soviet Union.

Stone exposed a conference of international businessmen who had been cartel partners with Krupp and IG Farben. He accused them of wanting to rebuild the German industrial machine and warned, "Not to punish German industrial and financial collaborators with the Nazis is to encourage their renewed participation in similar adventures after this war, and to leave secret nuclei of opposition and conspiracy both in Germany and abroad." He worried that the American businessmen sent to the conference could not be trusted; they had profited too handsomely from past associations with German capital. He accused State Department officials of protecting IG Farben's American cartel partners.

PM displayed pictures of Nazi horrors under the heading "This Is the Enemy: The Answer to Advocates for a Soft Peace." Richard Yaffe listed "Nazi rats" still to be caught. When the German generals who handled the surrender were praised for their correct bearing, Lerner reminded his readers that just because they handled the surrender, they were no "gentlemen." The novelist Howard Fast wrote a guest editorial attacking the dignified Junker image being promoted by some of the press coverage. "There was no honor in the fascist fight, for they waged not war, but murder." [159]

The paper wanted stiff war penalties against Japan and Germany. Its writers thought that unconditional surrender in Japan meant no emperor, whom Lerner attacked as the symbol of the military-industrial-feudal elite that had to be totally eradicated. The paper waged a long campaign to eliminate the emperor and believed that the United States had not achieved a political victory when it agreed to keep him on. As early as January 1944, *PM* identified a State Department faction that was "soft" on the emperor. Stone reacted to those who wanted to retreat from unconditional surrender as the terms for Japan in order to guard against a Soviet presence in the Pacific: "Is it so hard to remember that it was the Soviet Union which helped us to defeat Germany, that it was Japan that attacked us at Pearl Harbor?" The paper declared on page 1 "MacArthur Off to a Bad Start" in allowing the old industrialists and political cliques to retain power under American occupation.[160]

PM advocated war-crimes trials for Germany from late in 1942 and campaigned tirelessly for them until it was certain they would occur. The paper fought to make sure the German industrial giants would be indicted as well. Victor Bernstein returned to Nuremburg to attend the first trials. Bernstein had sent dispatches from Germany the previous year; he had also had his antifascist consciousness formed when he reported for the Jewish Telegraph Agency from Berlin during Kristallnacht. A fervent hatred for racialism had been acquired; it came through in his stories of white violence against American blacks and of Germany's atrocities.[161]

Though the paper reveled in the guilty verdicts for the leading Nazis and displayed photographs of their bodies after their executions, Bernstein was disappointed in the acquittals of collaborators like Schacht and Von Papen. More, he mourned a verdict which did not contain a denunciation of the fascist system.[162]

Eliminating fascism from the world was why *PM* had fought. If the war tribunal did not find fascism itself guilty, it validated its continuation in such places as Spain and Argentina. The world that emerged from World War II would not usher in the "Century of the Common Man." With the war won, antifascism ceased to be a crucible for American policy makers, who had a new enemy to confront. Instead, with a craven State Department, an unrepentant "Press Axis," Standard Oil, and Du Pont as powerful as ever, Franco undisturbed in his power, and with even Krupp out of jail, an uncertain and dangerous future continued to confront humanity.

4 | LABOR'S CHAMPION

> *PM* went into business on the theory that an aggressive, pro-labor paper could be fair and honest; that there was no need for a paper which lied to save labor's face, but for one which tells the truth—because the truth, in an awful lot of cases is on labor's side. And this truth is the truth not generally aired.
>
> —James Wechsler in *PM* [1]

*P**M*'s labor writers came to their subject after witnessing the depression-era tumult that had first driven most established unions to the brink of destruction and then, after the election of Franklin D. Roosevelt, had rescued the old organizations and recruited several million workers into new mass industrial unions. The paper was not on the scene to report the general strikes in San Francisco or Minneapolis, or to trumpet the dramatic news of sit-downs in the rubber and auto industries, but its writers had witnessed or heard about these events. Labor's right to organize was the credo to which *PM*'s young writers swore allegiance.

For many staff members the reversal of traditional governmental hostility to labor was the key to their own identification with the Roosevelt administration. Before FDR, strike activity had been regularly suppressed by a two-pronged governmental attack. Employers sought court injunctions against strikes as "restraints of interstate commerce"; federal courts invariably complied. If a strike continued, state and federal troops would be called out to disperse pickets, shoot and arrest determined strikers, and escort strikebreakers to work. Two Progressive Republicans—Nebraska senator George Norris and New York congressman Fiorello La Guardia—countered the court gambit even before Roosevelt was elected by sponsoring the Anti-Injunction Act of 1932; the new president moved to legalize collective bargaining in the omnibus National Recovery Act. When the Supreme Court, dominated by conservative Republican appointees, ruled the NRA unconstitutional, the president finally embraced the Wagner Act, which more than reaffirmed the NRA's guarantee of collective bargaining. It established the National Labor Relations Board to administer union elections and to protect against "unfair labor practices." These included company sponsored antiunion propaganda, antiunion firings, and of course antiunion thuggery, which had been established practice in most leading industrial firms.

PM's treatment of these advances was embodied in a piece by Weldon James and Hannah Baker welcoming the 150th anniversary of the Bill of Rights by saluting the extension of civil liberties to workers (and to blacks, too, though there was much less cause for celebration) in the 1930s. [2] "Industrial democracy" meant the right to organize, the right to redress inequitable economic distribution, and protection by the federal government for labor's just demands and needs. *PM* staffers saw these "rights" as being as fundamental to American democracy as any of the first ten amendments to the Constitution.

CIO president John L. Lewis actively campaigned for Roosevelt's reelection in 1936; after that victory young organizers in the auto, steel, and electric industries soon celebrated their first union contracts with corporate giants General Motors, U.S. Steel, and General Electric. Roosevelt certainly did not approve sitdown strikes anymore than he had endorsed the radical-led general strikes of 1934. His refusal to call in federal troops to crush labor's militancy, however, was a bold departure from the activities of all of his predecessors. Cleveland and Wilson (the other two post–Civil War Democratic presidents) had been as brutal as their Republican contemporaries in suppressing strikes.[3]

The Newspaper Guild, moved by the impressive gains in industrial unionism, switched from AFL to CIO in 1937. Guild veterans McManus, Randau, Crawford, Stewart, and Seeley were joined at *PM* by newer activists, like Kimball, Wechsler, and Baker. Their union consciousness was boosted by Ingersoll's commitment to labor. At this newspaper one could not only be a member of a union, but one could and should champion unionism.

The *Newspaper* dummy issue of April 1939, printed more than a year before mass circulation, featured the then-current coal strike. An unsigned news account told the story from the vantage point of the United Mine Workers. The union had offered to work under the expiring contract while negotiations continued; the operators, thinking they could break the union by using an American Federation of Labor scab unit, refused. The sympathies of the article were clear, but much more effective was the two page photo spread, with dramatic pictures of impoverished miners and unsafe working conditions. The captions under the photographs are a hymn to the need for labor to unionize:

> If in the United States you are a man like this . . . you make your living mining coal . . . 10 hours a day . . . and live in a town like this . . . after your day's work . . . you see whether you'll work tomorrow . . . and at home . . . you have a child . . . and another child . . . and a family . . . and a radio to listen to . . . and you can make music for yourself . . . or gamble away your substance if you like . . . but three things you never forget . . . your union . . . payday, when your pay may run from \$____ to \$____ [as this was a dummy issue, it was not necessary to provide actual figures], . . . and the man with the gun on his hip.[4]

The treatment presaged *PM*'s sympathetic coverage of the struggles of working men and women in the face of arduous jobs and powerful corporate adversaries.

JOHN L. LEWIS, UNITED MINE WORKERS, AND THE CIO

The politics of the labor movement were nowhere more difficult than in the arenas frequented by the imperious and impressive fallen hero, John L. Lewis.

The working conditions of the miners and the stormy politics of their union's president were a frequent focus of attention.

During the 1930s no union leader had been more identified with trade union organization than the majestic Lewis, who combined impressive physical stature (6 feet, 230 pounds, a granite chin, and fabulously full, pointing eyebrows) with a gift for flamboyant Shakespearean rhetoric. His response to FDR's equal damning of Little Steel and SWOC during the 1937 strike was classic Lewis oratory:

> Labor, like Israel, has many sorrows. Its women weep for their fallen, and they lament for the future of the children of the race. It ill behooves one who has supped at labor's table and who has been sheltered in labor's house to curse with equal fervor and fine impartiality both labor and its adversaries when they become locked in deadly embrace.[5]

Lewis seized on 1933's NRA legislation to reorganize the United Mine Workers. The union, which had withered away to about 100,000 members, responded to its president's energetic and fervent campaign. By 1936, the UMW had almost a half million workers, by far the biggest union in the nation. Lewis, determined to take full advantage of the prolabor political climate and the stirrings in the nation's unorganized industrial centers, had been the driving force in the organization of the AFL's Committee on Industrial Organizations. When the parent federation refused to proceed, Lewis led the CIO to independence. His single-punch knockdown of Carpenters Union president William Hutcheson at the 1935 AFL convention was typically dramatic and self-dramatizing. (Lewis believed in self-promotion. "He who tooteth not his own horn," he once said, "such horn shall not be tooted.")

While a determined union militant, Lewis shared little of the broader social views of the *PM* staff. He ran his union as an iron dictatorship, not hesitating to use the rankest forms of violence to maintain his control. His hatred of the open-shop principles of southern Democrats had made him a lifelong Republican. He endorsed Hoover in 1932; after the NRA and Wagner acts he campaigned for FDR's reelection in 1936. But as *PM* came into the world, he was publicly and bitterly anti-Roosevelt. He felt personally betrayed by the president' Little Steel remarks and by what he considered FDR's two-faced mediation during the General Motors strike. Moreover, he was an isolationist. Lewis held that the European crisis was best handled by American defense of the Western Hemisphere. He viewed Roosevelt's pro-British politics with disdain.[6]

For the prolabor, prowar, pro-Roosevelt *PM*, Lewis's politics were troubling. During the five months between *PM*'s creation and the CIO president's October endorsement of Republican presidential candidate Wendell Willkie, every Lewis move was debated by labor editor Leo Huberman and his ambitious assistant, James Wechsler. Huberman, entranced by Lewis's leadership in founding the CIO, did not foresee the growing split between FDR and Lewis becoming a permanent breach, but Wechsler was far more savvy. He predicted that Lewis would endorse Willkie because the CIO leader was committed to labor's independence but knew the movement was too weak to form a labor party. His meetings with FDR had failed to bridge the gulf between them, and Willkie gave him assurance of respect for labor's rights. He would risk endorsing FDR's rival and take the consequences, as he was ready to resign as CIO president anyway.

Wechsler's accurate reading of labor's attitudes continued after the Willkie endorsement, when he predicted that of the CIO national leadership, only Joseph Curran of the National Maritime Union would back Lewis, while the United Auto Workers and the United Electrical Workers would be united in backing President Roosevelt. (A far more impressive Wechsler prognostication occurred when *PM*'s labor editor gazed into his crystal ball and saw George Meany, then the head of New York state's AFL, becoming the eventual leader of a united AFL-CIO.)

While it was yet to be demonstrated that Lewis was isolated within the CIO, there was no question he was now anathema to *PM*. Amos Landman's account on 29 October saw most CIO unionists shocked by Lewis's support of Willkie and quoted many of their negative reactions, though the Newspaper Guild left endorsed no one for president and "expresses confidence in the leadership of John L. Lewis as head of the CIO." Stronger editorial guns were brandished on 1 November, when page 2 was devoted to the free-verse doggerel of John Beecher, grandson of Harriet Beecher Stowe, which called Lewis a "snake oil salesman" and bitterly described a 1932 Illinois coal strike where Beecher claimed Lewis had sold out to Chicago utilities monopolist Samuel Insull. Beecher professed to be not surprised.

Once FDR was reelected, *PM*'s labor pundits fell to probing the consequences of Lewis's endorsement of the loser. Wechsler had predicted early that Phil Murray would become CIO president, though he thought that Sidney Hillman's own ambition might be a stumbling block. Huberman, attending the CIO convention, still sang the praises of Lewis, seeing him handing over the reins of leadership to Murray peacefully and joining the CIO in fighting to prevent Wagner Act violators from getting defense contracts. Wechsler described the CIO as a nest of factional differences, since the only unity was based on organizing the unorganized. He thought Hillman would choose the CIO's next organizing venue.

Kenneth Crawford took on Lewis on several successive days in early December. He attacked him through the activities of his daughter Cathryn, who had become a vocal member of the antiwar and, in *PM*'s eyes, soft-on-fascism and anti-Semitic, America First movement. He found the anti-Semitism of America First a natural place for Lewis, remembering the CIO leader's famous repetition of "Dubinsky, Zaritsky . . ." when denouncing the trade unionists who returned to the AFL. He closed his attack with an endorsement of Roosevelt's warning about the dangerous consequences of the joining of extreme right and left by referring to the left-wing unions' support of Lewis's isolationist stance in the days of the Nazi-Soviet Nonaggression Pact. The following day Crawford reported UAW president R. J. Thomas's accusation that Lewis tried to have Thomas meet with Chrysler executive Howard Talboot, a Willkie supporter and public appeaser of Nazi activity in Europe. He attacked Lewis for staging the CIO convention as a grand gesture, but noted with satisfaction that the UMW president was out of power in the CIO for good.

The New York CIO, led by its left-wing faction, was so angered by Crawford's series that National Maritime Union president Joseph Curran cabled Ralph Ingersoll in London. *PM*, undoubtedly enjoying the attention, dutifully printed the text of Curran's wire.[7]

Though many factors were involved, the Lewis affair probably cost Huberman his job. It was already abundantly clear that Wechsler was a superior writer and had much more insight into the politics of the labor movement. Huberman, who had worked as labor editor at the *Nation* and as a college lecturer, had no newspaper experience before working for *PM*. Worried, he once furtively approached Bill McCleery to ask, "What's a zinc?" (*zinc* was newspaper lingo for a metal piece used in typesetting). His labor reputation was based on a book exposing antiunion activity, *The Labor Spy Racket*. He was handicapped, as was his boss, by an inability to type, but unlike Ingersoll he had no Zinny Schoales to take his dictation. His writing about Lewis reflects a sentimentality affecting his judgment. Richard Green says Huberman was fired for editorial lapses during the UMW convention. He was so taken by the appearance and speech of radical legend Mother Bloor that he wrote exclusively about her, neglecting to report or analyze the actual events of the assemblage.

Ingersoll's decision to fire Huberman became a minor event. Because *PM* was so publicly committed to unionism, it reported in detail on its own upheaval and the grievance brought before the Newspaper Guild. The case is also documented in a raft of Ingersoll memoranda. *PM*'s editor said he liked Huberman's writing but thought he was a poor editor. The guild announced it would grieve the matter; succeeding details were described in articles throughout January. Ingersoll took three-quarters of a page to describe Huberman's failings as a labor editor and labor writer. The readers had their say on both sides of the issue. Finally the guild and Ingersoll worked out a face-saving exit: Ingersoll reinstated Huberman with pay from the day he was fired—30 December 1940—but he resigned as of 2 May 1941, a week after the agreement was made.

The guild grievance unit defended Huberman vigorously for several reasons. Despite his lack of skills, he was universally liked. The firing, coming as it did after the economy purges of the previous summer, was a symbol of employees' jitters at the tenuousness of their positions. Finally, several staff members suspected that Wechsler was whispering red-menace warnings into Ingersoll's ear, and that *PM*'s founder, eager to put the instability of the previous months behind him, was too easily influenced. Still, there is little denying that Wechsler was the far more gifted analyst and writer. Huberman's reputation as an independent Marxist thinker was secured later, when he founded the *Monthly Review* with Paul M. Sweezy, whose wife, Maxine, left *PM* when Huberman was fired.[8]

Wechsler traveled tirelessly to several strike sites, there beginning a *PM* tradition of dramatic reporting from the field, and also attended AFL, CIO, and constituent union conventions wherever they were held. If the paper anticipated a major strike, Wechsler, and later others (most notably Tom O'Connor) would be on the scene with news and features about unionists' lives. O'Connor, who wrote for all departments, including ghostwriting for health columnist Albert Deutsch during the latter's early days as a journalist, became labor editor when Wechsler replaced Crawford as Washington bureau chief.[9]

Lewis was not to vanish from the scene so easily as Huberman. The first of his threatened strikes against the defense program took place before the attack on Pearl Harbor, but long enough after the Nazi invasion of the Soviet Union to disquiet the trade union movement and *PM*. Lewis called for a strike in late October 1941, damning Hillman for "casual indifference" to the plight of his men. Stone thought the miners had a good case, but an impassioned war speech by President Roosevelt put Lewis on the defensive. Lewis could probably win his case by submitting to arbitration, but this would validate the government's war mediation machinery, which Stone said Lewis was eager to discredit. Dr. Seuss pictured John Lord Lewis obstructing defense coal. When the UMW settled, Landman said it was "just in time" to prevent the miners from having to choose between Lewis and Roosevelt. In SWOC, long tied to the UMW because of the production links between coal and steel, and common employers, U.S. and Bethlehem Steel, Landman said the workers "revere" FDR, whose picture hung in every unionist home and office.

When the National Defense Mobilization Board decided against a closed shop in the Upton mines, the CIO withdrew from the board to back the mine workers. Wechsler wondered if Roosevelt's defense policy would collapse because of union opposition. "Pro–New Deal forces looked to FDR for leadership out of the painful paradox." The same day Harold Lavine explained the importance of the closed shop to protect unions from being destroyed.

Wechsler thought that a "split between the CIO and the New Deal contained the makings of a major national tragedy" and even allowed himself a rebuke of President Roosevelt for failing to involve the CIO to a greater extent in the defense effort. Still, he was confident FDR would find a way out.

But *PM* was taking no chances. It dispatched Amos Landman and photographer Morris Gordon to coal country, where Landman interviewed and Gordon photographed miners who were ready to strike if the UMW called for it. When the strike developed, Wechsler refused to blame Lewis, instead attacking the NDMB for "playing politics" and Bethlehem Steel for deliberate intransigence. From the mines, Landman said the miners were "deaf to threats"; they would stay out whether the army intervened or not. The following day H. R. Lieberman worried that a reactionary Congress would pass an antistrike bill which Roosevelt would use to end the coal strike and then seek to modify. Gordon illustrated the miners' unity with dramatic pictures of closed-down, captive mines.

Roosevelt's press conference attack on Lewis for the strike was reported without comment, but Landman's article detailed the succesful miners' action. Gordon photographed antiunion violence at the Red Lion Mine. Lieberman saw FDR moving cautiously; Landman wrote that the miners were furious at being called "Hitler's agents."

When Lewis decided to seek arbitration and end the strike, Crawford thought a union victory was forthcoming and attacked the other papers for focusing on Lewis's salary rather than on the union's case. Landman interviewed celebrating miners.

Without directly attacking President Roosevelt, *PM* once again stayed faithful to labor. Crawford's analysis partially blamed John L. Lewis for an "outraged public opinion"; he was glad the UMW had contracts until 1943, so there should be no more trouble from Lewis; likewise the Communist party, which he saw in retrospect as causing trouble at North American Aviation, would no longer be a problem. He hoped the CIO and AFL proposals for conferences to solve labor problems would be accepted by the Roosevelt administration. *PM* was relieved to find Lewis backing the war after the Japanese attack and welcomed him back to the labor movement. The welcome mat was not out long. When Lewis called for labor unity, Landman saw a transparent attempt to take over labor leadership, and Wechsler denounced Lewis as disloyal and dishonest. *PM* reported President Roosevelt, the AFL, and the CIO all felt the same way. Soon Wechsler accused Lewis of building an anti-CIO counterunion and hiring thugs. A "showdown" with the CIO was "inevitable." The following month, Wechsler charged:

> *PM* learned today that secret investigations have disclosed serious gangsterism and corruption among henchmen of John L. Lewis in his drive to create a new labor empire. . . . American labor is united now behind the war effort. The only threat to this unity is Lewis, with a movement that is foredoomed to failure. Revelation of the facts now caught labor on guard against the disunity which Lewis seeks.

Wechsler named several "organizers" with criminal records and aliases. CIO organizers were beaten by Lewis henchmen during a strike.

As Lewis and the CIO moved toward a break, *PM* backed the CIO and the anti-Lewis forces, including Phil Murray and his supporters, within the UMW. When Lewis ousted Murray from the UMW leadership because Murray had become president of the United Steel Workers (successor to the Steel Workers Organizing Committee), Wechsler denounced the "constitutional" issue as fraudulent. Lewis's grandiloquent pronouncement that "the issue at hand is the UMW vs. Communism" was cause for a sarcastic reminder of the unity between the U.S. Communist party and Lewis during the period of the Nazi-Soviet pact. Wechsler saw incipient anti-Semitism when Lewis men issued a leaflet attacking a CIO "Jewish" attorney, whom they also labeled a communist.[10]

STRIKE SUPPORT

It was on and around the picket lines that *PM* did its best work. Any strike in the New York area was covered fully and sympathetically. One of *PM*'s first crusades was the CIO's long battle with a businessman named Leviton, an electrical manufacturer who consistently defied National Labor Relations Board directives.

Leo Huberman's first Leviton article appeared on 11 September 1940—"1700 Strike for a Decent Life"—followed by three pages of pictures by *PM*'s photographers. The following day Huberman detailed Leviton's antilabor practices and the poor working conditions at his plant. Next was a feature on "The Hard Life of Leviton Workers," with contrasting photos by staff photographers of Leviton's house and a typical worker's house. On 17 September, Huberman reviewed the CIO's fourteen-week organization drive. Accompanying photographs of union organizers featured young Harry Van Arsdale, "one of the most militant leaders in the U.S.A. His men respect him because he never asks them to do anything he won't do himself." The next two days featured details of the NLRB hearings citing unfair labor practices by Leviton. Round one with Leviton seemed to be over when Huberman reported on the union's victory: Leviton promised to abide by the Wagner Act and hold a union election. The paper announced that the NLRB had ordered the balloting, but Morris Gordon's dramatic photographs of evicted strikers revealed that the company had not complied. Leviton, the CIO, and *PM* settled in for a long battle.[11]

The pattern established at Leviton would be repeated in many strike scenarios large and small: There would be news accounts which gave exhaustive details of the union's position and organizing history, lists of labor's grievances, dramatic photographs to display inequities, and features about the lives of the workers.

Some of the small scenarios included a striker dying of a heart attack on the picket line. *PM* blamed his employer—Triangle Cable—for refusing to go to arbitration. The next day James Wechsler did a feature column on the dead man's life and struggle. The most unlikely labor situations were given attention, as when Leon Goodelman reported on a union drive in Chinese restaurants against "Coolie Wages and Sweatshop Conditions." Later he reported on a soda jerk strike at Whalen's. John DeBiase did a photo-story on "Staten Island Clam Diggers on Strike for Higher Pay." Victor Bernstein gave early attention to the health of migrant workers on Long Island.[12]

EXPOSING LABOR'S ENEMIES

The treatment of these small strikes and obscure workers' struggles testified to *PM*'s commitment to labor. Much more important was the treatment of national strikes which focused on the great questions confronting the labor movement as the country moved to war. The economy and the politics of the United States were being transformed. Labor was at a crossroads.

The danger was that under the banner of "National Defense," labor's enemies would seek to undo the legislative victories of the Norris–La Guardia, Wagner, and Fair Labor Standards acts and the organizing victories of the unionists. Indeed the *Times* complained, "No matter how openly and undeniably labor union officials or members conspire to restrain trade, no matter how unreasonable their restraints or how anti-social their efforts, the government is powerless to do anything about it."[13] The *Herald Tribune* claimed that defense strikes were "a holdup of the nation to establish labor or certain of its leaders in a position to dictate to the government." The paper wanted the Wagner Act amended to stop union "intimidation of the worker," which meant that unions should be forbidden to bring pickets from outside a struck plant.[14] The *Sun* and *Journal-American*, which had no interest in the defense program anyway, nonetheless found it convenient to raise defense as an excuse to attack labor in their editorial columns.[15] In the *World-Telegram*, Hugh Johnson called for the government to take over any struck defense plants and to draft strikers.[16] His newspaper angrily disputed Roosevelt administration figures who did not think strikes had been more disruptive to the defense industry than normal worker absenteeism:

> Sickness or accident doesn't close down a whole great factory for weeks and months. Sickness or accident in one factory doesn't choke production in a dozen others. . . . And a country whose whole future may depend on production now, unimpeded by any avoidable cause, is not well served by attempts to prove that strikes are really an insignificant threat to its safety.[17]

A congressional coalition led by Virginia senator Harry Byrd moved to restrict labor's weapons. Wechsler warned that these men "believe that America can now be persuaded that the only way to save democracy is to give most of it up— especially the New Deal's labor legislation." He interviewed several anti–New Deal congressmen who wanted to strike at labor by curbing defense strikes and drafting defense workers. The paper fought against the antilabor efforts of such legislators as Howard Smith, Pappy O'Daniel, Hamilton Fish, Tom Connolly, Robert Taft, Eugene Cox, and Clare Hoffman. In the first week of December 1941, in response to the militant bargaining stance and three brief national strikes by the United Mine Workers, Representative Howard Smith of Virginia pushed through a noxious Defense Labor Bill. Wechsler was caustic:

> Smith analyzes the problems of the proletariat with the understanding he has acquired as a bank president. As he talked, the "people's war" against Fascism momentarily resembled a country gentleman's crusade. Representative Cox, Georgia's gift to the anti-labor front, applauded his man's effort to personify a mass movement. . . . You wondered as they recited their favorite anti-union prose decorated with anti-Hitler phrases, how the words would sound to the inarticulate citizens who crawl into mines and stand on assembly lines; how the debate would read in the dim light of a steel worker's shack.

When Smith's bill passed the House of Representatives, *PM*'s page 1 reaction was "Labor Haters Win; Ten Million Americans Lose." Inside Wechsler called it "a plagiarism of Dr. Ley's doughnuts for German workers . . . under the canopy of anti-Hitler 'national defense' slogans the House ran wild against labor yesterday. . . . There was earnest belief that FDR never would affix his signature to a bill which would turn the clock back to the dark ages of U.S. labor relations. . . . There ought to be dancing in the streets of Berlin today." Nathan Robertson was annoyed that the "President has completely lost control of the

House." He issued a complaint that would grow stronger as time went on. Roosevelt, he said, was so preoccupied with the war that he had forgotten New Dealers.

Managing editor John P. Lewis was more sanguine. He predicted that the Senate would never pass such a bill and that FDR would certainly veto it. The following day Wechsler thought "FDR is willing and able to halt the anti-labor stampede." He quoted an anonymous labor source: "If we can't beat Gene Cox and Howard Smith, democracy isn't going to win [the war against fascism] anyway." The bill never made it to the Senate, which was preoccupied with the events of the following Sunday. Although there was much antilabor posturing, labor's Wagner Act protection was not eliminated during the war.[18]

During the war, the paper fought for "equality of sacrifice" to guarantee that labor's newfound place in the world would not be eroded by its no-strike pledge while business took in record profits. It carefully responded to charges that labor unrest was sabotaging defense (part of what was seen as a broad campaign to strip labor of its rights under the banner of national defense). Many workers became restless with the no-strike pledge, and wildcat strikes (usually of a short duration) broke out. But when miners struck in January 1943, *PM* treated it as a major revolt against Lewis's leadership, with miners resenting high dues with nothing to show for them. *PM* writers said the miners wanted the federal government to intervene to force Lewis out, that he was losing control of his union, and urged miners to vote against him in the coming union elections. When the striking miners returned with no more fuss than wildcatting workers in other unions and failed to dislodge their longtime union president, the paper had nothing to say. The paper had again "substituted the wish for the deed."

Perhaps the wildcat strike taught Lewis that his men were ready for a fight. He waged a long campaign, threatening a strike throughout March and April after ignoring negotiations with operators in the bituminous coal industry and the government. His gift for oratory intact, he claimed that the U.S. government "fattens industry while starving labor." *PM* warily covered the preliminaries; Wechsler warned readers frequently not to confuse the miners' legitimate grievances with the political agenda of their union president.

Convinced a strike would occur, Wechsler teamed up with Mary Morris and traveled to Pennsylvania coalfields to interview miners. He found even those in political opposition to Lewis ready to strike because of the government's failure to keep prices down, and he charged that Lewis "succeeded in his campaign to confuse miners" into believing that the government's price and wage bureaucracy was made up of rich plutocrats who were controlling FDR. He affirmed that the miners had real grievances. Mary Morris's stark photographs of life in the coal towns provided compelling evidence.

With the strike set for 1 May, the paper geared up to provide blanket coverage. Wechsler, while denouncing Lewis, defended the miners:

I've talked to miners. They hate Hitler; they're not unpatriotic. . . . *PM* has consistently supported labor's fight for a fair break in wartime as well as peacetime.

We have resisted—and will continue to resist—The Holier Than Thou Brigade which has been ready and anxious to put a gun at labor's head.

The miners' legitimate grievances could not justify a strike during wartime, but this one revealed the anger throughout the labor movement at skyrocketing prices. The government should roll back prices, end inequalities in wages, and fight high corporate salaries by instituting ceilings. Wechsler called on President Roosevelt to visit the miners and talk specifically about how a coal shortage would hurt the defense effort.

Many pages were devoted to the two-day strike, with editorial opinion, features on the miners, and magnificent photographs. Wechsler sat by the radio listening to FDR with a miner who cried when the president appealed to his patriotism. Follow-up analysis included Max Lerner's taking Roosevelt to task for not discussing the miners' grievances. *PM* replied to coal operators' ads in other papers with a long defense of the miners' grievances, illustrated with telling charts. Gordon Cole exacted an admission from Office of Price Administration officials that prices in coal towns were above government ceilings. The paper noted that Roosevelt's new attempts to roll back prices would probably not have happened if labor—and especially the miners—had not forced the issue.

During the follow-up strike in early June, *PM* carefully separated its sympathies for the miners from its disdain for their leader. Both Lerner and Wechsler placed much of the blame for the June strike on corporate policy.

The paper hoped the miners would oust their president. Karl Pretshold covered a grass roots miners revolt beginning in May of 1944, which dwindled with the recognition that while the miners were sometimes coerced and sometimes intimidated by Lewis, they remained loyal to him.[19]

PM's careful distinction between legitimate miner grievances and its disdain for Lewis was not shared by the *Daily Worker*. The Communist paper, whose subhead now read, "National Unity over Nazism-Fascism," denied it was possible that legitimate reasons could exist for striking during the war. The only possible reason for a strike, according to George Morris, was that misleaders "interested in undermining the war effort and the CIO's part in it are actively promoting them." There was no chance that indigenous worker militancy could cause strikes; they were certainly "not unorganized, leaderless outbursts." Vicious leaders like John L. Lewis, Matthew Woll, David Dubinsky, and Walter Reuther were deliberately provoking them.[20] The *Worker* was outraged by *PM*'s sympathy for the miners. Under the headline, "*PM*'s Strike View Aids Lewis Line," Milton Howard attacked Max Lerner's statement that without the strike weapon and collective bargaining, labor was powerless. According to Howard, Lerner's logic made him the same as John L. Lewis. He defended the War Labor Board against complaints from *PM* that it ignored the miner's economic plight, concluding:

The "cause" of strikes in war industry today cannot be sought for in the economic conditions of the workers; it can only be sought for either in a lack of understanding as to what is labor's role in the war, or to the goading or encouraging propaganda of certain dubious leaders.[21]

The irony here is delicious. Only two years before the *Worker* had insisted that the War Labor Board was a capitalist attempt to draft labor for imperialist war. Now it condemned *PM* when that newspaper suggested the board might make a mistake.

Probably no daily paper had the impressively consistent antifascist, prowar credentials *PM* had maintained from the moment of its arrival in June 1940. At the height of the war, with a chorus of vilification surrounding the miners from papers ranging from the *Daily News* to the *Daily Worker*, *PM* had remained constant to the causes of the war and to labor by sharply disagreeing with the strike action and the motives of Lewis while supporting labor's traditional grievances. This was a particularly difficult road to travel because *PM*'s writers were busily trying to reconstruct the left-liberal united front against fascism. Most of the CIO fit easily into that model; the UMW did not. Fighting for the union's rights while distancing itself from Lewis's politics was a measure of *PM*'s devotion to labor.

Those who fought against labor's demands were foes of democracy, threatening the liberty and livelihood of the American majority. Sometimes, these foes threatened workers' lives. During the winter of 1941 Tom O'Connor's dramatic accounts from coal country highlighted one case:

> Mike Poloey was killed with 72 other miners in the explosion at the Willow Grove Mine of the Hanna Coal Company near Neffs, Ohio on March 16, 1940. I saw him and talked to him last week in a hospital room at Martin's Ferry, Ohio. I hope he never sees this newspaper because he doesn't know he was killed last March, and it will be easier if he never knows. . . . I couldn't keep my eyes away from his hands. They were white. They were white not in the way of sheets on the bed, fresh and laundered and clean looking, but white in the way of paste made of flour and water; in the way of maggots and grubs which never feel the sun. "New skin" someone explained.

And a miner searching for a villain said, "It'd be them congressmen who votes against the Federal Mine Safety bill. I guess they'd come as near to bein' the murderer as anybody you'd find."

O'Connor attacked the congressmen who had stalled the bill; facing his article was a full-page picture of embittered miners. O'Connor stayed in coal country to talk with mine widows and orphans. One wife blasted state investigators who okayed a mine two days before it blew up. Morris Engel supplied a moving photograph of miner's children. O'Connor stressed the importance of the UMW campaign to have federal inspections enforce safety regulations, inasmuch as many state regulations were then unenforced. Inspections took place only in areas specifically named in the individual state law. "Murder is a crime for which men are hanged. No man was even so much as brought into court for the murder of the 31 miners who died last November 29. The coal operators who lobbied against the federal mine safety bill and the congressmen who sabotaged it may well congratulate themselves." He interviewed a mine owner, James Hyslop of the Hanna Coal Company, who thought the UMW members were dangerous radicals "from Moscow," was against the mine safety law because it would "turn people to sheep," and who, despite Hanna's notorious use of speed-up techniques, blamed explosions on "the law of averages." *PM* followed the movement of the mine safety bill through Congress, announcing on 14 March 1941 that it had been finally passed.[22]

LABOR AND DEFENSE

The national hue and cry against labor's rights was most intense in the prewar period when workers struck defense plants. As the president moved slowly toward mobilization, his interventionist allies called for curbing the "excesses" of labor. The lofty editorialists of the *New York Times* and *Herald Tribune* waged a continuous campaign for mandatory "cooling-off" periods in defense-area strikes. The frequency and intensity of these editorials was second only to the two papers' advocacy of Lend-Lease aid to Great Britain. Defense strikes were broadly defined. The *Herald Tribune*, citing Martin Dies's charges of communist subversion, complained bitterly of the "senseless" strike at Bethlehem Steel, "a direct assault on defense production." The *Times* warned that the exorbitance of the Wagner Act mandated a review of all the New Deal's prolabor legislation; columnist Arthur Krock glibly explained labor "excess" by blandly describing the Roosevelt administration as a "Labor government." Krock's was a more polite version of the fulminations of Scripps-Howard columnist Westbrook Pegler, who denounced the dictatorial union "sub-governments" put into power by Roosevelt's diabolical actions. Pegler sang the praises of the racially split nonunion North Carolina workers supplying Fort Bragg. "Patriotism is rife among them and sabotage of a defense work as a means of advancing the narrow interests of a union" was unknown. Pegler's "moderate" New York patron, the *World-Telegram*, accused labor of "impeding defense" and charged the Bethlehem strikers with aiding Hitler. It joined in the call for mandatory cooling-off periods, suggesting that defense industry strikers should be drafted. The Hearst press railed against "New Deal socialism." The *Post*, which now flattered *PM* by imitating it with a Labor page of Associated Press or United Press wires, temporized. The paper was for a "cooling-off" period, if the labor movement wanted one.[23]

Three major strikes at defense firms were covered by *PM*, though all took place far from New York. The first, in the fall of 1940, was a recognition strike by the United Auto Workers against Vultie, a California defense contractor. To those who cried out that there was a national emergency, Wechsler replied, "The surest way to disarm democracy is to convince the workers they have no stake in its defense, that profiteers can't lose and that labor must lose in the coming months. . . . The right to strike is a basic part of America's moral and economic defense." He accused antiunionists of using the "emergency" gambit from the days "when Adolf Hitler was still painting landscapes."

When Attorney General Jackson accused UAW organizer Wyndham Mortimer of communist conspiracy, *PM* duly carried his denial. It reported the clash between Martin Dies and his House Un-American Activities Committee, and Mortimer, who called Dies's committee the "sounding board for every stool pigeon in the country," a position with which *PM* was in full accord.

On 27 November, *PM* reported that Vultie had signed with the UAW. The workers had applauded Mortimer and laughed at Dies. An accompanying analysis by George Reedy said Dies's attack had given comfort to the boss but had failed to move the workers. Tom O'Connor insisted there was no treason by striking workers.

Wechsler saw larger implications as the Vultie strike raised issues ripe for exploitation by the National Association of Manufacturers and antilabor congressmen. Ingersoll wrote that a "total crisis" meant preventing strikes by giving labor all of its rights. When General Motors called for a seven-day workweek to accommodate defense needs, *PM* smelled an anti-CIO rat.[24]

The next two defense strikes took place during the heated spring of 1941, when the CIO was moving swiftly to complete the unionization of major industry, discussed below. These strikes were troublesome for *PM* because they involved direct confrontation with the federal government's defense bureaucracy, which, as we have seen, was condemned in the paper for being insufficiently prepared. Amid the blanket coverage afforded strikes at Ford and Bethlehem and transit strikes in New York City and the daily coverage given to every labor conflict in the metropolitan New York area, the UAW's strike at the Allis-Chalmers turbine generator and electrical equipment manufacturing plant at Milwaukee escaped *PM*'s attention until it was suddenly under attack by National Defense Advisory Commission member and secretary of the navy Frank Knox and the Office of Production Management's William Knudson. The two men called for an end to the strike at the plant, which held $45 million in defense contracts with the government. When the strikers refused to obey the government's directive, it was front-page news, though *PM* stuck to reporting each side's position. But when Milwaukee police used tear gas on the strikers, the paper's sympathies were fully engaged. Wechsler blamed management, "a management which has stubbornly resisted every bid for a decent truce and brought down the official wrath of the OPM representative who intervened."

For *PM*'s writers, the strike at Allis-Chalmers had become a test of the company's ability to defy the law. OPM's plan had been accepted by the CIO, then challenged by the company. CIO vice president Sidney Hillman, labor's champion within the federal defense bureaucracy, was reported to be ill. Taking advantage of his absence, Knox and Knudson cracked down on the union. Wechsler insisted that the strike was the company's fault. The centerfold on 2 April featured "Police Brutality . . . Yesterday at Allis-Chalmers." Wisconsin's governor called for U.S. troops to "safeguard the population" at Allis-Chalmers, but *PM* noted that the only violence had been police violence, and it had come after Knox and Knudson had attacked the strike. *PM*'s staff was probably relieved to be able to report that Hillman and Labor Secretary Frances Perkins were angry at Knox and Knudson and that the government would mediate between the strikers and management, though the strike would continue. By 7 April, a pact had been signed, and the UAW had won a ban on antiunion activity by management.[25]

As usual, *PM*'s stance was a lonely one. Far more typical was the editorial position of the *World-Telegram*, which claimed the strike "smacks of sabotage against the government. . . . It is time it was dealt with acordingly." Nelson Harding's political cartoon in the *Journal-American* featured figures labeled "Communist Labor Disrupter" and "Communist Teacher" on separate telephone receivers connected to Stalin. The caption was "Party Line."[26]

Allis-Chalmers proved to be a rehearsal for an even more explosive confrontation that not only tested loyalties between the labor movement and its political friends, but also tested loyalties within the labor movement. Once again the union involved was the United Auto Workers. The strike was against North American Aviation, and the issue got into *PM* when UAW official Richard Frankensteen "fired" five "reds" from the union at the Inglewood, California, plant. He claimed communists were deliberately sabotaging national defense. Left-wing union leader Harry Bridges cabled his support of the walkout; the strikers heckled Frankensteen. President Roosevelt sent soldiers to break the strike, bringing in 2,000 scabs to replace 12,000 workers. Attorney General Jackson blamed "reds." The Selective Service, acting on Roosevelt's approval, threatened to reclassify all striking defense workers from 2-A to 1-A: draft bait.

PM's labor coverage faced a difficult divide. Its first response was to get the inside scoop. Under the headline "Leaders of North American Aircraft Strike State Their Case," strike leaders Lew Michener and Philip M. Connelly were interviewed by Ingersoll, Wechsler, and O'Connor. They reported that they began negotiating on 16 April with no progress until the mediation board intervened on 26 May. Frankensteen suggested a seventy-five-cent minimum wage, a ten-cent increase, and a strike vote with a deadline, but the company refused anything above fifty cents. The union continued to press for meetings to last at least two hours a day. Management failed to appear for a scheduled meeting in Washington, so the union team flew back to California. When picketing proved 100 percent effective, management closed the plant. Michener and Connelly claimed the mediation board had not been working as North American management had failed to show up for a week. They showed figures to prove North American could afford a raise; they attacked the government as being antiunion. Knudson's General Motors plant in Los Angeles paid workers eighty-five cents an hour, but he refused an increase at North American. Most controversially, they claimed that Roosevelt needed the aircraft industry, "more romantically tied up with war and war hysteria," as an excuse for federal intervention on communist charges (as opposed to taking action at Ford and Bethlehem, where the union leadership was not restricted to left-wingers); they insisted the communist issue was irrelevant to workers, as was aid to Great Britain. They claimed Frankensteen whipped up strike sentiment and then denounced the subsequent strike under pressure from Knudson.

Frankensteen was interviewed, too. He said the strike vote was just a tactic to push the mediation board.

Ingersoll sympathized with the men, who came across in the interview as forthright and logical. He attacked North American's management but concluded: "I do not think President Roosevelt could have taken any action at Inglewood other than he did. This country is in danger. The country is at war—whatever it's called in 1941. There is no longer any time to be wasted." Still, he hated to see bayonets pointed at workers; Secretary of War Stimson should not have eulogized the North American bosses. Ingersoll called on the government to "fire" ALCOA, which had provoked a strike in Cleveland. He thought federal troops would be stationed there next. The issue of the Communist party, he intoned, could no longer be avoided—and then he avoided it, saying nothing else on the subject.

The centerfold pictures were of the army at Inglewood; the most disturbing image was that of pickets being teargassed.

Kenneth Crawford predicted that FDR would bring out troops again to break strikes if it were necessary, but he did not want to. The president would have preferred to use the mediation boards but Communist party members dominated them; a battle to the finish between left and right in the CIO was now necessary to prevent a recurrence of defense strikes. Crawford praised the New Deal for allowing the Communists full civil liberties, "but they are now convinced that Hitler got, among other benefits, the services of the Soviet Foreign Legion out of his pact with Russia." Nonetheless Crawford conceded labor had a good case at North American.

Wechsler believed that many questions remained unanswered. What should CIO policy be to insurgent locals, to left-wing leaders, to the New Deal? "There are few unequivocal answers." Wechsler was now much less unequivocal, too, about strikes that hindered national defense. There was a wide gulf between Vultie and North American: between assuming that if the workers went out, it was the bosses' fault and the workers must be supported (Vultie), and assuming that if the workers went out, and President Roosevelt sent troops, it was because he did not have a choice (North American). Perhaps FDR, not the workers, should be supported.

Fortunately for the divided sympathies in the *PM* pressroom, this conflict would become mostly academic. When Nazi Germany invaded the Soviet Union, the Communist party and most left-wing unionists sympathetic to it took a different stance on defense work. Though Wechsler predicted that anti-Communist CIOers would continue organizing despite the war, when John L. Lewis attacked an FDR-Hillman-CIO conference, *PM* saw him in a tiny minority. The mediation board gave the North American workers their seventy-five cents an hour minimum and a hefty pay raise to boot. Wechsler said the CIO had "recovered" from a "savage internal war." The last of the fallout landed on the UAW convention where Allis-Chalmers delegates were banned, but union charges were dropped against Michener, who fought openly with Frankensteen about what had happened. At the end of the convention Michener was suspended from the executive board for one year by a narrow vote.[27]

Wechsler used the North American strike to indulge his own bitter feelings about the Communist party. On 24 June he wrote that the North American events, and a fight over them within the Newspaper Guild (where the New York local was led by the CIO left, and the national union was led by the CIO right), was a commentary on Communist party politics, where their "lies" were often tolerated because they were such good organizers. This bitterness appeared as a non sequitur to those who read *PM*'s coverage, but to other staff members it was not a surprise.

COMMUNISM AT *PM*?

Wechsler had become the house anticommunist at *PM*. All through the spring of 1941 he wrote the most passionate prolabor rhetoric in the paper. His public posture on labor was in no way different than the position taken by the other writers, including those associated with the left, few of whom were actually party members. (Hannah Baker, sympathetic to left-wing positions but never a Communist writes, "You couldn't fill a broom closet with party members.") As the eventful spring of 1941 went on, his ideas were changing. Rae Weimer remembers, "It's hard to understand Jimmy. Headstrong, he was pretty sure he was always right. He sure as hell became a violent anticommunist. He was a little difficult as he went through his transformation."[28] Where did Wechsler and Crawford's more subdued attack come from?

The most logical explanation is in the politics of the Newspaper Guild. Crawford was briefly guild president before being replaced by a left-winger supported by most of the *PM* guild unit in the spring of 1940. Wechsler lost his bid to become a member of *PM*'s delegation to the New York City guild organization. Crawford was in Washington, running the small bureau there with little involvement in staff politics. Wechsler sat in New York (until Crawford quit, when Wechsler became Washington bureau chief), warning Ingersoll of communism, and making himself unpopular to many staffers. John A. Sullivan recalled him "seeing Communists who weren't there."[29] Left-wing guild leader Jack McManus was adored by virtually everyone on the staff. Richard Green, who represented management at grievance procedures, cites the movie critic's uncommon friendliness; others have mentioned his charm and wit. Wechsler's dark charges of conspiracy alienated many on the staff. No one could deny Wechsler's talent, but most thought his obsessive anticommunism far more disruptive to the paper than the "communism" he saw lurking everywhere. The North American strike was Wechsler's first "principled" difference with the unnamed red faction at *PM*.[30]

Unfortunately, he would not write about it that way. His memoir of the period, written just after his appearance before the McCarthy committee, suggests that *PM*'s support for defense strikes was part of its softness on communism and implies that he was more attuned to the defense needs of the nation. *The Age of Suspicion* is an attempt to prove Wechsler a better American and a more astute anticommunist than Senator McCarthy. In his eagerness to make this proof, Wechsler distorts the record of his paper and glosses over his own impassioned support for labor's rights in its pages.[31]

There is evidence to suggest that the root of the North American strike and the discipline imposed by the UAW leadership was only tangentially related to "communism." Nelson Lichtenstein has demonstrated that all of the youthful national leaders of the union were finding it difficult to impose contract-to-contract discipline on the restive membership. The autoworkers were particularly prone to spontaneous walkouts and sit-down strikes, many over local grievances. Once movement began, union leaders could either condemn the actions or "lead" by following. In the already tangled factionalism of the UAW, "communism" became a convenient charge for local leaders less likely to rein in the militance of the rank and file. It is ironic that Michener was suspended from the union leadership for leading a strike which won its demands.[32]

Torn between conflicting loyalties, *PM* had striven to be sympathetic to the workers, to a massive war production program, and to President Roosevelt. The speedy resolution by the mediation board, which granted what the workers struck for, helped ease the controversy. Hitler's invasion of the Soviet Union, to be followed in a few months by Japan's attack on the United States, would make such conflicts rare.

1941: THE CIO VICTORIES IN AUTO AND STEEL

PM's best labor coverage of the prewar period came in the arenas of CIO unity where the federation forged ahead to complete the unionization process in the auto and steel industries. Defense was a related issue because all major industrial firms wanted to be included in lucrative war production contracts with the government. The CIO leadership sought to use the government's muscle by insisting that such contracts not be awarded to Wagner Act violators. Stone, in introducing the Reuther plan, had noted that Ford, as a holdout against unionization, had been excluded from the proposal.[33]

Ford was probably the most notorious "unfair labor practitioner" in the country. Using a massive company spy network, Ford fired all suspected union activists. Harry Bennett, Ford's spy chief, also ran a private police force of professional thugs. Their most infamous act was the ambush and beating of UAW leaders Richard Frankensteen and Walter Reuther during the aborted organizing campaign of 1937. Another Bennett tactic was to employ fairly large numbers of black workers in the lowest-paying jobs and to convince them the "white" union wanted to eliminate their positions. By 1940, Ford was in trouble, its market share in decline, while unionized GM and Chrysler gained. The CIO embarked on a massive organization campaign against the suddenly vulnerable company.[34] *PM* watched closely.

Wechsler declaimed "Ford Fires 100 UAW Organizers, Seeks to Provoke Strike. UAW Asks FDR for Aid," and he reported the next day that UAW members were celebrating FDR's intervention to force Ford to negotiate. By late December an unsigned piece welcomed the UAW's first victory, as Ford, eager to participate in defense contracts, had finally accepted the government mediator.

PM decided that labor history was about to be made and that the paper would be there to note it. Wechsler and photographer Alan Fisher were dispatched to Detroit, enabling *PM* to close 1940 with a brilliant prolabor series, "Revolt in Henry Ford's Empire."

PM heralded the articles with a front-page picture. A photograph of a UAW Ford worker and his family with faces covered by masks was captioned: "These Americans are afraid of Henry Ford." But Wechsler's prose needed no selling:

> In the capital of his far-flung empire, Henry Ford today faces open revolt among the 80,000 subjects who furtively call him King Henry.
>
> The capital is the River Rouge plant which sprawls spectacularly over 1096 acres of Dearborn, on the western edge of Detroit. It is the largest industrial plant in the world, with 100 miles of private railroad track, and the waters of the River Rouge running through it; with its own fire department and hospital; its own docks and traffic intersections—and its own private army.
>
> It is the shrine of the flivver, the real-life version of *Modern Times*, the greatest show on the machine-age earth. Here 80,000 souls—Italians, Poles, Negroes, Hungarians, Finns, Canadians, all the polyglot peoples of the world—work under a tyranny as incredibly efficient as the assembly lines that transform skeletons into high-powered V-8s.
>
> In this setting the first scenes of a miniature civil war are being enacted. And the plant is a fortress under siege from inside as well as outside.
>
> Rouge is the seat of the kingdom, with dependencies scattered throughout the nation; and if Rouge—plus the Lincoln and Highland Park plants in Detroit—yield to the CIO, the rest of the empire will capitulate.
>
> This is a war between a corporation that has spent unknown thousands of dollars in an eternal battle to prevent the organization of its employees (Ford ads published last week in Detroit papers were reported to cost $1500 each) and the United Automobile Workers Union (CIO), which is spending $20,000 a month to organize them.
>
> It is a war between Henry Ford's private army of "service men" (whose total membership nobody knows), distinguished for their ruthlessness in earlier skirmishes, and a band of CIO men risking immediate safety for ultimate security.
>
> It is a war in which spies flit between the lines carrying messages to the rival general staffs whose headquarters are separated by a one-mile wasteland.

Wechsler reported that 50,000 workers were reading the UAW's Ford paper, that Harry Bennett's goons were still on the scene, but that workers were no longer being intimidated, and he predicted that the UAW would win this battle for recognition.

Workers fired for union activity were featured under the headline: "Ford's 'Purges' Haunt Homes . . . 'Do I Go Next?'" while Alan Fisher's photographs told the story of six men: "These Were the Victims of Henry Ford's 'Firing Squad.'" The final day of the series focused on the UAW leader, Michael Widman, leading the Ford organizing drive.

Crawford wrote companion pieces to the series, assuring Ford workers that

Sidney Hillman would intercede with FDR to make sure that Ford got no defense contracts until it complied with the Wagner Act and reviewing Henry Ford's anti-Semitic campaigns of the 1920s. *PM* kept the heat on Ford, indicting him for reneging on his promise to rehire the two hundred UAW organizers he fired, and accusing him of stalling the union election in his Lincoln plant because he knew the UAW would win in a landslide. Ingersoll denounced Ford for selling out the workers on the consuming side, too, having shifted from the common man's car to a middle-class one. He was no longer interested in expanding the market among the working class by raising wages. Of course he was antiunion.

PM reported that federal pressure was working on the side of the UAW. Stone noted that a $10 million defense contract was awarded to Chrysler because Ford was continually defying the Wagner Act. Hillman had engineered this victory, and another: defense firms would not be exempt from paying overtime. Responding to rumors of a competing AFL union at Ford, Wechsler, by now labor editor, speculated that it was most probably a joint creation of Harry Bennett and AFL president William Green, but that it was missing a key ingredient: Ford workers. The paper used double-size print to report that the NLRB had ordered Ford to negotiate with the CIO and gave feature space to a worker suing the company for a beating he suffered in the 1937 organizing drive.

The issue returned to the front page in March. In double-size print Wechsler demanded "SEND FORD TO PRISON . . . 90,000 workers [are] set to strike. The truth is that Henry Ford faces the consequences of a violent career in law breaking. That law is the Wagner Act." Noting that the NLRB had condemned the automaker seven times, he advocated criminal proceedings against Ford for threatening and intimidating free speech and using a "technique of terror and espionage and anti-union discrimination." Wechsler cited a statute growing out of the bitter Harlan County coal strike of 1932. Inside was an R. J. Thomas speech attacking Ford. *PM* mapped the locations of Ford NLRB violations. Two days later, Thomas, having read Wechsler's piece, prepared a formal complaint to the Justice Department against Henry Ford. In two days in late March, Ford moved from defiance to deference. The paper reported his refusal to appear before the NLRB. He accused the board of communism, but the next day he scheduled early elections to avoid appearing. *PM* predicted a union victory, claiming 80 percent of River Rouge workers were wearing UAW/CIO pins.

When the showdown came the following week, Wechsler was in a valedictory mood. The front page heralded that Ford had to close his plant "pending settlement" with the UAW. The labor editor celebrated:

> In his lonely guarded Dearborn Estate, Henry Ford sat incommunicado today while revolt swept the 1096 acres of his auto empire's capital. . . . Outside the Rouge plant there were smoke-smeared, overalled men parading and picketing and singing where they hadn't dared to wear a union button some short months ago. The knowledge that untitled people whose names would make no future *Who's Who in America* were making history now dominates all Dearborn. The atmosphere was a little like the bravado of the Greeks as they defied Mussolini.

Wechsler remembered that Ford had vowed never to let the UAW close him down in 1937, but now the CIO had forced his hand. Ford imperiled the defense program. Bennett had precipitated a strike by declaring that bargaining would fail and by firing the CIO leaders inside the plant. Bennett chose the date, but the union was ready. Wechsler's only negative note was his disgust for the AFL's acting like scabs. Despite the older federation's disruptive role, life would never be the same. "Does Ford know that on April 2 at 12:15 AM an age and an illusion died at last?"

Coverage included assurances from Kenneth Crawford that FDR wanted the workers to get UAW recognition and a reply to Ford propaganda accusing the UAW of being pro-Nazi and pro-Communist. Under the title "Just Who Is Pro-Nazi?" *PM* printed two photographs. On the left was a UAW button. On the right was Ford's Order of the German Reich medal. Leon Goodelman wrote of "concentration camps for labor" at Ford plants; workers were suspended for smiling. Ford's NLRB violations were boxed. An unsigned article claimed that Goebbels liked Ford, as he should: both were antilabor and anti-Semitic. Centerfold pictures showcased police and scab violence against the strikers.

Blanket coverage of the Ford strike continued until *PM* celebrated the "Darkest Day in Harry Bennett's Life" with a photograph of Henry Ford signing an agreement with the UAW to hold an NLRB election. Several articles appeared each day. Penn Kimball went to Dearborn for firsthand news and features. He reported, "The world was built in seven days. The Ford workers spent ten finding their place in it." They were proud, happy, defiant, and no longer fearful. Wechsler warned of Ford's tendency to use violence and interviewed workers who gave dramatic accounts of beatings at Bennett's hands. The paper reported that 350 strikers were treated at the hospital. Crawford attacked the Washington politicians who wanted to break the strike, and Goodelman reviewed the brief and dramatic history of the UAW. When Walter White of the NAACP came to Dearborn to convince black workers not to let themselves be used as scabs, *PM* broke the story that he would convince them with the help of a thousand armed black prounionists. Wechsler interviewed GM and Chrysler workers who testified about the free atmosphere they worked in now that they were represented by the union and confidently and correctly predicted the outcome.

As a coda to the paper's own coverage, Wechsler introduced a memoir for serialization: *I Was a Ford Spy* by Ralph Rimar, under the headline, "How the Ford Gestapo Rules One of Democracy's Arsenals." *PM* took no chances getting Rimar's narrative. Wechsler secreted the former labor spy in a Manhattan hotel, hiding him from Harry Bennett, while Wechsler transcribed his account and *PM* attorney Richard Green checked it for libel.[35]

For those who had read the previous stories, there was little really new. Rimar had worked for Ford as a labor spy from 1932 to 1940. He reported that his employer was antidemocratic, antiunion, anti-Semitic, and sympathetic to Nazism. He charged that Father Coughlin worked with Ford bosses and called redbaiting a cover to confuse; he doubted that the NLRB election would happen. "Working as a Ford spy was like living in the underworld, amid constant fear and uncertainty and dread, never being able to trust anyone, always betraying the men who took you into their confidence." Ford took union names to the Dearborn police chief; the Detroit Red Squad worked with Bennett. Rimar attributed Ford's CIO firings to the list gathered by spies like himself. Ford underestimated the union allegiance of the workers, for despite spying, they "could not reckon with the intangible spirit that ultimately moved Ford men."

PM was counting on that spirit. When the UAW won the election, *PM* focused not on the outcome—a foregone conclusion—but on Paul Robeson's appearance to convince black workers to join the UAW. The attempts by Ford to use the race issue had failed.[36]

PM was able to capitalize on its unique status as the prolabor paper. Kimball remembers meeting with other reporters in Dearborn, swapping stories. Reporters from the mainstream press knew their editors would eliminate prolabor material; they donated their anecdotes to Kimball. Kimball reciprocated when he could, but there was not much in the way of pro-Ford anecdotes. Whatever pro-management material was available scores of other reporters were already assigned to uncover.[37]

In the five months between Wechsler's first dramatic accounts and the UAW's victory in May, *PM* fought two other major labor campaigns, involving the same attention and passionate commitment.

As at Ford, the CIO suffered a major setback in its attempt to organize "Little Steel" in 1937–1938. The Steel Workers Organizing Committee had been rebuffed but continued to wait for the right moment to act again. In late January 1941 Wechsler and photographer Mary Morris traveled to Bethlehem, Pennsylvania, where SWOC had struck against Bethlehem Steel, the most bitterly intractable foe of unionization. Under the headline: "5000 on Strike v. Little Steel," Wechsler wrote of

> thousands of anonymous steel workers—Hungarians, Poles, Italians, Pennsylvania Dutch, and the host of other smoke-smeared men who make America's steel. . . . We have been here only a day, but it takes only an hour to detect the tension. It may be that this will be the scene for the major showdown in the defense crisis. We think we will stay here for a while.

The following day he reported that a temporary truce sent the men back to work, as the union was not ready for a showdown.

Wechsler and Morris did stay for a while. In mid-February, Wechsler once again punctured the national defense rationale of antilabor idealogues:

> Whether "national defense" means a coupon-clipper's jag or a new sense of the workingman's dignity; whether "national unity" is a Kiwanis luncheon cliché or a revival of democratic traditions; whether 1941's arms boom is a prelude to another post-war hangover—bulging relief rolls and crying kids—or a real stride toward economic order; whether the anti-Hitler sermons preached by the local *Globe Times*,

Bethlehem's only daily, include the right of workers to join the CIO in Bethlehem, Pennsylvania.

Wechsler reported that of the town's 26,000 workers, 21,000 worked for the steel mill. While the company made record profits in 1940, it still needed legal action to force it to pay the minimum wage. He contrasted "the elegant homes on Bonus Hill (informally named after the bonuses Bethlehem Steel's 'dollar-a-year-men' snatched in the last war) and the wretched workers' shacks on the edge of the steel plant. . . . Outwardly, Bethlehem is the Marxist Manifesto."

He featured these homes the following day:

> While the stoic steel workers of boom-struck Bethlehem, Pennsylvania, deliver few public orations they inevitably point with pain to the homes in which thousands are doomed to live. . . . They point and they show you how from the windows of these dreary refuges, you can see the smoke pouring out of the profit laden Bethlehem Steel Works.

As many as 20 percent of the houses were without indoor toilets; 25 percent were without hot water; 276 homes had no water at all. After the CIO forced a referendum vote for federally funded housing, 700 new units were to be built —clearly not enough. Mary Morris deliberately snapped photographs of the plant through the ramshackle web of tattered clotheslines to prove Wechsler's point. Fifty years later she recalled the haunted look on the faces she captured for *PM*.[38]

Wechsler's next piece was an attack on the *Bethlehem Globe Times*, the only paper in town. It never criticized the steel company and soft-pedaled any strike activity. It advocated an open shop, claimed the workers were happy and characterized the CIO as a bunch of troublemakers. Naturally, there was no Newspaper Guild unit at the *Globe Times*, and Lehigh College students were told not to talk about labor, as the school depended on company support. (As we have seen, the New York press was generally as hostile as the *Globe Times* to the CIO's efforts.)

In his last article from Bethlehem, Wechsler compared the town to London. They were two cities fighting the enemies of freedom.

> The truth is that, despite the urgency with which the word *democracy* is uttered in Bethlehem, there has been no visible narrowing of the gap between rich and poor, steel baron and steel worker, middle class and lower depths. The lines between these remain outwardly frozen as if ordained beyond change.

PM moved on to Lackawanna, site of another Bethlehem plant, where B. C. Webster reported that SWOC was prepared to strike but offered to let FDR arbitrate. Webster announced, "Today this city is the first battleground in the long-feared war between Bethlehem Steel Corporation and the CIO." He thought martial law was possible and predicted scab violence. Wechsler again demanded to know, "Does national defense mean strengthening or surrender of New Deal labor policies?" He thought the strike would settle the issue. Blaming the company for the strike, he noted that record profits had had little impact on wages and that the Wagner Act had been ignored as a deliberate show of company support for Ford. The immediate cause was Bethlehem's refusal to meet with the CIO grievance committee, an NLRB violation. "Bethlehem refused to meet. It took the same route in 1918. So now the citizens and leaders of the United States will have to decide how far they think labor unions should go towards abandoning their own interest while Bethlehem Steel writes its own laws."

By the following day Wechsler was in Lackawanna, reporting on a compromise offered by the Office of Price Management: Bethlehem would rehire those fired for union activities, and would meet with the CIO to "explore" a union election. He thought the workers would not like this, but if the SWOC leadership agreed to it, there would probably be a revolt since the workers

> don't see Bethlehem Steel Corporation as merely a recalcitrant employer, but as a remote, absentee tyrant that has shadowed their lives and given them few breaks. They believe intuitively that the chance to win may be brief; that we may be at war or that the war may end. . . . So on a frozen front along Lake Erie they started something they had dreamed about a long time. Now they talk with a half joy, half fear; but they give no outward sign of caring that, in a couple of days, they have been transformed from anonymous steel workers, who nobody noticed, to leading characters in American journalism.

When the strike was settled on OPM terms, however, Wechsler found the workers elated, determined that the war against Bethlehem had just begun.

PM broke the news of the new strike in Bethlehem with an uncredited piece, but anyone familiar with the paper must have concluded it was written by Wechsler:

> There was a strange atmosphere in Bethlehem, home of the 18,000 man main plant of the Bethlehem Steel Co. This soot-covered town, grimy in a thickening mist, felt a new kind of organism growing within itself, something alien, though its roots lay in the city itself. Bethlehem employees are on strike, and they're discovering a dignity and strength they never knew they possessed. . . . Most of all they wanted a taste of freedom. . . . They had finally decided to take things in their own hands. That's what they're doing.

The article listed the issues: a company union forced on the men, lower wages than in CIO plants, war-boom profits for the company, steel-mill-owned tenements, Bethlehem's refusal to bargain, its evasion of the wage-hour law.

The front page was devoted to Bethlehem the next day. "State Troopers Ride Down Pickets at Bethlehem; Men and Women Trampled; One Victim Cries 'Is This the American Way?'" There was a photo of a mounted policeman charging the pickets and more dramatic action photographs by Alan Fisher in the center-fold. Wechsler reported,

> In an atmosphere of miniature civil war, thousands of striking employees of the Beth-lehem Steel Corporation's parent plant today faced the power of Pennsylvania's state police, who galloped here ostensibly to 'preserve order' and remained to clean the streets of pickets.

He described the military precision of the police, implying they had been training for this day and the anger of the men. This was the first strike since the 1919 losses, and police had come then, too. A companion article predicted that the Johnston plant would be on strike next.

Wechsler's featured editorial declared the morale of workers throughout the entire defense industry was at stake:

> For while the corporation for which they work stands convicted of violating the labor law of this land, only the strikers have been punished so far. . . . This war in Bethle-hem is no private skirmish or a labor sideshow. The thing that is really at stake is whether any corporation can live above the law; whether it can maintain its own feu-dal rules when democracy is in danger; whether it can break the hearts and spirits of the men who make our steel. And whatever the outcome of this strike this week in Bethlehem, that issue will face the country until Bethlehem Steel recognizes the rules of industrial democracy.

More dramatic strike pictures dominated the centerfold. Wechsler's news ac-count reported that SWOC's greatest fear had been an armed breaking of the strike; it would not happen as the police were allowing peaceful picketing. The few scabs were scared.

The settlement was front-page news. Wechsler reported that all strikers would return with guaranteed jobs and no harassment and that the company would meet with SWOC organizers. Despite the mayor's organizing of scabs, this was the first time Bethlehem could not break a strike.

SWOC's one-day strike against U.S. Steel and that giant's decision to bargain with the union helped push Bethlehem to set a union vote. On 16 May Wechsler proclaimed victory as SWOC was elected in Lackawanna, and Bethlehem had given up: it would recognize the union in all of its plants.[39]

THE TRANSIT WORKERS AND *PM* VERSUS NEW YORK CITY AND THE PRESS

The third labor crusade of the contentious spring of 1941 was not national news but received even more attention from all of the city's papers. This time the entire press corps, including the "liberal" *New York Post*, was arrayed against the workers and their union, while *PM* fought vociferously on labor's side.

When New York City's Transport Workers Union struck the then privately owned bus lines, *PM* devoted large segments of its paper each day to strike support. The paper sent photographer John DeBiase to cover the strike-vote meeting. The 10 March front page headlined "Bus Strike On in Manhattan," accompanied by a Morris Gordon photograph of TWU pickets and signs. The story inside quoted Mayor La Guardia's accusation that the union was itching for a strike since it had refused his offer to mediate, but the weight of the article and the accompanying photographs lay on the union side. The picket captain's orders were a "model of good form." A boxed philippic on page 18 attacked the bus owners as antiunion plutocrats. Steven Derry had two pages of photographs of striking drivers. Editor Wechsler commented the following day that "the strike has been conducted with a degree of order and discipline that makes elaborate police precautions look like comic opera." Landman found the other city newspapers, eager to attack the strike, exaggerating the inconvenience to New Yorkers.

Indeed, the New York City press was ferocious in opposing the strike and "Red" Mike Quill, TWU president. For Hearst's *Daily Mirror*, the strike was the "boldest and most brazen demonstration of Communist tactics ever known in this city. The Transport Workers Union is a Communist dominated, Moscow-directed outfit." The *Daily News* saw military sabotage: "One orthodox Red tactic is to hit at a large community's key points—transportation, power plants, water works and the like—in the hope of paralyzing the place and creating chaos so that a well organized knot of Reds can step in and take over." The *World-Telegram* also denounced a subversive power play: "Quill and his union leaders appear to put enforcement of their own powers far above the mere wages and welfare of the workers." The *Journal-American* called upon the city to break the strike violently. The *Herald Tribune* was not above red-baiting. The voice of business Republicanism threatened the TWU with an investigation by the Dies committee and accused Quill of using "his leadership to promote what he considers the 'class struggle' in this country and the 'class struggle' in turn to further his political ambitions. . . . The right to strike is not an absolute right. It may not be invoked against the government." The *Times* condemned an "unjustified strike"; under an editorial entitled "Good Men Misled," it accused Quill of indulging his "normal blind truculence. . . . He is destroying his own union." The "prolabor" *Post* complained that "the union's effort to settle the dispute by an abrupt strike is an effort to settle it without leaving time for the intervention of the informal, collective opinion of the people of New York." The *Sun* summed up the press establishment's fury. It asked rhetorically, "Who runs this town, the people or Quill?"[40]

PM printed in full the TWU's reply to bus company ads in the other New York City papers ("If You Had to Walk Today Blame the Transport Workers Union"). The other papers refused to carry the union response. Entitled "If You Had to Walk Today Blame John A. Ritchie" (owner of the bus lines), it stressed the contrast between the high profits of the companies and the low wages and poor benefits of the workers.

In double-size print, Ingersoll supported the strike and the union against editorials and bus company ads appearing in the other papers, despite having disagreed with TWU president Mike Quill's unwillingness to support FDR in the 1940 election.

> *PM* does not believe that all strikes are social calamities.
>
> In this calamity, *PM*'s heart goes out to the victims—the 3500 men who had to risk their future to stand up for what they believe in. They have courage and dignity.
>
> And *PM*'s heart goes out to their families, whose budgets have no capital structure in eight figures to fall back on.
>
> *PM* wishes them well, encourages them, believes in them.
>
> And of its readers and the public—in the names of these men, women and children—*PM* asks: patience, tolerance, sympathy.

Inside, Wechsler reviewed press treatment of the strike. He described a concerted "campaign to Break the Bus strike." Martin Dies had played the communist card, but Wechsler insisted Quill's politics were "irrelevant." Leanne Zugsmith and Tom O'Connor did feature pieces on individual strikers. Captions under eight bus drivers' photographs were the drivers' reasons for striking.

The following day Ingersoll urged unwilling pedestrians to be prostrike. John Hennessey Walker reported that La Guardia had persuaded the national CIO to help settle the walkout; O'Connor described how driving a bus in Manhattan turns a driver into a nervous wreck. Wechsler defended Mike Quill. Maybe he was a communist, but he was also an honest trade unionist whose principal contribution was building a union that protected its members. He sketched the TWU's history and its past successes and told Mike Quill's personal story beginning with his emigration from Ireland. Quill, Wechsler reminded his readers, made only fifty dollars a week and had taken off only fifteen days the previous year. O'Connor interviewed many bus workers, finding them increasingly angry at how the press was portraying them. "So now I'm a Red. Now I'm a Communist. Now I'm being misled. Well, I'll tell you, young man—you can put this in your paper—a man'd have to be pretty small, whether he's red or green or yellow, if he wouldn't stand and fight for what's due him." Amos Landman and Leon Goodelman ran parallel profiles under the headline, "Bus Baron Ritchie: $65,000 a Year . . . Conductor Sweeney: $1900!"

Coverage on 14 March began with a photo of a striking bus worker warming his hands over a street fire. Wechsler and Goodelman wrote, "To the 3500 striking busmen who walked out on Monday's snow-swept dawn, the strike today had become a kind of character test in which they affirmed their own dignity." Photographic portraits of proud strikers filled two pages. O'Connor, writing on the health and safety issues involved, began with a fantasy of what would happen if a driver lost control of a bus on a busy Manhattan street; the moral was that a driver's health is your health.

The 16 March issue devoted page 1 to the headline "Strikers: Be of Stout Heart." Ingersoll reported that the strikers offered concessions and that the owners, seeking a showdown, refused. O'Connor noted that the company used blacks only as menial workers, while Wechsler related that the company wanted to eliminate sick leave and vacations and wanted to pay four cents an hour less. The TWU would stick it out. Irving Haberman photographed strikers at a communion breakfast.

On 17 March, a front-page picture of the four-year-old son of a bus driver appeared under the headline "His Future Is at Stake in the Bus Strike." Wechsler claimed that this had become a "war of attrition . . . a knockdown fight for survival," as the company wanted to kill the union. Four other articles and features appeared on the strike, which made the front page and was again given blanket coverage on 18 and 19 March.

The front page on 21 March celebrated: "BUS STRIKERS WIN." Ingersoll congratulated the public for not being fooled by bus company propaganda printed in the other papers, while Wechsler proclaimed that the "Bus Strike Is Settled on CIO Terms": all rollback demands were withdrawn, and TWU wage demands were to be arbitrated. Accompanying photographs were headlined "Labor Writes a Happy Ending." Penn Kimball asserted through several interviews that the "Strikers Knew They'd Win."

Four days later Tom O'Connor attended a meeting in Harlem where black activists demanded that the bus company hire blacks as drivers. The TWU brass was also represented.

The fight against the bus company turned out to be a warm-up for the TWU leadership, which was headed for a confrontation with New York City about a new contract for the subway workers. *PM* reported that both the union and the New York State Assembly were getting ready for the showdown, the latter by passing a law, specifically aimed at the union, which banned city employees from striking. William P. Vogel's article featured an attack by American Labor party legislators on the new law.

A strike against the city government was politically more difficult to support than strikes against profit-making private companies. As we have already seen, *PM* was politically ambivalent about Mayor La Guardia, who was a defender of any labor struggle that did not involve public employees, but was adamant in denying that any union rights, much less the right to strike, could be extended to the public sector. The opening skirmishes between La Guardia and the TWU were dutifully reported by Tom O'Connor. La Guardia contended that the TWU could not collectively bargain with the city and the transit authority since it was legally forbidden to strike, but the CIO's Phil Murray said the Wicks Antistrike Law did not rule out collective bargaining. When Governor Herbert Lehman, a New Deal Democrat, signed the bill, he said it did not prevent strikes, but La Guardia used the occasion to attack the TWU again. In almost the same breath, the mayor attacked Leviton's ongoing antilabor position, thus appearing as both antilabor and prolabor on consecutive pages of *PM*.

As the clashes continued, Ingersoll weighed in. Here was the moment for the paper to take a strong position, but instead he called both La Guardia and Quill "able men" and promised *PM* articles in the next few days. Inside, however, the writers had made their decision. Tom O'Connor said the TWU would use *PM* to print "our side of the story" and asked Mayor La Guardia to "negotiate at the table—not in the news." John Hennessey Walker again presented a history of the union. Amos Landman contributed a portrait of the typical TWU member (an Irish family man whose salary of nearly $2,000 a year was due to the TWU's strength in 1937, suffering from an abnormally high number of respiratory diseases, attributable to work) and several such men were captured in the photographs of David Eisendirth, Jr. Ingersoll was being carried by his staff. Now he wrote, "While it's doctrinaire to say a strike is always right it almost always is," and reminded his readers that when workers strike they may be giving up their security in order to fight for principles. His words were surrounded by additional portraits of TWU men by John DeBiase and Irving Haberman. Ensuing photographs by these men were captioned "They have no quarrel with the people of New York." O'Connor praised the union for its democratic principles and procedures. Full participation was encouraged by committee meetings and frequent votes. He contrasted the union to several controlled by racketeers, once again referred to Quill's plebeian salary, and praised the low union dues structure and a spotless record on financial matters. "The TWU, insofar as its structure and activities are concerned, is a model of the democratic rank and file union. Charges to the contrary are totally unfounded." Quill, who would show a lifelong ability to rankle a succession of city mayors, reminded La Guardia that the mayor had publicly demanded a "100% union city."

When the Little Flower responded with wild charges of TWU adventurism in a wildcat bus strike that developed in Queens, Landman and O'Connor issued a long reply on behalf of the union and scolded La Guardia for misrepresenting the truth. O'Connor seized on the current Department of Labor *Monthly Review Press*, which showed solid salary increases since the TWU entered the subway field and which called strike action by the union "negligible." Landman's feature documented the general contentions in the *Monthly Review Press*, but it was the news from the next day that broke the mayor's will. Landman celebrated the successful end of the three-day bus strike, with drivers winning 10 to 18 percent wage increases. La Guardia began a two-month process of publicly offering the union concessions while denying that the city had to bargain collectively with the TWU. When the union, helped by the consistent public support of CIO president Murray, voted unanimously to authorize a strike, the mayor backed down and agreed to bargain. *PM*, of course, covered each moment as the battle unfolded.

Ingersoll looked as blustery and foolish as the mayor, because as late as 23 May he was still sitting on the fence (telling La Guardia to "appoint a commission") when his reporters' articles were ardently supporting the union. Only on 24 June did he finally conclude, "Well the union is right and the mayor is wrong. It's as simple as that."[41]

La Guardia moved on to attack the nascent organizing of the sanitation workers. *PM* followed the developing story, which at this early stage in the union's life merely illustrated the mayor's penchant for combating city unions. His continued sparring with the TWU was covered by *PM* through the end of his administration.[42]

PM's embattled support of the Transport Workers Union was later seized by Wechsler as another opportunity to rewrite retrospectively the paper's and his own history. Claiming the union's attorney had told him that the strike was important because "we're in a period of imperialist war and the workers have to be toughened up for the big fights ahead," Wechsler insists he "disqualified himself" from bus strike journalism. As noted above, Wechsler participated fully in the coverage, writing a pointed response to the red-baiting of Quill. Wechsler claims, "The bus enterprise was a failure because it was based on an essential dishonesty or naïveté—the notion that the communist-led Transport Workers Union was uninfluenced by the vaster politics of international communism and that its economic crusades could be divorced from its political designs." The TWU strike took place as Ford and Bethlehem workers were shutting down national bastions of antiunion activity. Should we now view these strikes as more plots by international communism, or as further evidence of widespread CIO militancy? The latter view is far more cogent. In the case of the transit workers, Wechsler's charge is particularly dishonest, for his own journalism had acquainted him with the actual history of the strike. As labor historian Joshua B. Freeman has pointed out,

neither the union nor the CP anticipated or desired a strike. Union members worked for nine days without a contract and did not take a strike vote until after the negotiations broke down. It was the companies' tough stand that precipitated the walkout. When TWU negotiators threatened a strike unless concessions were forthcoming— essentially a bluff, since they had made no strike plans—the president of the two companies, John A. Ritchie, refused to yield and told them to strike if they wished. Having already built up membership expectations, and unwilling to risk being forced through arbitration or mediation to accept any company demands, the union leadership decided that it would indeed have to call a strike. Only then were hasty preparations begun.[43]

Though Wechsler claims that "Mike Quill . . . must have been startled to discover all the justifications that *PM* invented for his capricious strike," Freeman sustains *PM*'s conclusion that the La Guardia fact-finding board settled it essentially on the union's terms.[44] La Guardia's men could hardly have been less susceptible to union "capriciousness" or communism.

It is true that Wechsler did not write about the TWU's contract dispute with the city. In June, it must be remembered, he lashed out against the North American strike. Finding communism as the motive for Quill's militant stand does not wash, however. Any reader of *PM* or the rest of the city press will find Quill as publicly intractable *after* 22 June 1941 (when the Nazi invasion of the Soviet Union made American Communists friendly to America's defense efforts) as before. It was not until 29 June, after Philip Murray interceded, that a settlement was arranged with the city. Though Freeman notes that the TWU leadership did seek the aid of Labor Secretary Frances Perkins to settle the dispute on 25 June (and were privately nervous about a potential strike for some time before), it continued to press for a prolabor solution. Quill worked closely with Murray throughout both disputes, and Wechsler would never have charged the devout Catholic, anticommunist Murray with "red" motives. Perhaps Wechsler cynically expected no one to remember the issues of the 1941 transit disputes and his own public support for the bus strike. The dishonesty is all too fitting for *The Age of Suspicion*, which tells how Wechsler "defied" the McCarthy committee, while supplying it with all the names of Communists the author knew from his youthful days in the party.[45]

The simpler explanation is the one that appeared in *PM*. Both bus company president Ritchie and Mayor La Guardia were determined to break the power of the TWU, which responded forcefully to defend its position.

PM was most successful with La Guardia in exposing teacher shortages and board of education budget firings. In at least one case—in June 1942—the paper's publicity helped contribute to a successful campaign to restore fired teachers to their jobs. The board of education was then a deeply conservative antiunion fiefdom. Arnold Beichman exposed the board's reactionary bias when it rejected an applicant for night school education director because, as an International Ladies' Garment Workers' Union leader, he had a "long record as a labor protagonist." Max Lerner devoted a column to lecturing the board of education on freedom of speech.[46]

Staffers might have hoped that *PM*'s militant defense of union rights would produce meaningful circulation increases among New York trade unionists. Penn Kimball, however, remembers telling striking transit workers he was from the only paper supporting their strike. They thanked him—and went back to reading Hearst's *Daily Mirror*. Ingersoll went to meet with International Ladies' Garment Workers' Union president David Dubinsky to complain of his newspaper's poor circulation in the garment center. Dubinsky "explained" that *PM* suffered from insufficient horse racing and sports analysis and police news. He offered to have the ILGWU subscribe to 50,000 copies, but Ingersoll turned him down. The editor was afraid the papers would simply be thrown away. He wanted 50,000 additional *readers*.[47]

Mike Quill was a favorite target of the city press because he was, in addition to being TWU president, an American Labor party city councilman and a frequent supporter of the CIO left. Whether he was a member of the Communist party or not, he worked closely with it and was publicly identified with many of its positions. Anticommunist attacks on Quill were always viewed as demagogic by *PM*, which insisted Quill be judged on the basis of his union record. While this provoked the "Press Axis" to near hysteria and even the *Herald Tribune* to open red-baiting, Ingersoll's paper looked at that record and found that it was good.

DEFENDING HARRY BRIDGES

PM assumed the same position in evaluating the political problems experienced by a national CIO leader whose base was on the West Coast. Harry Bridges, an alien from Australia, emerged from the ranks during the San Francisco general strike of 1934 when the national leadership of the AFL's corrupt International Longshoremen's Association had badly failed in representing the workers. Splitting with the ILA when the CIO left the AFL, Bridges brought the West Coast longshoremen into the International Longshoremen's and Warehousemen's Union. The honesty and militancy of his union was a constant rebuke to the established corruption of the East Coast's ILA. Although *PM* did not know it, it was President Roosevelt himself who furtively began a long series of unsuccessful attempts to have Bridges deported.[48] At each step in the deportation process, *PM* defended Bridges's civil liberties and his freedom of speech and angrily denounced the attempts to get rid of him, which began before the paper existed and continued through its final year. There were many moments during this period when *PM* was furious with Bridges's political stance, but at no time did it ever see the deportation attempts as anything other than a political attack on a successful and honest trade unionist. Wechsler wrote in February 1941:

> When Harry Bridges supported John L. Lewis in his Willkie boom, he was hopelessly wrong. He helped labor's enemies. He may do other things like that. Yet none of them will be as dangerous as the labor-baiting, flag-waving, witch-hunting parade that the West Coast shipowners have launched. . . . If the people clamoring for Harry Bridges' head win today, they will be demanding [Attorney General] Robert H. Jackson's scalp tomorrow.

Bridges's Communist party politics were beside the point, although Wechsler did attack those praising Moscow's current "peaceful" relations with Nazi Germany.

Harry Bridges handed Leon Goodelman a scoop in August 1941. Finding a wiretap in his New York hotel room, he blamed the FBI and called in *PM*. Photographer Gene Badger took a picture of it. Goodelman ensconced himself in a nearby hotel suite to watch for four days as the FBI spied on Bridges; knowing he was being watched, the ILWU president deliberately tore up papers and Goodelman observed as the FBI men pieced them back together. The hotel, colluding with the FBI, refused to rent Bridges another room. Not surprisingly, Bridges called for prosecution of the FBI for the illegal wiretap. Goodelman was among those appearing before the Senate Judiciary Committee to testify about the electronic eavesdropping; the attorney general–designate, Francis Biddle, repudiated the illegal technique. Nathan Robertson reported that the FBI had no records of wiretapping Harry Bridges.

When a deportation order for Bridges was issued, Wechsler sounded the alarm. "Unionists must be free to choose their own leaders; Bridges was hounded not for his politics but for his unionism. It will be a terrible day for the United States if the shipowners and manufacturers associations and G-men start choosing our union leaders." Tom O'Connor called similar deportation attempts against the TWU's John Santos "a retaliation for successful union building." American involvement in World War II seemed to put a temporary stop to the Bridges deportation proceedings, perhaps because the CIO left was now totally behind the war effort.

Unaccountably to *PM* (which never associated FDR with the ILWU president's difficulties), the Bridges case returned in May 1942 when Attorney General Biddle pressed for Bridges's deportation based on his communist sympathies. Crawford reported the CIO's united defense of Bridges for his prowar, prounion record, which Biddle himself had detailed, and Ingersoll asserted that Bridges "is the hard working and aggressive head of an organization on whose efficiency the lives of Americans fighting abroad depend." Ingersoll contrasted the rapid and wrong-headed action on Bridges with what he complained was slow action against fascist sympathizer Father Coughlin.

Ingersoll thought the Communist party issue was absurd.

> The fact that the poor bedraggled Communist Party of America is today doing all that it humanly or inhumanly can, not to overthrow, but to support the Government of the United States is obviously too small a fact for [Biddle] to notice. Would it concern him that one of the most gallant armies in history—the Army of Communist Russia—is the single greatest force supporting his right to live and write silly legalistic logic?

Ingersoll wrote that the American Communist party, though an important "nuisance" before the Nazi invasion of the USSR, was now totally loyal. *PM* printed a coupon for readers to send to the Justice Department demanding an end to the Bridges deportation efforts. On the same page editorial cartoonist Dr. Seuss depicted Biddle on his knees praying "and protect my bed from the Communist Boogey Man" while a Nazi grinned from under the bed. The following day an editorial from Marshall Field's *Chicago Sun* was reprinted condemning the deportation order. Victor Bernstein warned that the Bridges case was a threat to all liberals, as Biddle's brief was distributed to Justice Department bureaus as a guide for future deportation cases.[49]

As in many cases where the federal government was found wanting, *PM* did not attack Biddle's boss, President Roosevelt, for his appointee's sins. Biddle was treated as an independent agent, doing the kind of wrong the president was presumed to be incapable of.

AFL AND CIO

The American Federation of Labor adopted anticommunist resolutions in state and national federations and within many individual unions. *PM* generally reported this without comment, but when the New York Teachers Union struggled to achieve recognition and foundered, *PM* blamed red-baiting for undermining union efforts. From Albany, Vogel attacked "a new legal weapon against labor unions, which would make possible the wholesale blacklisting of union members being forged by the legislative committee investigating the school system." When the American Federation of Teachers revoked the charters of the New York Teachers Union, the College Teachers Union, and the Philadelphia Teachers Union for being "communist controlled," Vogel thought they were giving in to the odious pressure of the New York state legislature's Rapp-Coudert committee (see Chapter 3 above).

The CIO was faction ridden, but John L. Lewis, while he was president, and then Murray consistently refused to engage in red-hunts. *PM* supported the CIO's position, despite Wechsler's occasionally expressed frustration and anger with CP politics and tactics within the unions.[50]

PM was far more sympathetic to the CIO than to the AFL, being naturally drawn to the broader class implications of the industrial-organization approach and was often angry that the AFL's hatred of the CIO would induce that group to unite with notorious antilabor figures like Ford. The paper reported that AFL scabs "crashed" CIO picket lines at International Harvester. The AFL wired Ralph Ingersoll, threatening a boycott if *PM* were to become a "CIO propaganda sheet." Ingersoll responded with an attack on name-calling. Nor was *PM* through with attacks on the AFL. Wechsler condemned AFL institutional complacency against racketeerism and racism. "The AFL is ready for a shooting war with Adolf Hitler, but it still treats Jim Crow as if he were one of the boys." A. Philip Randolph raised his annual charges of jim crowism within AFL unions at the federation convention, always to be met with the standard annual silence. One year Bill Hutcheson of the Carpenters' Union had replied, "We don't care if you're an irishman, a jew or a nigger." Wechsler commented, "Yes, he said, 'nigger.'"

AFL protection of racism was nowhere more apparent than at the Kaiser defense plant, where the AFL local insisted on jim crow unionism, with no protection for the plant's black workers. The black workers tried to organize a CIO local with Kaiser's consent. This was the only case in all of *PM*'s history where the paper showed a marked partiality to an employer in a labor dispute. Henry Kaiser was that rare creature: a liberal industrialist. He was committed to racial equality in his plant, only to have his efforts blocked by the union local.

After the 1944 election campaign, I. F. Stone, writing for *PM*'s editors, attacked the AFL for its neutrality in the presidential race. "There are crucial battles ahead—battles for a permanent peace and for full employment, battles against bigotry and fascism. . . . What are the AFL leaders going to do in these battles? Be neutral?" John T. Moutoux analyzed the differences between the two labor federations. The CIO was actively committed to politics, while the AFL abstained; the CIO fought jim crow, while the AFL hid under the facade of "autonomous" union policy; the CIO had a progressive tax plan and the AFL did not. *PM* clearly preferred the CIO's approach.[51]

Stone exposed racism in the Railroad Brotherhoods, when the unions eliminated the category of "firemen," a relic in the era of diesel locomotives, so as to avoid promoting these mostly black men to be engineers, peers of the white workers. Under the brotherhoods' plan, the black workers lost their jobs.[52]

LABOR POLITICS

As the labor movement prepared to deal with the "dollar-a-year men" recruited from industry to manage the wartime economy, *PM*'s sympathies were with the unionists, not the businessmen on the government's boards. I. F. Stone was enthusiastic: "But the real focal point and storm of the [Office of Price Management] meeting was youthful, sandy-haired Walter P. Reuther of the United Auto Workers, CIO," who had been attacked in corporate ads as a sit-down disrupter and author of "other forms of production sabotage." Stone defended Reuther when he claimed it was industry which was sabotaging the war effort.

In the Sunday Magazine two weeks later, Wechsler wrote a flattering profile of Reuther. Noting that the "age of the fire-eaters is drawing to a close" (an allusion to John L. Lewis), Wechsler predicted that Reuther represented the future of labor: someone sophisticated enough to help set guidelines for production and to move the economy along the lines of workers' needs.

The first big battle was for a standard for wage increases during the war. The agreement arrived at was based on the increases achieved by the steelworkers in their government-supervised negotiations with Bethlehem and other steel mills. The "Little Steel" formula (forty-four cents a day), once adopted by the labor movement, was supported by *PM*. When, later in the war, labor grew restive because that increase came nowhere near matching price and profit inflation, *PM* charted and argued the union position. On 20 July 1942 page 1 announced:

LABOR IS FED UP
  • *Congressional Defense of Special Interests*
  • *Inequality of Sacrifice*
  • *Big War Profits*
  • *Manufacturing Inefficiency*
  • *Waste of Materials*
That's Why We Have Wildcat Strikes

Harold Lavine warned that if Congress failed to enact FDR's "equality of sacrifice" program, the country would be paralyzed by wildcat strikes the CIO leadership would not be able to stop.

PM fought labor's enemies in Congress, in the army and navy bureaucracy, and in the press whom it accused of encouraging antilabor legislation under the cover of fighting the war. Generally more sympathetic to the War Labor Board than the War Production Board, the paper fought industry spokesmen on both and rallied behind such public members as Wayne Morse, who emerged as a labor ally.[53]

Only once in its history did the paper feel shaken in its confidence in the trade union movement in general and the CIO in particular. After the Fair Employment Practices Committee forced the Philadelphia transit system to hire blacks throughout the system in jobs previously held exclusively by whites (as engineers and conductors, for example), a wildcat strike to protest the decision effectively closed down the system for five days. *PM*, as horrified as the national TWU and CIO leadership, sent Karl Pretshold and Charles A. Michie down for firsthand reports. The TWU blamed paid Nazi agents; Victor Bernstein echoed the union's claim that the Philadelphia Transportation Company colluded with the strikers by turning off electrical power when the strike was announced, despite the availability of men eager to work. Still, the unassailable fact that thousands of workers had joined a racist strike was gravely disquieting. Bernstein wanted the men punished; I. F. Stone admitted that a canon of liberalism had been toppled. The common people were sometimes disastrously and viciously wrong.[54]

The Montgomery Ward department store chain proved to be a flagrant violator of National Labor Relations Board rules, trying to use the war emergency to get away with union busting. The unions struck. *PM* called for the government to seize Ward's and applauded when that happened twice.

A side issue arose in the Montgomery Ward case. All unions honored the Ward picket lines, except an unlikely one—Harry Bridges's Longshoremen, which had a Great Lakes section whose members (following union policy) crossed the lines. This was during a bizarre Communist party policy period following the dissolution of the Communist International, when the American Communist party forswore the class struggle and even dissolved itself as a political party, becoming briefly the Communist Political Association. Wechsler joined Philip Murray and R. J. Thomas in condemning the lack of solidarity and made clear its disapproval of the new CP policy. An impassioned piece signed by "the Editors of *PM* "declared, "Unlike the left-wing analysts, however, we are not persuaded that American business has experienced a great revelation during the war and is prepared to lie down in blissful amity with genuine trade unionism." In fact, the editors continued, the war had produced plenty of evidence to the contrary. It was as foolish to see all businessmen as progressive as to call them all fascists. It would be great if the Soviet Union and the United States were to become trading partners; that hardly meant U.S. workers should abandon the fight for their own interests. *PM* reaffirmed its contention that the right to strike was fundamental to democracy.[55]

Only once was the paper taken to task by a union for being less than faithful to that belief. A grass-roots telephone strike among operators began in Ohio in late November 1944. Quickly "outlawed" by the War Labor Board, it spread rapidly throughout the Midwest and the East. Though many sympathetic features were written by *PM* reporters, Wechsler attacked the strike as "indefensible." A day later the union had called it off, but the New York local replied to Wechsler, in a letter that was printed prominently in the Labor section of the paper. "Coming from a paper which is opposed to seeing little people kicked around, this editorial comes as a big surprise and a kick in the teeth." John P. Lewis tried to find common ground, agreeing with the operators' grievances, but insisting on no strikes during wartime. *PM* continued to publicize those grievances at least in part because it gave the paper yet another excuse to take pictures of pretty young women, who were often called "phone girls" in headlines and captions.[56]

In supporting the activities of the War Labor Board, *PM* writers were endorsing an alliance of trade unionists and friendly government officials and actions. As wildcat strikes like those of the telephone operators were being suppressed by trade union leadership and government pressure, the rank-and-file democracy of shop-floor action was being replaced by a politically savvy bureaucracy, adopting policy to maintain "labor's influence" in Washington. Nelson Lichtenstein has written persuasively about this general trend.[57] At *PM*, where winning the war was still the most important priority, no one noticed.

A kind of sit-down antistrike grabbed *PM*'s attention in May 1944. A navy contract with the Brewster Defense Plant in Long Island City was canceled without warning, depriving 12,000 workers of their jobs. The paper's staff photographers interviewed a half dozen workers, who expressed their loyalty to their jobs and to the nation's defense. The UAW local asked FDR to reconsider the closing, but a spontaneous movement sent workers into the plant to produce planes after their dismissals. The workers continued unauthorized production without pay for over a week until President Roosevelt intervened, asking the navy to provide an explanation for the sudden cancellation. The War Production Board sent investigators; *PM* predicted more work would be found. Sophie Smollar did features on Brewster workers barely managing to stay ahead of living costs; Wechsler rebuked the navy for its precipitous dismissals. The UAW's Frankensteen foresaw a long delay before the workers would be back at their jobs. In fact, by mid-July all but two of the Brewster workers had jobs elsewhere—at lower pay.[58]

LABOR LOOKS AT THE POSTWAR ERA

As Wechsler noted in his attack on the navy, the Brewster strike had national implications. The country had been saved from unemployment and depression by war production. What would happen after the war? Following the lead of the United Auto Workers, *PM* often addressed the issue—with increasing urgency as the end of the war grew near. Ed Scott, with Dan Keleher photos, covered layoffs of 1,500 at a Newark shipyard. Management was explicit; it would not rehire the women workers. Stone campaigned for a reconversion plan which would study industrial capacity, human needs, and resources, and then plan the economy accordingly to provide for full employment. Without using the words, he seemed to be envisioning a planned socialist economy. The paper reprinted depression pictures to support Senator Kilgore's full-employment jobs bill. In a first and last for *PM*, the paper printed a long speech by its owner, Marshall Field, before the Advertisers Club of Cincinnati, in which he echoed Henry Wallace's call for sixty million jobs. Citing a "maladjustment" of income, Field declared that all Americans needed security, and the government must intervene for its people. He wanted loans available to working people, taxes cut at the bottom end of the income scale, subsidized housing projects, and more public works. *PM*'s own editors charged the press and Congress with being "blind" to the need for job creation. The paper gave extensive coverage to the reconversion plans of labor unions, especially the UAW.

Health and science editor Albert Deutsch was far less worried than his colleagues, writing that with women returning to their traditional jobs as housewives, students going back to school, and old workers retiring, the anticipated unemployment crisis might not materialize. He thought the economic structure "sound," but he saw particular problems in the lack of societal protection, lack of opportunities for blacks, and the concentration of defense industries on the West Coast. But a V-J Day headline expressed the prevailing fear at *PM*: "Labor Shortage Is Over—Unemployment Is Back." The day before, Wilbur Baldinger had predicted the loss of eight million jobs with the war's end. Moutoux wrote, "2 Million Are Laid Off in the First 10 Days of Peace." President Truman made friends at *PM* by endorsing the latest full-employment bill. Nathan Robertson thanked him profusely, and Stone found the endorsement "only a little less momentous than peace itself." [59]

PM devised its own way of helping the transition. Beginning on the back page on 5 July 1944, and continuing every single day of publication until it ceased operation, the paper made "Situations Wanted" ads available at no cost for returning veterans. Sometimes running over a full page, many of the ads succeeded, as witnessed by occasional articles following the successful job search of several who had been helped by *PM*. Even after the paper started accepting paid advertising in November 1946, the "Free Want Ads for Vets" continued.

PM's unique position in the world of daily journalism was nowhere more apparent than in its role as labor's champion. Its commitment was apparent when it dispatched journalists and photographers to central labor conflicts in the industrial heartland, when it insisted on telling "labor's side" no matter how clamorous or unified the opposition, and when it refused to cede ground to "national defense" patriots or anticommunists. Insistent on fighting Nazis, the paper never failed to consider defense workers' battles. It was equally adamant about the rights of labor when the communist-influenced unions seemed ready to abandon those rights. It carefully differentiated between its view of John L. Lewis as destructive to the nation's antifascist, pro-Roosevelt labor coalition and its support for the grievances of miners. When President Roosevelt seemed unduly unresponsive to workers' needs, *PM* gently chided him for it. By 1940, antilabor journalists and politicians had begun a counteroffensive against the encroachments of labor, particularly those of the CIO, into political leadership and respectability. *PM*, often alone, defended labor. It is one of the ironies of the ugly period to follow that some of *PM*'s finest journalism should be condemned as reprehensibly abetting communist duplicity by no less a personage than the man who wrote so much of it. The charge does not stand up to examination; that it became the fashionable verdict about *PM* is more revealing of McCarthyism's success in recasting the New Deal years than it is about the newspaper.

If *PM*'s labor journalism was naive, it was in entrusting trade union defense to a federal bureaucracy increasingly less committed to "New Deal" programs. Nor did the paper pause to examine the internal dynamics of the labor organizations, to consider what it meant when the spontaneous drama of sit-down militancy was replaced by the new generation of clever, politically minded union leaders. Labor writers were too busy battling labor's enemies in each strike situation, in the halls of Congress, or in the established New York newspapers.

In the last major strike in New York City before the war ended, *PM* had the field to itself. On 1 July 1945 all of the other newspapers in New York were struck by their delivery unions (this is the strike for which Mayor La Guardia is fondly remembered for reading comic strips on his radio show). The job action lasted about three weeks. The circulation of *PM* shot up from its normal 160,000 or so to 500,000. The paper ran a steady column to explain the striking workers' grievances and printed the official statements of both sides. It warned the publishers against hiring scabs and was furious when the War Labor Board announced the old contract was dead, allowing the owners to employ strikebreakers. As an additional service, a full page each day was devoted to summarizing important news from each paper's missing edition.

It was a violent strike. The circulation manager at the *Daily News* had mob connections. As he rounded up muscle to try to break the strike, deliverers from the *News* and the other papers began preparing for a war. Some isolated incidents occurred. When Arthur Leipzig went to take photographs at the *News* picket line, drivers saw the flashbulbs go off and assumed he was a scabbing journalist. Only the rapid intervention of *PM* drivers, on the picket lines to support their striking brethren, prevented Leipzig from being beaten.[60]

Max Lerner analyzed the resulting settlement as a union victory. It was a missed chance for *PM*. Despite being in a position to make advances in its own battle for self-sufficiency, the paper quickly returned to its prestrike circulation levels. It had run off half a million papers daily; all had been sold. The combined circulation of the missing papers was in the neighborhood of 4 million. How many people would have read *PM* had that number been printed is unknowable; the newspaper's presses and work force could handle only 500,000 issues. The rapid retreat to the approximately 150,000 copies (which was *PM*'s normal circulation) indicates that, although New York was a union town, the animating political perspective which made *PM* labor's champion did not ensure it commercial success.[61]

In fact, labor would find all of its allies weakened. A contentious postwar America awaited the trade unions. They were shortly to discover that like *PM*, they could no longer count on friends in Congress or the White House for protection against their common foes.

5 | CRUSADING AGAINST PREJUDICE

"Doesn't anybody have any trouble except Jews and the colored people?"
—Trial subscriber to *PM* [1]

Committed by its perspective to being "against people who push other people around" and to fighting against religious and racial prejudice, *PM* distinguished itself as a champion of the victims of bigotry abroad and in the United States. The paper's writers interpreted Roosevelt's "common man" rhetoric as promising a nation without discrimination or ethnic violence. With the same vigor the newspaper brought to its wars against consumer fraud, fascism, and labor exploitation, *PM* proclaimed its egalitarian principles, sought out and exposed enemies, enumerated the grievances of the abused, and crusaded for justice. The staff believed that racism was not only a violation of the spirit of democracy but was also an echo of the fascist menace imperiling world civilization.

In New York's always boiling ethnic cauldron, this meant paying special attention to the plight of the Jewish and black populations. New York was home to more than half of the nation's Jews; the massive arrival of Eastern European Jews during the 1880–1920 immigration wave made Jews the single most numerous ethnic group in the city. By 1940, the rebirth of the garment unions and the college education of large numbers of first- and second-generation Jews pointed to an end to mass poverty among them; New Dealer Herbert Lehman's election as New York's governor signified a new level of political acceptance. (Mayor La Guardia illustrated the same point. A balanced ethnic ticket all by himself, La Guardia's mother was Jewish. When he was a congressman seeking reelection, La Guardia was once challenged by a Jewish opponent who made the mistake of calling the Little Flower an anti-Semite. La Guardia buried charges of anti-Semitism forever by challenging the hapless candidate to a debate, "to be conducted entirely in the Yiddish language," on who would make the better congressman. Since the Democratic nominee could not speak the European tongue, he had to decline the invitation. He was swamped in the ensuing election, losing almost as badly among the Jewish voters as among the Italians.)

The newfound respectability did not guarantee acceptance. Young Christian Front hoodlums in the German, Irish, and Italian communities were fond of Jew-bashing; the genteel Protestant establishment maintained its white Christian exclusivity with written and unwritten quotas on jobs, housing, and educational opportunities.[2]

The black population had expanded exponentially after World War I as part of the exodus from the South which transformed the urban Northeast and Midwest. Fleeing an ever more depressed farm economy, African Americans sought job opportunities in mass industry. Those who found work were assigned the bottom tier as janitors in the factories, rack-pushers in the garment center, or day domestics in white homes. The craft exclusivity of the American Federation of Labor kept most unorganized. Though the Harlem Renaissance produced a vibrant political and cultural elite, most blacks were victimized by absentee landlords, police and vigilante violence, and the indifference of many politicians. The rigid legal segregation then at its zenith of power in the South was replicated by unwritten "understandings" in the North. The depression made those at the bottom most vulnerable; black unemployment soared. The federal bureaucracy offered little hope; though Eleanor Roosevelt and Harold Ickes were influential voices against discrimination, Washington (a segregated city) maintained jim crow in the armed forces throughout the fight against fascism.[3]

During its eight-year history, *PM*'s zeal to uncover instances of discrimination was constant. Violence against Jews in Europe and in New York and against African Americans in the North and South was reported with a frequency unparalleled in the rest of the daily press. Daily stories throughout April 1945 included horrific photo-essays of the concentration camps; using all of *PM*'s photographic clarity, they were probably the earliest vivid record of the death camps available to the American mass audience. Howard K. Smith and Edward R. Murrow transcribed their radio reports detailing Nazi brutalities against Jews for *PM*; Richard Boyer, Victor Bernstein, and Irving Brant traveled to Europe to document anti-Semitism. The New York office of the NAACP and Rabbi Stephen Wise of the American Jewish Congress were regular sources for stories of national and European racism.[4]

Bernstein and Tom O'Connor traveled to flash points of racial violence in the United States. Bernstein reported from Mobile, Alabama, when white workers rioted against black shipyard employees. O'Connor went to Fort Bragg, South Carolina, after racial incidents were reported. He interviewed black colonel Charles Eliot, who was initially referred to as "Negro," but found the whites slipping into "nigger." All of the facilities were segregated. Originally, O'Connor had thought the deaths of two soldiers were unrelated to race, but

> now I think it's a lie. Now I think that two soldiers died and four more went to the hospital because a young punk Southerner, now dead, had been given a gun and a club and he felt he could use them on "niggers" without fear of consequences, whether the black men wore the uniforms of the military defenders of the American way of life or not.

A white MP clubbed a black drunk; when four black soldiers said he was hurt, the MP beat them, too. One shot the MP and a little war broke out, leaving the black shooter dead as well. The following day, MPs terrorized every bus of black soldiers. Some were beaten; others were marched to their barracks with MPs shooting at their feet. O'Connor's exposé resulted in the removal of the racist colonel in charge of Fort Bragg.[5] His story was related to a major theme covered by the paper throughout the war: the humiliation of African American troops in the U.S. armed forces by virtue of segregation, local violence, or the racism of the military brass.[6]

When the U.S. Army faced combat, *PM* told stories of the heroic actions of black units. Some of these stories were written by *PM*'s reporter Roi Ottley, recruited by the army and the newspaper at the same time. Ottley wrote of black/white tensions in England and Italy. He demanded combat assignments for black troops in Europe.[7]

A dramatic exchange developed when a black inductee refusing entrance to the army wrote to *PM*. John P. Lewis replied under the headline "Why Negroes Should Serve in the Army":

> *I believe this to be a two-front war.*
> * *The military front against the Fascist armies in the field.*
> * *The political front to improve and broaden and strengthen our democracy at home.*

O'Connor wrote that the drafted man, Winfred Lynn, was in jail for denying the draft. Lynn would fight imprisonment on the basis of jim crow's being illegal according to the Selective Service Act.[8]

In Philadelphia a black man was arrested for shouting in public, "This is a white man's war." Penn Kimball noted:

> Somewhere else a Negro mechanic is being turned away from an aircraft job. He's already been refused by the U.S. Navy. He gave a pint of blood to the Red Cross and watched it carefully segregated from that of white donors. His brother is in an Army Hospital, a southern constable's bullet in his lung. They buried his cousin in Missouri last month, what they could find after the lyncher torched off his gasoline soaked body. . . . We can't lock up 13,000,000 Negro Americans for saying the words we put in their minds. We can't put doubt in their minds and expect democracy to win the war. Out in Malaya nobody gave the natives a chance to fight either.

For about a year after the Japanese attack on Pearl Harbor, *PM* ran a series, "What Are We Fighting For?" to which guest columnists were invited to contribute. For the ten-day period between 31 March and 9 April 1942, the columns tied the struggle for black equality to the task of defeating fascism. Stella Garvin detailed Hitler's antiblack racism. Wendell Willkie insisted on the ending of all bars to racial equality. Lester B. Granger had a narrower focus: "When William Green and the Executive Council of the American Federation of Labor begin to hate discrimination as much as they have hated the CIO, we shall get action on the 18 internationals and the 1000 or more union locals that now bar Negro workers." A. Philip Randolph advocated a boycott of racist employers, invoking the slogan "Don't Buy Where You Can't Work."[9]

PM conducted a crusade combining labor, Jewish, and black causes when an ILGWU organizer who had been drafted was jailed for protesting segregated and unequal facilities for black GIs. Originally covered by Gordon Cole, the story was adopted by national editor James Wechsler, who wrote pointed questions to the army brass about the Levy case. The ILGWU had Senator Wagner intercede, but the generals at first turned a deaf ear. When they did reply to Wechsler, he pointed out that their answers were evasive. The NAACP asked FDR to review the case. Months later Levy was freed suddenly; the army never replied to his charges.[10]

PM's campaigns against racism were often dramatic, front-page affairs. After two years of detailing racist and anti-Semitic violence in metropolitan New York—replete with striking photographs, interviews with the victims, and confrontations with local authorities including Mayor La Guardia, who denied a pattern of racist violence—John P. Lewis introduced a "Declaration of War on Hate-Mongers" with a coupon for *PM* readers to return, renouncing religious and racial hatred and vowing to pursue criminal proceedings against anyone seen violating these principles. Despite the fanfare with which the campaign was introduced, it surprised no one when anti-Semitic and antiblack violence continued in New York.[11]

If the coupons appear foolishly futile in retrospect, some of the journalism was brilliant, though equally futile. Amos Landman traveled up to a black women's "slave market" in the Bronx, where they waited to be hired as domestic servants for ten to twenty-five cents an hour. Months later, O'Connor took on the same story, headlined on page 1 as "Negro Maids Hired at Slave Pay":

> Those who have labor to sell begin to make their appearance about 7 o'clock in the morning, at the busy corners of the Bronx. Their badge is a dark skin and a brown paper parcel under the arm containing work clothes. They stand around huddling in doorways or vestibules when it's cold or snowing or raining until some housewife comes along and offers work. They may get work right away, they may wait half a day, they may come back and wait for one another. They get paid whatever sum they can command through individual bargaining with the housewife who hired them.

Typically such wages were $1.05 a day. O'Connor tried to bring union-era representation to the household workers, suggesting voluntary agreements between housewives and domestics stipulating wages, hours, and working conditions.[12]

THE HATE-ADS CRUSADE

The loudest campaign against racism was a spring 1942 crusade to eliminate bias from advertisements in the rest of the city's newspapers. It began early, in the first week of the newspaper's publication, with an exposé of racism in classified ads from several of New York's dailies. The issue returned a year and a half later on the letters and editorial page under the angry headline, "What in

Hell Has a Man's Religion to Do with Winning the War?" Want ads asking for white or Christian applicants were reproduced and attacked.

As a warm-up for the main event, *PM* publicly battled with the *Saturday Evening Post* over a noxious article titled "The Case against the Jew" by Milton Mayer, the substance of which was that Jews were too pushy for their own good. Ingersoll decided this was front-page news. The day's featured headline was "Answer to Yesterday's Attack on the Jews in *The Saturday Evening Post.*" Page 2 was devoted to offensive passages from the article, followed by Ingersoll's invocation of the Declaration of Independence and its newest offspring: "We as a people created what is known as the New Deal." Ingersoll enjoyed his rhetoric enough to reprint it five days later. Mayer was condemned for prewar isolationist remarks. Albert Deutsch and Tom O'Connor coauthored a column comparing Mayer's remarks with Goebbels's speeches, asking, "Is there anything here that Herr Hitler wouldn't agree with?" *PM* claimed victory when the *Post*'s new editor and Curtis Publications, the magazine's publisher, admitted on successive days that the article was destructive.

Perhaps encouraged by reader response to the *Post* series, *PM* turned over many pages of the daily paper to exposing the competition during May and June. Under the headline "The Hate Season Is On," John P. Lewis attacked restricted hotel advertising in New York papers; ads from the previous day's Sunday editions with the papers' mastheads were reproduced. *Journal-American* offenses took the rest of page 3, the *Times* all of pages 4 and 5, the *Herald Tribune* page 6, and the *Sun* page 7. All of the ads were connected by lines to an enormous circle containing the single word *Hate!* The next day *PM* reported that the other New York newspapers' advertising directors refused to discuss the issue with its reporters.

The following Monday, *PM* returned to the attack. Lewis again editorialized against the ads; several of the offending ones were reproduced. Arnold Beichman reported that "restricted" ads brought $381,465 to the New York press; a companion article noted that the Jewish War Veterans had joined *PM*'s crusade by decrying similar ads in Brooklyn weekly papers. When the *New York Post* announced it would forswear such ads, *PM* decided this was front-page news. Lewis celebrated in an editorial titled "Victory over Hate," urging the other papers to follow the *Post*'s example. The following Monday more of the previous day's "hate ads" appeared with instructions asking readers to call the other newspapers to voice their disapproval. The *New York Daily Mirror* was confronted with its "news" columns' boosting the resorts of restricted advertisers. A photograph of a *Juden Verboten* sign in Vienna was paired with a restricted ad from the *New York Times*. Photographs of anti-Jewish restrictions from Italy and Germany made this comparison again in successive days, as *PM* demanded rhetorically, "What's the Difference?"

PM's suggestion that its readers write or telephone the other newspapers resulted in a war of words between advertising managers at the *World-Telegram* and the *Times* and *PM*'s editorialists. It was an unequal struggle. Ingersoll intoned, "What we are fighting in hate ads is *the social sanction of racial discrimi-*

nation they imply." Hate ads meant Hitler was right. *PM* would not stop the campaign; to do so would be to wave a "white flag" to religious and racial intolerance and to Hitlerism. The paper tried to make it economically unprofitable to run the ads. Reprinting Macy's, Wannamaker's, and McCreery's ads from the *World-Telegram*, *PM* suggested, "If you advertisers don't like the 'restricted' ads, why not ask the *World-Telegram* to stop them?" Roy Howard's promise in 1931 (when the *World* and *Telegram* were united)—"We will essay the difficult role of being tolerant with the intolerant"—was paired rhetorically with more ads and the question "Is This What He Meant?" When the unfortunate *World-Telegram* billed its "Travel and Resorts" section as "patriotic," *PM* replied with "bunk . . . because" of the notorious restricted ads. The Scripps-Howard newspaper promoted the restricted resorts in its news columns; *PM* claimed this proved its point about integrity and advertising. A *Times* editorial on 30 May attacking prejudice was compared with its acceptance of the offending ads.

The *Brooklyn Eagle*, at this point still the host of *PM* at its Dean Street publishing plant, waved a half-white flag, sending a letter to its advertisers requesting permission to delete "restricted" and "Christian management," and suggesting instead "churches nearby." Lewis congratulated the *Eagle*, but did not understand the need for churches to be mentioned at all. Lewis decided to be appear tactful the next day, mollifying his rivals by assuring them that *PM* would not gloat when papers changed policy, but it would stay on the attack against those which did not. Nonetheless, the campaign was all but over by early July, though except for the *Post* and Ingersoll's old employer, the *New Yorker*, there were no victories. It was not until the following January that New York State's Democratic legislators introduced bills which banned such advertisements. Four years after the campaign, *PM* surveyed the results. Most resorts were complying, but some had taken up the *Eagle*'s suggestion of "churches nearby." One blurb read, "The clientele is still carefully selected, if you know what we mean." [13]

The restricted-ads campaign unmasked *PM* as well as its competition. One could not argue with the principles involved, but the intensity, shrillness, repetitiveness, and massive space devoted to this crusade shows questionable judgment. It is hard to imagine how this could ever be considered front-page news. Though both Ingersoll and Lewis wrote for the campaign, it is more typical of Ingersoll's self-promoting, melodramatic style. [14] By mid-July 1942, Ingersoll was in the army, Lewis was running the paper, and the campaign—though not the abuses it condemned—was over. *PM* would continue to focus on racial and religious intolerance, but its reporting was more appropriately focused.

BOSTON, DETROIT . . . AND HARLEM

A series of anti-Semitic incidents took Arnold Beichman to Boston. He linked the violence to the Christian Front and despite personally angering Massachusetts governor Saltonstall, made enough of a fuss to have the governor order an investigation. When the Massachusetts attorney general issued his report, he blamed the Boston police commissioner for indifference to anti-Semitic violence. Beichman's quarrel with the Massachusetts governor and the subsequent exposure of organized violence was newsworthy enough to be covered by the rival *New York Post*.[15]

The events in another American city were profoundly disturbing. The 1943 race riot in Detroit was more frightening than southern racism, which was an understood fact of American life. But Detroit was home to the CIO's United Auto Workers and the scene of labor battles much celebrated in the pages of *PM*. The events in Motor City frightened the staff to the core.

It began on a small scale, when whites stoned black families moving into federally funded defense housing. Albert Deutsch and Tom O'Connor wrote, "The Sojourner Truth housing riot is the direct fruit of domestic appeasement toward elements which consciously or unconsciously are doing Hitler's dirty work here. . . . Race prejudice has no place in our public policy." The government, Deutsch and O'Connor claimed, fed the crowd's anger by describing the housing as units built for black defense workers, instead of saying it was built for defense workers of any color. A citizens commission attacked the Detroit riot squad as hostile to blacks. Tokyo Radio played up the racial implications of the housing riot. To put the lie to Japanese propaganda, Deutsch and O'Connor wanted federal action to ease racial tension in the city. No preventive action was taken, and when fourteen black families moved into the project, the National Guard was summoned to disperse pickets and allow the families entry. Three white men were arrested for incitement to riot. Deutsch was satisfied with the prompt policing action: "The Detroit incident symbolizes the government's intention to crack down on instigators of race hatred, who divide Americans and weaken the war effort."

Over a year later, no one was satisfied. Page 1 headlined, "24 Dead in Detroit: This Is a Victory for Fascism." Staffer Edward Levinson reported that police, tired of protecting blacks against white vigilante violence, had fired a hundred shots into a crowd of blacks. White mobs had jumped at the opportunity to demonstrate violently; some blacks had fought back. Wechsler and Bernstein thought the riots helped fascism. The centerfold acknowledged this view: "First Pictures of Mob Violence in Detroit . . . As Native Fascism Does a Good Job for Hitler." Lerner agreed that the rioters were "doing Hitler's work." He advocated prompt federal and local action against those who spread violence; Coughlinites, Klansmen, and Bundists had lit the match, but there was plenty of fuel. America was paying the price for its failure to eliminate discrimination and prejudice.

Beichman blamed the auto companies for their resistance to helping or hiring black workers. The writer traced the root of the problem to massive emigration from the South to Detroit of thousands of white and black workers, seeking the jobs vacated by those in the armed forces. The whites brought with them their anger at black claims to equality and resented blacks in auto jobs they wanted. The automakers ignored the racial hostility in their plants.

PM printed nine pages of Detroit pictures. Editor Lewis said they demonstrated "how hatred can make fools of men." Lerner commented two days later, under the headline "Program for a Racial Peace":

> The paradox of the relations of the white to the Negro is that they deny him a chance at a job and then call him shiftless; they segregate him in the worst slums under conditions that breed animality and then call him vicious; they deny him education and then call him ignorant.

He believed black integration into American economic life was already occurring. Americans needed to respond politically and socially. Lerner's comments made good rhetoric but hardly constituted a program.

Deutsch mocked the FBI, which discovered no evidence of planned white violence. Willard Wiener found Federal Housing Administration and Justice Department documents which testified to increasing racial tension in Detroit, but no governmental action had been taken. Wechsler slammed Martin Dies's promised "investigation" into the matter. Dies sought to blame Detroit civil rights groups for attacking inequities. The centerfold paired racial-violence pictures from Germany and Detroit under the heading "Racism Is the Seed of Fascism, and Fascism Means Death to a Nation."

PM was shaken enough to print an attack on President Roosevelt by Thomas Sancton of the *New Republic*. FDR was too passive. He must give a great national speech outlining a broad national antiracist policy, and he must appoint a cabinet-level race relations officer. Wechsler condemned the Detroit special prosecutor when the latter blamed the NAACP for the riots; he upheld the statements of UAW president R. J. Thomas and NAACP leader Walter White against the Detroit DA and provided a list of incidents of violence against Detroit blacks by policemen and vigilantes. He supported a young Detroit politician who risked his seat in the Detroit City Council by attacking those who blamed blacks for the riots. Wechsler provided his own analysis: There were no new housing starts, the city council had zoned Detroit into segregated neighborhoods, and police racism was unchecked.

Detroit's official explanation was summarized in *PM*'s headline: "Final Detroit Report Blames Blacks for Riot; Governor Says 'Desire for Equality' Was Cause." Bernstein issued the sarcastic rejoinder: "You know what we should do? Keep mum." Incredibly to *PM*, the Detroit City Council "Calls Riot Case Closed."

PM touted the UAW's policies to unite black and white workers in the city and attacked Detroit's Mayor Jeffers, who accused the union of conspiring with blacks to take over. The paper condemned Jeffers and his major opponent in the upcoming election for playing to fear of blacks; Beichman reprinted ugly racist posters supporting each candidate.[16]

From the first, the greatest fear at *PM* was a replay of the riot in New York. Lerner endorsed La Guardia's plea to prevent "snakes" from causing riots here. For several days running, the newspaper printed a coupon for readers to clip out and send to the mayor pledging they would not engage in racism. Harry Braverman, identified as a Los Angeles businessman (he would much later replace Leo Huberman at the *Monthly Review* when *PM*'s first labor editor died), asked the Office of Civilian Defense to prevent race riots in New York.

And then it happened anyway. The shooting of a Harlem boy by a policeman caused rioting in Harlem. La Guardia appeared on the streets immediately and then called for calm on the radio. His speech was printed in full; another coupon appeared renouncing racial violence.

By the next day, La Guardia was seen as part of the problem. Victor Bernstein was grim: "It *did* happen here." Blacks everywhere thought cops were the enemy. Police brutality was an everyday part of life North and South. An African American delegation had met with La Guardia a year before to report their complaints of police violence, and he had done nothing. Bernstein warned New Yorkers they could not be "isolationist" about life "behind 110th Street."

Deutsch parceled out the blame to city and federal governments. FDR said there would be no discrimination in hiring, but the government did not discipline those firms which practiced discrimination. The United States itself fielded a segregated army. If a black New Yorker visited a relative in the south he saw jim crow everywhere. His blood was not good enough for the Red Cross; he heard congressmen denouncing "black savages." There was plenty of propaganda to "liberate Europe" but no mention of liberating the domestic ghettoes. Bernstein acidly replied to Arthur Krock, writing in his *New York Times* column that blacks were treated so well in the armed forces that they were demanding equality at home; this lead to riots. Bernstein wondered if Krock had heard of jim crow.

Patricia Bronte found life in Harlem "back to normal" two weeks later, and thought that meant trouble, as no one was taking action against the conditions that spawned riots. Bernstein echoed her. Now it was nineteen days and nothing had been done. "We are now 19 days nearer the next outbreak in Harlem."[17]

PM itself could not be accused of ignoring racist abuses. From the earliest days, the city desk took on the New York area's racism. O'Connor covered a boycott campaign to force private bus companies in Manhattan to hire black drivers. The campaign was ultimately successful. He followed an NAACP drive against tenement slumlords. There he met Adam Clayton Powell, Jr., whom he profiled favorably as the young Powell campaigned for a city council seat. O'Connor publicized Powell's challenge to the City College of New York, located in Harlem, for having no black faculty members; the city council demanded that CCNY's president respond to Powell's charges.

O'Connor, Deutsch, and Arnold Beichman replied to scare stories in the other papers about a Harlem "crime wave" by detailing the poverty they insisted caused crime. Morris Engel and John DeBiase presented vivid photos of Harlem squalor to illustrate the point. Deutsch attacked the press for identifying the race of black criminals and failing to use race identification for the white ones. He insisted there would be no crime wave in Harlem when its citizens were fully welcomed into American democracy. Beichman showed how African Americans were excluded by quoting public school textbooks that were filled with black stereotypes. The board of education promptly promised to eliminate the offensive texts. Beichman proved retail prices were higher in Harlem than in other parts of the city. He attacked proposed budget cuts by Mayor La Guardia as disproportionately handicapping Harlem's citizens.

Deutsch returned often to the total picture of Harlem life. He found widespread tuberculosis, venereal disease, and one awful public hospital; citizens lived in overcrowded housing and were offered only the dregs of employment. Children went to ancient, crumbling schools. He battled antiblack admissions policies in medical schools and in New York's public and private hospitals. He cheered when the state legislature banned race quotas at medical schools. Elizabeth Wilson had an exclusive about a black nurse hired in a phone interview by a Buffalo hospital, which had advertised about its nursing shortage. When she arrived, the hospital rejected her. *PM* printed a copy of the "urgent" telegram the nurse received requesting her services.

Deutsch questioned the sensitivity of the city bureaucracy. Writing about black/white clashes in the city's high schools, he thought the teachers were culturally so different from the students that they could not begin to communicate with them. He documented an upswing in anti-Semitic and antiblack incidents in the schools. It is frightening how little things have changed.[18]

PM was an active pioneer in an area that was to have historic results: putting pressure on baseball commissioner K. M. Landis and the major league owners— especially the New York area clubs—to break the color line. Sports editor Joe Cummiskey and writer Tom Meany exposed the hypocrisy of Landis and baseball executive Larry MacPhail. They celebrated when Dodger president Branch Rickey signed Jackie Robinson to his contract with the Dodgers' Montreal farm club.[19]

When New Yorkers seemed to be moving toward racial harmony, *PM* touted the achievement. One such story sent Sally Winograd and photographer Irving Haberman to watch an integrated group of schoolchildren examine blood under a microscope, where they found no difference in blood based on the skin color of the donor. The American Red Cross proved harder to convince. Deutsch waged a long battle against its refusal to accept black donors' blood, pointing out the policy was another way of making black Americans feel removed from the war effort. When it finally did accept it, the Red Cross segregated the blood for use only by other blacks. Did this mean, Deutsch and O'Connor asked sarcastically, Irish American donors would give only to recipients of Irish descent? The Red Cross accepted the blood of criminals and of Japanese Americans, but not of its black citizens.[20]

The Philadelphia transit strike had a small replay at a Brooklyn war plant. An ugly wildcat strike against black workers kept the factory closed for four days before the union succeeded in getting the men back to work and then attacked those responsible for the walkout.[21]

FIGHTING SEGREGATED SCHOOLS IN NEW YORK

Perhaps the best local coverage *PM* provided of the race issue was in its full treatment of the struggle by black parents and students and the NAACP to create an integrated high school in Rockland County, New York. The conflict anticipated the struggle more than a decade away in the South. At the beginning of the 1943–1944 school year, Patricia Bronte accompanied NAACP officials as they protested the tiny number of black students in Hillburn High School. Fifty-six black students who were denied enrollment were offered a chance to attend an all-black school. They refused. The complacent mayor, captured in all his arrogant buffoonery by John DeBiase's photographs, suggested that abolishing slavery "was a great mistake. All a Negro wants is a full belly." Boycotting the jim crow school, black parents set up their own in a local church and staged rallies to gather support. The township of Ramapo charged the black parents with truancy in state court; the parents told *PM*'s Evelyn Seeley and John DeBiase they would face jail rather than accepting a jim crow solution. The local court fined the parents, but the State Education Commission investigated, granting the parents immunity from prosecution while the probe was conducted. When the state education commissioner found in favor of the Hillburn parents, *PM* put the story on page 1; Hillburn's black teachers prepared to move into the main high school. White parents pulled their children from the now integrated high school and sent them to private schools instead. Months later, Evelyn Seeley returned to write an exclusive. She interviewed white parents who wanted to return to the public schools but were afraid of ostracism if they did so. *PM* covered the story with full news accounts, on-the-scene photographs, and revealing features about black parents and students and the local politicians. The coverage matched the dramatic bravery and tragedy of the story it told.

It is useful to contrast *PM*'s treatment with that of the "newspaper of record" and the other liberal paper in town. The *Times* buried the story in the back pages with four- or five-paragraph unsigned accounts; the *Post* gave it more attention though never star billing; only one story featured photographs, which were tiny and uninformative. The *Post*'s view was similar to *PM*'s. Its final story began, "Prejudice rose to new heights here today as the parents of all except one white child in Hillburn withdrew," but without the features and photographic saturation so characteristic of *PM*'s journalism, the story lost much of its intensity. It is no wonder that Thurgood Marshall's correspondence contains a letter from an associate, congratulating him on his "successful result" in the Hillburn case, and noting that he "watched its development carefully in the reports given in *PM Daily*."[22]

One of the most effective of *PM*'s campaigns on behalf of New York's Jewish community occurred when health and science editor Albert Deutsch broke a story which escalated in a few months and had lasting impact on New York's educational system. He was given a copy of a private letter from the American Dental Association calling on Columbia University to put quotas on the number of Jewish applicants it accepted into the dental school; the ADA claimed that

New York was being swamped by Jewish dentists. The next day he reported that other dental groups were furious with the ADA, repudiating its position. Deutsch charged that the ADA was following the lead of medical schools, notorious for their quotas on Jewish and black doctors. The furor was now directed at all New York City area colleges and beyond. Were they discriminating in admissions or in job placement on the basis of religion or race? New York University dropped religious affiliation as a question on its job application. Deutsch attacked the *Journal of Clinical Psychology* for advocating limits on Jewish psychiatrists, lest they "take over" the field. The City College of New York, where enrollment was celebrated as a rite of passage for thousands of Jewish students, was attacked for limiting the number of Jews it hired as faculty. *PM* charged that ABC Radio censored an attack on Dartmouth for its Jewish quota.

The political storm forced the New York state legislature to open hearings into creating a New York State University which would be bias free. The effort was directly related to the CCNY revelations, which were followed by similar ones at other City University colleges. Stephen Wise and the American Jewish Congress provided more evidence of CCNY discrimination. *PM* pressured Mayor O'Dwyer to investigate the charges. The American Labor party demanded a state probe into Columbia's admissions policy. That effort turned up a quota system in place at Cornell. Eventually the committee would discover that Cornell burned its files to escape exposure.

The projected state university would have an "anti-discrimination code of ethics." The proposal drew the immediate support of Max Lerner. Another bill in the state assembly would remove tax exemptions from colleges guilty of bias in admissions or faculty hiring practices. Deutsch got Mayor O'Dwyer to back that proposal, and John K. Weiss found Republican legislators being forced to back their Democratic and American Labor party counterparts in establishing the state university. Investigative committees for both state and city recommended the new school complex, which is today one of the largest and most prestigious state university systems in the country.[23]

CRUSADING AGAINST JOB DISCRIMINATION

PM's consciousness had been forged by the depression's nearing its end as the paper began publication. That fact and the deliberately prolabor policy it adopted made job discrimination a major source of interest. The first exposure was of a natural enemy. The National Association of Manufacturers blocked Jews from jobs in its legal department. Sutherland Denlinger printed letters to an applicant asking "if you are gentile." NAM's president apologized in a letter to *PM*, promising it would never happen again.

But it was on the nation's most rapidly expanding new field that the paper concentrated its coverage. Defense contractors were investigated, interviewed, and castigated if they failed to show integrated staffs. Tom O'Connor applauded President Roosevelt's decree that all defense jobs be made available without race discrimination, contrasting the new policy with discrimination against Jews in Germany. When A. Philip Randolph and others announced plans for a march on Washington to protest job discrimination, *PM* offered support, but was overjoyed when FDR announced the creation of a Fair Employment Practices Committee to prevent job discrimination, which canceled plans for the march. *PM* warned that many firms flouted the FEPC's intent by simply hiring more black janitors, and intrepid reporters dug up several additional examples of job discrimination. One such *PM* exposé moved President Roosevelt to promise an investigation. Dr. Seuss drew a "Disunity Employer" who pulled "Negro Labor" and "Jewish Labor" far behind in separate small tanks, saying, "I'll run Democracy's War. You stay in your Jim Crow tanks."

As was shown in Chapter 4, the struggle by blacks to break the jim crow unionism at Kaiser was given close attention. Beichman pretended to be looking for work and took a job at Kaiser to follow the story, reporting, "AFL Still Lily White at Kaiser." Other AFL locals which engaged in discriminatory practices were rebuked. *PM* annually reported the yearly ritual at the AFL convention: anti—jim crow resolutions introduced and rejected.[24]

After its creation, FEPC reports were given thorough attention. *PM*'s investigative tandem of I. F. Stone and Nathan Robertson poured through the committee documents and attended all FEPC hearings, citing the recalcitrant employers, including industry giants like General Motors. The FEPC was grateful: It singled out *PM* as the only newspaper to cover its work consistently. As the FEPC's historian has noted, "Only a handful of newspapers throughout the country treated it in the manner warranted by its importance."[25] FEPC attorney and later *New York Star* owner Bartley Crum complained, "Except for *PM* we are getting a nice case of freeze-out in the press."[26]

A showdown between Paul McNutt of the War Manpower Commission and the FEPC found *PM* in a fighting mood. McNutt blocked an FEPC report on railroad discrimination as "too explosive." Wechsler worried that the FEPC "May Fold." John P. Lewis demanded McNutt reverse himself; both AFL and CIO national leaderships agreed. Walter White of the NAACP charged that the White House must have known; McNutt agreed to meet with labor and civil rights groups but did not reverse himself. The National Lawyers Guild demanded a totally independent FEPC. *PM* insisted on its strengthening, summarizing its accomplishments. A. Philip Randolph threatened civil disobedience, which seemed to go too far for John P. Lewis, at least in wartime. Wechsler summarized the compromise, which endorsed the FEPC powers, but allowed McNutt to prevent the release of the railroad report. Undeterred, the FEPC announced its intention to investigate again discriminatory practices of the railroads and their unions and soon settled with Virginia railroad companies. After the FEPC announced its decision, the national railroads proclaimed their defiance; *PM*, reminding railroad workers it was a prounion paper, pleaded with them to support antidiscrimination measures. When President Roosevelt seized the railroads during a wage impasse, Wechsler was delighted, saying FDR could now enforce FEPC guidelines. In fact he did no such thing, though *PM*, often blind where the president was concerned, did not notice.[27]

In addition to recalcitrant employers, the FEPC faced another enemy: an increasingly hostile Congress, which had the power to destroy the agency by limiting its funding. Southern senators began semiannual filibusters beginning in June of 1944 to kill the agency, in the beginning settling for compromises which limited its funds. *PM* consistently campaigned for the FEPC and urged its readers to wire their representatives and senators in behalf of it. It denounced the anti-FEPC senators in profiles written in acid. The outrageous racial slurs and lies of Mississippi senators Eastland and Bilbo were printed, including their claim that black troops abroad had committed mass rape and their insistence that the Democrats were a "white man's party." Russell of Georgia was fingered as the man orchestrating the destruction.

During the 1944 campaign, the Democratic platform did not mention the FEPC, to "avoid a flare-up." Nathan Robertson warned that blacks might revolt because of the Democratic party's deliberately vague platform.

Covering the final showdown, Stone warned the nation, "Make no mistake about it. The battle over FEPC in Congress is as fundamental a fight as we Americans will be called upon to wage in our time. This country can no longer survive half free and half racist than it could survive half slave and half free." The filibuster was out to prove "that this is a white, Protestant, Anglo-Saxon country. . . . Racist ideas have deeper roots in the South than anywhere in the world except South Africa." He condemned both national parties for refusing to provide national leadership against the strangling. When the southerners finally won, *PM* was most disgusted with "moderate" senators like Fulbright of Arkansas, who participated in the filibuster, and Taft of Ohio, who refused to be present to vote for cloture.[28]

Defeated nationally, *PM* carried on a more successful struggle within New York State. It backed American Labor party efforts to establish a statewide FEPC, printing the earliest proposals in double-size print and charting out the functioning of the proposed bill. Before the 1944 convention it strenuously attacked New York's Republican governor Thomas Dewey, who was named the "Little Brain of Albany" by Victor Bernstein for stalling pro-FEPC measures in order to appease southern delegates to the Republican National Convention.

After the 1944 elections, pressure for a New York State FEPC began again. Once more *PM* cheered the proponents and attacked the opponents, urging the public to keep the pressure on Dewey and the legislature. After the law was enacted, the paper reported on similar measures in other states and prominently featured the first uses of the New York State statute.[29]

SOUTHERN JUSTICE

Of course, *PM* campaigned against southern racist practices before the FEPC was born. Particularly loathsome southern politicians were given close examination, as when the Sunday Picture News invited readers to "Meet [Georgia governor] Gene Talmadge—You Won't Like Him." Hodding Carter, who had written for *PM* during its earliest days and was now the editor of a Mississippi paper, was invited to profile Mississippi senator Theodore Bilbo. His portrait of Mississippi described a fundamentalist state in the grip of almost universal poverty, with a population terrified that all challenges to the present system were inspired by the North's desire to reimpose Reconstruction. Bilbo had used "cunning" to nurture these prejudices for years, and the widespread illiteracy and ignorance in the state made his ugliest and most deceitful speeches believable.

Tom O'Connor charged that Talmadge's return to power in Georgia had started a new cycle of Klan violence, with four blacks dead and their killers known but unprosecuted. His "Portrait of a Lynch Town"—Monroe, Georgia—profiled a dozen people he interviewed who had no compunctions about sharing their violently racist attitudes. It makes chilling reading. O'Connor's reports sparked a *PM* symposium asking, "Should Negroes Abandon Georgia?" Deutsch argued the affirmative, but national civil rights leaders and O'Connor thought the idea impractical and vowed instead to continue the fight.[30]

Southern justice was closely examined when *PM* sent Elizabeth Wilson to Jackson, Mississippi, to witness the trial of four white men accused of murdering a sixty-six-year-old black preacher. Dating her story eight days in the future, Wilson wrote that the grand jury "dismisses indictments" against the accused. Lewis editorialized that this was *PM*'s prediction, but it hoped to be proven wrong. A separate article condemned FBI indifference, ignorance, and incompetence in the case. When witnesses failed to appear for fear of reprisal, the headline read, "*PM*'s Story Coming True." A happier ending seemed to be on the horizon when this headline appeared: "*PM* Is Pleased to Make This Correction: 6 Men *Are* Indicted in Murder in Mississippi . . . 'Missing' Witnesses Were in Hiding for Protection." Unfortunately, all too typical southern justice prevailed: One suspect was found not guilty when a black witness did not appear, and the case against the others was abandoned.

Lillian Smith's prose poem, "Portrait of the Deep South," a frightening portrait of terror-enforced inequality, was reprinted in the Sunday Magazine. Victor Bernstein was given generous space for a portrait of the South. He doubted that the war was for the Four Freedoms when racism and racial violence ruled there. He charged that the North shared the blame because the National Association of Manufacturers profited from racist salary scales. He claimed that the Klan was getting stronger in Alabama and that unions were handicapped by intense racism. The following day he interviewed Roy Wilkins of the NAACP. Wilkins advocated widening the FEPC's powers, eliminating the poll tax, and passing an effective antilynching law as basic elements in a policy to change the South. Bernstein journeyed to Mississippi to interview politicians who all claimed to oppose lynching but were united in opposing a federal law to that effect.

In matters of interstate commerce, national firms, particularly the railroads, allowed policy to be set by southern practices. William Fisher reported that "Jim Crow railroad trains leave from Penn Station daily." The white cars were air-conditioned and modern; blacks shared their cars (which were not air-conditioned or heated) with baggage. Irving Haberman's photographs illustrated the differences in accommodations as the trains rode through Georgia.

When *PM* photographer Wilbert H. Blanche traveled to Atlantic City to receive a photographic award, he was unable to find accommodations in New Jersey's jim crow resort. Blanche, who was light skinned, narrowly escaped racial violence in Brooklyn when drunken sailors from the South announced to a small group of *PM* photographers that they were looking for some "niggers" to beat up. Blanche kept mum, while his comrades gathered around him and rapidly moved away.

NAACP and other efforts to combat the system were given ample coverage. *PM*'s Picture News devoted three consecutive issues to College of William and Mary students who dared to suggest that the South should change its ways. The student newspaper called for racial equality, only to find itself under attack by the school's administration, which removed the editors.[31]

Though southern Democrats could arouse *PM*'s ire for a variety of reasons, ranging from supporting antilabor legislation to giving lukewarm support to our Soviet ally, nothing made *PM*'s staff angrier than their successful defense of the poll tax, the system which forced voters to pay for their right to vote, sometimes "grandfathering" in poor white voters, while leaving the blacks disenfranchised. (In other communities, many whites were deprived of their votes as well.) An organized campaign in Tennessee to fight the poll tax won an early endorsement. Jennings Perry, who would rejoin the paper as a columnist in late 1946, wrote a series analyzing how the poll tax had progressively disenfranchised voters since the 1890s. Representative Howard Smith's reactionary politics were frequently paired with the low voter registration in his district made possible by the poll tax. Beichman reported on the NAACP's Thurgood Marshall's challenging the detested levy in federal court in Texas.

Senator Claude Pepper, the rare progressive southern Democrat, became a *PM* hero when he began hearings to write anti–poll tax legislation. When Pepper wrote his findings into a bill, his proposal was front-page news. Bernstein's editorial was accompanied by a revealing chart showing how the poll tax undermined representative democracy. Rhode Island cast 314,023 votes in the 1940 elections and had two representatives; Mississippi, Alabama, Georgia, and South Carolina had a combined population of 9,300,00, but only 264,419 votes had elected thirty-two representatives. *PM*'s most hated congressmen were pictured with their small percentages of the votes compared to the overall adult population: Martin Dies of Texas, 13 percent; John Rankin of Mississippi, 10 percent; Smith, 13 percent; Virginia's Harry Byrd, 10 percent. *PM* printed a coupon backing Pepper's bill. Readers were asked to send the coupons to their congressmen and senators. The coupons were printed on several consecutive days. Even after they stopped appearing, readers were periodically reminded to pressure the Congress. Nathan Robertson was certain the bill would pass in the House but was alarmed by the power poll-tax senators wielded. He demanded the bill be reported out of the Judiciary Committee and voiced fear of a filibuster to kill it.

When the feared filibuster became reality, *PM*'s writers vented their anger. Robertson attacked the "anti–poll tax" senators who were "unavailable" to vote for cloture. Harold Lavine's headlines revealed his fury: "Southern Windbags Distort Democracy"; "Windbag Marathon Enters Its Fifth Day." On the same page, *PM* printed the names of the absent senators who were pledged to end the poll tax, hoping to embarrass them. With a picture of a lollipop on page 1, John P. Lewis denounced "Suckers for Senators," and claimed "the greatest deliberative body in the world" had been turned into a "pre-school nursery." Having brought legislative business to an end, the poll-tax backers made a deal: they stopped the filibuster as the Pepper bill was withdrawn. *PM* was angriest at the liberals and moderates who had been absent for the cloture votes. Senator Pepper charged that defeat of his bill showed the Senate did not back the nation's war aims. Referring to the defeat of the League of Nations, Kenneth Crawford agreed, saying that as in World War I, we would win the war and lose it in the U.S. Senate.

The same scenario was followed in each succeeding year. *PM* rallied its readers, the bill made it through the House, the Senate filibustered, and the bill died. It was a disgraceful spectacle, but *PM* never tired of the battle. The paper printed an anti–poll-tax ad turned down by the *Boston Herald-Traveler*, *Newark News*, *Detroit Free Press*, and *Cleveland Plain Dealer*. Stone fulminated that the vote in 1944 was a "farce. A majority of the Senators were pledged in writing to vote against the Poll Tax. They found a way to break their word by refusing to vote cloture and prevent a filibuster." As postwar European politics turned confrontational, Victor Bernstein wanted Secretary of State Byrnes, himself a southern politician, to explain why Bulgarians should vote when blacks in the south could not.[32]

ANTI-JAPANESE XENOPHOBIA

The zeal with which *PM* campaigned for America's entrance into World War II and its total commitment to the war effort once the nation was at war clashed with its commitment to battling racism, especially in 1941 and 1942.

Even before the attack on Pearl Harbor, *PM* noted with approval that the FBI was ready to "crack down" on Japanese living in Hawaii, to force them to register as agents of Japanese business or government. Dr. Seuss's offensive drawing just before the war began can be summarized by his caption: "I can be velly dangerous when aroused." After the bombing Dr. Seuss drew thousands of slanty-eyed cats lurking and sneaking everywhere. *PM* enjoyed Bob Miller's jingle, "We're Gonna Slap the Cheeky Little Jap." A more serious analysis came from Peggy Wright, writing in the Sunday Magazine, who described, in the "Japanese National Character," people resigned to poverty, longing to die heroically on the front. Lying, she claimed, was allowed in the moral code. Men were fitness fanatics who kept their women in third-class positions.

Some on the staff worried about Japanese civil liberties from the beginning.

Tom O'Connor interviewed second-generation Japanese Americans in the immediate aftermath of the Pearl Harbor bombing. He heard several declarations of loyalty to the United States and promises to enlist to defend it. Ironically, *PM* took FBI promises of due process at face value: "There was no sign that federal agents, now sifting our Japanese population for dangerous elements, were sharing the war-spy hysteria which gripped some Washington Departments in the early days of World War I." Kenneth Crawford attacked the FBI for not doing enough to close down the Japanese operatives in Hawaii. Did Hoover know his business? Selwyn James denounced British foreign secretary Anthony Eden for getting worked up about Japanese rape of "white women," reminding Eden the Japanese had been conducting similar atrocities against the Chinese for ten years. This was not about race. A Sunday Magazine story defended a Japanese American WPA artist who was being treated as a "dangerous alien."

But if a picture was worth a thousand words, Dr. Seuss's cartoons more than counteracted efforts by O'Connor and James. He drew a huge stream of Japanese from Washington, Oregon, and California lining up for TNT at a house called "Honorable 5th Column." One Japanese man carried a spyglass. The caption was "Waiting for the Signal from Home." The Sunday Magazine assured readers, "The Jap swells with cruel arrogance once he puts on a uniform."

When the American Civil Liberties Union commented on wartime abuses, it was fairly satisfied with American conditions, with the exception of the treatment of America's Japanese citizens. This might have been the time for *PM* to apologize for some of its own offensive material. That did not happen then or at any other time.

In fact the subject vanished from the newspaper for almost a year and a half. When it came up again, *PM*'s treatment of Japanese Americans was squarely in line with all of its reports on racism. Interior Secretary Harold Ickes wrote to *PM* to complain of Mayor La Guardia's attempt to bar a Japanese American hostel in New York. Hostels were being established as the worst abuse of the war—the Japanese internment camps—were being phased out. *PM* gave Ickes's letter prominent space, and Harold Lavine editorialized, "No racism, please, Mr. Mayor." A follow-up feature sympathetically profiled a Japanese American family, "part of the group La Guardia wants gone." Helen Pleasants covered the opening of the hostel in Brooklyn Heights, and the following day Natalie Davis exposed racist sentiment in the neighborhood in a piece called "Clinton Street Grumbles as Japanese Americans Move In." Arthur Leipzig photographed a Japanese American GI band entertaining at a Staten Island hospital.

Carey McWilliams wrote a lengthy piece in the Sunday Magazine describing the prejudice, evacuation, and relocation centers that confronted many loyal Japanese Americans. He liked the idea of a Japanese unit in the army and endorsed FDR's speech restoring belief in Japanese American loyalty. Nowhere in the piece does he denounce racism in the government's decision to intern these citizens in the first place. His next article attacked jingoism in the California press.

PM condemned the actions of a Washington state American Legion post for removing the names of Japanese Americans from its honor roll. Months later Charles A. Michie traveled there. He reproduced a newspaper ad which read, "So sorry please. JAPS are not wanted in Hood River," and quoted local politicians who made openly racist statements. *PM* printed the diary entry of an American soldier in Burma, defending the civil liberties of Americans of Japanese extraction. Michie detailed several anti-Japanese shooting incidents in California.

Represented at its worst in Dr. Seuss's cartoons, *PM* came fully around to supporting the struggle of Japanese Americans against prejudice. But the worst outrage—the roundup and interning of an entire ethnic group—was never condemned by the newspaper. Comparing the detention with Nazi concentration camps would probably have been unthinkable for the staff.[33]

PM's journalists had much to be proud of in their tireless efforts to battle racial and religious prejudice. The paper's exposés had forced changes in racist practices of the *New York Post, Brooklyn Eagle*, New York City's board of education, the state legislature, the National Association of Manufacturers, many individual firms, and even the United States Army. O'Connor, Deutsch, Beichman, and Bernstein wrote distinguished articles and editorials uncovering injustices and presenting detailed descriptions and histories of American racism. The NAACP and other New York civil rights organizations cited *PM* "for conspicuously fair treatment of the Negro in its news, editorials, and pictures." A panel organized by the New School for Social Research agreed, declaring that the New York City press was anti-Negro except for *PM* and the *New York Post*.[34]

PM should be applauded for its consistent attention to the denial of equal rights to America's black and Jewish citizens at a time when most of the media expressed interest only when racism erupted into rioting. Despite its call for long-term solutions, its own analysis was more frequently a denunciation of the way things were than a program for social change. Irving Brant came closest to presenting a program. His two-part series advocated New Deal economic proposals in the South which would attract black and white voters. This would break the alliance between Republicans and southern Democrats controlling the Congress. He described racism as the tool of oppressors to keep blacks and whites poor.

If *PM*'s writers had their collective heart in the right place but were unable to enunciate a programmatic response that would cure the nation of its racial woes, they were not alone. The small number of black civil rights organizations were themselves divided and uncertain about which way to turn. The NAACP, whose activities, as we have seen, were recorded faithfully by *PM*, was committed to confronting segregation where legal challenges could be mounted and to pressing the Roosevelt administration wherever jim crow activities were prevalent in the government or its business partners in the war industry. In the 1930s, NAACP officials Walter White, Roy Wilkins, and *Crisis* editor W.E.B.

Du Bois often found the New Deal sorely remiss in attacking racial discrimination. Early Roosevelt programs in both industry and agriculture left jim crow intact or even strengthened, and FDR's reliance on powerful congressional Democrats from the South hardly augured well for the future.

By the time *PM* came into existence, the broad social changes created by the nascent war economy made the struggle for the FEPC possible. NAACP officials were cautiously hopeful about the FEPC's potential to change the direction of American racial politics. As we have seen, no newspaper in America gave the FEPC the consistent attention of *PM*. Indeed, there is little difference in NAACP broadsides on racial matters in the United States and the antifascist racial rhetoric of *PM*.

What cannot be found in *PM* is any sign of the black-nationalist perspective then reflected in semi-Marxist intellectuals like Doxey Wilkerson, Ralph Bunche, and, for much of this period, the American Communist party. Though the Communists could be counted on to provide militant leadership against racial injustice and economic hardships, spearheading drives against Harlem landlords or propagandizing, as did *PM*, for the integration of baseball, the CP still paid lip service to the notion of an autonomous black belt in the South. As we have seen, the only time *PM* came close to suggesting geographical alternatives was when Albert Deutsch advocated *abandoning* Georgia to avoid the racial violence encouraged by Gene Talmadge. There was not a whisper of political or economic black nationalism in any of *PM*'s racial broadsides.[35]

Nor could there be any. *PM*'s antifascist perspective was a drive to democratize one America, to advocate consistently an egalitarian century of the common man. Racial injustice could be cured within the framework of a more democratic, more just, single society. As with other problems, racial injustice would be solved by expanding the premise and promise of the New Deal.

The invocation of the New Deal illustrated the problem. Loyalty to Rooseveltian politics limited the analysis, as when Albert Deutsch, perhaps the most resolute proponent of civil rights on the staff, observed, "Negro's Social and Political Status Raised by New Deal."

In fact, Roosevelt was ambivalent about combating racism. The FEPC had been forced on him by the threat of a march on Washington; he alternated between supporting and undercutting its activities. Though he had targeted some southern racists in the failed Democratic party "purge" primaries of 1938, he allied himself with many others. After 1938, he never attempted to confront the racists within his own party again. He had encouraged even the noxious Theodore Bilbo when he was worried about the threat of Huey Long. Never did he commit himself to the anti–poll tax fight so loudly championed in *PM*. He never attacked southern segregation. (Nor, despite her well-known sympathies, did Eleanor Roosevelt while her husband was president. She spent one anguished evening with Louis Weiss and his wife discussing the pros and cons of openly denouncing jim crow. The following day she received a reassuring letter from

PM's attorney, agreeing with her that more harm than good would come from her taking a public stand.) Roosevelt's commitment to political power convinced him of the need to get along with the racists *PM* fervently condemned.[36]

Nonetheless, real opportunities were available to blacks during the war. The status of many was changed with their assignment as combat (if still jim crow) troops. The rapid expansion of defense industries during the war boom's full employment economy created thousands of new jobs. W.E.B. Du Bois, who had earlier criticized the failure of the New Deal to address the South's racial inequities, campaigned energetically for Roosevelt's reelection in 1944.[37] If *PM* exaggerated Roosevelt's commitment to racial equality, it was in good company. The condemnation of Dewey for temporizing at the Republican convention on the FEPC was not matched by an equal condemnation of the Democratic candidate's identical inaction. Though Nate Robertson censured Democratic silence, his newspaper's overall perspective was embodied by Deutsch's analysis. As in the struggles to defeat fascism and to secure labor its rights, *PM* attributed racial progress to the common man's friend in the White House. Whatever the reservations, Roosevelt remained "the Champ."

6 | Voice of the New Deal

Roosevelt has no integrity, none at all.
—I. F. Stone in private conversation, 1944.[1]

Our country, our children, the world, owe him more than we can yet realize. We are humbly grateful not merely for his humanity, for his quick instinctive sympathy with the oppressed, for his sense of justice, but also his masterly sense of politics, the toughness of fibre, the flexibility, the capacity for compromise.
—I. F. Stone for the editors of *PM*, 13 April 1945

*P*M's writers identified the New Deal not as a political slogan or even as a specific program but as a broad movement transforming American society. By correcting the most egregious inequities and by empowering social classes never before represented by political elites, the New Deal was seen as fulfilling the promise of American democracy.

PM's view was hardly unique. Republican rule in the 1920s had alienated much of America's literary and intellectual circles long before the depression; that calamity and the rise of fascism made the intelligentsia take urgent interest in politics. Hoover's personal rigidity combined with his calcified policies made him a symbol of all that was wrong with the country. Although many disaffected thinkers, like Wechsler and Stone, began Roosevelt's term of office with a suspicious disregard of the new president, the air of experimentation he brought to Washington and the liberal thinkers whose ideas he encouraged, like Columbia's Rex Tugwell and Harvard's Felix Frankfurter, eroded their hostility. Frances Perkins, Henry Wallace, and Harold Ickes opened their departments to welcome an influx of idealistic young reformers. Eleanor Roosevelt actively courted voices of change among college students and civil rights organizations. The social legislation championed by FDR was inextricably linked to the legitimization of trade union aspirations.[2]

When *PM* came into the world in June 1940 with the help of Franklin Roosevelt, many like-thinking intellectuals were working for his administration. Archibald MacLeish, who had assisted Ralph Ingersoll's political education, moved from being Librarian of Congress to directing the Office of Facts and Figures. When Elmer Davis of CBS was named to run the Office of War Information, he chose *PM*'s original managing editor, George Lyon, as his first deputy.

As we have seen, many Roosevelt administration figures read *PM* regularly. Even as it foundered below the 100,000 circulation level, the new paper was studied in government offices in Washington. Creekmore Fath, working for the OSS, says that in the White House "we all read *PM*. We all loved *PM*."[3] Lerner churned out a steady correspondence with Roosevelt's appointees to the Supreme Court, including Felix Frankfurter, who remained a Roosevelt adviser even after donning the black robes. Mrs. Roosevelt's friendship with James Wechsler occasionally resulted in his being used as an intermediary by John P. Lewis when Ingersoll was in the army. Ingersoll himself had relatively easy access to the president, seeing him three or four times between *PM*'s birth and his enlistment.[4]

The heady feeling of being heeded at the White House could only strengthen the allegiance most staff members felt to Rooseveltian politics. As the new paper came into existence, the president was arranging a "draft" to renominate him for an unprecedented third term in office at July's Democratic convention. Before the new paper was a week old, the Republican National Convention was taking place in Philadelphia. Kenneth Crawford and guest writer Lillian Hellman wrote from the convention for *PM*. Their hostility to the GOP was hardly disguised. Crawford and Weldon James chortled about FDR's "cleverness" in appointing Republican interventionists Henry Stimson and Frank Knox to the cabinet. Crawford thought FDR had strengthened internationalists in both parties; James believed that Republicans were now hopelessly "confused." *PM*'s photographers pictured the stereotypical smoke-filled rooms; Hellman, after describing civil rights violations in Philadelphia, wrote, "Uptown, the party of Abraham Lincoln is making deals in a city in which at least three white men and two black men are too frightened to exercise their primary right of free speech. I thought that Lincoln might not like that." Until the actual balloting, the *PM* writers at the convention thought conservative Robert Taft would be the Republican choice, though they rooted for the eventual nominee, Wendell Willkie.[5]

PM billed the Democratic National Convention precisely as Roosevelt would have wanted. The opening story was headlined, "Roosevelt Will Accept Draft; He Would Prefer Not to Run but New Dealers Have Persuaded Him No Other Democrat Can Defeat Willkie." Crawford's analysis was that the president "will make the sacrifice." There were no smoke-filled rooms in *PM*'s coverage of *this* convention; instead, the huge banners of FDR's portraits were reproduced with maximum effect. The analysis provided was uneven. Crawford's column one day accurately described the Democratic party as a mix of New Dealers, city bosses, and southern Bourbons; the next day he asserted that, with FDR running, "the New Deal is in charge." The nomination of Henry Wallace for vice president was a "rout" of the old guard; Nathan Robertson was convinced Roosevelt would be able to control the direction of his party.[6]

PM did not mention that the Roosevelt "draft" was stage-managed by the Chicago Democratic party machine; that the microphone booming "We Want Roosevelt" was held by Chicago's commissioner of sewers, leading to much Republican fun about "the voice from the sewers," or that Wallace was both so personally unpopular among old-line Democrats and representative to them of being manipulated by the president that the new vice-presidential nominee was treated rudely and prevented from speaking before the convention. Of the two national conventions, there can be little doubt that it was the Democratic which was "boss" controlled, with the boss being the most powerful politician in the United States. The Democrats had renominated FDR because they wanted to win. Crawford was whistling in the dark when he claimed that "what happens today in Chicago may produce the long-awaited realignment of American political parties."[7]

Ingersoll wrote a series of editorials in August endorsing FDR. A third term, he argued, would force industrialists to recognize that their days of sole power were over. The government was strong enough to force industry to share its profits with working people. By September the paper had become a campaign journal. Walter Winchell moonlighted from his *Daily Mirror* gossip duties, writing a frankly partisan campaign diary under the pseudonym "Paul Revere II." Though *PM* had been pleased by the Republican selection of the liberal Willkie, he was now attacked as lacking courage. Crawford claimed he talked out of both sides of his mouth (true enough, but it was no easy task being sympathetic to interventionism and labor's rights while carrying the Republican standard). Was he a New Deal supporter or critic? The Sunday Magazine did a seven-page photographic essay on depression squalor under the headline, "Before Roosevelt Things Were Like This." *PM*'s writers were delighted by FDR's campaign oratory excoriating "Martin, Barton, and Fish." The paper turned over three pages to the text and another three pages to pictures of the New York rally where he spoke. Dorothy Thompson, in a column that was killed in the *Herald Tribune*, wrote that the Axis powers wanted Roosevelt beaten. This became *PM*'s major theme in the last days of the campaign. By 30 October, the page 1 headline asked rhetorically, "How Will Hitler Vote?" There was no doubt about the answer.[8]

The flush of victory gave rise to a honeymoon of increased expectations. No one at *PM* noticed that the margin was considerably closer than in the landslide of 1936. Writers were convinced their man's liberalism was stronger than ever. They predicted tougher anti-Nazi policies and strung together several denunciations of such reactionary Democrats as Millard Tydings of Maryland and the ambassador to Great Britain, Joseph P. Kennedy. The Republican opposition was accused (justifiably) of championing isolationism, regressive tax policies, and antilabor strategies. Robertson foresaw forceful presidential action to cut down industry price-gouging. Ingersoll, Wechsler, and Crawford gave the president credit for halting the stampede to antilabor legislation; when William Knudson and Frank Knox recommended precisely such policies, no one remembered how "clever" it had been to bring them into the cabinet. All through *PM*'s fanatically interventionist spring of 1941, no direct criticism of Roosevelt accompanied the campaign. Tabitha Petran and William Walton briefly thought that enlightened liberalism and compassion was being forced on the State Department. Crawford engaged in hagiography: Although the president was tired, he worked anyway. After the bombing of Pearl Harbor, Jack McManus journeyed to Washington to hear Roosevelt speak. "He looked ten years younger than his age." The film critic was rhapsodic about the famous smile. The centerfold on FDR's sixtieth birthday used yearly photographs beginning in 1933 to prove that "Photos Show He Hasn't Aged."[9]

By early 1942, grumblings on the paper accompanied the recognition that the New Deal was in political retreat before increasingly powerful foes on the right. Robertson was angry that Roosevelt had not fought hard for the Farm Security

Administration. "He played into the hands of his enemies." A few days later Robertson apologized after FDR attacked congressional critics of the FSA. Ingersoll, Crawford, and Wechsler backed the anti-inflation plan, even wage controls. Ingersoll implored labor to "have a little faith in your President." Crawford wanted to correct any wrong impression that all of *PM*'s warnings about unpreparedness may have given: The president had the country moving in the right direction. Although the paper attacked many War Production Board policies, Crawford explained why FDR himself had been exempt. He was a "stream that never has ceased flowing toward liberal objectives." When Roosevelt endorsed the Tammany Democratic nominee in the New York governor's race instead of the American Labor party candidate, *PM* gently chided him. Roosevelt knew more than *PM* did about the country, but *PM* knew more about New York.

Roosevelt's unexpected swipe at media critics on the left found Robertson bewildered and "depressed." *PM*, in pointing out the anti–New Dealers in government, was engaging in criticism, but it was "offered by those who consider themselves his best friends. It is offered by people who have faith in Franklin D. Roosevelt, the man who has done so much to make a better America."

PM campaigned energetically for a liberal Congress in the elections of 1942. It ran a series of exposés of the toughest opponents of the New Deal. Before election day, Robertson urged voters to save the nation from the isolationists: "Today the lives of millions of Americans are in jeopardy in a war to save the nation from slavery." Though the first postmortem was in the form on a front-page headline—"FDR Holds Congress"—ensuing analysis by Robertson and Crawford was grimmer and more accurate. Robertson headlined his article "Reactionaries May Rule New Congress." Crawford closed the year warning that if "you think this congress was bad," wait until next year.[10]

Though the main thrust of the newspaper's editorial position was always pro-Roosevelt, anguished murmurs of discontent rumbled through *PM* in 1943. Michael Straight of the *New Republic* wrote that *PM* should apply criticism to the president when necessary. "Our job is not be apologists but to fight with all our power to hammer out a militant progressive program." Harold Lavine replied that the enemy was fascism, not Roosevelt. While Picture News devoted half of a late-January issue to commemorating FDR's sixty-first birthday with stirring quotes from his speeches, Lerner distinguished between the overall record and what he saw as a bankrupt North Africa policy. Robertson complained about the president's failure to fight for a more equitable tax plan.

When Roosevelt ended the public quarrel between Vice President Wallace and Secretary of Commerce Jesse Jones over wartime economic policy by removing jurisdictional control from both men, the murmurs became impassioned denunciation. Wallace's "Century of the Common Man" speeches had crystallized wartime New Deal thought in *PM*'s editorial offices and throughout the liberal-labor constituency. Page 1 insisted that "New Dealers Rally to Henry A. Wallace." Victor Bernstein claimed, "New Dealers were seriously questioning their feelings about President Roosevelt and a fourth term in the light of the blow he gave to Vice President Henry Wallace and all that the New Deal has stood for."

Lerner used double-size type to charge that the president was no longer interested in the New Deal but only in winning the war. Liberals would have to fight for Wallace's renomination if a progressive domestic policy was to triumph. He warned FDR that a third-party option should be carefully studied by the liberal left. Wechsler thought veteran Democratic hacks had more pull with the president than ever before. Stone was most bitter: "The President, by his manner, invites the inference that he took this way to say to reactionaries, 'I, too, dislike this fellow's talk of TVAs on the Danube, and a quart of milk as a human right.' " FDR might be most savvy politically, "but how good a peace can he make surrounded by the men he has chosen to replace his old progressive lieutenants?" Prominent space was given to analysis by Robert La Follette, who declared that the New Deal was dead. The Wisconsin progressive claimed FDR's veto of the Smith-Connally antistrike law had been overridden because the president made no effort to rally enlightened forces. Wechsler began a several-months-long series documenting the exit of New Dealers from the federal bureaucracy and their replacement by mediocrities and careerists. Lerner touted Willkie as a possible presidential alternative. Similar discontent within the leadership of several CIO unions—most notably the UAW—was reported sympathetically.[11]

Their fury vented, *PM*'s editorialists began moving back into the president's corner. Stone admitted that Roosevelt was a puzzle. Would his next move be progressive or conservative? In early 1944 FDR began campaigning for reelection by citing his New Deal record. When he "explained" that "Dr. Win-the-War" had temporarily replaced "Dr. New Deal" the paper breathed a relieved sigh, asking, "Why didn't you tell us?" Wechsler polled labor leaders and found that a substantial majority would back the president for reelection. When House Speaker Alben Barkley briefly resigned after Roosevelt promised to veto a regressive tax package, Robertson ran a series denouncing the congressional revolt against the New Deal, claiming the "US People to Decide Historic Conflict Between FDR and Congress." The paper replayed congressional quarrels with the president since 1938, finding him on the progressive side of every argument.

Lerner sounded a warning note. Guard against hero worship; FDR was unpredictable. Still, the United States was more reactionary than "any country where the fascists are not openly in power." The military bureaucracy, the State Department, and business interests were powerful; labor was split and unable to defend itself against a postwar corporate crackdown. The "bitter and blind" press polluted public discourse. A new Congress, not a new president, was the main liberal agenda.

To further that objective, *PM* ran a new series exposing their old enemies in Congress and praising young New Dealers. Representative J. William Fulbright was considered an exemplary southerner because he had attacked Clare Boothe Luce's isolationism and Martin Dies's committee. Lyndon Johnson was excused for his reactionary voting record "because of sentiment in his district"(a credulous reporter was being deftly manipulated by a young master).

When Willkie lost in the Wisconsin primary in early April, the anti-Roosevelt revolt was over. Page 1 headlined "Roosevelt Must Run Again." The editors of

PM explained, "He must run because he alone still holds the loyalty and faith of the great mass of common people, both here and in other countries of the world."

Stone explained the reconciliation. "The President has made many compromises which we don't like and have quite properly criticized. That's our job. But his is to find that common denominator not merely for his reelection but for some minimum cooperation with Congress that can make some continuation of his policies possible."

The triumph of pro–New Deal Democrats in senatorial primaries convinced Wechsler that the "anti–New Deal tide is ebbing." As the nominating conventions of both parties neared, Carl Sandburg wrote, equating Roosevelt and Lincoln. Charges of dictator had been hurled at the Great Emancipator, too.[12]

Though dissatisfied with Roosevelt, *PM*'s editorialists had few alternatives. As part of a restive liberal-CIO coalition, the feisty tabloid sought to influence power, but no one in a Republican White House would be reading *PM*. Furthermore, Roosevelt's left turn as campaign time neared indicated he had not abandoned his supporters.

There is evidence that the impassioned denunciations of the previous year were limited to the editorial writers. Staff members Arthur Leipzig, Sally Winograd, and Louise Levitas do not remember ever feeling angry at FDR. For the bulk of *PM*'s liberal but less ideological staff, in 1943 as in 1940, "Roosevelt was It."[13]

The 1944 presidential election was strictly a good-guys-against-the-bad-guys affair. *PM* had ample time to build hatred for eventual nominee Thomas Dewey, whose nomination Lerner foresaw as early as January. As Republican governor of New York, he was a well-known entity. *PM* damned him for his equivocation on the Fair Employment Practices Committee; if FDR had similarly equivocated, the FEPC was still his creation. Dewey was portrayed as a narrow, ambitious politician. After Bernstein dubbed him the "Little Brain of Albany," John P. Lewis embraced the sobriquet as his own. Since he had supported much of the New Deal, Willkie's possible candidacy had been troublesome. Dewey, who had to mollify the Republican right wing to be nominated, allowed no praise of FDR to pass his lips. The relationship of the president to the Congress had deteriorated to the point that Republicans felt at ease making personal attacks on FDR. Wechsler thought the Republicans expected to lose; it explained the viciousness of their position. Attending the Republican National Convention for *PM*, Wechsler, Nathan Robertson, Eleanor Donahue, and Charles A. Michie described the dominance of Babbitt-like boosterism, small-town xenophobia, and hatred of the president. Wechsler found Republican delegates swamped by a "terrific gloom," nominating a man they did not even like. Lerner characterized the Republican ticket of Dewey and Ohio governor John Bricker as a slate of "two little men." *PM* treated them as contemptible. Roosevelt biographer James MacGregor Burns seems to agree. Although he claims, "All agreed that the two men made a strong ticket," he writes that Bricker's "mind had been compared to stellar space" and that Dewey "had acquired a reputation for being stiff, humorless, overbearing."[14]

One major issue remained to be settled at the Democratic National Convention. Would Wallace be retained? Although committed to Roosevelt regardless of the outcome, *PM* joined the liberal coalition actively campaigning to maintain the vice president. Wechsler was savvy enough to realize that Roosevelt's letter, which claimed he would have supported Wallace had he been an individual delegate, was not the endorsement the convention needed but was instead a friendly desertion. While the paper's writers tried to rally the convention, Marshall Field was one of many Wallace boosters on the convention floor. When the fight had been lost, *PM*'s owner received a gracious note from the vice president, thanking him for his support and asking Field to pass on to Lerner Wallace's gratitude for "his splendid support in *PM*. Max is a great encouragement to many people." Still Truman, whose selection had been predicted by Lerner the previous May, was greeted warmly as a "New Dealer." Given the close relationship between Stone and Robertson and Truman's Special Committee to Investigate the Defense Program in 1941, *PM*'s support was not surprising.[15]

By fall, *PM* was a Roosevelt campaign sheet. Lerner was on the board of directors of New York's CIO Political Action Committee, but the newspaper did not restrict its electioneering to editorials on page 2. *PM*'s artists were recruited to the campaign effort. After Dewey gave a Labor Day speech in which he tried to represent himself as a friend of unionism, he was pictured in a tuxedo and top hat; his stiff collar was drawn to resemble former president Hoover's. Mary Morris, who had moved to Los Angeles, did several features on "Hollywood for Roosevelt," accompanied by her own photographs of the stars; Cecelia Ager met Frank Sinatra as the young singer campaigned for the president. Jack McManus did double duty as film critic and organizer of a two-page daily spread for Roosevelt which included "Deweyisms," featuring noxious quotes from the Republican candidate and *PM*'s refutation of them. "The Champ's Corner" was decorated with a caricature of FDR in boxer trunks. Willkie had called Roosevelt "the Champ" when the utilities executive had been the challenger; now *PM* adopted the slogan as proof he would win. McManus began a month-long education drive in early October explaining to voters the mechanics of registration and voting. The paper did troubleshooting in districts heavily populated by new voters, quarrelling with Mayor La Guardia for not making the process simpler. (Of course La Guardia was campaigning for Roosevelt, too.)

The editorialists had a field day, particularly when Dewey decided to use red-baiting as his primary weapon. When he charged that Roosevelt had not prepared the nation for war, *PM* was ready with charts which illustrated how Republicans had voted against defense appropriations from 1939 to 1941. When Arthur Krock's description of how Roosevelt okayed the Democratic party's vice-presidential choice, "Clear it with Sidney" (that is, CIO/PAC leader, Sidney Hillman), was seized upon by Republican campaigners for thinly veiled antilabor and anti-Semitic innuendos, Wechsler denounced "the dirtiest political war since the Ku Klux Klan's crusade against Alfred E. Smith." Roosevelt must have been reading. In Boston to conclude his campaign, he remembered how in 1928, "all the bigots in those days were gunning for Al Smith"; now they were gunning for him.

PM fought with the opposition press. When the *Journal-American* banned the mention of Sinatra's name because he backed FDR, *PM* denounced censorship. For a couple of weeks, the *Daily News* printed a daily "GOP Battle Page." When this feature ceased, *PM* printed some suggested "Battle Pages" in which it published embarrassing Republican quotes, such as John Foster Dulles's suggestion that his party's senators not cooperate with FDR's peace plans if he were to be reelected.

A page 1 drawing of a grave marked "1929 to 1932" was marked "15th Anniversary of the Great Hoover Depression. DON'T LET IT HAPPEN AGAIN." The centerfold illustrated with charts, photographs, and drawings.

The best campaign material was, of course, President Roosevelt himself, who "disproved" the whisperings about his ill health by waging a great campaign. He began in September with the hilarious Fala speech, replying to charges that millions of dollars had been spent sending a battleship to retrieve his dog. "These Republican leaders have not been content with attacks on me, or my wife, or my sons. No, not content with that, they now include my little dog, Fala. Well of course, I don't resent attacks, and my family doesn't resent attacks, but Fala *does* resent them. . . . His Scotch soul was furious. He has not been the same dog since." All of Roosevelt's campaign speeches were printed prominently.

The only way to disprove the charges that he was dying was for FDR to campaign energetically. His full-day campaign tours of New York and Philadelphia were electrifying. Riding in an open car though pouring rain, he was greeted by millions of loving supporters in both cities. *PM* followed him through New York as Weegee, Irving Haberman, and Martin Harris took pictures of the massive throngs. Harris snapped a close-up of the thinner face with the still triumphant smile under the plain hat, drops of rain on the glasses. It is *the* classic photograph of the 1944 election, created for the newspaper most technically friendly to photography and most politically friendly to Roosevelt.

Wechsler again showed his skill as seer by predicting Roosevelt would win thirty-five states, with ninety-three electoral votes going to Dewey (Dewey actually won ninety-nine electoral votes). After the election, the page 1 photo of the president was headlined, "And Still the Champ." The paper was delighted that many Senate liberals were retained; with all the rejoicing, *PM* ignored the fact that, in the words of James MacGregor Burns, "Roosevelt's popular-vote margin of 3.6 million votes out of 48 million cast was the narrowest since Wilson's hairline victory over Hughes in 1916." Liberal thinkers should have been worried. The United States was about to defeat Germany, Japan was losing, the nation was riding a war boom, and yet the brilliant politician with the devoted personal following had his narrowest win. Being on the winning side, however, had its own rewards. Within days of the election, the Democratic National Committee sent John P. Lewis a letter thanking *PM* for its help.[16]

No repetition of the 1941 honeymoon followed; the editorialists had grown wary. The storm over Stettinius's appointments to State began in December, as was discussed in Chapter 3; *PM* writers were on guard to make sure Henry Wallace got the secretary of commerce post he wanted. By January, Wechsler wondered publicly if the president was still a New Dealer, inasmuch as conservatives were running the State Department and businessmen had taken charge throughout the federal bureaucracy.

Others were more romantic. Dorothy Parker accepted a guest assignment to cover the fourth-term inauguration. She reported, "The sky was still gray, but you could see the sun."

The universal shock Roosevelt's death caused his followers was powerfully conveyed by *PM*. A reprint of Martin Harris's 1944 picture with no text or headline filled page 1. Twenty-one of the twenty-four pages were devoted to FDR's passing. Whitman's "O Captain! My Captain!" and evocative photographs of mourning people congregating in Times Square conveyed the all-consuming sense of tragedy. The following day Lerner assessed Roosevelt's leadership, claiming, "He grew with each occasion." Guest writer Howard Fast extolled FDR with religious fervor: "If he were standing among us—and I for one believe he stands among us, more alive than ever," he would have no doubts about America's commitment to the war, international peace, and the New Deal. Wechsler led off a photographic retrospective with a paean to Roosevelt's "courage." No criticism of the thirty-second president would find its way into *PM*'s editorial columns again. His legend would be the yardstick by which living politicians would be measured; inevitably they fell short of the mark.[17]

The newspaper backed Roosevelt because he often appeared as the leader of the antifascist and egalitarian coalitions it was committed to. Criticism when the president seemed to abandon these movements, especially in 1943, could be vigorously expressed. For others on the left, that criticism was betrayal. The *New Masses* responded to *PM*'s attack on the class-friendship line of the Communist party by denouncing the newspaper's "baiting of Secretary Hull and the advocates of a fourth term for Roosevelt." (The magazine also imagined all sorts of implied attacks on the Soviet Union, which is surely a bizarre reading of its wartime coverage.) Communist party leader Earl Browder was equally incensed. He wrote to Eleanor Roosevelt to complain about excessive carping at her husband by the "Trotskyites" on *PM*. The first lady, we have seen, had her own reservations about her husband's politics. She was not about to share those doubts with Browder, but she vigorously defended the honesty of the young journalists at *PM* who voiced their disagreements with the Roosevelt administration.[18]

Any threats to forsake Roosevelt vanished at election time. The single-mindedness with which *PM* campaigned for FDR was as intense as any crusade in the paper's history, including its declaration of war in the spring of 1941.

The dichotomy between anguished dissent in non-election years and vigorous support at crunch time illustrates a problem for idealists then and now. How serious is "opposition" when it melts in the heat of practical politics? Lerner, like generations of leftist intellectuals before and after him, often mused about a labor or third party. The timing never seemed to be right.

More troubling was the tendency to romanticize. Roosevelt's "first class temperament"[19]—his charismatic jauntiness, warm speaking ability, expressive face, and giant laugh—allowed him, as Penn Kimball observed, to be a great performer. He mesmerized masses of people. Independent thinkers should have kept a wary eye, even at election time. Lerner had been right to warn of hero worship; after Roosevelt's death he joined all of *PM*'s writers in elaborate myth-making. It reflected both an understandable nostalgia and an equally understandable yearning for a great leader who would respond to the ideas and the principles of a broad liberal movement, a movement given voice by the fiercely partisan journalism of *PM*.

7 | Crusading in the Postwar World

"Lost causes, Mr. Payne, are the only ones worth fighting for."
—Senator Jefferson Smith, *Mr. Smith Goes to Washington*[1]

As World War II came to an end, *PM* writers confronted the future with joy, anxiety, and doubt. Unbounded joy greeted the defeat of the monstrous Nazi Reich by the victorious United Nations. Anxiety and doubt about whether that coalition could hold together were justified by rumblings between the powers even as the war progressed. Would the United States and the Soviet Union lead the world into an era of international understanding and peace? Was a Europe of both political and economic democracy possible? What would become of the survivors of Nazi genocide?

In the United States the death of President Roosevelt just as the war was ending left the political scene strewn with questions. Would President Truman prove faithful to the principles of the New Deal? Could he hold the liberal-labor coalition together against an increasingly partisan and hostile attack from the right? Would the great gains of labor in the 1930s hold against a Republican-corporate attack?

The newspaper itself faced major life questions. All staff members serving in the military had been guaranteed the right to return. Could the fragile economics of *PM* survive dozens of returning veterans? One veteran in particular might turn the whole applecart upside down. Ralph Ingersoll had left the newspaper wars to battle in the real thing in July 1942. There was never any doubt that *PM* was his paper. What would he think of it now? What changes would he want?

The tabloid had changed. War rationing had reduced its size on most days to twenty-four pages. Though the war was over, there was no thought of returning to the original thirty-two. *PM* was still losing money. John P. Lewis and Rae Weimer never considered approaching Marshall Field about expanding.

Lewis and Weimer had a realistic understanding of what the paper accomplished and what it did not. It was never able to deliver on Ingersoll's promise of supplying all the news that readers needed in a timely fashion. Handicapped by a small national staff and an almost nonexistent international one, *PM* had been deliberately excluded from the Associated Press, which "chose" the papers that could subscribe to its service. The AP, like the New York newsstand dealers in 1940, knew where the money was. The hostility of the McCormick-Patterson,

Hearst, and Scripps-Howard publishing groups to the liberal tabloid was reflected in the AP's refusal to grant *PM* a franchise.

When Marshall Field began publishing the *Chicago Sun* in 1942, the AP similarly denied Colonel McCormick's new rival access. Louis Weiss, acting for both Field publications, sued the Associated Press for antitrust violations. In late 1944, the Supreme Court upheld Field's case. As the war ended, the *Sun* and *PM* could finally anticipate making use of the nation's largest wire service.

Nonetheless, with a only a small bureau in Washington and stringers serving urban areas throughout the country, *PM* had not and could not challenge the resources of the news giants. No one would ever confuse it with "the newspaper of record."

What readers of *PM* could anticipate was thorough and sympathetic treatment of labor and of those confronting prejudice. The Washington bureau, particularly the canny Nathan Robertson, carefully untangled the intricacies of political debate and mapped the labyrinths of proposed legislation. News from abroad was culled from *PM* editorialists taking turns touring Europe, from United Press dispatches, and from independent left-liberal correspondents seeking a friendly forum. The photography and graphic art remained uniquely evocative; even in reduced form the consumer news provided an uncommon service. The paper continued to help veterans find jobs and aided every reader to locate radio and movie choices. But most *PM* readers probably read the paper for its commentary, or the left-liberal feeling that permeated all of the newspaper. Max Lerner continued to be the chief editorialist, but I. F. Stone, Alexander Uhl, Albert Deutsch (in his pioneering role as the daily press's first health and science columnist), Victor Bernstein, and two newcomers, Irving Brant and Saul Padover, all regularly produced critiques from a variety of liberal and radical perspectives. *PM*'s readers were more politically committed and more liberal than the average New York newspaper reader. A substantial majority were Jews. Despite *PM*'s justified reputation as labor's champion, the city's workers were far more likely to read the *News* or the *Mirror*. Lewis and Weimer knew who their audience was. In Weimer's words, "We had found our niche." The editors were dubious about how Ingersoll would now fit in.

It became obvious Ingersoll himself was not at all sure about his role. Discharged from the army in July 1945, *PM*'s founder was expected back on 1 September, after a honeymoon following a whirlwind romance and marriage. Marshall Field encouraged his return. Instead, after raiding the newspaper office for secretarial help, Ingersoll holed up in his house in Connecticut, dictating his second set of memoirs about his war experience, *Top Secret*, to Sally Winograd. (Typically, the book would be controversial. Ingersoll attacked the reputations of General Patton and Field Marshal Montgomery and extolled General Omar Bradley. His assessment would later be regarded as accurate, but Montgomery was furious. The book rode the publicity to the best-seller list.) As the months went by, the erstwhile guiding spirit of *PM* remained in exile. He did not return until January 1946.[2]

Back at the office, *PM*'s editorial writers approached postwar politics as a continuum of the antifascist perspective which made World War II its greatest crusade. Fascism represented the ultimate threat to democracy; the antifascist coalition was the basis for establishing a permanent peace and international understanding. Problems that were anticipated long before war's end—such as what kind of governments would emerge in the nations liberated from Nazi rule—were understood from the same perspective as the unexpected—such as the shocking dawn of the atomic age. In all cases *PM* advocated joint action by the victorious United Nations, a cooperative attitude toward the Soviet Union, establishment of broadly democratic governments in Europe, and a speedy end to colonial rule.

AGAINST THE NASCENT COLD WAR

From the moment the United States entered the war, *PM* writers assumed that their nation would have to play a major role in the reconstruction of Europe. In a December 1942 series, Gordon Cole asserted that without American help in Europe, "the decline of the West will become a reality." He thought that the American military would be forced to "police" Europe and foresaw that economic collapse in war-ravaged Europe would turn the need for American food into a political weapon.

Max Lerner urged an antifascist coalition of labor, peasant, and liberal intellectuals as the basis for postwar European governments. He and Victor Bernstein demanded that Nazis and Nazi collaborators be banned. The basis of U.S. actions had to be principle, not profit. As the Italian invasion reached Rome, Lerner and I. F. Stone insisted that the kind of government Allied military forces installed in Italy would test America's commitment to antifascist war aims. Lerner worried that British industry wanted a strong German trading partner and was pressuring Churchill to abandon principle. He found evidence in Churchill's reluctance to recognize de Gaulle as the leader of a future French government. Richard Yaffe interviewed Edward R. Murrow, returning home from London. Murrow reported, "What is worrying the people in Britain and France is whether or not Britain and the U.S.A. propose to build a crust over revolutionary Europe in an effort to maintain the traditional system." Britain's left-Labour leader and Lerner confidant, Harold Laski, wrote a *PM* exclusive accusing Churchill of playing the old power politics in Europe, attempting to win the United States to his approach by encouraging America's economic dominance. He charged that in Greece, Churchill "has killed the Atlantic Charter with his own hand." Alexander Uhl decided the trend in Europe defied Churchill's desires; Yugoslavia's resistance-based government proved traditional British foreign policy would fail. Lerner accused Churchill of wanting to use American aid as a bribe against the triumph of democracy. "Churchill fears social democracy in Europe more than he fears anything else." He advised British voters to defeat the Tories in the upcoming British elections. *PM* celebrated Labour's triumph in July 1945.[3]

PM equated resistance movements with democracy. The paper was a forceful advocate for a Yugoslavian government based on Tito's guerrilla fighters, a position made easier by British support for first King Michael, and then Sergei Mihailovich, both collaborators with fascism. The paper denounced State Department support for anti-Tito forces. In the light of recent events, the most tragic piece was Alexander Uhl's report that only Tito, as a minority Croat, could heal the ethnic tensions in Yugoslavia and unite its disparate peoples. When the new Belgian government ousted resistance leaders, Uhl warned "to destroy the Resistance is to destroy Europe's hope."

To *PM*'s writers, destroying that hope precisely defined British policy in Greece. They watched in shock and then in anger as British occupying forces campaigned for the restoration of yet another quisling king, disarmed the Greek resistance, placed a government in power loaded with men who had previously collaborated with Nazi occupation, and then sought to enforce that government's rule by engaging the resistance in a shooting war. London correspondent Frederick Kuh claimed Great Britain's "hysterical" policy resulted from "fear" of a "democratic regime." John P. Lewis reprinted the Atlantic Charter as a rebuke to British policy in Greece. *PM* explained British policy there as stemming from three reprehensible causes: forcing the continuation of Great Britain's traditional control over Greece, seeking compliant capitalist bankers who would favor British commercial interests, and securing the Mediterranean for its all-important commerce with its Indian colony. Roi Ottley landed a scoop by interviewing a Greek communist leader who was waging war against British troops. He attacked the new Greek government as controlled by fascists. When the British staged elections under their military control, an Alexander Uhl exclusive interview with Greek American newspapermen accused the British of rigging the vote. After the Labour party replaced the Churchill government in Great Britain but followed the same foreign policy, *PM* denounced it for betraying social democracy in Greece.[4]

Looking at the composition of the indigenous antifascist forces in the Balkans, *PM* predicted socialists and communists would be leading democratic governments there. Moscow correspondent Ralph Parker reported, "Europe Going Left," but insisted "Russia has no hand in it." Uhl answered his front-page question "Is Europe Going Communist?" by asserting that new governments were simply following New Deal trends in guaranteeing freedom from want. All the European left parties wanted to cooperate to create economic democracy. Without such policies, the industrialists, who were mostly fascists or fascist collaborators, would be rewarded in the reconstruction of Europe. Lerner was not afraid to define what he meant by "economic democracy": "The best impulses in Europe today are those that look toward a democracy which not only has democratic political forms, but a democratic political base. Americans are generally hesitant about calling this 'socialism,' but Europeans don't regard the word as a bogey. They want economic socialism, just as they want political democracy." Lerner saw socialism ascendant in Great Britain, Belgium, France, and Italy. CBS correspondent Howard K. Smith, writing in *PM* from Europe, reported that conflict there was between "people who live by investment and dividends from ownership and people who live by wages from labor." After Labour ousted the Tory government, Stone hoped that "socialist" Great Britain could mediate between the capitalist United States and communist Soviet Union so that the three Great Powers would support the leftward direction of Europe.

Uhl thought it natural that the left should lead the new Europe; it was the right that had failed to protect Europeans from Hitler. If the United States did not understand this, it would be isolated. But Stone and Max Werner looked at the past and came to a different conclusion. It was true many Eastern European governments were not democratic; the profascist sentiment that had produced the prewar governments was not eliminated yet. The most important task was the eradication of fascism; this the new Eastern European governments would accomplish. Stone found British policy hypocritical: British policy in Greece was as undemocratic as Russian policy in Eastern Europe, but the British supported fascists in the government.[5]

Clashes with the Soviet Union about the nature of governments in Eastern Europe focused most on Poland, where the issue arose earliest. Even before the Red Army crossed the Polish border, the Soviet government's diplomatic clashes with the London-based government-in-exile distressed *PM*, which recognized early that arguments about Poland could threaten American friendship with the USSR. When the Soviet Union executed two Polish Jewish socialists on charges of Nazi collaboration, Uhl worried that the charges might be unsubstantiated and that the action could divide American labor-left support for our Russian ally. The paper wasted little sympathy on the London-based government, which fully represented Poland's own ultranationalists. *PM*'s writers hoped for a new government combining London and Lublin Poles, a second government-in-exile which had Soviet backing. When it became clear the two groups could not cooperate, the paper leaned strongly toward the Lublin group. It was not anti-Soviet and had no quasifascists in its coalition.

PM was friendly to Soviet desires to move Polish borders westward. Stone used maps of Eastern Europe over the last hundred years to argue that Poland's borders had changed constantly and that Poland's most recent eastern boundary was the result of Western hostility to revolutionary Russia after World War I. Lerner and Irving Brant contended that it was natural for the Soviets to desire placing additional territory in the way of any future German invasion. The Red Army's arrest of sixteen Polish underground leaders affiliated with the London Poles on charges of anti-Soviet activity created doubt and fear in Frederick Kuh and Max Lerner, but the subsequent trial, convictions, and light sentences reassured them the Soviets were right and fully eliminated the legitimacy of the London Polish government, at least in the editorial pages of *PM*.

Irving Brant's trip to Poland reinforced *PM*'s friendliness to the postwar Polish government, which he saw fighting battles against still venal anti-Semitism and an "anti-Soviet psychosis." While Brant worried about laws preventing procapitalist parties from participating in parliamentary elections, Saul Padover believed that, given the virulent strains of fascism and anti-Semitism remaining in Poland, the government was as democratic as it could be. He congratulated the Soviet Union for not interfering in Poland's politics.

Reporting from Czechoslovakia followed a similar pattern. CBS correspondent Richard C. Hottlelet wrote, "Here in Czechoslovakia there is no doubt about democracy and freedom. They are not in danger. There is no question of any totalitarian system being set up here on any pretext." The Red Army was not interfering with the creation of a new government. Czech democratic procedures were more encouraging than in Poland: voters elected communists and socialists. Padover was not surprised. The British and French had betrayed Czechoslovakia to the Nazis; no wonder the people rejected capitalist parties.

In Romania, however, democracy was troublesome. Yalta called for "free and unfettered elections" in all formerly occupied nations. The Romanians were still fascistic. While understanding that the Soviet Union would not allow fascists in power, Padover was disturbed. "The Russians have everywhere made their choice—they have sacrificed scruples for power and embraced political evil for what they believe to be the ultimate good." He counseled "stock-taking" in light of their approach, but had no further advice.[6]

It was a painful dilemma. *PM* staff members tended to be romantic about the politics of resistance movements; after all, they had participated in the good fight despite the awesome power of the Wehrmacht. Nonetheless, the paradox of antifascists from Churchill to Stalin demonstrating themselves to be antidemocratic confronted the newspaper throughout Europe. If antifascism meant democracy, how could people choose fascism? What should antifascists do about it? *PM* might have reflected that the Germans themselves had elected Nazism. It was a quandary that had no easy solution, for *PM* in 1946 or for Eastern Europe now amid the "democratic" violence and race hatred left triumphant in the rubble of Stalinism.

Stalinism was not the term used by *PM* to describe the Soviet system. While carefully distinguishing its "economic democracy" from its lack of "political democracy," *PM* viewed the Soviet Union with friendship for leading the military battle against Hitler. The only way to prepare for peace was to continue American cooperation with the USSR in the postwar era. Lerner stressed Henry Wallace's view that friendship could be built on trading ties. He replied to the growing Republican and Hearst press claim that war with Russia was inevitable by demonstrating such a war to be impossible. Would the United States return its troops to Europe, to fight against the great Red Army which had just beaten the Wehrmacht? And for what cause? The Soviets had occupied Nazi lands and been as democratic in their occupation policy as Great Britain or the United States. War with the Soviet Union was a "daydream war" which equaled "the daydreams of the beaten Nazis. . . . War with Russia is impossible as well as lunatic." Victor Bernstein insisted that a de-Nazified, democratic Europe was in the interests of the Soviet Union and all of Europe.

The paper's insistence on tolerance and friendship for our great wartime ally has been a powerful ideological bludgeon for critics ever since. Were the writers blind, naive, or indifferent to Soviet dictatorial and expansionist policy?

In the earliest days of the cold war—in 1946 and 1947—many understood

Soviet action in Eastern Europe as protection against past and future antagonists. The Germans invaded Russia twice in this century; now the British seemed determined to restore fascists to power in Greece. Italian communists were being prevented by American occupiers from participating in interim local and national postwar governments, despite their leadership in the resistance. The earliest Soviet moves seemed to be defensive, especially given the sacrifices made by the Russian people during the war. In an argument over Poland, it seemed natural to defend the Soviet position instead of that of the London Polish group, which included extreme nationalists and anti-Semites.

Still, despite Lerner's call for democratic socialist forms, *PM*ers were willing to give the Soviets the benefit of the doubt; the early Czech coalition of communists and socialists provided hope for the restoration of prewar popular-front groupings. Again it is necessary to stress that this leniency was extended to everyone who fought fascism—MacArthur, de Gaulle, and Chaing Kai-shek included. As each component of the good fight displayed antidemocratic principles, it was reluctantly abandoned. As we shall see, by the end of 1947, Lerner and Padover were both denouncing Soviet practices in Eastern Europe.

No *PM* writer would ever endorse the developing cold war, for no matter what one thought of the Soviet Union's internal politics, only a cooperative relationship could produce world peace. As hostility between the two great victorious nations increased, most *PM* writers bemoaned the foreign policy of both.

PM fought for American-Soviet friendship against increasingly strident U.S. policy. Churchill's "iron curtain" speech was roundly condemned. The front-page headline "Churchill Calls for a New Anti-Russian Axis" was followed by Lerner's analysis that the "call for America to join Britain in an anti-Comintern pact . . . furnishes the Russians with a confirmation of some of their worst fears." This was the Churchill of the 1920s who praised Mussolini's effective anti-Leninism. "The one time he saw the danger whole can be matched by the many times he conjured up an unreal enemy and embraced the real enemy as friend and protector." Lerner thought the aim of the speech was to get the United States to bolster British imperialism. Americans would not buy it. Follow-up articles maintained that the speech "provides the basis for Soviet justification of expansion," and wondered, "Did Churchill catch Truman napping?" expressing a fervent hope that Truman was too stupid to know what Churchill would say. Stupidity would be better than the Briton's blatant bellicosity. Whether Churchill spoke for Truman, Lerner wrote, "*PM*'s position is unchanged. We never believed that Russian imperialism was out to conquer the world and we do not now believe it." Saul Padover agreed, finding Soviet policy to be isolationist, not imperialist, and rooted in the fear of invasion. Ralph Ingersoll, finally back at the paper and by now writing editorials once or twice a week, was not surprised at Soviet fear of American intentions. Once he had campaigned for more and better U.S. bomber planes for Europe; as record numbers arrived in 1946, Ingersoll knew they were not necessary for policing Germany. The inescapable conclusion was that they were aimed at the USSR.[7]

The planes were not alone. By the time Ingersoll editorialized about bomber planes aimed at the Soviet Union, it was clear to *PM* writers that the American monopoly on atomic weapons was being used to threaten our onetime ally.

Appropriately, *PM* devoted half of its paper to Hiroshima, beginning with the front-page headline "Atomic Bomb Opens New Era! It Will End All War—Or All Men." Irving Brant wanted nothing more to do with the bomb. "America must join and lead in a world-wide renunciation of this weapon by a world-wide renunciation and prevention of war." Weapons expert Willy Ley called the new armament "the biggest news of the century." John P. Lewis was cautiously hopeful. "There is no choice but to believe that men are good enough and wise enough not to misuse the knowledge that has come to them. For if they are not, it will mean the end of man."

It developed that men were not "good enough and wise enough." Although at first supportive of President Truman's decision to keep the weapon secret "from a lawless world," editorialists soon took another view. Atomic scientists quickly disabused *PM* of the notion of a secret. A group of the scientists led by Albert Einstein, Robert C. Urey, and J. Robert Oppenheimer called for international control of atomic energy and for banning its use in war. Einstein claimed FDR would never have used the bomb against Japan. *PM* wanted the UN to control atomic energy, but it was sympathetic to Soviet suspicion, given its minority status in the international organization. Lerner tried to walk a middle path between the Baruch plan, which allowed the U.S. to give the UN the bomb in stages while maintaining control each step of the way, and the Soviet position, which did not allow for inspection. He wanted the U.S. to cede control to the UN immediately but insisted that inspections would be necessary. Powers Moulton contributed a long, illustrated verse which endorsed the paper's view. It ended:

> *The moral is*
> *What God hath wrought*
> *To monkey with*
> *We hadn't ought*
> *But since we have*
> *We would be wiser*
> *Not to be*
> *An atom-miser.*

It is grimly amusing to read assurances that atomic testing in New Mexico was not radioactive. That canard lasted until Mark Gayn, reporting from Tokyo, recounted watching a film which showed the effects of radiation on people in Hiroshima and Nagasaki.

By October 1945, it was apparent to *PM* that Truman was using the bomb to challenge Soviet policy in Eastern Europe. Under the headline "We'll Hold A-Bomb as Political Weapon," Elizabeth Donahue wrote:

Official Washington is speechless for once in the face of the climactic agreement among three national leaders [of the U.S., Great Britain, and Canada] that they could hold the elusive "secret" of the atomic bomb as a lever to coerce international good will. . . . Careful analysis of the White House statement caused the inescapable conclusion that Britain and the USA view the bomb as their political and military weapon to wring special commitments from Russia.

After the press (ironically including *PM*) reported that atomic testing on Bikini atoll was a scientific wonder, Saul Padover wrote:

It is now clear that (*a*) while the gentlemen talk peace, we are preparing for war; that (*b*) the Bikini test is not strictly a scientific experiment, but a curtain raiser for an ultimate world conflict; that (*c*) there is a danger that atomic energy, which can be a blessing to mankind in providing the cheapest possible fuel and power, will fall into the hand of the monopolists of destruction.[8]

The "monopolists of destruction" seemed increasingly to include the United States government.

In the early days of the cold war, *PM* analysts blamed Great Britain for establishing anti-Soviet policy. This was rooted in centuries of imperialist thinking, which sought to dominate Europe and perpetuate colonial possessions in Asia and Africa. *PM* believed the liberation ideology of World War II meant an end to all colonial empires. The paper campaigned tirelessly for independence for India, Dutch Indonesia, French Indochina, French Arabia, and the American Philippines. If revolutionaries were communists, as in Vietnam or the Philippines, their causes were no less legitimate. One story predicted, "A lot of people seem destined to be killed in Indo-China," but no one on *PM* could have foreseen how true that would turn out to be. Lerner was particularly revolted by French and British socialists who fought to maintain their nations' colonial empires. "The duty of holding empire comes first, and takes priority over the duty of extending socialism. . . . You cannot enter the house of socialism by the murderous gateway of imperialism."[9]

While Great Britain was implicated, it was American policy that seemed hell-bent on support for Chiang Kai-shek, who found that the defeat of Japan enabled him to concentrate even more fire on the Chinese Red Army than during wartime. Several times in 1945 and 1946, Chiang opened war on Mao's forces, despite that group's consistent call for broad coalition government. *PM* contrasted Chiang's corrupt dictatorial rule with agrarian reform, mass education, and town-meeting style democracy in Red Army–held areas. The paper exposed Koumintang use of Japanese puppet troops to attack the Communists. When Chiang prevailed on his American ally to fly troops to Manchuria in order to fight Mao's forces, the front page sent a "Memo to Honorable Harry S. Truman, Commander in Chief: What Are American Troops Doing in the Middle of the Chinese Civil War?" The paper repeatedly claimed that the issue was not Chiang against communism so much as it was Chiang against "democratic forces there."[10]

Elliot Roosevelt's memoir of his father accused Churchill of wanting to use American power to bolster British imperialism. *Look* had the serialization rights, but *PM* summarized extensively. Nonetheless Lerner's review of the book replied not only to *As He Saw It*, but to much of *PM*'s writing on the nascent cold war. It was the United States that emerged as the most economically and militarily powerful nation after World War II. Talk of Truman's mindless following of British imperialism ignored American motives in anti-Soviet hostility. What Truman feared in Russia was "the spread of radical ideas all over the world," which would empower labor in the United States. That fear was leading to a deplorable result. "It would be tragic folly if we continued to hand to the Russians the initiative in supporting the cause of the masses of the people against the oligarchies." This allowed the Soviets to become the democrats, even though "they ignore the democratic form." Saul Padover agreed. He condemned the 44 percent of the budget being spent in both the U.S. and USSR for military purposes and demanded a reversal of American policy. Only by meeting the Soviet Union's "vigorous . . . opposition to colonialism, racism, anti-Semitism, imperialism, clericalism and landlordism" with support for "social economic democracy" could we prevail.

Unfortunately, powerful forces in the United States had no interest in progressive foreign policy. In an editorial called "The Road to Militarism," Lerner cited a large war budget, peacetime conscription, "using displays of naval power as an instrument of national policy," and the permanent institutionalization of the Joint Chiefs of Staff as creating a dangerous new grouping. "The partnership between a military caste and an industrial caste spelled fascism in Japan and Germany both. Can it spell anything less in America?" Lerner thought a new American "empire" was being built. Too subtle for colonial possessions, American imperialists used food and loans to coerce policy changes in weaker nations. Military bases springing up all over the world and monopoly control of the atomic bomb provided the muscle behind American policy.

THE RETURN OF LABOR'S CHAMPION

While *PM* frequently took President Truman to task for not following a mythologized Rooseveltian vision of international amity, his foreign policy during his first year in office seemed to move inconsistently from hostility to the Soviets to expressions of friendship. It was in domestic politics that Truman was most severely criticized. There Truman's inability to further labor's postwar objectives, and indeed his spring 1946 role as labor's antagonist, turned the newspaper against him.

The hostility was not immediate. Analyses by Stone and Wechsler after Truman's first five days, Lerner after ten days, Robertson after six weeks, and Stone again after five months were all positive. The writers thought the new president was committed to the New Deal; they cited his endorsement of full-employment and unemployment-compensation legislation as proof.

By late September 1945, the honeymoon was over. Congressional opposition to the two labor measures were destroying them. *PM* faulted Truman for failing to play presidential power politics effectively. Given FDR's problems with Congress after 1938, this analysis seems unfair. But Robertson was alarmed by more than ineffectiveness. Claiming "Liberals Worried by Truman's Recent Moves," Robertson attacked the president for appointing political hacks, botching anti-fascist reformation in Japan, failing to combat price inflation, and for not battling for unemployment compensation.

Most of the blame was parceled out to Congress. Robertson was bitter:

> The same Congress and the same [Ways and Means] Committee which have permitted industry to roll up $47,000,000,000 in profits during the war, that have voted billions for manufacturers whose war contracts are cancelled, that have given industry a right to draw refunds of $60,000,000,000 of war taxes to recoup losses during the next two years—now have flatly refused to provide a single penny for the war worker who is discharged when war contracts are cancelled. . . . This is the chance for the President to show *his* true colors and his leadership.

Lerner and the entire Washington bureau repeatedly faulted Truman for failing to press Congress on behalf of labor.[11]

In December, as Ingersoll was preparing to return to his newspaper, he was able to secure an appointment for himself, Lewis, and Lerner to meet the president. The meeting did not inspire the threesome with confidence. Lerner wrote to Wechsler, then doing his own army stint, "We were even more dismayed than we had expected to be."[12]

The major strike wave of 1945–1946 turned dismay to outrage.

Many feared that racial and labor strife would return to Detroit. Wilbur Baldinger analyzed conditions there. The end of FEPC-supervised hiring seemed to bode ill for white/black relations now that the defense industry was eliminating jobs. A quarter of a million had already been laid off. Housing throughout the city was inadequate and run-down. Fortunately, the UAW was "Detroit's Most Dynamic Force" and perhaps a think tank for the nation. The union's plans for reconversion "will do much to determine the pattern of labor relations and peace production all over the country." Once again, Walter Reuther was singled out for particular approbation.[13]

It was a brief step from the intimation of labor trouble ahead in Detroit and the explosive contract impasse between the UAW and General Motors that ushered in the great strike wave of 1946. The impasse, which Baldinger began covering in mid-October 1945, occupied center stage at *PM* for months. The automaker seemed to be provoking a strike, eager to test labor's strength after FDR's death and the war's conclusion. The union (and *PM*) countered with economic analysis that showed record profits enabling corporations to handle major wage increases without raising prices. Reuther and CIO President Murray, like GM, saw this struggle as setting a pattern for the nation. They called for national uniform wage increases throughout major industry; more radically, they wanted labor to fight against price increases. The AFL and John L. Lewis refused to go along with the broader social vision of the CIO leaders. *PM* emphatically endorsed the CIO view and the subsequent strikes. Baldinger's headlines made clear where *PM* stood: "GM Opens Undeclared War on Labor"; "GM Fiddles While Workers Vote on Strike"; "GM Has Choice of Peace or War after Getting Final UAW Briefs Today"; "Strike Appears Inevitable as GM Ignores UAW Case." The paper prepared charts to illustrate the union case against GM. Nathan Robertson, using figures supplied by GM and Chrysler to the federal government, proved that the companies had enjoyed huge war profits. Baldinger uncovered a document written to stockholders which argued for an attack on the UAW.

The strike itself was covered in daily articles between 21 November 1945 and mid-March 1946. For the first several weeks they were written by Baldinger; eventually the paper began using Associated Press or United Press wire stories. Max Lerner was enamored of UAW strategy and its political orientation:

> By insisting on the links between wages and profits, wages and prices, wages and full employment, the auto union is in effect declaring that the nation's economy is indivisible. . . . Labor is leaving behind it the narrow trade unionism of the past. . . . What we see of the Big Corporate mentality as shown by GM's Wilson and others reveal them as men lost in the dusk of an irresponsible capitalism, blind in their strength, arrogant in their anti-union passion; and in their blindness and arrogance, tearing down the pillars of their own house of power.

As an increasingly hostile Congress responded to the strikes with antilabor legislation, *PM* expected President Truman to defend the union. His first responses were inconsistent, saying the workers deserved raises but warning the American people that sharp price increases would result if the wage demands were met. Nathan Robertson exhorted Truman to back the GM strike, and Lerner wrote that the president "blundered" by not consulting with labor before talking publicly. The paper printed in full Philip Murray's response to industry and congressional critics: "Industry can raise wages 24 percent and still earn more than twice the take home profits it did before the war"; the corporate threat of major price increases was an industry "hold-up" of taxpayers and consumers. John Moutoux noted caustically that antilabor bills were rushed to the White House for Truman's signature while the full-employment and unemployment-compensation bills were stalled in committee. When Truman proposed a commission to investigate the GM strike, the UAW immediately accepted. Lerner warned GM that if the corporation's executives failed to respond positively, "they stand convicted before the people of what the UAW has been accusing them all along: of an arrogant sense of power and contempt of the national welfare." But Baldinger correctly predicted that same day that GM would decline the suggestion. After Truman ignored this reaction, Lerner was worried. "It would be a grave thing if the only group that Truman chose to fight hard was labor."

By early January the United Electrical Workers were out, the United Steel Workers were about to strike United States Steel, Western Union employees walked picket lines in New York, and a host of smaller strikes were cramming *PM*'s news and picture columns. In all cases, the unions were claiming their needs had been put on hold during the war; they now sought major wage increases warranted by record wartime profits. Mediation boards were recommending hefty increases in all the major strike areas, but the corporations were rejecting their suggestions. Industry refused to budge off of its initial bargaining position. Max Lerner found labor's arguments compelling. Industry spokesmen and cynical politicians, he wrote, were deliberately fomenting strikes to test labor's strength. A strike was "a final resort in an unequal struggle," and workers were being forced to act by deliberate provocations. "We are moving back to the law of the economic jungle." But Ralph Ingersoll thought the strike wave was a positive expression of American democracy. "This 'unrest' feels good to me," he confided.

As the confrontations multiplied, *PM*'s coverage became increasingly dramatic. Shirley Katzander did a graphic exposé of the "notorious" working conditions at meat-packing plants, describing in detail numerous skin diseases and the high accident rate suffered by workers. A page 1 photograph showed how a "plainclothes cop clubs a helmeted picket wearing service stripes as Los Angeles turns back the clock to the violent old days," under the headline, "Slugging of Pickets Begins in Los Angeles."

PM's best scoop came during the Western Union strike. Under the headline, "I Was a Strike Breaker at Western Union," Robin Lord told her own story. Hired during October fresh from her move to New York from the Midwest (she wondered if the company was deliberately bringing in workers from outside New York to prepare for a strike), she went in one day to see what work was like during the walkout. She found the scabs frightened, surrounded paramilitary-style by supervisors. Cots were placed in the room so no one would have to leave; the strikebreakers did extra work because there was nothing else to do. She pretended she was ill so that she could depart and decided to tell her story to *PM* because she had liked only that paper's coverage of the strike. To a reader of the paper, it seemed more than coincidental when Western Union's resistance collapsed just four days later and the union claimed victory.

GM's tough stand against labor was imitated by U.S. Steel, which similarly ignored union demands, refused to open its books (the unions at both firms were confident the financial data would reveal record profits), and rejected a compromise suggested by President Truman. Moutoux repeated Philip Murray's attack on a "Big Business Plot." Baldinger thought GM would welcome a U.S. Steel strike, since its competitors would be unable to produce without its basic raw material. Lerner was sure of the company's motives.

> It is transparent that their decision was based . . . on considerations of power. They are forcing a showdown . . . not only with labor in the steel industry. It is with labor throughout the American economy. And in the end it is a showdown with the American government and the American people.

U.S. Steel, Lerner asserted, wanted to return to its victory in 1919, when steelworkers' wages fell from five dollars to three dollars a day. This time labor had led the way, showing it would compromise, and industry was slamming a door in a "united front of industrial reaction. . . . The Marxian theory of class revolution turned topsy-turvy, the pyramid standing on its head." These industrial policymakers were "the gravediggers of America."

I. F. Stone knew how to stop the corporate attack. Under the page 1 headline "How to End All the Big Strikes; *PM*'s Plan: Stop Subsidizing Economic Sabotage by Industry," Stone blamed the confrontational stance by business on the 1942 "carryback" tax policy that protected industry against the "uncertainties of war production." "This is the $20,000,000,000 'kitty' on which US Steel and General Motors and other industrial recalcitrants can draw if they fail to make 'normal' profits this year because of strikes." Why should they settle? "They have a chance to break the labor movement at treasury's expense." He advocated repealing the 1942 war rules.

Four days later, he went further. In advising President Truman on "How to Make Steel Surrender," he suggested three presidential letters. One would appoint *PM* hero Henry Kaiser to head all government-owned or -controlled steel manufacturing, which Stone estimated to be 10 percent of the industry. This group would, of course, settle with the United Steel Workers and speed production. The second letter would direct the secretary of the treasury to kill all bank loans or credit to U.S. Steel, and the third would direct Attorney General Tom Clark to investigate industry to see if it was practicing

> a conspiracy under the Civil Rights Act to deprive American citizens of their rights, in this case . . . collective bargaining under the Wagner Act. . . . Truman and his advisors have encouraged US Steel to defy the country by acting like a group of weaklings who do not know what they want or where they are going.

A steel strike would hit industrial production everywhere, causing massive unemployment. "Send those letters and make steel surrender."

Unfortunately, it was Truman, not Stone, who made government policy. Wechsler (back from his stint in the army) had just attacked the president's "failure to put heat on corporations," which he attributed to having "no labor-industry strategy" and a "mild, muddled Administration policy." *PM* grew more impatient with the president. After U.S. Steel announced a major price increase, the page 1 headline read "Truman Silent—Big Steel Grows Bolder." Wechsler commented:

> Yesterday marked the 13th day of Steel's resistance, the 20th of GM's holdout. . . . Steel and General Motors were no longer just defending themselves; they were taking the offensive. . . . The President ignored the challenge. . . . The real issue was whether price control would be destroyed as industry's price for industrial peace. . . . Will U.S. Steel and General Motors continue their defiance of governmental recommendations regardless of the cost to the country? . . . Will they be allowed to blow up the nation's anti-inflation machinery?

Two weeks later, Wechsler had still less confidence in Truman. "With the steel strike in its fourth week and with White House announcements still 'postponed,' the picture of conflict and confusion inside the Administration was reaching perilous proportions." He feared labor's worst scenario: abandoned price controls and new wage controls.

Though action from the White House continued to disappoint, the labor battles were generally won with 18 percent wage increases for the unions in auto, steel, electric, Western Union, and in some unusual arenas, such as the walkout of tugboat crews, an action *PM* covered with many features and wonderful photographs. The struggle to maintain price levels, however, was abandoned.[14]

Municipal workers were hardly about to win such heady increases, but Mayor O'Dwyer, though a much more traditional politician than his predecessor, was not so hell-bent on confronting city labor's organizing efforts. He met with the fledgling Federation of State, County, and Municipal Employees local organizing in New York City and appointed a fact-finding board which would find most of the TWU's new contract demands entirely reasonable. During the presettlement posturing between the city and the TWU, Ingersoll finally came out forthrightly for that union's and all public employee unions' right to strike. *PM* replied at length to attacks on the TWU and Quill in the other city papers.[15]

PM thought labor had been the winner in the postwar battles—a marked difference over events after World War I. Wages were up and unionism was intact, but Gordon Cole warned, "The cards are stacked against the people in Congress."

When John L. Lewis prepared to lead his men in the first postwar strike in the coalfields, *PM* was firmly in the UMW's corner, while expressing its dislike for the union president. Lerner, looking wistfully across the sea to Great Britain, called for permanent nationalization of the mines, saying coal was profitable only in wartime. Ingersoll agreed with Lerner's proposal after Truman seized the mines to end the strike. One day the paper looked mildly schizophrenic. Gordon Cole, calling Lewis a "czar" and comparing him to Hitler, nonetheless supported the miners' grievances but detailed violence directed at union dissenters. Meanwhile Hy Engel attacked the rest of the press because it "Blasts Lewis as No. 1 Issue; Blandly Ignores Real Mine Evils."[16]

The railroad strike of May 1946 was the last great labor campaign for Ingersoll's *PM*. The paper turned over its first eleven pages to the issue on the first day of the strike, under the page 1 headline, "US Paralyzed." Ingersoll wrote in support of the strikers, their negotiations and demands were explicated, and the history of the grievances dating to before the war was told. Features on stranded commuters and the lives of individual strikers were accompanied by photographs. The paper responded to "Truman Cracks Down on Train Strikes" with "The R.R. Workers' Side." Ingersoll lectured Truman that FDR would never have publicly supported the operators. Montana senator Murray's speech in the workers' defense was printed in full. Three *PM* photographers had the best journalism of that day's paper, however, with photo captions of thirteen unionists who told their own stories and explained the strike. Wechsler noted, "The railway labor strike has provoked the greatest crisis in relations between the White House and organized labor since the Republican Party was driven out of power"; he warned of repercussions in the 1946 and 1948 elections.

Ambivalent about the president for many months, *PM* now turned its guns on him. Godal's cartoon showed figures of "Antilabor Sentiment" and "Robber Barons" with Truman over a caption reading "United We Stand." Ingersoll thought the antilabor legislation passed by the House made the "democratic forces" appear hopeless, and he could not believe it.

> No man can deny that what happened over Sunday is the work of men who have lost their faith in democracy, men who are cynically ready to abandon it. They are revealed as seeking a showdown with progressive democracy. I think they'll get it— and lose.

Saul Padover called Truman's oratory "a great Republican speech. . . . It leaves a lingering memory of bad taste and unfairness." It was "morally disturbing" to blame the weaker side against the press-backed bosses. A true friend of labor would have outlined the railroad men's grievances and talked about the railroad owners' life-style. Nathan Robertson reported with grim satisfaction that the railroad brotherhoods would spend every last cent of the union reserve fund to beat Truman.

When Truman summoned a joint session of Congress to demand a law to draft the railroad men (and other strikers he designated as threatening the national interest) and to enforce that draft and railroad peace with troops, *PM* headlined a response by Max Lerner as "An Appeal to Reason: A Program to Save America from Truman's Plan for Military Fascism." Inside, Lerner wrote: "The Nation is caught in a hysteria over the labor crisis. The President, incapable of handling labor relations through the regular channels, has asked Congress for a blank check which would give him a dictator's life and death power over American labor." The representatives cheered Truman as if he were attacking a foreign enemy. Instead of cheers, the Truman bill

> deserves the unmitigated opposition of every American who cares for freedom. . . . The President's hysterical performance this weekend is no happy augury of how he could be trusted to keep his head in the future. . . . You can't head a nation in peacetime by laying hold of a military remedy every time you find it hard to solve a civilian problem.

He ended by calling for permanent nationalization of the railroads and mines. Padover endorsed this solution the next day, while warning of a residue of labor hatred in the country, but the paper was relieved to report that Congress and Truman himself seemed to be abandoning the proposal.

Managing editor John P. Lewis, who rarely wrote, now embarked on a five-part series based on the confidential minutes of the railroad brotherhoods, which showed Truman to be erratic, impulsive, and disposed to confrontation in his negotiations with the union. He stopped mediating after having a friendly session with the unionists; at his next session he smashed his fist down on the table and demanded the union accept a sixteen-cent increase. The president promised railroad concessions and new negotiations if the unions waited for five days; though the unions complied, neither promise materialized. He called off official negotiations to settle the strike—though the union had told him it would offer the necessary concessions there—in order to make his frenzied appearance before Congress. It was a damning picture, meticulously detailed in Lewis's careful way rather than in the dramatic rhetoric of Wechsler, Stone, or Lerner. All the more sobering was the conclusion that "President Truman's concern was not so much to save or spare the country from the effects of a railroad strike as to establish himself as a dictatorial master of American labor for the remainder of his term in the White House." Roosevelt, Lewis claimed, had settled the 1943 railroad strike fairly; his formula—"a maximum of fairness,"—was lacking from his successor's attitude toward labor.[17]

PM would continue to back labor and to celebrate its victories, as in the maritime strikes of August through October, and the truck strike of September, but Lewis, like Ingersoll before him, had identified the problem. It was Truman, not Roosevelt, in the White House. When Sidney Hillman died in July, John K. Weiss worried that labor could never replace his political savvy and influence. The attitudes that *PM* staffers shared—that "the truth is on labor's side"—was no longer the popular consensus in the nation.[18]

PM's STAFF IN CRISIS

Meanwhile, *PM* went through a mini–labor crisis of its own, surely the nastiest and most well publicized confrontation in its history. At its root were the tangled motivations of two ambitious men.

James Wechsler ran the Washington bureau until his induction into the army in January 1945. Unlike the earlier round of draftees, Wechsler attempted to stall the army; when he failed, he seems to have entertained the notion that his service selection was caused by factional enemies at *PM*, including John P. Lewis. Before he left, he had already demanded that Lewis fire I. F. Stone for writing too friendly a piece about Cordell Hull and U.S. North Africa policy. A review of that material indicates that generally Wechsler and Stone argued a similar critical position; on this occasion Wechsler was afraid that Stone's stance undercut his own. Lewis had defended Stone's independence, citing the latter's numerous contributions to the paper. He tried to mollify Wechsler by admitting that Stone could be personally "difficult" though the editor's own calm temperament was ruffled when Wechsler referred to Rae Weimer as "brainless."

Wechsler and Ingersoll both returned to the paper in January 1946. Each had to cope with changes which undercut his previous power at the tabloid. Wechsler had left two political allies at *PM*, men who agreed that "communism" was making sneaking attempts to control the paper and were warily watchful for such conspiracy. Through Wechsler's influence, both men had achieved leading positions. Harold Lavine had filled in for Rae Weimer as assistant managing editor when the latter had broken a leg; Arnold Beichman had become city editor. But Lavine had been drafted when Wechsler was inducted; he did not return. Beichman was fired, ostensibly for economic reasons; actually, he was a victim of a secret study.

While Ingersoll bided his time in the fall of 1945, he asked executive secretary Virginia Schoales to evaluate the staff for him. Her memo rated everyone from A to F. There were few superlatives and few outright failures. Beichman came close to the latter. She thought he was a poor writer and a D as an editor. She believed his incessant factionalizing alienated the reporters he worked with.

Ingersoll decided to come back with as big a splash as he could. He wrote a long letter to Marshall Field, excoriating their newspaper. It is a fascinating letter because it is both insightful and blind at the same time. The insight is that the tabloid was more of a liberal crusading sheet than a newspaper; Ingersoll thought *PM* had become ideologically predictable. The blindness, of course, is that the paper had become that way largely at Ingersoll's insistence. A reader today is struck by how much the Ingersoll of 1946 is attacking the Ingersoll of 1938–1942.

To change the paper, Ingersoll wanted to make major staff changes. He claimed that this was because there was too much staff incompetence; it is logical to infer that he wanted to bring in a new group of "Ingersoll" loyalists to challenge the Lewis-Weimer organization which had maintained *PM* for three years. He suspected he had been usurped. Lerner's presence as editorialist seemed to him a personal affront, yet Lerner's editorials had become so fully identified with *PM*'s reputation that it was impossible to eliminate the columnist. He began a flurry of "economy" firings; Lewis reminded him gently that it seemed ludicrous to fire dozens of people for financial reasons before embarking on a major expansion.

Undeterred, Ingersoll homed in on the Washington bureau, staffed almost entirely by veteran Nathan Robertson and young reporters trained by Wechsler. Stone and Alexander Uhl, who worked out of Washington, were not part of the bureau, since they were considered editorial writers. Claiming that *PM* did not need many Capital reporters—because it could rely on the Washington staff of the *Chicago Sun*—Ingersoll decided to fire three protégés of Wechsler. Not only did Wechsler not agree, he claimed that the Washington bureau had been incompetent during his stay in the army. To repair morale, he wanted to raise the wages of some of his staff members.

Lewis tried vainly to head off a confrontation, warning Ingersoll that to antagonize Wechsler unnecessarily would not only deprive *PM* of Wechsler's talent but would probably embroil the paper again in public communist/anticommunist turmoil. Ingersoll steamed along heedlessly. In a meeting with Wechsler, he once again demanded the three be fired. Wechsler thought he was being stripped of power. (He was probably right.) He made a ludicrous demand of his own: that

Stone and Uhl be fired instead. Lewis was at least able to offer a compromise: he offered the three journalists jobs in the New York office. Wechsler advised the three to seek Newspaper Guild protection. Jack McManus represented them at the grievance hearing; the arbitrator ruled there was nothing wrong with their transfer. The three reporters decided to leave *PM*.

It was at this point that Wechsler's behavior became as destructive as Ingersoll's and proved John P. Lewis to be prescient. He arranged for the rest of the Washington staff to resign and issued a press release, picked up for major stories in *Editor and Publisher* and the *New York Times*, which claimed that the root of the quarrel lay in Ingersoll's susceptibility to communist domination. The Washington staff was leaving because *PM* had become too gullible about the Soviet Union and communism. Almost simultaneously, the *New Leader*, a violently anticommunist socialist journal, printed an attack on communist subversion at *PM* by "Karl Collins." It was obvious to many at the paper that Kenneth Crawford was using an alias to open old wounds. "Collins" accused O'Connor, McManus, Uhl, and Stone of being party-liners. Ironies abounded: McManus had defended the Washington writers; Stone's North Africa analysis, which embarrassed Wechsler, was more in agreement with Crawford's when the latter exited from the paper.

The charges were just not true. Uhl was simultaneously criticizing the Soviet Union in *PM* for vetoing the UN's mild action against Franco. Stone and O'Connor, whatever their politics, were not following anyone's discipline, and had already demonstrated themselves to be great assets. Creekmore Fath, reading the tabloid from the White House, made the same discovery as thousands of *PM* readers: "Stone was a unique reporter. He had all the necessities to make him the best." Any reader of *PM* must agree. As Rae Weimer says, "Izzy knew Washington better than anyone else. . . . He was always coming up with material marked 'Confidential.' " McManus's duties as radio-page editor and movie critic hardly portended communist subversion. The principal editorial voice at *PM* was Lerner's. Though arguing forcefully for peaceful relations with the USSR, he was no "Stalinist"; nor would anyone make such a claim. But the broad brush of *PM*'s opponents still found it convenient to paint the paper red, just as the July 1940 leaflet had identified Wechsler as one of the communists plotting for control. At any rate, Wechsler would shortly find his exit professionally fruitful. Within six months, he would become editor of the *New York Post*.[19]

PALESTINE

At the very moment Wechsler was demanding Stone's ouster, Izzy was not in Washington or even in the country to defend himself. He was in the midst of a conspiratorial assignment—one that had nothing whatever to do with communism but that reflected his newspaper's passionate interest in the survivors of the Holocaust.

After the war, bureaucratic stupidity or political insensitivity to the condition of the remaining European Jews incensed *PM* staffers. Bernstein reported furiously that General Eisenhower had demanded eleven weeks before that Jewish refugees be given special treatment, but that nothing happened. John P. Lewis claimed that while U.S. and British bureaucrats "investigated" the plight of the refugees, more of them were dying. Lerner demanded that the United Nations Refugee Relief Administration fire British General Sir Frederick E. Morgan, who thought there was a Jewish "conspiracy" to leave Europe. *PM* celebrated his resignation the next day. Stone believed Morgan's statement was testimony to British panic in the face of a political situation they neither understood nor had solutions for. Ralph Ingersoll's first strong editorial on his return from Europe was an attack on UNRRA administrator Herbert Lehman, who rehired Morgan. Bernstein was incredulous that U.S. Army policy forbade Polish Jews from traveling to the American Zone in Germany. When some of these unfortunates were allowed entry, Bernstein accused the U.S. Army of mistreating them.

Palestine emerged as a center of attention early. *PM* reported the desires of Palestinian Jews to fight against Hitler in their own division of the British army. The British, anxious to avoid upsetting the Arabs under their colonial purview, spurned these desires, earning *PM*'s contempt. The paper continued to press for such an army. When the British claimed they had no equipment to spare for the Zionists in Palestine, Bernstein called for Lend-Lease Aid to provide it. He wrote that British imperialism was making Arabs friendly to the Axis, thus imperiling Jews. American policy in North Africa also appeared to be aimed at appeasing Arab opinion, according to Stone, who attacked the failure of the American occupiers to repeal the Nuremburg racial-purity laws. The policy was especially ridiculous and reprehensible, he argued, because Arabs did not mind such a repeal. When the laws were finally repealed, the U.S.-installed Giroud regime did not grant Algerian Jews citizenship.

As news of Nazi genocide and the lack of a safe port for Jewish refugees became widespread, *PM* embraced the campaign to open Palestine to Jewish emigration, attacking State Department officials and the *New York Times* for their opposition. When equality for the Jews of Algeria was legally established, Stone claimed it proved the Arabs were not anti-Jewish. They had not revolted in North Africa, and they would not if the Jews came to Palestine. The paper deplored Stern Gang terrorism in Palestine and in Great Britain, but it consistently blamed such terrorism on the British white paper which cut off Jewish emigration to Palestine. Alexander Uhl reported bitterly as the United Nations gathered in San Francisco that Arab states were given seats while the Zionists were called "consultants."

President Truman was applauded for pressuring Great Britain to allow Jewish emigration. Frederick Kuh broke a story on page 1 that the British had arrived at a new solution: "British Propose to Send 50,000 Jews to Algeria." Lerner dubbed this policy "Mr. Atlee's Ghetto—and America's" and demanded U.S. and British financing for massive Jewish immigration to Palestine as the only way to "burn away the moral blindness and the political cowardice."

When European Jews forced the issue by beginning that immigration, *PM* gave the effort strong support. John P. Lewis reminded Great Britain that an open door to Palestine might have saved thousands or even millions of Europe's Jews. From Warsaw, Irving Brant wrote that the remaining Polish Jews desperately needed Palestine.

Stone made the first of several trips to the "promised land," proclaiming no Jewish/Arab tensions but cautioning that "Arabs Friendly to Jews Fear Own Extremists." He attacked British delay, saying "Palestine has had enough of 'inquiries.'" For the European Jews, it was either go to Palestine or "Mars, via the Pearly Gates." He repeated what was already becoming a cliché, "Pioneers Made Deserts Bloom."

Of the *PM* writers, Stone was most interested in avoiding a confrontation with the Arabs, though John R. Wilhelm had already presented "The Arab Case in Palestine Dispute," reminding readers that Palestinian Arabs had been promised independence, but if Jewish refugees flooded Palestine, Arabs would be outnumbered. They were only a generation removed from Ottoman tyranny, which they associated with European politics. Stone accused the British of using anti-Zionism to unite the Arabs against Jews and Russians. Arab patriots and Jewish settlers had a natural enemy: British imperialism. He called for a binational state in Palestine that would recognize Arabs and Jews. Months later he claimed the British Foreign Office needed Arab/Jewish hostility to justify a bankrupt policy. He proposed a Jordan River Valley Authority, modeled on the TVA, to solve the problems of Jews and Arabs alike.

PM continued to decry deliberate British delay. When terrorists kidnapped five British officers, Saul Padover attacked Great Britain for blaming the whole Jewish community in Palestine. This was imperialist thinking. Padover echoed Stone's call for unity between Arabs and Jews against British imperialism. Padover thought all three Great Powers were failing Europe's "displaced persons," but the British were by far the worst. *PM* carried an AP story accusing Great Britain of arming Arab opponents of Jewish emigration.

Refugee horror stories included pictures of Jews, having escaped Nazi death, once more behind barbed wire. This time Great Britain was the warden.[20]

Stone's second trip to Palestine was a journalistic coup. The story was the journey, made in May and June of 1946, not the destination. He followed the Jewish underground trail out of Poland to Palestine, taking every illegal step that the refugees trod. Each border crossing was fraught with danger. The journey was serialized in *PM* as *Through Europe Underground to Palestine* and was later published as a book. Stone went from Poland through Czechoslovakia and Austria to Italy. There the refugee band took one and then another illegal boat to Haifa. The anecdotes are filled with vivid word pictures of many of the refugees, the guides, and the boats' crews. Stone learned Yiddish expressions and songs. He witnessed other refugees who were not able to go and reported on the mixed background of the refugee exodus ("Aboard a Floating Tower of Babel"). The danger of discovery makes every day's installment inherently dramatic. The lesson it taught him, Stone warned the British, was *"Nothing will stop the people I traveled with from rebuilding a Jewish community in Palestine."*[21]

INGERSOLL'S FINAL CRUSADE

Stone's tale raised *PM*'s circulation, just as Ingersoll's trips to London and Moscow at the height of their peril had. The timing was helpful to Ingersoll, who had just fired his last grandiloquent cannon. On the sixth anniversary of *PM*'s birth—18 June 1946—Ingersoll had the newspaper print a special second section. Billed as a "Prospectus to sell 100,000 more *PM*s a Day," the front page frankly appealed for "100,000 Additional Readers, the equivalent of 100,000 Additional Shares in Itself." Admitting that Marshall Field had lost $4 million, it reminded its readers that they had spent far more: $14 million to purchase their copies of the paper over the last six years. Why not view their purchase as an investment, and find additional investors?

Though unsigned, the prose had the old breathless rush of the founder's longest memos. Ingersoll retold the story of the creation of the paper and of the attempts of the *Daily News* to kill it, defended *PM* against charges of communism, attacked the paper's early chaos, took credit for journalistic pioneering for labor and for Harlem's citizens, and actually rehashed the Huberman affair (undoubtedly to prove Ingersoll was no red). He glossed over the three years he was absent, deprecated advertising and a price increase, and advocated massive circulation growth instead. He promised readers expanded sports coverage and an improved front page. Half of the last page was a coupon readers were to fill out, asking for more copies of the supplement and pledging the purchase of additional papers.[22] Field, Lewis, and Weimer allowed the self-aggrandizing performance to go forward, expecting it to accomplish little.[23]

The campaign was a failure. Circulation figures rose slightly during the Stone serialization; they held at the 150,000 to 165,000 level throughout the year. The sports coverage was expanded; the new front page was dreadful. In attempting to match the busy front pages of the competition, *PM* now highlighted several stories instead of one. Clelland's clean and elegant look became an ugly maze. It was the worst design decision the editors ever made. Fortunately, they did not tamper with the look of the paper inside.

TRUMAN, WALLACE, AND ISOLATION

Nor was the content much different. In an increasingly hostile world, *PM* continued to press for its view of Rooseveltian politics. During the summer of 1946 those politics were greatly endangered by a ferocious Republican opposition and by Truman's split with the last of the Roosevelt holdovers in his cabinet—Henry Wallace.

PM had watched warily as the old FDR team left the new president's cabinet. Interior Secretary Ickes's resignation at the height of the strike wave was cause for brooding. "The Old Curmudgeon" had issued a broadside against Truman's failure to control inflation. Wechsler had bemoaned Wallace's "lonely spot as [the] last of [the] New Dealers." He was granted a "40 minute session" with the former vice president, "the living image of the character who emerged as the leader of the Democratic Party's New Deal bloc during the last tumultuous months of FDR's regime."

PM longed for Truman to press liberalism. Lerner wrote, "The Republican bosses have in effect declared that the congressional elections of 1946 will be a struggle between liberalism and reaction. Let us take up the challenge boldly and squarely." The paper endorsed the work of CIO/PAC and NCPAC, an allied organization of liberals without ties to the labor federation. When the two organizations held a joint meeting with the new Independent Citizens Committee, Lerner cheered, insisting that liberals need not be tied to the Democratic party.

For *PM*'s writers, Wallace's retention in Truman's cabinet was its only saving grace. In March, after the Democrats' annual Jackson Day celebration, Wechsler was impressed:

> Wallace more closely approached selflessness than any other big-time political figure. . . . The unmistakable Messianic quality in Wallace is a basic clue to his conduct. . . . Wallace's rhetoric had a fire that Truman's lacked, and the audience seemed to sense the contrast. The two men did not disagree, but Wallace's words seemed to stem from greater personal conviction and from a more dramatic vision of the future. . . . He is likely to baffle political sages for a long time.

By May, Roosevelt's old friend and former treasury secretary, Henry Morgenthau, publicly attacked the president for breaking with Roosevelt's legacy on labor and foreign relations; within days Lerner nominated "Seven Choices to Replace Truman in '48." After leading man Wallace, Lerner suggested two of his friends on the Supreme Court—Justices Black and Douglas—followed by others on the left of the Democratic party (charter *PM* investor Chester Bowles was among them). Still furious about the president's railroad-strike intervention, which he characterized as "President Truman's incredible performance last week in the role of a potential little corporal," Lerner nonetheless warned against third-party speculation. He wanted to beat the hundred worst members of Congress in 1946 and then "blast President Truman out of the 1948 Democratic nomination."

Saul Padover likewise condemned third-party preparations, all the while pressing for what was clearly a social democratic platform. He called for nationalization of public utilities, "joint government-private control of big payroll industries [steel and automobile] . . . a national health service . . . free higher and professional education," massive spending on public housing, a "national economic planning board . . . democratic foreign policy." How Padover ever thought such a program compatible with the Democratic party of 1946 is a mystery. Despite reporting that the Democratic primaries "Show Trend to Liberalism," the paper reported that Truman was deserting the New Deal and adopting an overt anti-Soviet policy. Under the headline, "The Wages of Mismanagement," Ingersoll decried the new president's foreign policy:

> Roosevelt's foreign policy—in aiding Britain, but not the British empire, and in making a friend of the Soviet Union, even though he disagreed with the political

system of the Russian state, saved the world from domination by the armed forces of Germany and Japan. . . . Roosevelt was hardly buried before the undoing of his policies began. . . . So Truman sold his heritage of sound national and international policies—that had stood the test of peace and war—for a mess of half-baked advice at home and for some twice-burned British porridge [that is, the old balance-of-power politics] abroad.

PM's editor was no kinder on the domestic front. Wondering if the United States was on the brink of the "Truman Depression," Ingersoll remembered thinking after his only meeting with the chief executive that he was "no President of the United States at all—no president with a brain, a personality, and a character of his own." The United States was a rich country after a successful war, yet it was "arming in peacetime as never before, for a war no sane man thinks is unavoidable. . . . People can't get food despite a record harvest."

Just when it seemed things could not get worse, they did. Wallace, campaigning for the New York Democratic ticket, made the keynote speech at a Madison Square Garden rally. Before he spoke, he cleared the speech with the president. A postwar recitation of the "Century of the Common Man," Wallace's words were tailor-made for *PM*, which gave over the first four pages of the 13 September issue to them. The "Editors of *PM*" affirmed that the remarks summarized the paper's views. Wallace's manifesto called for American commitment to the elimination of racism and the industrialization of the undeveloped world. He warned against relying on the British to create American foreign policy, because he thought the interests of empire were antagonistic to his overall world view. In the comments most frequently cited later, Wallace claimed to be neither anti- nor pro-British; neither anti- nor pro-Soviet. Comparing Soviet interest in Eastern Europe with American interest in Latin America, he reminded his listeners that "Russian ideals of social-economic justice are going to govern a third of the world." Instead of talking tough, he proposed a peaceful competition of the two social systems.

Though embraced by *PM*, Wallace's views were immediately under fire from all sides. The *Daily Worker* was dissatisfied with the equating of British and Soviet interests. Far more significant was the attack on their colleague's remarks by other members of the Truman cabinet. The president himself disavowed them.

A suspenseful ten-day period ensued. Stone and Lerner urged Wallace to fight for his world view within the Truman administration; in a long interview with Stone, the commerce secretary reviewed his last several months in office, including Truman's request that he write up his criticisms of Secretary of State Byrnes's foreign policy; now Byrnes was furious to discover that such criticisms existed.

Stone managed another exclusive. Wallace would not talk, but *PM*'s intrepid investigator ferreted out a Truman promise to Wallace to meet with Stalin personally if Byrnes's mission to Europe failed; hours later the chief executive called apologetically to ask for Wallace's resignation.

Wallace's departure from Truman's cabinet marked the end of progressive hopes for the foreseeable future. Lerner analyzed the political scene:

The Democrats are a party without a leader, while Henry Wallace is a leader without a party. . . . In personal terms Wallace emerged from the ordeal a more massive figure than he has ever been, with a more distinctly Presidential stature than any man in public life today.

The world was in danger, for there was a "race between world catastrophe and the awakening of the American people."[24]

END OF THE DREAM

World catastrophe seemed to hold the edge. In campaigning for control of the Congress, Republicans were fiercely denouncing Roosevelt, labor, and the Soviet Union. No advocate embracing the New Deal outlook remained at the White House.

The feisty New York tabloid no longer had friends in high places. It was also facing a new economic crisis. As 1946 began, the paper seemed on the brink of breaking even. Then the inflation it decried took its toll. Huge increases in the cost of paper plunged *PM* back into the red. Business manager Lowell Leake had been advocating the acceptance of advertising for months; now Lewis and Weimer backed his plans. Alone, Ingersoll objected. Finally, Marshall Field decided it was time to try the traditional approach. On election day 1946, *PM* announced it would accept advertising. The newspaper's founder, Ralph Ingersoll, resigned. Once again John P. Lewis would be editor.

Ingersoll's public letter to Marshall Field reminded the publisher that Roosevelt's initial welcome to issue number one had expressed support for an adless paper. While the paper might continue to be valuable, the "idea man" was too wedded to its founding principles to continue. It made great copy, but Ingersoll, other than chasing Wechsler off the paper, had been almost a passive bystander in the editorial shaping of *PM* during 1946. Weimer speculated that the advertising decision was Ingersoll's excuse to leave a newspaper which never achieved its most ambitious dreams and, moreover, had become one he no longer controlled. Though some bemoaned his departure, no one left with him. Lewis and Weimer, while recognizing the pivotal role he had played in creating the paper, were delighted to see him go.

Although the paper was essentially committed to the same political perspective it had always embraced, there was enormous symbolism in Ingersoll's resignation on election day. That day ushered in the first Republican Congress since before Roosevelt. A snarling, explicitly anti–New Deal party had control of both houses. The dream of the independent, liberal paper died on precisely the day Americans forswore liberalism (and banished antifascism forever) at the ballot box. Marshall Field blamed the Republican victory on Truman's failed leadership. His *Chicago Sun* editorial calling for the president's resignation was reprinted in *PM* on the editorial page, together with a countereditorial by Lerner claiming that the owner of his newspaper was foolish and advocating new efforts to place a liberal in nomination for 1948.[25]

In continuing to believe in the right to organize, in demanding justice for the propertyless rather than the propertied, in demanding a planned economy with a broad social net (as Stone had), or in advocating nationalized industry and even socialism (as Lerner had), *PM* was defining in Henry Wallace's words, an "economic bill of rights." It was a kind of liberalism that was vanishing, amid an avalanche of Republican votes and rhetoric, from the United States. Similarly, in championing social democracy in Europe, *PM* was whistling into the wind. Though the newspaper would continue to publish as *PM* or the *New York Star* for two and a half more years, it was more than coincidental that the brave, defiant, crusading journal which had trumpeted "that adlessness was next to godliness" surrendered to conventional wisdom on the day regressive Republicanism had its greatest triumph until the election of Ronald Reagan more than a generation later.

8 | Epilogue

Two days after Ralph Ingersoll resigned, John P. Lewis published a new credo under the title "Answering Questions about the New *PM*."

> We believe in people.
> We believe in democracy. . . .

ECONOMIC DEMOCRACY, for only when all men have a chance to earn a decent living can democracy itself be made to work. Poverty still is the greatest shackle on human freedom.

> POLITICAL DEMOCRACY . . .
> RACIAL AND RELIGIOUS DEMOCRACY . . .
> SEX DEMOCRACY. . . .

PM unequivocally opposes Communism in the United States of America. We want no part of a political party which orients itself by the interests of another government. We have only contempt for any man who permits his political thinking to be dictated to him by a party or under penalty of expulsion, humiliation and social ostracism. We have, of course, no respect for a conspiratorial party that seeks to impose rather than to convince.

By the same sign, we refuse to join up with the rabidly hysterical anti-Communists, whether they be disillusioned former party members, or that hysterical band of reactionaries, which seeks power by attacking any and all progressive movements as communistic. We refuse to judge issues and men by phony labels attached by their enemies . . .

Internationally, *PM* believes that the Capitalist democracy of the U.S.A. can live in peace with the Communist Soviet.

PM wants to prevent war with Russia and to build a progressive movement here.[1]

Lewis was going out of his way to disavow communism specifically as a way of avoiding the personal and ideological disputes that had disrupted the paper in its early days and to stave off charges of communist domination from the paper's enemies. No ideological discipline had ever shackled any *PM* writer; no such discipline was applied now. Other than the specific noncommunist avowal, Lewis's declaration was a restatement of the paper's historic principles.

The only visible change in the tabloid was caused by the acceptance of advertising. An "Advertising Display Rates Card" on 7 November offered bargain-basement prices, pennies a line.[2] Even so, advertising did not pour in. It was not until the spring of 1947 that ad copy was significant. Nonetheless, the impact was immediate. To accommodate advertisers, the paper was altered with deleterious consequences to its appearance. The four-column page printed in nine-point Caledonia type gave way to a more traditional tabloid format: five columns in smaller print size. This reduced the pleasing clarity which had made *PM*'s design uniquely reader-friendly. Pages that were entirely devoted to news, however, maintained their overall beauty. Those which shared space with advertising were often unattractive. The paper expanded its available type styles to assist advertisers, who often selected the plainest bold type to grab the reader's attention. Most of the ads were simply ugly. Pages that were given over entirely to advertising could be hideous. By 1947, page 5 was frequently rented by S. Klein's, Union Square's discount department store. One day a perfectly composed adless page 4 faced a full-page ad from Klein's dominated by the two-inch word, GIRDLES; the price screamed in four-inch bold: $2.22.[3] No traditional newspaper reader—then or now—would be surprised at the juxtaposition; but anyone who had been attracted to Ingersoll's dream of a beautiful newspaper and who had left New York for a year would have been shocked at the visual assaults now contained in *PM*.

The paper's editorial staff felt assaulted by a world increasingly inhospitable to the vision of economic and political democracy central to its perspective. The new Republican majority of the Eightieth Congress aggressively attempted to undo the New Deal. By mid-January, congressional committees were in a "Race for Anti-Labor Law." Robert Shelton, *PM*'s new labor correspondent, reported the genesis and development of the Taft-Hartley Act, which barred labor's open political involvement (a deliberate attack on CIO/PAC), permitted the president to declare eighty-day cooling-off periods in national strikes, insisted that all labor leaders sign a noncommunist oath, and allowed states to declare themselves right-to-work. The last proviso meant that states in areas like the South could easily kill closed-shop contracts and thus unionism. Shelton was joined in fierce denunciation of the law by Padover, Uhl, Lerner, and Stone, who made unusual use of the new political vocabulary by terming the anticommunist provisions "totalitarian." Truman's veto message was given great play, and a new coupon campaign to uphold the veto was organized. The ability of the Republican–southern Democrat alliance to override the veto caused Lerner to lose faith momentarily in the direction of American history.

Even in "liberal" New York, the state legislature acceded to Governor Dewey's request to enact the Conlin-Wadlin Law, which prohibited strikes by municipal workers and mandated prison terms for union leaders who engaged in them. Though CIO organizing in sanitation and among municipal clerks had picked up strength, *PM* was right to assume the law was primarily aimed at Mike Quill and the Transport Workers Union.[4]

The Republican domination of the House Un-American Activities Committee revived the aggressiveness of that group. As the committee hunted "communists" in labor unions, government, Hollywood, and among teachers, *PM*'s writers defended the civil liberties of all the accused, whether they were communists or victims of absurd guilt-by-association charges, reproduced and condemned the witch-hunt atmosphere of the hearings and recognized early that *communist* was often code language for "Roosevelt" or "Jew." As Lerner put it: "The Communist hunt has become a Republican show. [Attorney General] Tom Clark and the FBI may have started it, but if they did they must feel now like the sorcerer's apprentice." But Stone was not letting the Democrats off the hook. He carefully noted the activities of the Truman administration's own loyalty program, which he insisted planted the hysteria HUAC deliberately mined. He scorned Clark's "subversive" organizations list, writing deadly feature pieces exposing the trumped-up nature of the charges against scores of individuals. The paper documented the early stages of the Mundt-Nixon Communist Registration Bill, which was compared to Nazi legislation. When leaders of the Communist party were indicted for conspiracy to advocate the overthrow of the government, the paper—by now the *New York Star*—defended them against the hysteria and hearsay at the root of the case. The CP leaders posed for an evocative Irving Haberman photograph in the shadow of Manhattan's Federal Court Building.[5]

The impassioned denunciations of President Truman in 1946 were replaced by more ambivalent reporting. In his State of the Union message that began the new year, he advocated anti-inflation measures and again called for a full-employment bill. His spirited veto of the Taft-Hartley Act won him a friendly response (but not from Stone, who saw the new law as the logical outcome of his 1946 attack on labor's rights). It was the Presidential Commission on Civil Rights which won the biggest raves. That commission endorsed *PM*'s civil rights agenda, demanding antilynching and anti–poll tax legislation and an end to legalized segregation. The Sunday Magazine gave over its first twenty-four pages to a reprint of the entire report. Truman's decision to appoint the commission and his endorsement of its views was widely supported. His executive order barring discrimination by the federal government was cheered as a "bold act for civil rights."[6]

Although the developing cold war was covered copiously, the most thorough foreign affairs attention was lavished on the struggle of Jewish Palestinians to establish an independent state. Every British delay was furiously denounced; Victor Bernstein, who seemed to be living at the Lake Success headquarters of the United Nations, wrote scores of editorials imploring the Truman administration to force its British ally and the UN to grant immediate independence. Every equivocation brought forth a fresh denunciation. Stone thought British and American interest in Arab oil explained the dallying. Attacks on Soviet policy in Eastern Europe were mitigated by warm regard for its support for the proposed Jewish state. Truman's meeting with Chaim Weizmann and his promise for aid to Israel as the state achieved independence was cheered. Stone returned to

Palestine in 1947 and once again was part of the story: the British seized and held him for several hours. He also made his way to areas officially off limits. He reported on the scene during the 1948 war with the Arab states. These well-publicized reports focused on the struggles of a kibbutz in the Negev, providing both dramatic war correspondence and a record of a new socialist effort.[7]

The president's decision to assist the right-wing Greek government against communist-led guerrillas and to justify that aid by enunciating the Truman Doctrine, an international declaration of American anticommunist hostility, was roundly condemned. The Greek government had been handpicked by the British, who had restored many collaborators of fascism to power. To support it with American arms was to betray the cause of the war. In addition, to view world politics as a series of confrontations between the United States and "international communism" meant abandoning the dream of peaceful cohabitation with the Soviet Union.

The European program most passionately proposed in early 1947 called for massive American economic aid to reconstruct the shattered continent. All of the paper's editorial writers advocated this approach; they were pleasantly surprised by the Marshall Plan. They campaigned actively against Republican reservations, particularly those expressed by presidential hopeful Robert Taft, who was accused of old-fashioned isolationist politics. Though supporting the adoption of the European Recovery Program, Padover, Lerner, Uhl, and Stone were aware that the economic aid was being offered with political strings. They condemned American attempts to oust socialists and communists throughout Western Europe. Lerner thought the United States was constructing a noncolonial imperialism by virtue of its hegemonic economic strength. He watched the cold-war budgets support military-industrial growth. Without using Eisenhower's famous phrase of the future, he was frightened by the military-industrial complex. Padover bemoaned the downfall of European social democracy as "mark[ing] an epochal crisis in Western civilization."[8]

The paper bemoaned the increasing bellicosity of the Soviet Union, both the strident tone of Foreign Secretary Molotov's speeches and the imposition of stricter controls in the nations of Eastern Europe. The removal of socialists from coalitions with Eastern European communists was regarded as cynical manipulation. The ouster of Czech socialists in a bloodless coup in March 1948 was particularly agonizing. Lerner claimed the Czech coup provided "final proof that when the Communist lion and the Socialist lamb lie down together, the lion has no peaceful intentions." Lerner saw the suicide of Czech democrat Jan Masaryk, amid speculation that he had been pushed rather than had jumped from a window, as

> the symbol of the plight of European man today, caught between the Russians who cynically kill him unless he turns anti-capitalist, and the Americans who just as cynically let him die unless he turns anti-communist. . . . The humanist tradition of Europe is nearing an end.

Increasingly, Lerner defined the postwar struggle as a battle between two imperialisms. We had entered, he intoned, "An Age of Lost Confidence."[9]

As the 1948 presidential campaign began (almost as soon as the Republicans had won the 1946 congressional elections), the paper was indeed lost. Sympathetic to virtually everything being said by former vice president Wallace and the Progressive Citizens of America, *PM*'s editorialists were of several minds about his presidential candidacy. Lerner speculated that Wallace, whose integrity and decency he defended consistently, was hopelessly naive about the Communist party members supporting him. He and Padover reviewed American history to find third-party movements ineffective. This particular third-party movement, they reasoned, could "succeed" only enough to allow a Republican candidate to win. Lerner's correspondence with Idaho senator Glen Taylor, who would eventually become Wallace's running mate, argues that he would have been sympathetic to a third-party which could sink roots in American political life; he thought the Progressive party would vanish quickly. As 1947 progressed, it seemed increasingly likely that *PM* would endorse the president. Truman's feints to the left were encouraged by Shelton.

But Albert Deutsch, Jennings Perry (who had become a featured columnist in 1946), and Stone would not have it. Stone was particularly emphatic. "I just can't bring myself to vote for Harry Truman. As long as Wallace speaks, millions abroad may be assured that older America is not yet dead. . . . Wallace is the rallying point for those who believe that—as he said last night—'peace, jobs, and freedom are indivisible.'"

As the campaign heated up, so did Stone's support for Wallace. Referring to the communist-dupe charge which burdened the Wallace candidacy throughout, Stone replied, "I don't think I'm quite as big a dupe as those who are going to vote for Truman and the bi-partisan Cold War, and expect to get peace, housing, and better prices."

When Truman's response to the Czech events was to increase American military posturing against the Soviets, his potential support from any *PM* editorialist was gone. The paper was as solidly against him as it had been during the spring of 1946. Lerner, writing for the editors, was explicit: "Under no conditions will we give our support to Harry Truman and his cabal." John P. Lewis began a new coupon campaign, this one directed at the Democratic National Committee. The object was to produce another nominee. The budding movement to draft General Eisenhower for the Democratic nomination was given support; Lerner (with far better reason) advocated drafting Justice Douglas.

PM's real favorite was not available, but his presence was palpable. A drive to increase subscriptions promised a lavish picture book on the life of President Roosevelt. Another promotion offered cash for those who wrote the best essays denoting the finest quality in the late president.

Of course, Truman would totally control the 1948 Democratic convention. The draft movements were nothing more than hot air, though they reflected the popular consensus that Truman would lose the general election. Then, just as the Republicans were convening to name their candidate, *PM* ceased to exist.[10]

It surprised no one. The paper had always been in financial crisis. Arthur Leipzig left to work for Hearst's wire service, which he detested (and soon left) in early 1946, because "the handwriting was on the wall." Advertising had grown slowly, but not enough to make up for inflation. Full-page ads in *PM* soliciting still more advertising provided ample evidence that the paper's financial prospects were bleak. Shortly after Ingersoll left, Marshall Field warned the Newspaper Guild that the paper might die, though he continued to maintain his hands-off editorial policy.

In mid-1947, Lewis and Weimer thought the experiment was over. They had tried Ingersoll's circulation-alone method; after many months of advertising plus circulation, the paper continued to lose money. They approached Field; Weimer says they told him, "We didn't want to stay on a subsidized paper all our lives." They had another idea. They proposed a national newspaper on the *PM* model, perhaps coming out weekly instead of daily. Field was not interested in another effort. After some initial difficulties, the *Chicago Sun* was a success; he had been able to merge his paper with the *Chicago Times*; the *Sun-Times* was *his* newspaper. He told Lewis and Weimer he would need about a year to find a purchaser; he directed Louis Weiss to locate interested parties.

Clinton D. McKinnon, a California publisher and Democratic congressional candidate, appeared to be the new owner. The sale of the tabloid was announced in *PM* on 15 March 1948. The Newspaper Guild objected to the terms of the sale, because McKinnon would not abide by contract guarantees to the employees. McKinnon withdrew. The guild prevailed upon Field to extend his deadline while additional purchasers were located. The silent owner was finally losing patience. The paper printed his understatement, "I have met its losses for a period that has exceeded any reasonable limit." Still, April issues continually reassured readers that deadlines were extended. As the last one approached, the 29 April issue proclaimed the sale of *PM*. The transfer was effective on 1 May.

Bartley Crum, a liberal San Francisco lawyer, was the new publisher. Joseph Barnes—*Herald Tribune* foreign editor and a close aide to Wendell Willkie in the last two years of his life—became the new editor. They promised readers exciting changes, which they indicated would occur slowly. Tom O'Connor, who had helped work out the guild unit's relationship with the new management team, smiled wryly and said, "Here we go again." Ken Stewart found the staff relieved that the ordeal of transfer was over; he characterized the mood in the pressroom as "a second honeymoon." For seven weeks the ownership continued the paper as *PM*. On 23 June 1948, the *New York Star* appeared on the newsstands. Lewis and Weimer collected their belongings on the final day that *PM* appeared and left. Lewis began operating a small newsweekly in New Hampshire. Weimer worked for a year with his brother in Columbus, Ohio. Then the University of Florida hired him to create its journalism school, now a flourishing institution which bears his name.[11]

The *Star* cleaned up the front page, giving it a broadsheet look despite the tabloid format. Several articles began on page 1; Ingersoll's verboten "Continued on" was standard. Where possible, Caledonia was continued as the typeface of choice. New talent was brought in. John Lahr did an amusing anecdotal column; John S. Wilson began a "New York, N.Y." column of theatrical news and gossip. The editorial page was restructured. Looked at today, it appears to be the model for the editorial and op-ed double page of the *New York Times*. On the left page (usually page 10), was the unsigned editorial, written by Barnes or occasionally Crum. Underneath was a guest column called "The By-Line." Nunnally Johnson was the first guest; Edgar Snow the second. Twice *PM* veteran Amos Landman was featured, writing from India and China. On the facing page several of *PM*'s columnists—Lerner, Perry, and Stone among them—wrote regularly. Deutsch's health column continued to score impressive firsts. He reported a conversation he had held with a mouth cancer specialist who claimed statistical evidence was accumulating linking tobacco smoking and cancer—in November 1948. Victor Bernstein and Alexander Uhl, who had become regular reporters, wrote occasional editorial columns. Frederick Kuh, originally hired by the *Chicago Sun*, stayed as London correspondent for the New York paper. He contributed infrequently as an editorialist.

Editorially, the paper was more mainstream liberal than it had been. Stewart reports that many staff members were sorry the new ownership would not campaign for Wallace. Barnes and Crum steered the official editorial position to Truman. The *New York Star* was the only English-language daily in the city to support the president for reelection. Though Wechsler backed the president, the *New York Post*'s publisher, Dorothy Schiff, concluded he was a certain loser, and joined with the rest of the press to endorse Republican candidate Dewey.

If the *Star* was aboard the Truman Special, its whistle blew frequently in Wallace country. Stone and Perry were more forthrightly in favor of the Progressive candidate than ever; the continuing government security programs were roundly condemned. Lerner speculated that the Justice Department had timed the Smith Act arrests of Communist party leaders to damage the Progressive party convention. He condemned the arrests as a "reckless betrayal of the conditions of freedom and the traditions of decency." Progressive party advertisements competed with those of the anticommunist liberal Americans for Democratic Action, which advocated the president's reelection.

Lerner, no longer the voice of the paper, temporized about his choice for months, finally declaring himself for perennial Socialist candidate Norman Thomas. For someone who had decried the third party-movement as foolish because it could not hope to win, this was an inscrutable choice, but Lerner insisted that his differences with Thomas aside, at least he was casting a ballot for democratic socialism. Perhaps a more effective commentary was provided by Irving Haberman's magnificent photograph. Thomas was pictured sitting alone in a darkened hotel room while outside his door Progressive party stalwarts held posters of Wallace and Taylor, signaling the Socialist's dignity and his isolation.

In a perverse way, here was the old united front, now fractured and impotent whichever way it turned. While the *Star* officially insisted, "No one can deny that Mr. Truman's Democratic platform goes right down the line of New Deal tradition on Palestine, on civil liberties, on housing, social security, labor legislation, price control and scores of issues confronting us," Stone was incredulous that liberals could support Truman's civil rights record when he had helped fuel the witch-hunting hysteria poisoning the air. When publisher Crum attacked Secretary of State Marshall for canceling the personal diplomacy of Truman confidant Fred Vinson, who had offered to confer privately with Stalin, Stone replied in print that Marshall worked for Truman and reflected his boss's views.

No matter whom the liberals voted for in 1948, they did not win. Wallace best represented their politics; no one anticipated just how poorly he would actually do. Truman surprised everyone by winning the election; his dedication to the cold war was unabated. As Stone noted later:

> It was the complete absence of any perspective that made the Truman inaugural address so appalling. . . . To paraphrase Lincoln's second inaugural, Mr. Truman spoke with malice toward none, except half of mankind (Russia and China), and with charity toward all willing to give us military bases.[12]

The war for economic and political democracy was in retreat, in the United States and throughout the world. There was no longer any politician interested in the left Rooseveltian world view articulated by *PM* or the *Star*.

There were not enough readers, either. Field had sold the newspaper on generous terms. He received no cash, just an offer of stock options for later on. The signs of financial desperation were everywhere. A new campaign for 100,000 additional readers was launched; either Crum and Barnes did not know about Ingersoll's July 1946 drive, or they did not care about omens. To stimulate readership, coupons were printed; if enough were accumulated, lucky readers could purchase volumes of the *American Family Encyclopedia* for twenty-five cents a volume. Three pages in succession were reserved for trumpeting the circulation drive. Twice, Sunday's page 1 was disfigured by garish reproductions of the encyclopedia. An editorial note apologized for the intrusiveness of the promotion.

The coupon drive was still going on 28 January 1949 when page 1 carried the sudden announcement, "*The Star* Suspends Publication." Crum and Barnes had been trying to procure additional financing; no one was willing. As sports editor Jim Russell told *Newsweek*, "I was shocked, but I wasn't surprised." The second honeymoon ended with a jolt. Ironically, the biggest financial loss was absorbed by Marshall Field: there were no stocks to option.[13]

The *PM* staff departed. Many left journalism altogether. Ralph Ingersoll would team with Texan millionaire Charles Marsh to buy and restructure small newspapers to make them profitable. After a short hiatus Max Lerner turned up at the *New York Post*. His politics continued to move to the right. In retrospect he became a supporter of Harry Truman's "greatness" and backed the American war in Vietnam. A reader of his columns beginning in the 1950s would have been surprised to know of his earlier radicalism.

Lerner's shift to cold-war liberalism in the 1950s was one logical outcome of postwar politics. If Truman's loyalty purges marked the beginning of the end for a depression-era liberalism which believed in economic and political democracy, as Stone charged, then those who had adhered to the now-antiquated views had to reconsider. If they still wished to exercise influence in American politics, they had to rethink their views. The death of Harold Laski, Lerner's socialist mentor, probably helped to free the columnist from views no longer considered tenable in any area of government or in establishment circles. In the 1950s, Wechsler's anticommunist credentials allowed him to write speeches for Democratic presidential hopeful Adlai Stevenson.

For a brief time, yet another left-liberal newspaper made an appearance in New York. When Ted Thackery divorced Dorothy Schiff, she retained control of the *New York Post* and its cold-war liberalism. Thackery was sympathetic to the Wallace point of view. He purchased the *PM* presses and in May 1949 began publishing the *Daily Compass*. To attract the *PM/Star* audience he retained Albert Deutsch, Jennings Perry, and I. F. Stone as columnists. Cecelia Ager reviewed film. Tom O'Connor was hired as a reporter; before long he was the newspaper's managing editor.

The *Compass* looked just like the *Post*: Same typeface, same ads, same messy copy; just as unsightly; an audience leaning further to the left. In 1952 O'Connor was named as a communist by an associate from his days in Los Angeles as Newspaper Guild leader. Subpoenaed by the House Committee on Un-American Activities, O'Connor made use of Fifth Amendment protection against self-incrimination and refused to name any others. He told the committee that the Constitution allowed him to "think as I please, write as I please and edit a newspaper without interference from Congress." Thackery stood by his managing editor, who died two months later of a heart attack at the age of thirty-eight. It is tempting to write that McCarthyism had found another victim, but Penn Kimball, who had roomed with O'Connor when *PM* was new, testifies that the brilliant writer had suffered from tuberculosis as a young man. The *Compass* folded a year later; even in New York there was no longer an audience for a daily paper opposed to the cold war.[14]

The cold war, under James Wechsler's byline, wrote the official history of *PM*. That version told of an inept newspaper sabotaged by Communists, a day behind the rest of the press.

To anyone who reads *PM*, the account does not stand up. The communism charge is ridiculous. What the newspaper shared with the Communist party was abhorrence for fascism and a dedication to the rights of labor and the oppressed. As the principal voice of antifascist political culture, Ingersoll's paper agreed with the Communist party many times. But often the two outlooks clashed. For the first year of *PM*'s publication, it vigorously demanded increased participation in the war against Hitler; the *Daily Worker*, defending the German-Soviet pact, emphatically demanded "Peace." During the war, both papers backed the CIO's no-strike pledge, but when *PM* legitimized miners' grievances and supported Montgomery Ward workers, the *Daily Worker* attacked *PM*, and Harry Bridges scabbed on the Ward workers. *PM* was an emphatic supporter of the NAACP, covering virtually every struggle the organization initiated; the Communists battled with and belittled Walter White and A. Philip Randolph. *PM*, in today's terms, was integrationist; the Communists were attracted to the black nationalist conception of a "black belt." As the cold war began, editorialists Lerner and Padover attacked U.S. militarism and Soviet interference in Eastern Europe; for the Communists every Soviet action was justified. Only idealogues who do not read *PM* can fall for Wechsler's characterization.

What is true is that the antifascist outlook the paper championed was increasingly relegated to society's outcasts as the cold war waxed. Perhaps that is one of the tragedies of the period.

While *PM* failed to attract an audience to sustain itself and never had a strong enough national network to cover the news fully, the tabloid was a great innovator. It reinvented newspaper photography, demonstrating that superb reproduction was possible. Properly used, pictures *could* effectively tell many stories better than words. It redefined the "woman's" page, making consumer news a vital concern of journalism. It forced its rivals to carry radio, movie, and finally television listings as necessary news services. It legitimized the struggles of American labor and the nation's black citizens, affording eloquent news, feature, and pictorial coverage to outsiders the traditional press ignored.

Investigative journalism by *PM* did far more than expose "chicken ghouls." O'Connor's mining series was vital ammunition for members of Congress pressing for safety legislation and won him the 1941 Heywood Broun Memorial Award from the American Newspaper Guild. Stone's ghosting of Reuther's "500 Planes a Day" plan and his subsequent exposure of dilatory practices by American defense firms led to Senator Truman's special committee to investigate the industry. (One imagines that his contribution to Truman's career did not exactly give Stone retrospective pleasure.) Nathan Robertson virtually invented close scrutiny of tax legislation.

Many articles about *PM* presume it was a failure as a newspaper because it failed financially. Looked at this simplistically, a great majority of American newspapers are failures. By the time Ingersoll attempted to revolutionize journalism, newspaper publishing was already in crisis. Radio and the movies had taken their toll. The Hearst empire had begun to contract; the great Pulitzer newspapers had failed or been bought for merger. The New York press was afraid of the new paper. First the *News* tried to prevent circulation; then the established papers united to deny *PM* access to Associated Press wire services. Against their hostility to his experiment, Ingersoll never raised so much money as he had originally projected. With fourteen major investors, he was afraid of losing control by bringing in more.

Today, most newspapers still lose money. They are published by powerful millionaires seeking to influence those more powerful. In New York, the *Post* and the once mighty *Daily News* are financial disasters. The New York run of *Newsday* was made possible by the success of its Long Island edition. Marshall Field did not mind losing money when he thought *PM* was vital enough to sustain. His success in Chicago gave him personal satisfaction; *PM* was no longer important in Washington. It no longer made sense for him to funnel money into a project other powerful men ignored.

Why did the newspaper not attract more than its normal circulation of 150,000 to 165,000? Rae Weimer argued that the conservative habits of most newspaper readers make it difficult to establish a new paper. In a city that already boasted eight daily papers (or nine, if one counts the *Brooklyn Eagle*), the paper did not offer enough to a mass audience. "I don't think women want a paper without advertising; 'Best Buys' didn't satisfy." This seems more true today than ever, when readers purchase their papers on particular ad days of the week.

Perhaps the message was limiting. A *PM* reader, almost by definition, had to be more intensely ideological than the average citizen. Though anyone might be entertained by its beautiful graphic design or impressed by the quality of its photographs, to be a consistent reader of this tabloid was to spend a nickel a day to buy into the antifascist culture which was at its heart. The paper possessed more coherence than the traditional papers, except perhaps for the *Times*, which had and continues to have no problem presenting itself as the "newspaper of record." This coherence would not impress those who rejected the worldliness and earnestness of its antifascist commitment; for those who embraced the now-vanishing creed as central to their perspective, *PM* was indeed, their bible. [15]

Weimer, himself never an idealogue of any kind, found confirmation of the *PM* experiment in *USA Today*. Though poles apart politically, the two papers share a creative use of color, photography, and graphic art and the departmentalization of the news. [16] Regarded aesthetically, *USA Today* and the new look of much of the daily press is finally catching up to the standard set by *PM* in 1940. Since today's newspapers are all published on traditional newsprint, they will probably never be so beautiful. Attractiveness became an issue for the mass press forty-plus years after Ingersoll and his followers claimed that the look of a newspaper was important.

Despite Wechsler and company's bugaboo of communist domination, *PM*'s editorial stance showed it be infatuated by only one mythology: that of Franklin Roosevelt. Though the paper criticized individual aspects of FDR policy or performance, it helped create a New Deal legend: a great saga of democratic advance for the aspirations and needs of the common man. After Roosevelt died, even specific complaints were forgotten. This romance, which *PM* shared with most contemporary liberals and radicals, had a powerful allure. *We* had a president on *our* side. If Truman could not be supported by *PM* veterans, the longing to influence power had brought the newspaper close to an endorsement in 1947. Wechsler and Lerner would find fewer principles separating them from mainstream politicians. Both were charmed by John F. Kennedy. The dilemma of practical politics as opposed to principle, of the eventual third party as opposed to the reality of Democrats versus Republicans is confronted at every election. The Roosevelt aura helps to induce most, while hesitating, to pull the lever under the donkey.

I. F. Stone had different impulses. He remained faithful both to the crusading tradition and to the politics of the century of the common man. When the *Compass* folded, he went back to his boyhood roots to publish his own newsletter. *I. F. Stone's Weekly*, begun during the heyday of McCarthyism, challenged all the verities of the "bi-partisan cold war." It continued until his impassioned dissent from the war in Vietnam helped him temporarily to radicalize the *New York Review of Books*. His rhetoric of crusading opposition continued a tradition he had come to cherish.

When *PM* ceased publication, Stone wrote:

Ralph [Ingersoll] and John [P. Lewis] had something else. It is not enough to be bright. It is also necessary to care, and to care deeply about a lot of things.

They believed in giving a break to the poor sucker getting the dirty end of the stick. They enjoyed a good fight, and they felt that the only kind of a good fight was a fight in which the odds were against you. (Somebody—I think it was Napoleon—once said that God fights on the side of the strongest battalions. That's an inglorious place to be.) Ingersoll and Lewis collected their kind of staff. None of us would fit into a Calvert whiskey ad but even the office boy had strong views. For all of us *PM* was a chance to do the kind of newspaper job small boys dream about, mixing it up with windmills and knights errant. [Westbrook] Pegler would say we were a bunch of do-gooders, bleeding hearts and worse. The paper was often sloppy, screwy and exasperating. But it wasn't dull. It got people mad, sometimes mad enough to get results. It had excitement. In between endless griping, we were proud to be *PM*ers.[17]

NOTES

CHAPTER ONE: THE ROOTS OF *PM*

1. Penn Kimball, tape recorded interviews by author, New York, 21 May 1985, and Washington, D.C., 21 February 1994. Portions of Kimball's letters to his parents were shared with the author. See also idem, *The File* (New York: Harcourt Brace Jovanovich, 1983).

2. William E. Leuchtenburg, *Franklin D. Roosevelt and the New Deal* (New York: Harper Torchbooks, 1963), 108.

3. Earlier hagiography of Franklin Roosevelt by Rex Tugwell, *The Democratic Roosevelt* (New York: Doubleday, 1957), and especially by Arthur Schlesinger, Jr., *The Crisis of the Old Order, The Coming of the New Deal*, and *The Politics of Upheaval* (Boston: Houghton Mifflin, 1957, 1958, and 1960, respectively), has given way to a more critical analysis, though criticism of the president as more wily politician than committed liberal go as far back as James MacGregor Burns, *The Lion and the Fox* (New York: Harcourt Brace, 1956). Most recently, Kenneth S. Davis has painted Roosevelt as a politician who rode the crest of events while providing little leadership. His most recent volume, *FDR: Into the Storm, 1937–1940* (New York: Random House, 1993), is a devastating indictment of political impotence and timidity against reaction at home and fascism abroad. Frank Freidel's *Franklin D. Roosevelt: A Rendezvous with Destiny* (Boston: Little Brown, 1990) is far less severe, endorsing Schlesinger's evaluation of FDR's greatness without being quite so reverential. Anthony J. Badger's *New Deal: The Depression Years, 1933–1940* (New York: Hill and Wang, 1989) concludes that the period marked major advancements for immigrant groups and industrialized labor in part by keeping southern workers and blacks effectively disenfranchised.

4. Kenneth Stewart, *News Is What We Make It* (Boston: Houghton Mifflin, 1943), 142–150.

5. Davis, *FDR:Into the Storm*, 441–443.

6. The newspaper collection at the Forty-second Street branch of the New York Public Library is invaluable. All of the New York dailies, including much of the foreign-language press, are completely represented on microfilm from at least as far back as early in this century. *PM* writer Kenneth Stewart mixes the story of his progress as a newspaperman in the 1920s and 1930s with a casual history of the press and the Newspaper Guild in *News Is What We Make It*. A marvelous article by Jim Bishop in the January 1968 *Playboy*, "The War of the Tabloids" (162–164, 254–264), tells the exciting and hilarious tale not only of the tabloids but of the whole New York press in the 1920s and early 1930s. See also Betty Winfield, *F.D.R. and the News Media* (Urbana: University of Illinois Press, 1990).

7. Ralph Ingersoll, *In and Under Mexico* (New York: Century, 1924).

8. Ralph Ingersoll, *Point of Departure* (New York: Harcourt, Brace and World, 1961), 186.

9. Wolcott Gibbs, "Profiles: *Time . . . Fortune . . . Life . . . Luce,*" *New Yorker,* 28 November 1936, 20–25.

10. Stewart, *News,* 170–171.

11. Ralph McAllister Ingersoll papers, Special Collections, Mugar Memorial Library, Boston University; *PM* papers, Special Collection, Nieman Center, Walter Lippmann House, Harvard University; Ingersoll, *Point of Departure*; Roy Hoopes, *Ralph Ingersoll: A Biography* (New York: Atheneum, 1985); Wolcott Gibbs, "Profiles: A Very Active Type Man" [Ralph Ingersoll], *New Yorker,* 2 May 1941, 19–28, and 9 May 1941, 21–30; Laura Z. Hobson, *Laura Z: A Life* (New York: Arbor House, 1983), 160, 173–175, 186–187, 208, 227, 233–236; idem, *Laura Z: A Life—Years of Fulfillment* (New York: Donald I. Fine, 1986), 19–22.

12. Kimball interviews; Richard Green, tape recorded interview by author, New York, 12 January 1994; William McCleery, tape recorded interview by author, Princeton, New Jersey, 19 January 1994; Rae Weimer, telephone interview by author, Gainesville, Florida, 16 April 1994; Ralph Ingersoll, letter to Ed Stanley, 25 August 1938; agreement between Ralph Ingersoll and Ed Stanley, 20 October 1938 (both documents in *PM* papers, Harvard University); Ken Stewart, "The People Who Made *PM* and the *Star*" (unpublished report commissioned by Marshall Field, 1949), Ken Stewart Collection, American Heritage Center, University of Wyoming.

13. Hodding Carter, *Where Main Street Meets the River* (New York: Rinehart and Co., 1952), 108–121; Stewart, *News,* 261–283; Kimball interviews; Stewart, "The People," 87.

14. Snowden Herrick, tape recorded interview by author, New York, 20 December 1993.

15. Hannah Baker, letters to author, 15 January 1994 and 12 February 1994.

16. There are many works on the Jewish socialist experience. An excellent summary, partially invalidated by the author's passionate anticommunism, is available in Irving Howe, *The World of Our Fathers* (New York: Harcourt Brace Jovanovich, 1976). For the Jewish communist perspective, see Michael Gold, *Jews without Money* (New York: Sun Dial Press, 1930). A brilliant, evocative memoir of emerging from an immigrant-family household and embracing radicalism is Alfred Kazin's *Walker in the City* (New York: Harcourt Brace Jovanovich, 1951). See also Deborah Dish More, *At Home in America: Second Generation New York Jews* (New York: Columbia University Press, 1981).

17. James A. Wechsler, *The Age of Suspicion* (New York: Random House, 1953).

18. Robert C. Cottrell, *Izzy: A Biography of I. F. Stone* (New Brunswick: Rutgers University Press, 1992), 1–101; Andrew Patner, *I. F. Stone: A Portrait* (New York: Pantheon, 1988), 9–15, 29–53, 73–79.

19. Sally Winograd Berger, tape recorded interview by author, Glen Cove, New York, 5 January 1994.

20. McCleery interview.

21. Mary Morris, tape recorded interview by author, Oakland, California, 31 March 1994; Charles Norman, *Poets and People* (New York: Bobbs-Merrill, 1972), 177–185.

22. Stewart, *News,* passim.

23. Kimball, McCleery interviews.

24. Cecilia Youngdahl, tape recorded telephone interview by author, Miami, Florida, 14 December 1993.

25. John A. Sullivan, telephone interview by author, Vashon Island, Washington, 6 January 1994.

26. John Kobler, interview by author, New York, 16 December 1993.

27. Stewart, "The People," 21–24.

28. Stewart, *News,* 234.

CHAPTER TWO: THE CREATION AND EARLY DAYS OF *PM*

1. Ralph Ingersoll, *A Discursive Outline of a Proposition to Create a Daily Newspaper* (mimeographed; 16 April 1937), available in the *PM* papers at the Nieman Center, Harvard University.

2. All circulation figures for the New York press come from *Editor and Publisher*, 27 January 1940, 63–64.

3. *New York Times*, 17 June 1940, 14.

4. *Editor and Publisher*, 6 January 1940, 6; 20 January 1940, 11.

5. *New York Herald Tribune*, 14 June 1940, 22.

6. Ibid., 18 June 1940, 24.

7. *New York Sun*, 3 June 1940, 18.

8. Ibid., 4 June 1940, 22; 5 June 1940, 22; 6 June 1940, 22.

9. Ibid., 7 June 1940, 20.

10. Ibid., 17 June 1940, 12.

11. Ibid., 14 June 1940, 22.

12. Bishop, "War of the Tabloids."

13. *New York Daily News*, 7 June 1940, 27.

14. Ibid., 8 June 1940, 19.

15. *New York Daily Mirror*, 1 June 1940, 5.

16. Ibid., 10

17. Ibid., 1 June 1940, 24.

18. Ibid., 3 June 1940, 19.

19. *New York Journal-American*, 1 June 1940, 12.

20. Ibid., In the News, 1, 5.

21. Ibid., 4 June 1940, 12.

22. Ibid., 5 June 1940, In the News, 1.

23. *New York World-Telegram*, 10 June 1940, 17.

24. Ibid., 12 June 1940, 25.

25. Ibid., 1 June 1940, 18; 7 June 1940, 24; 8 June 1940, 18.

26. *Editor and Publisher*, 20 January 1940, 4.

27. *New York Post*, 1 June 1940, 10.

28. *Daily Worker*, 3 June 1940, 6.

29. Ibid., 1 June 1940, 4.

30. Ingersoll, *Discursive Outline*.

31. Ralph Ingersoll, diary, entry for 30 November 1940; Ingersoll, letter to Ed Stanley, 25 August 1938; agreement between Ralph Ingersoll and Ed Stanley, 20 October 1938 (all the foregoing in *PM* papers, Harvard University); Green interview; Hoopes, *Ingersoll*, 187–212 passim; Hobson, *A Life*, 233–236; Hobson, *Years of Fulfillment*, 21.

32. Winfield, *F.D.R. and the News Media*, 130. On Roosevelt and the press, see Burns, *Lion*, 241, 317; Tugwell, *Democratic Roosevelt*, 321, 364, 450–453, 540, 548; Freidel, *Roosevelt: Rendezvous*, 99, 123, 146, 203.

33. Hoopes, *Ingersoll*, 187–194.

34. Ralph Ingersoll, *A Financial Proposal: A New Type of Newspaper* (mimeographed), Ingersoll papers, Boston University.

35. Ralph Ingersoll, *The Blue Book: A New Kind of Newspaper; The Brown Book: A New Kind of Newspaper; Fundamental Requirements of a Stockholder* (mimeographed), Ingersoll papers, Boston University.

36. Kobler, Green interviews. All of the quoted material is from the Green interview; *PM* papers, Harvard University; Ingersoll papers, Boston University; Hoopes, *Ingersoll*, 187–

212; Stephen Becker, *Marshall Field III: A Biography* (New York: Simon and Schuster, 1964), 61, 199–206.

37. *Editor and Publisher* (1940): 20 January, 4; 16 March, 6; 5 May, 6; 8 June, 68.

38. Green, Kimball interviews; Ralph Ingersoll, *Memorandum to Mr. Henry Root Stern* (typewritten), 14 September 1940, *PM* papers, Harvard University.

39. Ralph Ingersoll, *Proposition to Create a Newspaper* (mimeographed), *PM* papers, Harvard University.

40. Ingersoll, *Point of Departure*, 192–194; Hoopes, *Ingersoll*, 66.

41. Boyce, Hughes, and Farrell, *The Newspaper "PM": Report on Examination*, 28 December 1945, *PM* papers, Harvard University.

42. Arthur Leipzig, tape recorded interview by author, Sea Cliff, New York, 13 December 1993.

43. Stewart, "The People," 17–20.

44. Morris interview.

45. *Newspaper* can be read on microfilm with the rest of *PM* at the Forty-second Street library; to savor its beauty, the reader can see several copies of the original in the *PM* papers, Harvard University.

46. Ralph Ingersoll, *Reprint of a Confidential Memorandum to the Staff of "PM": Subject—This Paper as of April 22, 1940* (New York: Publications Research, 1940).

47. Kimball interview, 21 February 1994.

48. *PM*, 23 April 1944, 14.

49. Ibid., 13 July 1943, 16; 19 July 1943, 16; Hoopes, *Ingersoll*, 216.

50. Kimball interview, 21 February 1994; Morris interview.

51. *PM*, 19 April 1944, 14–15.

52. Leipzig interview.

53. Carter, *Main Street*, 108–121.

54. Green, Kimball, Berger interviews.

55. Sullivan interview.

56. Green, Kimball, McCleery interviews.

57. Kimball, Green interviews.

58. *PM* (1941): 6 January, 16–19; 7 January, 14–16; 12 January, 10; 15 January, 13.

59. Ibid. (1941): 4 August, 10; 5 August, 10; 7 August, 11; 8 August, 12.

60. Ibid., 16 March 1942, 27.

61. Kimball, McCleery interviews.

62. Green interview; Stewart, "The People," 7.

63. Jonathan King, letter to author, 17 January 1994, Ingersoll papers, Boston University.

64. Berger, Green, Kimball, Youngdahl interviews; letters from Baker; Stewart, *News*, 240-241.

65. Kobler interview.

66. Ralph Ingersoll, *Notes on Where We Stand Politically* (11 May 1939), Ingersoll papers, Boston University.

67. *PM* (1940): 1 July, 10; 8 July, 13; 9 July, 14; 10 July, 10–11; 11 July, 16–17; 29 July, 10; 2 August, 10.

68. Ibid., 8 December 1940, 62–63.

69. Ibid., 19 April 1942, Picture News, 6–7; 30 November 1942, 11; 21 January 1943, Picture News, 18; 11 February 1943, 18.

70. Berger, Youngdahl interviews; Morris interview, 7 January 1994; Adele Goldberg, telephone interview by author, Brooklyn, 9 January 1994; Jean Evans, telephone interview by author, Portsmouth, New Hampshire, 9 January 1994. Mary Morris, letter to author, 8 January 1994; Louise Levitas Henriksen, letter to author, undated (January 1994).

71. McCleery interview.

72. Green interview; Hoopes, *Ingersoll*, 217.

73. Issues of 14, 15, 16, and 17 June 1940 are part of the Forty-second Street library's microfilm collection.

74. Ingersoll, *Memorandum to Henry Stern*.

75. Ibid., Green, Kimball, McCleery interviews.

76. Berger, Green, Kimball, McCleery interviews; Ingersoll, *Memorandum to Henry Stern*.

77. Stewart, *News*, 232, 240.

78. Stewart, "The People," 14.

79. Weimer interview.

80. McCleery interview.

81. *PM*, 12 July 1940, 21.

82. Stewart, *News*, 236–244; Stewart, "The People," 39.

83. Penn Kimball, telephone interview by author, Washington, 26 March 1994; Weimer interview.

84. Ingersoll, *Memorandum to Henry Stern*; Robert A. Miller, *The Newspaper "PM," Inc.: Financial Report* (31 August 1940), in *PM* papers, Harvard University.

85. Ingersoll, *Memorandum to Henry Stern;* Green interview; Becker, *Marshall Field*, 215–217; Hoopes, *Ingersoll*, 236–237.

86. Herrick interview.

87. Green, Kobler interviews.

88. R. A. Lasley, *Editorial Survey for the Newspaper "PM" (20 March 1941)*, PM papers, Harvard University.

89. Kimball interview, 21 February 1994.

90. Ingersoll, Memoranda to the Staff (1940): 22 June, 27 June, 8 July, 17 July; George Lyon, Memorandum, 16 July 1940, PM papers, Harvard University.

91. *PM*, 21 October 1941, 12.

92. Ibid. (1940): 7 August, 1, 26–27; 8 August, 1, 26–27; 11 August, 1, 27, 12 August, 1, 11; 13 August, 27; 15 August, 27; 2 September, 1; 3 September, 1, 10–12; 4 September, 10; 5 September, 10–11; 6 September, 11; 10 September, 11; 11 September, 2, 12; 12 September, 12; 18 September, 2; 19 September, 11; 23 October, 8; 10 November, 10; 13 November, 8.

93. Kimball interview, 21 February 1994.

94. For example, see Lewis Donohew, "*PM*: An Anniversary Assessment," *Columbia Journalism Review* (Summer 1965): 33–36.

95. Cited by Carter, *Main Street*, 116; Hoopes, *Ingersoll*, 247.

96. *PM* (1940): 10 October, 1, 8; 15 October, 8; 16 October, 11; 17 October, 9; 21 October, 8; 22 October, 8; 23 October, 9; 24 October, 11; 9 December, 9; 7 January 1941, 10.

97. Ibid. (1940): 1 November, 10; 3 November, 10; 4 November, 9; 5 November 9; (1941): 1 January, 8; 16 February, 13; 6 May, 6.

98. Franklin Roosevelt's personal correspondence includes letters from Washington editor Ken Crawford in 1942 urging FDR to send the telegram and Ingersoll's thanks after it was received. In April 1941 business manager William Baumracke, Jr., asked if FDR could support a drive to have people buy *PM*. Press secretary Early responded, "I regret to advise you that the President cannot write promotional letters even for friendly publications" (Franklin D. Roosevelt, Personal Correspondence, *PM* File, Roosevelt Library, Hyde Park, New York).

99. *PM*, 18 June 1941, 1, 14–15; 18 June 1942, 1–4.

100. Ibid., 12 February 1941, 6.

101. Eleanor Roosevelt, Personal Correspondence, 1943 "W" File, Roosevelt Library, Hyde Park, New York.

102. *PM*, 5 February 1941, 12; 25 June 1941, 20; 8 July 1941, 20; 15 March 1942, 2–7.

103. Ibid. (1942): 24 June, 19; 25 June, 20; 26 June, 12; 12 July, 18–19; 15 July, 20; 31 July, 1–4; 2 August, 2.

104. Franklin Roosevelt, *PM* File, Roosevelt Library.

105. Shana Alexander (Cecelia Ager's daughter), telephone interview by author, Los Angeles, 1 February 1994; Creekmore Fath, telephone interview by author, Houston, 2 February 1994.

106. Baker letter, 15 January 1994.

107. Weimer interview.

108. John A. Sullivan, letter to author, 22 January 1994.

CHAPTER THREE: FIGHTING THE WAR AGAINST FASCISM

1. *PM*, 17 June 1940, 7–9.

2. *Daily Worker*, 16 March 1941, section 2, page 1.

3. Ibid., 26 May 1941, 6.

4. *New York Times*, 17 June 1941, 8.

5. Sullivan, Green, Kimball interviews; Stewart, *News*, 214; Wechsler, *Age*, 154–155; Kimball, letter to parents, 12 October 1938.

6. *PM* (1940): 21 June, 19; 1 July, 1–2; 3 July, 1; 12 July, 18.

7. Ibid., 9 July 1940, 18; 10 July 1940, 8, 18.

8. Ibid., 5 August 1940, 11–13, 16–17.

9. Ibid., 8 August 1940, 6. As both Richard Green and John A. Sullivan pointed out, *PM* was the first newspaper to make extensive use of radio transcriptions as news sources. CBS provided a wire transcript, and *PM* used it the way it did the United Press wire, assigning Sullivan to follow the transcriptions and suggest which ones were useful as articles. Broadcasts by Edward R. Murrow, William L. Shirer, and Howard K. Smith (among others) became major news stories for *PM* (Sullivan, Green interviews).

10. *PM* (1940): 8 August, 13; 9 August, 13; 11 August, 9; 26 August, 2; 30 August, 2.

11. Ibid., 10 September 1940, 2; 24 September 1940, 2.

12. Ibid. (1940): 25 August, 9; 26 August, 6; 5 November, 7; (1941): 24 April, 7; 25 September, 6–7; 26 September, 4–5; 8 December, 2, 8; (1942): 8 February, 1; 3 May, Picture News, 3–7; 12 August, 2; (1943): 5 March, 4; 11 May, 13.

13. Ibid., 30 September 1940, 1, 5–6.

14. Ibid., 4 October 1940, 5; 8 October 1940, 5; 9 October 1940, 5.

15. Ibid., 23 September 1940, 8; 10 October 1940, 7.

16. Ibid., 30 September 1940, 2.

17. Ibid., 1 October 1940, 2.

18. Ibid., 4 December 1940, 2.

19. Kimball interview, 21 May 1985.

20. *PM* (1941): 27 January, 2; 28 January, 6–7; 30 January, 8; 4 February, 2; 10 February, 11; 23 April, 10.

21. *New York Times*, 19 April 1941, 14.

22. *New York Herald Tribune*, 3 April 1941, 26; 15 April 1941, 24.

23. *New York Journal-American*, In the News, 16 May 1941, 1.

24. Daily Worker, 27 May 1941, 1.

25. *PM* (1941): 16 March, 1, 7–8; 28 May, 1–16, 18; 29 May, 11; 2 September, 1–3, 6; 12 September, 1–10; 28 October, 1–4.

26. *New York Times*, 28 May 1941, 18; *New York Herald Tribune*, 28 May 1941, 24; *New York Sun*, 28 May 1941, 18; *Daily Worker*, 29 May 1941, 1.

27. James MacGregor Burns, *Roosevelt: The Soldier of Freedom* (New York: Harcourt Brace Jovanovich, 1970), 90–92, 100–101.

28. *PM*, 25 April 1941, 1–17.

29. Stewart, "The People," 61–63.

30. *PM*, 27 April 1941, 6–10, 15.

31. *New York World-Telegram*, 19 April 1941, 12; *New York Journal-American*, In the News, 22 May 1941, 1.

32. *PM*, 1 May 1941, 1, 8, 11–16.

33. Ibid., 4 May 1941, Picture News, 33–48.

34. Ibid., 15 May 1941, 2–6.

35. Ibid. (1941): 8 May, 9; 3 August, 3; 15 August, 10; 21 August, 8; 5 September, 1; 10 September, 3; 12 September, 3; 22 October, 8; 2 November, 3.

36. Ibid. (1941): 11 November, 1–2; 12 November, 6; 8 December, 2; 9 December, 1; 11 December, 2.

37. Ibid., 6 March 1941, 1–2; 10 March 1941, 2.

38. Ibid., 1 December 1943, 2.

39. Ibid., 5 May 1941, 9; 5 January 1942, 22; 9 March 1942, 14.

40. Ibid. (1942): 7 May, 12; 10 May 12–13; 12 May, 12; 21 May, 14.

41. Henry Wallace letter to Marshall Field, May 1942, Henry Wallace papers, microfiche, Roosevelt Library, Hyde Park, New York.

42. *PM*, 15 December 1942, 2–3; 16 February 1943, 18; 7 March 1943, Picture News, 19.

43. Neal Gabler, *Winchell: Gossip, Power and the Culture of Celebrity* (New York: Knopf, 1994), 291–292.

44. *PM* (1940): 22 July, 18; 23 July, 7; 12 August, 13; 13 August, 7, 11; 3 November, 7; 14 November, 7; 15 November, 7; 16 November, 6; 18 November, 10; 19 November, 6; 21 November, 6; 22 November, 6; 25 November, 5; 3 December, 7; 9 March 1941, 8.

45. Ibid. (1940): 10 July, 6; 10 September, 7–11; 12 September, 6; 13 September, 6.

46. Ibid. (1940): 22 December, 8; 23 December, 9; 29 December, 8; (1941): 7 February, 6; 21 February, 8; 13 March, 9; 14 March, 9; 1 April, 14; 2 May, 10.

47. Ibid. (1941): 1 June, 1, 10–11; 10 June, 12; 11 June, 9, 12; 13 June, 11; 4 August, 9; 7 August, 13.

48. Ibid. (1941): 25 August, 10; 28 August, 11; 29 August, 10; 31 August, 12; 2 September, 10; 4 September, 11; 5 September, 12; 8 September, 13; 9 September, 9; 10 September, 8; 11 September, 9; 14 September, 10.

49. Ibid., 10 April 1946, 8.

50. Ibid. (1941): 14 November, 3; 16 November, 12; 20 November, 11; 23 November, 6; 24 November, 11; 30 November, 8; 5 December, 9; 7 December, 11.

51. Ibid. (1941): 22 December, 4; 23 December, 5; (1942): 11 January, 2; 12 January, 2; 15 January, 1, 3–7; 12 February, 12; 13 February, 12.

52. Stewart, *News*, 295–297.

53. *PM* (1942): 29 January, 11; 18 February, 13; 25 March, 14; 27 March, 2–6; 29 March, 10–12, 19; 31 March, 13; 1 April, 10; 2 April, 11; 3 April, 11; 5 April, 9; 6 April, 12; 7 April, 12; 8 April, 13; 9 April, 14; 10 April, 13–14; 20 April, 12; 22 April, 14.

54. Ibid. (1942): 5 April, 8, 10; 6 April, 13; 7 April, 13; 8 April, 14; 9 April, 15; 12 April, 12.

55. Ibid. (1942): 16 November, 10; 18 November, 10; 19 November, 12; 22 November, 11; 22 December, 7; (1943): 15 January, 12; 18 February, 8; 25 April, 3–4; 26 April, 4; 27

April, 4; 4 May, 5; 20 June, 4; 21 June, 5–6; 26 June, 3; 11 July, 3, 6, 18; 13 July, 2; 15 August, 3; 16 August, 3; 17 August, 3; 18 August, 5; 19 August, 5–6; 7 September, 5; 5 December, 6–8; (1944): 4 February, 3; 7 February, 2; 11 February, 2; 13 February, 5; 17 February, 5; 18 February, 3; 21 February, 4; 22 February, 3, 5; 13 March, 2; 5 April, 7; 8 May, 3; 15 May, 3; 4 June, 3; 30 July, 6; (1945): 1 January, 2; 2 January, 2; 7 January, 11; 16 January, 2; 19 March, 2; 1 July, 1–3; 1 August, 2; (1946): 11 February, 2; 23 October, 7; 24 October, 7.

56. Ibid. (1943): 30 June, 3–5; 1 July, 3; 5 July, 1–2.

57. Ibid. (1943): 1 April, 2; 11 May, 2; 12 May, 2; 1 June, 2; 28 July, 2; 9 September, 2.

58. Ibid. (1940): 11 July, 18; 4 August, 8; 19 August, 7; 30 August, 5; 1 October, 8; 11 October, 7; 13 October, 7; 14 October, 1, 8; 18 October, 9; 8 November, 8; 21 November, 7; 22 November, 6; 3 December 7; (1941): 30 June, 16–17; 4 September, 14; 9 September, 12; 9 October, 9; 8 December, 14; 10 December, 12; (1942): 5 April, 11; 8 June, 8–9; 28 June, 1; 29 June, 3, 5; 30 June, 11; 3 July, 10; 8 July, 6; 10 July, 20; 19 July, Picture News, 4–5; 2 August, 18; 9 August, 6; 6 September, 18; 13 September, 2–5; 1 November, 19; 1 December, 19; (1943): 5 January, 8; 9 May, 11; 2–18 June, daily centerfold, 14–15; 27 July, 3; (1944): 2 January, 3, 5–6; 8 March, 6–7; 28 March, 10; 6 April, 12–13; 17 April, 7; 19 April, 3–5; 20 April, 3–5; 21 April, 3–4; 24 April, 3; 25 April, 3; 26 April, 4–5; 27 April, 3–4; 1 May, 7–10; 17 May, 3–4; 18 May, 3–9; 22 May, 2; 23 May, 2–5; 2 January 1945, 9; 21 January 1945, 10.

59. Ibid. (1940): 1 August, 11; 23 August, 7; 6 September, 7; 24 September, 8; 26 September, 8–9; 27 September, 7; 2 October, 7–8; 8 November, 6; 8 December, 2; 18 January 1942, 11.

60. Kimball interview, 21 February 1994.

61. *PM* (1942): 10 February, 1–15; 11 February, 3–8; 12 February, 2–3; 13 February, 10; 15 February, 18; 18 February, 1–5.

62. Ibid. (1940): 15 June, 10; 24 June, 10; 1 August, 12–13; 12 August, 10; 13 August, 11; 19 August, 9, 14–17; 3 December, 7; (1941): 26 February, 12; 12 December, 17; (1942): 10 March, 14; 23 March, 8; 2 April, 2–3; 12 May, 11; 22 May, 21; 2 June, 15; 16 June, 19; (1943): 25 July, 3; 1 August, 4; 9 August, 11–13; 15 August, 12; (1944): 8 August, 2; 5 October, 12; 8 October, 13; 25 March 1945, 12.

63. Kimball interview, 21 February 1994.

64. *PM* (1940): 6 August, 1–2, 9; 8 August, 21; 15 August, 2; 16 August, 11; 26 August, 11; 24 October, 11; (1941): 24 April, 16–18; 25 April, 19; 28 April, 22; 12 September, 14; 14 September, 7; 15 September, 1, 9–10; 16 September, 10–11; 17 September, 11; 18 September, 1, 8–10; 19 September, 7; 22 September, 7; 23 September, 10; 26 September, 8; 2 October, 2–4; 3 October, 6–8; 9 October, 8; 12 October, 10; 31 December, 5.

65. Norman M. Littell, *My Roosevelt Years* (Seattle: University of Washington Press, 1987), 66.

66. Franklin Roosevelt, Personal Correspondence, *PM* File, Roosevelt Library.

67. *PM*, 8 May 1941, 7; (1942): 11 March, 13; 12 March, 11; 25 March, 15; 30 March, 1–10; 31 March, 1, 14–15; 1 April, 2; 6 April, 2–3; 9 April, 13; 15 April, 1–7, 22; 17 April, 2; 18 April, 2–6; 21 April, 6–8; 4 May, 14; 5 May, 3–7; 7 May, 10; 19 June, 5; 24 June, 19.

68. *New York Times*, 19 March 1941, 20.

69. *New York Herald Tribune* (1941): 7 March, 20; 8 March, 10; 14 March, 18; 19 March, 24; 25 March, 20. *New York Journal-American* (1941): 10 March, 18; 14 March, 16; 19 March, 18; 20 March, 16; 27 March, 16; 29 March, 6. *New York Post* (1941): 17 March, 14; 18 March, 10; 26 March, 14. *New York Times* (1941): 14 March, 20; 19 March, 20. *New York World-Telegram* (1941): 12 March, 26; 14 March, 26; 15 March, 14; 16 March, 16; 18 March, 18; 20 March, 20; 25 March, 18; 26 March, 22; 27 March, 22; 28 March, 25; 31 March, 16.

70. *PM* (1941): 15 January, 13; 21 March, 13; 24 March, 13; 25 March, 2; 23 April, 14; 20 May, 10; 12 June, 12; 19 June, 10; 20 June, 11.

71. Ibid. (1942): 10 June, 2–3; 15 June, 13; 16 June, 12; 17 June, 14; 21 June, 11.

72. *National Guardian*, 14 March 1963. *Daily News*, 31 May 1941, 13. For Hood and Bismarck, see ibid., 28 May 1941, 29; 29 May 1941, 19.

73. *New York Journal-American*, In the News, 23 May 1941, 1–2.

74. Ibid., 29 May 1941, 1–2.

75. *PM*, 15 June 1940, 9; 26 February 1941, 15; (1942): 19 April, 9; 28 April, 1, 4–7; 29 April, 1–11; 30 April, 1–7; 1 May, 1–5; 3 May, 2; 6 May, 8–11, 13; 14 May, 13; 21 May, 2–6; 22 May, 1–6; 23 May, 2–5; 23 May, 10; 26 May, 11; 27 May, 13; 28 May, 12; 29 May, 11; 9 July, 10; 12 July, 10; 3 August, 10; 4 August, 12; 6 August, 4–8; 7 August, 2–5; 9 August, 2; 10 August, 4–6; 11 August, 6–9; 19 August, 1–7; 7 September, 2–7; 9 May 1944, 8.

76. Weimer interview.

77. *PM* (1942): 10 August, 2–5; 11 August, 2–5; 12 August, 3; 13 August, 3; 14 August, 2–3; 16 August, 2–3; 17 August, 2; 18 August, 2.

78. Ibid., 21 December 1943, 2; 7 January 1944, 6; 1 February 1944, 5–8; 21 December 1944, 4; 20 February 1945, 3–4.

79. Ibid. (1944): 11 August, 6; 30 August, 12; 31 August, 8–9; 11 September, 9; 12 November, 6–7, 9; 18 December, 11–13; (1945): 15 April, 11; 16 April, 4; 18 April, 15; 19 April, 11; 23 April, 7; 24 April, 8; 25 April, 12–13; 26 April, 12–13; 27 April, 11–12, 30 April, 9, 24; 25 June, 7.

80. Ibid., 9 March 1944, 2.

81. Ibid. (1943): 31 January, 1–6; 14 February, 6–7; 7 March, 18.

82. Ibid. (1943): 27 January, 2; 2 February, 2; 1 November, 3–4; 2 December, 2; 6 December, 3–6; 7 December, 2; (1945): 8 January, 2; 13 February, 1–11; 9 March, 2.

83. Ibid. (1944): 3 August, 2–9; 11 August, 2–14; 13 August, Picture News, 10–11; 14 August, 9; 15 August, 12; 16 August, 14; 17 August, 18; 18 August, 12; 20 August, Picture News, 14–15; 22 August, 17; 23 August, 17.

84. Ibid., 2 April 1941, 23; 16 September 1942, 4.

85. Ibid. (1944): 1 February, 2; 21 September, 6; 26 September, 6; 4 October, 2; 17 November, 2.

86. Ibid. (1940): 10 July, 18; 17 July, 5; 21 July, 16–17.

87. Ibid. (1940): 25 July, 7; 29 July, 13; 7 August, 8; 22 August, 2; 15 October, 1, 16–17; 16 October, 1, 7–10; 29 October, 1, 9; 30 October, 8; 28 November, 14; 16 September 1942, 8–9.

88. Ibid., 4 August 1941, 14; 25 March 1942, 22.

89. Green, Kimball interviews; Penn Kimball, letter to author, 1 April 1944.

90. Sullivan interview.

91. Kimball interview, 21 April 1985.

92. Louise Levitas Henriksen, interview by author, New York City, 7 April 1994.

93. Kimball, McCleery interviews; Baker letters; Stewart, *News*, 232; idem, "The People," passim. Lewis's pieces on the letters page could not be more different than Ingersoll's. He could be aroused—usually on the subject of racism—but those infrequent editorials were kept distinct from his regular feature. Ingersoll never recognized any boundaries.

94. Weimer interview.

95. Ibid.; Green interview.

96. Weimer interview.

97. Eleanor Roosevelt papers, 1943 "W" File, Roosevelt Library.

98. Max Lerner papers, Sterling Library, Yale University; the story of "You'll never be a newspaperman" is in Lerner's introduction to Hoopes, *Ingersoll*. The difference between

Ingersoll and Lerner is apparent in the condition of their personal papers. Ingersoll's collection at Boston University is chaotic; one box labeled *"PM"* has nothing in it but childhood toys. Lerner saved and cataloged everything. Letters from correspondents who appear to be deranged are filed alphabetically and chronologically next to letters from Albert Einstein, Elizabeth Taylor, and Harold Ickes. Part of this may be a tribute to the careful work of Yale archivists, but Lerner's decision to save every piece of writing to and from him from his days as a graduate student is itself a fascinating comment on his mind and character. Morris interview.

99. Weimer interview.

100. Ibid.; Kenneth Stewart, "Interview with John P. Lewis for *PM-Star* Project," 23 May 1949, Stewart Collection, University of Wyoming.

101. Franklin Roosevelt, Personal Correspondence, *PM* File, Roosevelt Library.

102. *PM* (1940): 31 July, 13; 8 December, 13; 10 December, 7; 12 December, 7; 15 December, 8; 17 December, 9; (1941): 23 February, 12; 2 March, 6–7; 2 June, 7–11; 19 August 1942, 11; 18 October 1942, 6–7.

103. Leipzig interview. For a typical Ley piece, see *PM*, 9 January 1942, 20.

104. *PM* (1940): 22 December, 9; 23 December, 8; 24 December, 8; 27 December, 8; 29 December, 8; 3 January 1941, 7; 13 January 1941, 13.

105. Nelson Lichtenstein, *Labor's War at Home: The CIO in World War II* (Cambridge: Cambridge University Press, 1982), 269.

106. *New York Times*, 31 January 1941, 18.

107. *PM* (1941): 10 January, 1–3; 27 January, 13; 13 July, 18; 17 November, 5; 18 November, 5–8.

108. Ibid., 30 June 1941, 12–13; 2 September 1941, 1; 30 March 1943, 14–15.

109. Burns, *Soldier*, 176; Davis, *FDR: Into the Storm*, 412.

110. *PM*, 22 December 1941, 12; (1942): 5 March, 21; 25 March, 16–17; 7 June, 8; 16 June, 2–3.

111. Franklin Roosevelt, Personal Correspondence, *PM* File, Roosevelt Library.

112. *PM*, 2 April 1942, 21.

113. Ibid. (1942): 9 February, 21; 6 March, 2–4; 8 March, 2; 9 March, 11; 14 May, 1, 12; 28 May, 2–5.

114. Ibid. (1945): 12 January, 10–11; 14 January, 12; 26 January, 15.

115. Penn Kimball reported that the war caught *PM* with no foreign correspondents. The paper improvised well. Kimball interview, 21 May 1985.

116. Franklin Roosevelt, Personal Correspondence, Ben Robertson, Jr., file, Roosevelt Library.

117. Stewart, "The People," 78–82.

118. Leipzig interview.

119. *PM*, 26 August 1940, 5; 24 September 1940, 5; 11 November 1941, 3; 8 December 1941, 12, 16–17; 22 June 1942, 1–5; 23 June 1942, 2–4; 7 December 1942, 18; (1943): 6 April, 9; 27 April, 9; 10 May, 8; 19 May, 7; 16 June, 8; 19 July, 7.

120. Ibid. (1941): 7 April, 2, 6; 12 June, 2; 13 June, 4; 15 June, 4; 19 June, 4; 22 June, 18.

121. Ibid., 21 November 1941, 14–17; 13 February 1942, 21; 24 March 1942, 15; 31 March 1942, 15; 2 August 1943, 5; 8 September 1943, 7; 25 September 1943, 12; (1944): 16 April, 6; 11 June, 1, 10–11; 21 July, 11; 28 July, 4; 13 August, 3; 24 September, 3; 11 February 1945, 8.

122. Ibid., 1 September 1941, 1–32.

123. Ibid. (1944): 5 June, 1–8; 13–15; 6 June, 1–22, 24; 7 June, 1–22, 24; 8 June, 1–16; 9 June, 1, 3–8; 12 June, 1, 3–12; 13 June, 1–12; 14 June, 1–10; 15 June, 1, 3–10.

124. Ibid., 19 November 1940, 14.

125. Green interview; Robert A. Miller, *The Newspaper "PM," Inc.: Balance Sheets*, 1 November 1940 and 29 November 1940, *PM* papers, Harvard University.

126. *PM*, 22 December 1941, 14; (1942): 18 March, 1, 8, 14; 19 March, 10, 14; 22 March, 15; 23 March, 5; 26 March, 15, 6 July, 2–3.

127. The first date for each serialization in *PM* is, respectively, 2 January 1943; 11 May 1943, 11 July 1943, 24 November 1943, 2 January 1944, and 7 September 1943.

128. *PM* (1943): 5 January, 2–3; 6 January, 2–3; 8 January, 7; 9 January, 6; 11 January, 8; 12 January, 8; 14 January, 8; 15 January, 6; 17 January, 8.

129. Ibid. (1941): 27 January, 6–7; 30 January, 6–7; 31 January, 6–7; 1 February, 7; 5 February, 8; 6 February, 8.

130. Ibid., 10 June 1941, 4–5.

131. Ibid., 24 November 1941, 8–10; 19 February 1943, 11; 2 March 1943, 2–3, 18.

132. Ibid., 4 April 1943, 5; 25 April 1943, Picture News, 12; Alexander interview.

133. *PM* (1944): 20 October, 3–5; 30 October, 8; 21 November, 8; 12 December, 8–9; 8 July 1945, 2, 5; 25 July 1945, 4; Burns, *Soldier*, 540–544.

134. *PM* (1940): 10 November, 5; 11 November, 5; 12 November, 5; 13 November, 5; 14 November, 5.

135. Ibid. (1942): 5 November, 2–5; 6 November, 15–17, 8 November, 1–4, 16–17; 9 November, 8; (1943): 1 March, 12; 5 March, 2–3; 8 March, 3; 9 March, 7; 17 March, 6; 26 April, 8; 17 May, 9; (1944): 29 May, 2; 8 October, 4; 16 June, 11; 18 June, 5; 22 June, 10; 11 July, 5; 18 March 1945, 20.

136. Ibid., 26 December 1941, 2; 14 September 1942, 7; (1943): 22 January, 2; 24 January, 2–3; 27 January, 2; 28 January, 13; 31 January, 13; 2 February, 13; 26 February, 2–3; 4 April, 8–9; (1944): 9 February, 7; 16 March, 7; 29 May, 2, 6; 1 June, 8; 12 June, 2; 18 June, 2; 12 October, 4.

137. Stewart, *News*, 181.

138. *PM* (1941): 3 February, 1, 6–7; 6 March, 6–7; 1 April,4; 8 June, 6; 9 June, 4; 7 November, 13; 18 November, 13; 27 November, 12; (1942): 26 February, 12–13; 14 October, 2–4; 9 November, 18; 20 November, Picture News, 3–6; (1943): 10 October, 8; 25 October, 6; 4 November, 6; 14 November, 6; (1944): 22 February, 6; 25 February, 8–9; 28 February, 8; 5 March, 6, 8; 6 March, 6; 7 April, 7; 4 May, 7; 19 August, 5; 29 October, 3–4; 30 October, 12; 14 November, 9; 24 November, 8; 26 November, 3; 28 December, 2; (1945): 19 February, 8; 27 April, 7; 30 April, 2.

139. Davis, *FDR: Into the Storm*, 15–16, 30–31, 119–126, 249–251, 395–399. The quoted passage is on page 399.

140. *PM* (1944): 15 October, 3; 23 October, 3–4; 25 October, 7; 26 October, 2; 27 October, 7; 29 October, 3; 1 November, 8; 2 November, 8; 14 November, 2; 14 December, 9; 7 January 1945, 4; 17 April 1945, 9.

141. Ibid., 3 February 1941, 6–7; (1943): 18 January, 18; 28 February, 18; 1 March, 2; 3 March, 9; 7 June, 3; 8 June, 6; 9 June, 4; 11 June, 6; 12 November, 2; 26 December, 3; (1944): 21 January, 6; 6 February, 2, 6; 20 March, 2; 3 April, 8–9; 7 April, 7; 8 April, 2; 13 April, 8; 2 May, 6; 4 May, 7; 20 August, 2; 4 December, 8, 10; 30 April 1945, 2; 13 November 1945, 2–3.

142. Ibid. (1946): 29 January, 8; 28 February, 9; 1 March, 2; 5 April, 2; 12 April, 8; 18 April, 3; 21 April, 2; 5 May, 5; 4 June, 9; 9 June, 8.

143. Ibid. (1941): 3 February, 6–7; 4 February, 6–7; 25 February, 6–7; 26 February, 6; 4 March, 6; 17 May, 4; 8 June, 2; (1943): 21 April, 2; 29 July, 2; 1 September, 2; 14 September, 2; (1944): 1 January, 2; 6 February, 2; 28 February, 2; 15 March, 2; 27 March, 2; 21 May, 2; 23 August, 2.

144. Ibid. (1944): 5 December, 1, 3–4; 6 December, 3; 7 December, 1, 3–4; 10 December, 2–4; 11 December, 3; 12 December, 3; 13 December, 3; 14 December, 2–4; 15 Decem-

ber, 1–3; 17 December, 8; 18 December, 3; 19 December, 4, 19; 20 December, 2–4; 4 January 1945, 7.

145. Franklin Roosevelt, Personal Correspondence, *PM* File, Roosevelt Library.

146. *PM*, 10 August 1941, 4–9; 11 September 1941, 2; 12 July 1942, 2–4; 21 September 1943, 8; (1944): 2 January, 7; 12 January, 11–12; 23 April, 6–7; 24 April, 10–11; 15 May, 9; 16 May, 7; 26 May, 10; 30 May, 2; 31 May, 3–4.

147. Ibid (1940): 17 June, 4; 28 June, 2; 2 July, 5; 11 October, 2; 14 October, 3; 11 November, 6; (1941): 15 January, 5; 29 January, 8; 25 March, 7; 8 April, 6; 13 April, 6; 23 June, 18; 25 June, 5; 4 July, 2; 6 July, 4; 7 July, 6; 9 July, 5; 14 July, 6; 16 July, 4; 29 July, 1, 4; 19 August, 3.

148. Ibid., 19 August, 3; Franklin Roosevelt, Personal Correspondence, *PM* File, Roosevelt Library.

149. *PM* (1941): 21 September, 2; 24 September, 2; 16 October, 2, 4; 20 October, 4.

150. Ibid. (1941): 27 October, 1–7; 29 October, 6–8; 31 October, 5–9; 5 November, 6–7; 6 November, 6–7; 7 November, 7–10.

151. Ibid. (1942): 12 January, 22; 26 January, 22; 18 May, 13; 19 May, 2–3; 20 May, 3; 24 May, 14; 25 May, 16–17; 16 July, 18; 19 July, 16–17; 31 July, 16; 2 August, 14; 4 August, 13; 9 August, 13; 26 August, 18; 10 September, 3; 15 September, 18; 16 September, 18; 20 September, 13; 25 September, 14; 5 October, 16–17.

152. Ibid. (1943): 14 January, 3; 26 January, 15; 3 February, 14–15; 14 February, 14–15; 17 February, 3; 24 February, 15; 19 March, 9; 1 July, 9; 8 July, 7; 16 July, 7; (1944): 2 March, 2; 7 April, 2; 22 June, 9.

153. Ibid., 6 November 1941, 3; 14 November 1941, 6–8; (1942): 22 March Picture News, 3–4; 8 April, 2; 8 May, 20; 5 July, Picture News, 3–5; 12 July, 16–17; 15 July, 18; 23 July, 14; 30 July, 21; 17 August, 14; 31 August, 18; 17 September, 14; 27 September, 13; 28 September, 19; 27 October, 2–5; (1943): 23 February, 14–15; 17 March, 9; 11 April, 16–17; 16 April, 8; 13 May, 11–14; 30 May, 12; 22 June, 14–15; 27 June, 9; 2 August, 5; 23 August, 2; 26 August, 2; 5 September, 5; 9 September, 5, 12; 26 September, 12; 10 February 1944, 6.

154. Ibid. (1942): 27 September, 1–4; 29 September, 2; 2 October, 8; 5 October, 9; 23 October, 13; 1 November, 8. Harold Ickes to Donald Nelson, 30 September 1942, Franklin Roosevelt, Personal Correspondence, *PM* File, Roosevelt Library.

155. *PM*, 22 April, 1942, 1–5.

156. Ibid. (1943): 1 February, 2–6; 2 February, 18; 8 March, 2; 9 March, 2.

157. Ibid. (1943): 10 March, 2; 14 March, 2; 16 March, 2; 15 August, 2; 20 September, 2; (1944): 2 February, 2; 3 February, 2; 4 February, 2; 22 February, 6.

158. Ibid. (1943): 19 March, 17; 30 April, 20; 1 July, 2; 9 July, 17–18.

159. Ibid. (1943): 4 January, 2–3; 5 January, 2–3; 10 January, 21; 20 July, 21–22; 21 July, 3; 22 July, 4; (1944): 10 April, 12; 8 May, 7; 9 May, 2; 12 May, 8; 1 September, 2; (1945): 28 January, 12; 19 February, 2; 4 March, 3–4; 6 March, 2–3; 7 March, 8; 18 March, 6; 19 March, 2; 26 March, 2–3; 30 March, 6; 8 April, 10; 13 April, 5; 17 April, 10–11; 4 May, 3; 6 May, 5; 13 May, 2; 23 May, 8; 3 June, 2–3; 1 July, 1–3; 3 July, 2; 4 July, 3; 19 July, 2; 6 August, 2.

160. Ibid., 9 January 1944, 6–7; 3 December, 1944, 7; (1945): 11 April, 6; 18 April, 8; 15 June, 2; 20 July, 4; 22 July, 2–3; 23 July, 2; 24 July, 2; 29 July, 2–3; 13 August, 2–3, 7; 16 August, 2; 31 August, 2; 2 September, 3–5; 9 September, 8; 10 September, 1, 3–5; 11 September, 1–4; 12 September, 2–3, 5; 13 September, 2; 14 September, 1, 3.

161. Stewart, *News*, 317–319.

162. *PM*, 29 December 1942, 16; 22 March 1943, 12–13; 7 September 1943, 10–11; 23 October 1944, 10; 29 November 1944, 7; (1945): 26 January, 8; 20 February, 2; 21 February, 2; 22 February, 2; 23 February, 2; 21 March, 2; 16 April, 2; 13 May, 2–3; 8 June, 3;

13 June, 9–11; 30 August, 11–13; 8 October, 5; 29 November, 2; 9 December, 4; 12 December 3; (1946): 24 April, 2; 3 October, 8; 4 October, 2; 24 October, 11–13; 25 October, 10.

CHAPTER FOUR: LABOR'S CHAMPION

1. *PM*, 6 January, 1941, 13.

2. Ibid., 17 February 1941, 2.

3. Burns, *Lion*; Davis, *FDR: Into the Storm;* Leuchtenburg, *Roosevelt and the New Deal*; Lichtenstein, *Labor's War at Home*; Schlesinger, *Crisis of the Old Order;* idem, *Coming of the New Deal* idem, *Politics of Upheaval*; Tugwell, *Democratic Roosevelt*; Irving Bernstein, *The Lean Years: A History of the American Worker, 1920–1933* (Boston: Houghton Mifflin, 1960); idem, *Turbulent Years: A History of the American Worker, 1933–1941* (Boston: Houghton Mifflin, 1970); Melvyn Dubofsky and Stephen Burwood (eds.), *The Great Depression and the New Deal: Labor* (New York: Garland, 1990); Melvyn Dubofsky and Warren Van Tine, *John L. Lewis: A Biography* (Urbana: University of Illinois Press, 1986); Steve Fraser and Gary Gerstle (Editors), *The Rise and Fall of the New Deal Order, 1930–1980* (Princeton: Princeton University Press, 1989); Steve Fraser, *Labor Will Rule: Sidney Hillman and the Rise of American Labor* (New York: Free Press, 1991); Charles P. Larrowe, *Harry Bridges: The Rise and Fall of Radical Labor in the United States* (New York: Lawrence Hill and Co., 1972); Sidney Lens, *Left, Right and Center: Conflicting Forces in American Labor* (Hinsdale, IU.: Henry Regnery, 1949); George Martin, *Madam Secretary: Frances Perkins* (Boston: Houghton Mifflin, 1976).

4. *Newspaper*, 26 April 1939, 8–9.

5. Cited by Davis, *FDR: Into the Storm*, 91.

6. Dubofsky and Van Tine, *Lewis*, passim; Bernstein, *Turbulent Years*, 363–368, 390–392, 419–427, 435–441, 470–472, 534–544, 714–722.

7. *PM* (1940): 16 June, 22; 19 June, 15, 22; 21 June, 14; 23 June, 15; 15 July, 15; 16 July, 15; 17 July, 14; 18 July, 15; 31 July, 14; 7 August, 15; 13 August, 13; 24 October, 10; 25 October, 10; 28 October, 10; 29 October, 12; 1 November, 2; 5 November, 10; 13 November, 10; 17 November, 11; 20 November, 10, 12, 19–21; 2 December, 10; 3 December, 12; 4 December, 9; 6 December, 11.

8. Green, Kimball, McCleery interviews; Baker letters; Sullivan interview. *PM* (1941): 15 January, 13; 17 January, 14; 19 January, 15; 21 January, 15; 30 January, 26; 16 February, 2; 25 April, 5. Ingersoll memoranda to the Newspaper Guild (1941): 14 January, 16 January, 30 January, in *PM* papers, Harvard University; Stewart, "The People," 49–54; Wechsler, *Age*, 163–168.

9. Berger interview.

10. *PM* (1941): 26 October, 18; 28 October, 14; 30 October, 21; 30 October, 19; 10 November, 15; 12 November, 19; 13 November, 5, 21; 17 November, 14–15; 18 November, 18–19; 19 November, 18, 20; 20 November, 18–19; 23 November, 10; 1 December, 8; 9 December, 11; (1942): 20 January, 3; 22 January, 3; 20 February, 10; 16 March, 11; 24 March, 12; 12 May, 11; 15 May, 11; 27 May, 12; 29 May, 13; 5 June, 9; 28 June, 9.

11. *PM* (1940): 11 September, 13–16; 12 September, 13; 13 September, 13; 14 September, 13- 15; 17 September, 13; 18 September, 10; 19 September, 10; 2 October, 11; 10 October, 11; 3 November, 13.

12. Ibid. (1940): 26 July, 12; 24 September, 10; 25 September, 10; 4 November, 10; 14 November, 11; 5 February 1941, 20.

13. *New York Times*, 10 April 1941, 22, repeated verbatim 15 April 1941, 22.

14. *New York Herald Tribune*, 1 April 1941, 20.

15. *New York Sun* (1941): 1 April, 22; 2 April, 24; 3 April, 24; 8 April, 22, 17 April, 20; 18 April 22; *New York Journal-American*, 16 May 1941, 16; 29 May 1941, 12.

16. *New York World-Telegram*, 2 April 1941, 25.

17. Ibid., 21 April 1941, 16.

18. *PM*, 9 December 1940, 11; (1941): 31 January, 21; 11 March, 9; 18 June, 20; 31 July, 18; 2 December, 18; 4 December, 1, 10, 21; 5 December, 19; (1942): 8 February, 11, 12; 15 February, 11; 25 February, 11; 17 March, 10–11; 12 May, 11; 14 May, 14; 15 May, 3–6; 17 May, 10; 20 May, 14; 21 June, 1–6; 1 July, 3–6; 4 October, 10; (1944): 17 April, 2–6; 26 May, 3–4; 2 June, 3.

19. Ibid. (1943): 6 January, 10; 8 January, 5; 18 January, 11; 21 January, 2; 26 February, 9; 4 March, 10; 7 March, 9; 16 March, 4; 18 March, 3; 25 March, 2; 28 March, Picture News, 1, 3–8; 30 March, 5; 4 April, 3; 26 April, 3; 28 April, 4, 13; 29 April, 3; 30 April, 4; 2 May, 1–4, 13; 3 May, 1–5, 13–15; 5 May, 20; 7 May, 3, 5; 10 May, 5; 12 May, 3; 31 May, 5; 1 June, 6; 2 June, 3; 3 June, 3; 6 June, 4; (1944): 22 May, 5; 28 May, 6; 3 July, 4; 13 September, 14; 14 September, 13; 20 September, 15.

20. *Daily Worker*, 25 May 1943, 5.

21. Ibid., 29 May 1943, 5.

22. *PM* (1941): 20 February, 10–11; 21 February, 16–17; 23 February, 16–17; 24 February, 16–17; 26 February, 18–19; 7 March, 20; 14 March, 20.

23. *New York Herald Tribune* (1941): 4 March, 20; 5 March, 20; 8 March, 10; 15 March, 10; 17 March, 22; 21 March, 20; 22 March, 10; 26 March, 24; 27 March, 22; 28 March, 20; 29 March, 14. *New York Journal-American*, 1 March 1941, 6; 15 March 1941, 6. *New York Times* (1941): 15 March, 16; 20 March, 20; 27 March, 22; 30 March, E3, E8. *New York World-Telegram* (1941): 1 March, 14, 15; 4 March, 17; 5 March, 26; 6 March, 10; 8 March, 14; 10 March, 13; 11 March, 17; 13 March, 23; 14 March, 25; 15 March, 14; 19 March, 26; 20 March, 22; 24 March, 15; 25 March, 17; 27 March, 21, 22; 28 March, 25, 26; 31 March, 16. *New York Post*, 7 April 1941, 12.

24. *PM* (1940): 19 November, 9; 24 November, 9; 26 November, 5; 27 November, 9; 29 November, 6, 9; 9 December, 2; 19 December, 13.

25. Ibid. (1941): 28 March, 19; 29 March, 1, 19; 1 April, 18; 2 April, 16–18; 3 April, 14, 19; 7 April, 19.

26. *New York Journal-American*, 29 March 1941, 6. *New York World-Telegram*, 19 March 1941, 26.

27. *PM* (1941): 9 June, 19; 10 June, 13–17; 11 June, 12–15; 24 June, 11; 2 July, 21; 3 July, 15; 8 July, 19; 4 August, 20; 6 August, 12; 12 August, 19.

28. Weimer interview.

29. Sullivan interview.

30. Berger, Green, Kimball, Sullivan interviews; Baker letters; Stewart, *News*, 240–241; idem, "The People," 21–24.

31. Wechsler, *Age*, 162. The charges about *PM*'s treatment of the defense strikes were first made by Wechsler in a two-part postmortem he wrote for the *Progressive* ("The Life and Death of *PM*"), March 1949, 9–12; April 1949, 15–17. A reader of those articles or *The Age of Suspicion* would have been astounded to know that the most frequent and most eloquent spokesperson for defense workers in the pages of *PM* was James A. Wechsler.

32. Lichtenstein, *Labor's War at Home*, 53–63.

33. *PM*, 22 December 1940, 9; 23 December 1940, 8.

34. Bernstein, *Turbulent Years*, 570–571, 657–659, 734–751.

35. Green interview.

36. *PM* (1940): 19 December, 13; 20 December, 12; 22 December, 13; 29 December, 1, 7, 13–15; 30 December, 8, 14–15; 31 December, 16–17; (1941): 9 January, 10; 13 January, 2; 17 January, 16; 31 January, 13; 3 February, 15; 4 February, 18; 21 February, 7; 25 Febru-

ary, 20; 9 March, 1, 19; 11 March, 18; 25 March, 19; 26 March, 19; 3 April, 1, 13–17; 4 April, 18, 20; 6 April, 18–19; 7 April, 18–19; 8 April, 13, 15; 9 April, 19; 10 April, 12; 11 April, 14; 13 April, 20; 17 April, 20; 4 May, 9; 20 May, 13.

37. Kimball interview, 21 February 1994.

38. Morris interview.

39. *PM* (1941): 26 January, 18; 27 January, 17; 10 February, 19–21; 11 February, 18–20; 12 February, 18–19; 16 February, 18; 25 February, 20; 26 February, 20; 27 February, 21; 28 February, 18; 2 March, 18; 25 March, 18; 26 March, 18; 28 March, 1–2, 18; 6 April, 20; 7 April, 9; 8 April, 15; 16 May, 18.

40. *New York Daily News*, 11 March 1941, 31. *New York Daily Mirror*, 11 March 1941, 23. *New York Herald Tribune* (1941): 11 March, 22; 12 March, 24; 13 March, 22; 18 March, 22; 21 March, 20; 23 March, 8. *New York Journal-American*, 18 March 1941, 14; 22 March 1941, 6. *New York Post* (1941): 11 March, 10; 12 March, 14; 13 March, 10; 18 March, 10; 21 March, 14; 25 March, 10; 31 March 10. *New York Sun*, 11 March 1941, 9. *New York Times* (1941): 12 March, 20; 18 March, 22; 22 March, 14. *New York World-Telegram* (1941): 11 March, 8; 20 March, 22; 24 March, 16.

41. *PM* (1941): 9 March, 19; 10 March, 1, 18–20; 12 March, 1, 11–14 ; 13 March, 12–14; 14 March, 13–14, 18–20; 16 March, 1, 18–19; 17 March, 1, 18–20; 18 March, 1, 18–20; 19 March, 1, 12–13; 21 March, 1, 2, 18–19; 25 March, 20; 31 March, 21; 4 April, 20; 9 April, 18; 10 April, 12; 15 April, 19–20; 16 April, 18, 18 April, 19; 20 April, 1; 23 April, 1, 13; 24 April, 10–12; 25 April, 6, 11–12; 28 April, 6–7; 29 April, 6–7; 30 April, 6–7; 1 May, 7; 2 May, 6; 10 May, 13; 12 May, 12; 13 May, 21; 14 May, 20; 15 May, 18; 19 May, 13; 20 May, 15; 21 May, 13; 22 May, 18–20; 8 June, 20; 17 June, 19–20; 24 June, 19, 21; 26 June, 13, 18, 19; 27 June, 18; 29 June, 6, 15, 19, 20.

42. Ibid., 12 May 1941, 12; 26 May 1941, 20; 2 July 1941, 20; 17 December 1942, 17; 24 December 1942, 16; (1943): 1 January, 8; 6 January, 17; 7 January, 17; 26 January, 16; 10 February, 16; 10 December 1944, 11.

43. Joshua B. Freeman: *In Transit: The Transport Workers Union in New York City, 1933–1966* (New York: Oxford University Press, 1989), 212.

44. Ibid., 213–214.

45. Ibid., 218–223; Wechsler, *Age*, 170–171. For an extended analysis of Wechsler's appearance before the McCarthy committee, see Victor Navasky, *Naming Names* (New York: Viking, 1980), 58–68.

46. *PM* (1942): 8 June, 19; 18 June, 18; 25 June, 19; (1943): 26 March, 3; 28 March, 2; 30 March, 3; 1 April, 13; 2 April, 10; 4 April, 10; 6 April, 10; 7 April, 11; 12 April, 11; 13 April, 12.

47. Green, Kimball interviews.

48. Schlesinger, *Politics of Upheaval*, 206; Larrowe, *Harry Bridges*, 104, 106.

49. *PM*, 14 June 1940, 15; 21 June 1940, 15; 17 July 1940, 15; (1941): 17 February, 20; 31 March, 21; 25 August, 14–15; 29 August, 19; 4 September, 12–13; 10 September, 14; 30 September, 13; 5 December, 12; (1942): 6 January, 4; 29 May, 2–4; 31 May, 2; 2 June, 2–4; 3 June, 22; 11 June, 10.

50. Ibid. (1940): 27 June, 15; 6 August,15; 7 August, 14; 21 August, 10; 26 August, 10; 10 September, 18; 17 September, 12; 19 September, 19; 4 December, 9; (1941): 8 June, 12; 17 June, 9.

51. Ibid. (1941): 4 February, 18; 24 March, 18; 21 May, 2; 10 October, 13; 5 October, 12; (1942): 18 October, 19; 25 November, 18; 14 December, 12; 2 July 1943, 3; 13 November 1944, 2; 3 December 1944, 11.

52. Ibid., 22 December 1943, 2.

53. Ibid., 5 January 1941, 3; 18 January, 44–45; (1942): 15 February, 5; 24 February, 10; 26 February, 13; 1 March, 11; 18 March, 12; 20 March, 1, 12–13; 22 March, 9–10;

23 March, 11; 24 March, 11; 25 March, 11; 17 April, 13; 1 May, 12; 5 May, 14; 10 May, 11; 20 May, 11; 23 May, 8; 9 June, 18; 10 June, 10; 26 June, 11; 30 June, 9; 2 July, 10; 5 July, 19; 10 July, 10; 12 July, 12; 17 July, 9; 19 July, 10; 20 July, 1–2; 21 July, 10; 28 July, 11; 5 August, 14; 6 August, 14; 20 August, 10; 23 August, 10; 4 September, 12; 7 September, 10; 16 September, 11; 29 September, 13; 29 October, 4–5; 5 November, 14; 8 November, 9; 8 December, 13; 15 December, 2–3; 17 December, 8; 22 December, 18; 25 December, 11; 30 December, 7; (1943): 29 January, 2–3; 22 February, 17; 23 March, 3; 25 March, 3; 30 March, 3; 28 April, 3; 29 April, 4; 7 May, 5; 10 May, 5; 26 May, 2; 17 November, 3; (1944): 27 January, 4; 14 February, 3; 12 March, 3–4; 28 March, 6–8; 24 May, 12.

54. Ibid. (1944): 16 July, 3; 2 August, 10; 3 August, 8–13; 4 August, 2–4; 5 August, 3–5; 7 August, 3–4.

55. Ibid., 1 December 1942, 9; (1944): 14 April, 3; 23 April, 2; 1 May, 1–5 (page 1 headline: "Montgomery Ward's War against the Nation"); 5 May, 4–5; 7 May, 6; 17 May, 5; 21 May, 5; 29 May, 3; 30 May, 4; 20 July, 15; 13 December, 6; 14 December, 5; 15 December, 6; 24 December, 10; 26 December, 7; 29 December, 9; 5 January 1945, 10.

56. Ibid. (1944): 21 November, 14; 22 November, 9; 23 November, 8; 24 November, 10; 3 December, 14; (1945): 3 January, 16; 25 January, 12; 16 January, 11.

57. Lichtenstein, *Labor's War at Home*, 178–202.

58. *PM* (1944): 23 May, 15; 24 May, 12; 25 May, 6; 29 May, 11; 30 May, 13–14; 31 May, 12–14; 1 June, 11, 14; 2 June, 2, 11; 14 June, 6; 15 June, 15; 25 June, 2; 17 June, 15.

59. Ibid. (1944): 9 August, 1–7; 14 November, 5; 24 November, 2; (1945): 8 March, 2–3; 13 March, 6; 18 May, 8; 3 June, 10; 4 June, 2; 5 June, 2–5; 13 June, 4; 22 June, 14; 2 July, 8; 3 July, 10; 12 August, 11; 13 August, 7; 30 August, 14.

60. Leipzig interview.

61. *PM*, daily, 1–18 July 1945, 10–13; Boyce, Hughes, and Farrell, *The Newspaper "PM,"* *PM* papers, Boston University.

CHAPTER FIVE: CRUSADING AGAINST PREJUDICE

1. A. J. Liebling, "The Wayward Press," *New Yorker*, 12 February 1949, 53–58.

2. Gold, *Jews without Money*; Howe, *World of Our Fathers*; Kazin, *Walker in the City*; More, *At Home in America*; Nathan C. Belth, *A Promise to Keep: A Narrative of the American Encounter with Anti-Semitism* (New York: Schocken Books, 1979); C. Bezalel Sherman, *The Jew within American Society* (Detroit: Wayne State University Press, 1965); Arthur Mann, *La Guardia: A Fighter against His Times* (Philadelphia: Lippincott, 1959), 150–158.

3. Badger, *New Deal*; Burns, *Lion*; Leuchtenburg, *Roosevelt and the New Deal;* James Baldwin, "The Harlem Ghetto," in *Notes of a Native Son* (Boston: Beacon, 1955), 57–72; Barton J. Bernstein, "The New Deal: The Conservative Achievements of Liberal Reform," in idem (ed.), *Towards a New Past: Dissenting Essays in American History* (New York: Vintage, 1969), 278–281; W.E.B. Du Bois, *The Crisis Writings* (Greenwich: Fawcett, 1972); idem, *Against Racism: Unpublished Essays, Papers, Addresses, 1887–1961* (Amherst: University of Massachusetts Press, 1985); Joanne Grant (ed.), *Black Protest: History, Documents, and Analyses, 1619 to the Present* (Greenwich: Fawcett, 1968), 175–250; Charles E. Silberman, *Crisis in Black and White* (New York: Random House, 1964); Howard Zinn (ed.), *New Deal Thought* (Indianapolis: Bobbs-Merrill, 1966), 309–353.

4. For Nazi and other European violence against Jews, see *PM*, 18 September 1940, 5; (1941): 19 September, 4; 1 October, 7; 9 November, 4; (1942): 17 March, 18; 18 May, 14; 12 November, 19; 25 November, 1, 13; 26 November, 12; 9 December 1, 18–19; (1943): 19 January, 6; 15 February, 19; 2 March, 4–5; 3 March, 18; 10 March, 14–15; 25 May, 7;

18 June, 6; 27 August, 12–13; 29 September, 9; 24 November, 7; (1944): 30 January, 7; 9 April, 12; 18 April, 11; 20 April, 10; 9 May, 8; 6 July, 9; 11 August, 6; 30 August, 12; 31 August, 8–9; 11 September, 9; 13 October, 6; 12 November, 6–7; 18 December, 11–13; (1945): 15 April, 11; 16 April, 4; 18 April, 15; 19 April, 11; 23 April, 7; 24 April, 8; 25 April, 12–13; 26 April, 12–13; 27 April, 11–12; 30 April, 9, 24; 4 May, 6; 25 June, 7; 5 July, 6; 2 October, 1–2; 30 December, 2; 23 August 1946, 7. On racial violence against southern blacks, see *PM*, 28 November 1940, 9; 20 December 1940, 10; (1941): 15 August, 10; 25 August, 12; 1 October 13; (1942): 12 January, 4; 21 January, 4; 1 July, 13; 9 August, Picture News, 6; 31 July, 14; 6 August, 6; 30 August, 9; 9 September, 2–8; 10 September, 8; 28 October, 2–4; 22 November, 12; 14 July 1943, 11; 15 July 1943, 3; (1944): 26 April, 9; 16 July, 6; 7 December, 12; 24 June 1945, 13; 12 July 1945, 9; (1946): 1 March, 3; 6 May, 9; 20 August, 13.

5. *PM* (1941): 10 August, 12; 11 August, 11; 12 August, 11; 10 October, 9; 31 May 1943, 4.

6. Ibid., 22 August 1940, 6; (1941): 9 February, 14; 10 February, 7; 6 May, 19; 8 May, 8–9; 6 August, 12; 31 October, 12; 30 November, 11; (1942): 5 January, 4; 9 April, 1, 9; 15 June, 8–9; 23 July, 19; 10 December, 2–3; 29 May 1943, 11; 4 October 1943, 13; (1944): 20 March, 3–4; 21 March, 3–4; 3 April, 6; 12 July, 16; 20 October, 11; 22 October, 15; 21 December, 12; 29 December, 14; (1945): 21 January, 12; 5 March, 20; 3 April, 9; 19 April, 5; 24 June, 13; 27 June 9; 30 June, 4.

7. Ibid. (1944): 16 April, 11; 31 July, 6; 21 September, 10; 22 September, 7; 13 November, 10; (1945): 1 January, 3; 4 January, 20; 7 January, 2; 10 April, 8; 10 June, 8; 11 June, 11; 11 July, 6.

8. Ibid., 5 October 1942, 2; 27 November 1942, 18.

9. Ibid. (1942): 16 February, 13; 31 March, 12; 6 April, 13; 8 April, 12; 9 April, 14.

10. Ibid. (1943): 8 September, 4; 28 September, 5; 30 September, 4; 7 October, 5; 8 October, 2–3; 10 October, 3; 11 October, 6; 14 October, 5; 15 October, 2; 18 October, 3; 26 October, 3; 14 November, 4.

11. Ibid., 28 July 1940, 12; 29 July 1940, 4; 4 February 1941, 14; 5 August 1941, 15; (1942): 3 May, 19; 18 May, 4–5; 15 June, 1–3; 16 June, 4; 18 June, 20; 19 June, 5; 25 June, 19; 21 September, 20; 23 September, 19; 25 September, 19; 14 October, 7; 16 November, 2–3; 25 November, 7; (1943): 23 March, 12; 6 June, 11; 21 June, 2; 1 October, 12–13; 27 October, 14–15; 29 October, 12–13; 31 October, 2; 30 December, 8–10; 31 December, 9; (1944): 2 January, 12–13; 11 January, 11–12; 14 January, 2; 17 January, 8; 7 February, 9; 14 February, 9; 23 April, 13; 15 October, 8; 16 October, 15.

12. Ibid., 15 July 1940, 13; 16 January 1941, 1, 18; 20 January 1941, 14.

13. Ibid., 23 June 1940, 23; (1942): 16 January, 18; 26 March, 2; 27 March, 2; 29 March, 2; 1 April, 22; 15 April, 13; 16 April, 16; 4 May, 3–7; 5 May, 22; 11 May, 2–3; 14 May, 21; 15 May, 1, 20–21; 18 May, 19–20; 20 May, 10; 21 May, 22; 22 May, 22; 29 May, 20; 31 May, 6; 1 June, 20–21; 4 June, 20–21; 5 June, 20; 12 June, 21; 17 June, 22; 18 June, 20; 23 June, 20; 26 June, 21; 29 June, 19; 1 July, 21; 7 July, 22; 31 January, 1943, 16; 2 June 1946, 11.

14. John A. Sullivan says Ingersoll, "was given to crusades" (Sullivan telephone interview). Penn Kimball strenuously objected to my assessment. Still reflecting his own commitment to being "against people who push other people around," Kimball told me, "If you're gonna fight the bastards, you've got to fight 'em with everything you've got" (Kimball interview, 21 February 1994).

15. *PM* (1943): 18 October, 5; 19 October, 3–5; 20 October, 4–5; 22 October, 5; 11 November, 3. *New York Post*, 20 October 1943, 5.

16. *PM* (1942): 1 March, 10; 2 March, 12; 9 March, 9; 30 April, 10; (1943): 22 June, 1, 3, 12–13; 23 June, 2, 10–19; 25 June, 2, 11; 27 June, 3–5; 28 June, 3–5; 29 June, 12–13;

2 July, 2; 23 July, 10; 28 July, 3; 29 July, 6; 1 August, 3; 12 August, 5; 20 August, 5; 24 October, 3; 29 October, 4; 31 October, 7.

17. Ibid. (1943): 24 June, 2; 4 July, 2; 2 August, 2, 10, 12–15; 3 August, 2 (double-size print); 4 August, 12; 5 August, 2; 16 August, 12–13; 20 August, 2.

18. Ibid. (1941): 20 March, 20; 1 April, 20–21; 2 April, 20; 20 April, 1, 20; 21 May, 14; 31 October, 18; 2 November, 19; 9 November, 18; 12 November, 12–13; 13 November, 8; 14 November, 13; 2 December, 11; 3 December, 10; (1942): 3 February, 19; 4 February, 20; 23 February, 6; 23 April, 18; 26 May, 21; 6 January 1943, 17; (1944): 13 January, 10; 3 February, 11; 15 December, 11; (1945): 5 February, 12; 24 May, 11; 28 May, 12; 17 August, 12; 15 October, 8; 16 October, 15.

19. Ibid. (1942): 17 July, 30; 19 July, 29; 28 July, 30; 31 July, 30; 3 August, 30; 30 January 1943, 3; (1945): 18 March, 14; 1 October, 23; 25 October, 13; 7 April 1946, 14.

20. Ibid., 31 February 1941, 14; (1942): 9 January, 15; 29 January, 20; 3 March, 20; 20 May, 21; 15 January 1943, 2.

21. Ibid., 10 June 1943, 11; 13 June 1943, 11.

22. Ibid. (1943): 10 September, 10; 12 September, 10; 14 September, 12–13; 16 September, 10; 17 September, 10; 20 September, 9; 24 September, 10; 29 September, 16; 1 October, 9; 5 October, 11; 10 October, 16; 12 October, 1, 10; 13 October, 11; 19 October, 12; 21 October, 2; 24 December, 11; *New York Post*, (1943): 12 September, 8; 14 September, 6; 15 September, 4; 17 September, 8; 21 September, 4; 29 September, 4; 30 September, 14; 5 October, 16; 6 October, 18; 13 October, 4; 18 October, 4. *New York Times*, (1943): 10 September, 25; 24 September, 19; 30 September, 42; 1 October, 36; 2 October, 9; 4 October, 25; 5 October, 30; 12 October, 29; 19 October, 21. Theodore M. Berry to Thurgood Marshall, Box B-145, Folder on Hillburn Correspondence, NAACP Collection, Library of Congress.

23. *PM* (1945): 30 January, 11; 31 January, 12; 8 February, 9; 2 March, 16; 8 April, 9; 19 April, 12; 20 August, 7; (1946): 24 January, 9; 25 January, 2; 27 January, 13; 1 February, 9, 13; 20 March, 12; 17 March, 12; 14 April, 10; 19 May, 10; 2 July, 14; 23 October, 14.

24. Ibid. (1940): 10 October, 9; 13 October, 10; 22 October, 9; 26 December, 12; (1941): 20 January, 14; 8 May, 8; 12 May, 13; 14 May, 20; 15 May, 19; 16 May, 20; 16 June, 21; 17 June, 19; 18 June, 8; 26 June, 19; 30 June, 20; 2 July, 21; (1942): 20 January, 4; 1 February, 11; 3 February, 13; 18 February, 19; 14 April, 19; 16 April, 22; 20 September, 18; 1 October, 15; 5 October, 2; 8 October, 2; 18 October, 18; 21 October, 18; 29 October, 20; 13 November, 20; 23 November, 12; (1943): 31 January, 10; 29 June, 11; 19 July, 3; 27 July, 3; (1944): 3 February, 10; 4 February, 9; 27 November, 13; 29 November, 9.

25. Louis Ruchames, *Race, Jobs and Politics: The Story of FEPC* (New York: Columbia University Press, 1953), 21.

26. Ibid., 63. *PM*, 17 September 1943, 4.

27. *PM* (1942): 15 April, 11; 27 May, 21; 23 November, 12; (1943): 11 January, 12; 12 January, 10, 22; 13 January, 12; 14 January, 11; 15 January, 11; 17 January, 6–7; 19 January, 8; 20 January, 8; 21 January, 8; 22 January, 8; 25 January, 10; 31 January, 8; 12 March, 11; 5 September, 9; 10 September, 8; 17 September, 4; 28 October, 5; 29 October, 3; 4 November, 3; 14 December, 4; 15 December, 3; 16 December, 4; 22 December, 2; 28 December, 3.

28. Ibid. (1944): 12 June, 15; 13 June, 13; 21 June, 12; 18 July, 4; 17 July, 5; 24 November, 12; 30 November, 8; (1945): 26 April, 14; 27 April, 14; 18 May, 8; 3 June, 12; 5 June, 11; 7 June, 8; 17 June, 8; 20 June, 6, 24; 26 June, 24; 28 June, 5; 30 June, 1, 4; 1 July, 11; 2 July, 7; 3 July, 9; 4 July, 9; 5 July, 8; 10 July, 5; 13 July, 7; 18 July, 8; 19 October, 3; 17 December, 4–5; (1946): 13 January, 8; 23 January, 6; 3 February, 2; 5 February, 1–3; 7 February, 3; 11 February, 3; 1 July, 8.

29. Ibid. (1944): 9 March, 12; 10 March, 11; 12 March, 13; 17 March, 14; 19 March, 11;

23 March, 10; 27 March, 9–10; 15 November, 10; 29 November, 12; 3 December, 23; (1945): 9 January, 11; 29 January, 11; 9 February, 12; 13 February, 12; 15 February, 11; 16 February, 9; 18 February, 13; 19 February, 11; 21 February, 15; 28 February 11; 6 March, 12; 15 March, 11; 18 March, 5; 20 March, 12; 24 July, 9; 21 March 1946, 9.

30. Ibid. (1942): 23 August, Picture News, 25–27; 11 September, 11; 13 November, 11; (1945): 5 August, 10; 6 August, 6; 7 August, 14; 8 August, 10; 24 August, 2; 1 November, 3; (1946): 5 July, 7; 28 July, 4; 29 July, 3; 5 August, 2–4; 8 August, 10–13.

31. Ibid. (1942): 9 August, Picture News, 6; 9 September, 2–8; 10 September, 8; 28 October, 2–4; 31 December, 9; (1943): 3 June, 11; 13 September, 9; 16 September, 4; (1944): 31 March, 16; 4 May, 3; 1 June, 4; 11 June, 12; 5 July, 3–4; 6 July, 4; 8 October, 9–10; 17 October, 9; 27 October, 10; 5 November, 6; (1945): 12 February, 7; 15 February, 9; 13 May, Picture News, 12–15; 20 May, Picture News, 12–14; 27 May, Picture News, 12–14; 3 March 1946, 7. Leipzig interview.

32. *PM* (1941): 29 January, 10; 20 March, 9; 21 March, 9; 22 March, 10; (1942): 13 March, 21; 13 May, 8; 2 July, 1–3; 12 September, 12; 9 October, 4–5; 13 October, 12; 14 October, 10; 15 October, 2; 18 October, 2–3; 20 October, 10; 27 October, 13; 2 November, 8; 4 November, 13; 15 November, 12; 17 November, 12; 18 November, 9; 19 November, 1–2; 20 November, 2–3; 22 November, 2; 24 November, 10; 25 November, 21; (1943): 7 March, 7; 7 May, 3; 24 May, 5; 25 May, 4; 26 May, 5; 17 October, 3–5; (1944): 4 April, 3; 12 April, 3; 12 May, 2–3; 17 May, 2; (1945): 21 January, 11; 24 January, 9; 26 February, 1; 27 February, 2; 22 October, 2.

33. Ibid. (1941): 4 August, 10; 1 December, 20; 10 December, 14; 8 December, 11; 9 December, 9, 11; 14 December, 42–50; (1942): 1 January, 4; 11 March, 15; 13 February, 21; 5 April, Picture News, 15; 21 June, Picture News, 25; 27 December, 16; (1944): 28 April, 14; 2 May, 10; 10 May, 11; 11 May, 11; 23 May, Picture News, 9; 12 September, 17; 26 September, 8–10; 31 December, 10; (1945): 15 January, 6; 25 February, 11; 22 April, 24; 29 April, 8.

34. Ibid., 13 February 1942, 10; 30 March 1943, 13.

35. Ralph Bunche, *The Political Status of the Negro in the Age of FDR* (Chicago: University of Chicago Press, 1973); Walter A. Jackson, *Gunnar Myrdal and America's Conscience: Social Engineering and Racial Liberalism, 1938–1987* (Chapel Hill: University of North Carolina Press, 1990); Mark Naison, *Communists in Harlem during the Depression* (Urbana: University of Illinois Press, 1983); Ruchames, *Race, Jobs and Politics*; Harvard Sitkoff, *A New Deal for Blacks: The Emergence of Civil Rights as a National Issue—The Depression Decade* (New York: Oxford, 1978); Raymond Wolters, *Negroes and the Great Depression* (Westport, Conn.: Greenwood Press, 1970).

36. *PM*, 25 August 1944, 2; 27 August 1944, 2; 6 November 1944, 9; Burns, *Lion*, 198, 214, 285; idem, *Soldier*, 124, 264, 265, 421, 431, 462–466; B. J. Bernstein, *Towards a New Past*, 278–282; Eleanor Roosevelt, Personal Correspondence, 1944 "W" File, Roosevelt Library.

37. Walter White, "U.S. Department of (White) Justice," in Zinn, *New Deal Thought*, 331–344; W.E.B. Du Bois, "For the Reelection of Franklin Delano Roosevelt," in idem, *Against Racism*, 253–254; National Negro Congress, "The Call," in Grant, *Black Protest*, 240–243.

CHAPTER SIX: VOICE OF THE NEW DEAL

1. Stone's conversation with Sidney Elsner, Cleveland stringer for *PM*, in the fall of 1944, recounted in Sidney Elsner, letter to author, undated, (late December 1993).

2. Burns, *Lion*, 153–157, 165–288 passim; Schlesinger, *Crisis of the Old Order*, 145–269 passim; idem, *Coming of the New Deal*, 68–84, 136–151, 282–419; idem, *Politics of Upheaval*, 325–443; Tugwell, *Democratic Roosevelt*, 270–497 passim.

3. Fath interview.

4. Lerner papers, Yale University; Eleanor Roosevelt, Personal Correspondence, 1943 "W" file, Roosevelt Library; Franklin Roosevelt, Personal Correspondence, *PM* File, Roosevelt Library.

5. *PM* (1940): 21 June, 6, 8; 23 June, 7; 25 June, 1, 6; 27 June, 6–7.

6. Ibid. (1940): 14 July, 1, 8; 15 July, 18; 16 July, 8; 17 July, 6; 18 July, 6; 19 July, 6; 21 July, 8.

7. Ibid., 17 July 1940, 6; Burns, *Lion*, 426–430; Davis, *FDR: Into the Storm*, 593–603.

8. *PM* (1940): 1 August, 9; 25 August, 2; 27 August, 6; 29 August, 2; 17 September, 2; 27 September, 8; 29 September, 7, 33–39; 4 October, 1; 14 October, 2, 6; 18 October, 7; 21 October, 7; 22 October, 7; 23 October, 7; 29 October, 9–11, 15–17; 30 October, 1–2; 1 November, 1, 7–8; 3 November, 2; 4 November, 7.

9. Ibid. (1940): 6 November, 1–6; 10 November, 8; 28 November, 6; 12 December, 8; 19 December, 8–9; 26 December, 7; (1941): 7 January, 2, 7; 9 January, 10; 10 January, 12–13; 15 January, 6; 16 January, 11; 21 January, 9; 31 January, 21; 7 February, 7; 24 February, 6; 5 March, 20; 6 March, 8; 7 March, 8; 8 March, 1–2, 9; 11 March, 9; 30 March, 9; 21 April, 10; 4 June, 12; 18 June, 10; 1 July, 9; 3 July, 11; 7 July, 21; 9 July, 20; 16 July, 12; 31 July, 13; 28 August, 14; 14 September, 10; 19 September, 9; 26 September, 9; 29 September, 8; 7 October, 11; 11 November, 12; 10 December, 6; 30 January 1942, 14.

10. Ibid. (1942): 8 January, 2, 22; 4 February, 14; 8 February, 11–12; 11 February, 15; 15 February, 11–12; 18 February, 11; 20 February, 11; 25 February, 11; 27 February, 12; 1 March, 11; 10 March, 12; 17 March, 10–11; 18 March, 11; 29 March, 12; 12 April, 11; 21 April, 13, 21; 28 April, 12, 21; 12 May, 11; 14 May, 14; 17 May, 10; 20 May, 14; 27 May, 2; 1 June, 1–6; 1 July, 3–6; 9 July, 13; 9 August, 20; 7 September, 17; 23 September, 2–4, 6–8, 21; 30 September, 2–5; 2 October, 2–5; 4 October, 11; 6 October, 13; 7 October, 14; 27 October, 2; 1 November 20, Picture News, 3–5; 3 November, 11; 4 November, 1, 3, 21; 5 November, 12; 10 November, 11; 2 December, 2; 11 December, 10; 14 December, 11.

11. Ibid. (1942): 3 December, 11; 6 December, 19; 27 December, 9; (1943): 24 January, Picture News, 1–11, 28; 31 January, 18; 8 February, 8; 11 February, 3–4; 6 April, 3–4; 9 April, 3; 14 April, 2; 17 May, 2; 18 June, 4; 2 July, 2; 18 July, 1, 3; 19 July, 2; 20 July, 3, 6; 25 July, 2; 18 August, 4; 25 August, 3–5; 29 August, 3; 3 September, 2; 13 September, 2; 27 September, 2–3; 4 October, 3; 8 October, 4; 31 October, 3.

12. Ibid. (1943): 3 September, 2; 5 November, 2; 8 November, 4; 29 December, 2–3; (1944): 2 January, 2; 26 January, 2; 20 February, 3–6; 24 February, 1–3, 7–8; 25 February, 4; 27 February, 1, 3–4, 29 February, 2; 5 March, 2; 8 March, 4; 20 March, 11; 21 March, 10; 4 April, 6; 6 April, 1–2; 14 April, 2; 4 May, 3; 7 May, 1–3; 9 May, 3–4; 16 May, 3; 23 June, 2.

13. Berger, Henriksen, Leipzig interviews.

14. *PM* (1944): 26 January, 2; 25 June, 3–5; 26 June, 3; 28 June, 3–5; 29 June, 2; 2 July, 2–3. Burns, *Soldier*, 501–503.

15. *PM* (1944): 2 May, 2; 18 July, 3, 5; 20 July, 4; 21 July, 3–4; 23 July, 11–12; 1 September, 11; Lerner papers, Yale University; Wallace papers, Roosevelt Library.

16. *PM* (1944): 3 September, 3; 19 September, 12–13; 22 September, 14–15; 25 September, 13; 1 October, 2; 2 October, 12, 14, 17; 3 October, 17; 4 October, 10; 6 October, 1–4, 12, 17; 8 October, 2; 9 October, 1, 2, 8–13; 10 October, 2, 16, 17; 11 October, 17; 12 October, 15, 17, 23; 13 October, 2; 15 October, 8; 17 October, 9–10; 18 October, 10–11; 19 October, 16, 24; 20 October, 13–14; 22 October, 19, Picture News, 2–4; 23 October, 2–5; 24 October, 2; 26 October, 1–2; 27 October, 12–15; 29 October, 1, 10–11; 31 October,

3; 1 November, 6; 2 November, 2–3; 3 November, 2; 5 November, 2; 6 November, 13; 8 November, 1. Franklin Roosevelt, Personal Correspondence, *PM* File, Roosevelt Library; Burns, *Soldier*, 521–532.

17. *PM*, 28 November 1944, 2; 4 December 1944; 1–4; (1945): 10 January, 13–14; 11 January, 11; 14 January, 9; 22 January, 2; 13 April, 1–20, 24; 15 April, 2, 8; 16 April, 9–15; 17 April, 3, 8–10.

18. A. B. Magil, "*PM* and the Communists," *New Masses*, 11 April 1944, 15–17; Eleanor Roosevelt, Personal Correspondence, 1944 "B" File, Roosevelt Library.

19. Oliver Wendell Holmes's assessment, on meeting FDR just before his first inauguration, cited effectively by Burns, *Lion*, 157.

CHAPTER SEVEN: CRUSADING IN THE POSTWAR WORLD

1. Frank Capra (producer), *Mr. Smith Goes to Washington* (Los Angeles: Columbia Pictures, 1939), screenplay by Sidney Buchman, from a Lewis R. Foster story; directed by Frank Capra.

2. Rae Weimer, telephone interviews by author, Gainesville, Florida, 16 April 1994 and 3 May 1994; Berger interview; Max Lerner letter to James Wechsler, 14 December 1945, in Lerner papers, Yale University; Lerner's introduction to Hoopes, *Ingersoll*; *PM* papers, Harvard University; Hoopes, *Ingersoll*, 311–332.

3. *PM* (1942): 20 December, 2–3; 21 December, 8–9; 22 December, 8; (1943): 11 May, 2; 12 May, 2; 28 July, 2; 30 July, 6; (1944): 7 May, 2; 29 May, 2; 28 November, 5; 6 December, 8; 24 December, 4; (1945): 2 January, 3; 15 May, 2; 3 July, 4; 27 July, 1–3, 6.

4. Ibid. (1944): 30 May, 2; 6 October, 8; 25 October, 8; 1 December, 6; 5 December, 8; 6 December, 7–8; 7 December, 9; 8 December, 10; 11 December, 2; 31 December, 2; (1945): 8 January, 5; 8 March, 9; 22 April, 6; 17 June, 6; 25 June, 6; 19 July, 4; 5 August, 7; 2 September, 7; (1946): 4 February, 8; 5 February, 7–8; 7 February, 6; 2 April, 8; 12 June, 2; 16 June, 7–8; 17 June, 7; 2 September, 6, 8–9; 3 September, 9; 15 September, 8.

5. Ibid., 8 October 1944, 4–5; 16 October 1944, 6; (1945): 3 January, 1, 3; 4 January, 2; 8 January, 5; 14 January, 3; 12 March, 2; 1 April, 2–3; 14 May, 2; 22 August, 2; 23 August, 2; 23 September, 3; 22 July 1946, 7; 4 August 1946, 2.

6. Ibid. (1943): 14 March, 2; 18 March, 16–17; 27 April, 2; (1944): 26 July, 10; 18 September, 10; 30 November, 6; 24 December, 5; (1945): 1 January, 8; 11 March, 5; 15 March, 10; 29 March, 6; 17 April, 17; 23 April, 2; 25 April, 3; 6 May, 6; 7 May, 2; 14 May, 3; 16 May, 11; 17 May, 2; 31 May, 2–3; 1 June, 2–3; 3 June, 7; 18 June, 4; 21 June, 10; 22 June, 2; 17 September, 5–6; 31 October, 11; 7 November, 15; 30 December, 2; (1946): 27 May, 6; 7 June, 2; 10 July, 2; 19 July, 2; 3 November, 2.

7. Ibid., 15 March 1943, 2; (1945): 4 May, 2; 6 May, 2; 22 May, 2; 26 August, 6–7; 4 September, 6; 24 September, 2–3; 21 October, 1–3; 2 November, 8; (1946): 15 January, 2; 5 March, 2; 6 March, 1–2; 7 March, 5; 10 March, 1, 5; 26 March, 2; 28 April, 2; 3 June, 2.

8. Ibid. (1945): 7 August, 1–12, 23; 10 August, 3; 12 September, 10; 18 October, 2–4; 22 October, 2, 7; 28 October, 4; 29 October, 2; 15 November, 8; 16 November, 3–4; (1946): 25 January, 2; 7 March, 4; 8 March, 3; 10 March, 8; 13 May, 8; 3 July, 2; 19 August, 5.

9. Ibid., 14 August 1940, 6; 9 December 1943, 12–13; (1944): 1 October, 9; 5 October, 5; 11 December, 2; (1945): 27 April, 6; 1 May, 3; 30 May, 7; 13 June, 12–13; 26 August, 6; 30 September, 7, 10–11; 12 November, 6; 2 December, 3; 9 December, 11; (1946): 22 January, 11; 11 February, 7; 24 February, 10; 28 February, 2; 17 March, 2–3; 20 March, 1–2, 6; 5 April, 5; 17 May, 6; 27 August, 2.

10. Ibid., 23 August 1944, 2; (1945): 8 June, 2, 10; 11 June, 2; 14 August, 5; 15 August,

10; 16 August, 7; 18 August, 7; 22 August, 4; 24 August, 3; 29 August, 2, 4; 4 September, 6; 10 September, 2; 5 October, 4; 24 October, 7; 29 October, 3; 31 October, 6; 1 November, 1, 8–9; 8 November, 5; 11 November, 9–11; 13 November, 6; 14 November, 5; 18 November, 9; 28 November, 3; 2 December, 3; 19 December, 5; 23 December, 8–9; 26 December, 3; (1946): 11 January, 11; 15 March, 5; 15 April, 5; 22 April, 4; 8 May, 7; 10 July, 8; 12 July, 8; 28 July, 2; 11 August, 2; 14 August, 8; 20 August, 9; 27 August, 2, 9; 27 October, 11.

11. Ibid. (1945): 15 April, 5–6; 17 April, 2–3; 18 April, 2–3; 19 April, 4; 22 April, 2; 27 May, 4; 8 June, 7; 31 August, 7; 6 September, 7; 7 September, 2–7; 9 September, 2; 13 September, 7; 23 September, 1, 8; 24 September, 7; 26 September, 2; 27 September, 2–3; 28 September, 6; 30 September, 2–3; 7 October, 3; 25 October, 2; 28 October, 2–3; 4 November, 3; 17 December, 2–3; 25 January 1946, 3.

12. Lerner letter to Wechsler, Lerner papers, Yale University.

13. *PM* (1945): 5 September, 7–8; 9 September, 6; 10 September, 9.

14. Ibid. (1945): 23 October, 5; 24 October, 4; 26 October, 3; 28 October, 3; 31 October, 2–5; 4 November, 5; 11 November, 10; 18 November, 6; 23 November, 2; 28 November, 2; 5 December, 2, 9; 6 December, 3; 13 December, 2–3; 19 December, 2; (1946): 7 January, 2; 8 January, 3; 11 January, 3; 13 January, 3; 14 January, 2; 17 January, 3; 18 January, 3; 20 January, 7; 21 January, 2; 23 January, 2; 25 January, 2; 27 January, 2; 1 February, 2; 6 February, 8–9; 10 February, 12; 13 February, 8; 14 February, 11–13.

15. Ibid. (1946): 20 February, 10; 21 February, 2; 24 February, 12; 25 February, 9; 26 February, 2–3, 13; 27 February, 3–4; 3 March, 10; 13 March 10; 16 April, 9; 17 April, 4; 18 April, 12; 19 April, 9–11.

16. Ibid. (1946): 18 March, 4; 22 March, 2; 2 May, 7; 7 May, 2; 9 May, 2–3; 10 May, 4; 12 May, 4, 13; 22 May, 2.

17. Ibid. (1946): 24 May, 1–11; 26 May, 1, 4–7, 9; 27 May, 2–3; 28 May,1–3; 29 May, 2–3; 30 May, 3–5; 31 May, 3–4; 2 June, 5; 3 June, 4–5; 5 June, 2–3.

18. Ibid. (1946): 11 July, 3–6; 21 August, 14; 6 September, 13; 8 September, 9–10; 11 September, 2–3; 12 September, 5; 17 September, 2, 9; 18 September, 11–13; 1 October, 10; 2 October, 11.

19. Weimer and Fath interviews; Ingersoll's letter to Marshall Field and memo to John P. Lewis, Lewis's memo to Ingersoll, and Virginia Schoales's evaluation of the staff are in the *PM* papers, Harvard University. See also Lerner's letter to Wechsler; Lerner's introduction to Hoopes, *Ingersoll*; Stewart, "The People," 89–118; *Editor and Publisher*, 22 June 1946, 54; *New York Times*, 15 June 1946; Wechsler, "The Life and Death of *PM*: II. The Editor Who Thought He Was God," *Progressive* (April 1949), 15–17.

20. *PM* (1941): 8 May, 17; 10 June, 8–10; 26 November, 3; 27 November, 2; 28 November, 6; (1942): 23 January, 4; 3 February, 18; 26 June, 2; 18 November, 18; (1943): 18 January, 18; 11 February, 13; 18 March, 6; 2 April, 8; 19 April, 14–15; 12 August, 8; 2 September, 9; (1944): 31 March, 2; 14 May, 7; 17 May, 8; 2 August, 2; 12 November, 11; (1945): 16 January, 7; 15 March, 2; 23 March, 7; 11 April, 8; 21 September, 9; 1 October, 2; 2 October, 3; 10 October, 7; 11 October, 4; 12 October, 7; 15 October, 3; 17 October, 19; 19 October, 6; 22 October, 3; 23 October, 7; 24 October, 2; 8 November, 2; 11 November, 2; 13 November, 4; 14 November, 2; 15 November, 3; 27 November, 8; 4 December, 5–6; 5 December, 5–6; 11 December, 7; 24 December, 8–9; (1946): 3 January, 2; 4 January, 9; 6 January, 2; 10 January, 9; 30 January, 8; 28 March, 6; 1 May, 1–4; 2 May, 3; 3 May, 3; 13 June, 2, 12–13; 17 June, 2; 19 June, 7; 30 July, 2; 13 August, 6; 14 August, 6; 15 August, 2, 7; 19 August, 2; 25 August, 6; 30 August, 7; 4 September, 3; 10 October, 12–13.

21. Ibid. (1946): 22 July, 3–4; 23 July, 3–4; 24 July, 3–4; 25 July, 8–9; 26 July, 8–9; 28 July, 10; 29 July, 10; 30 July, 9; 31 July, 7; 1 August, 8; 2 August, 9; 4 August, 8; 5 August, 11; 6 August, 9; 7 August, 15; 8 August, 4; 9 August, 9; 11 August, 9; 12 August, 8; 13 August, 7; 14 August, 7; 15 August, 8; 16 August, 7; 18 August, 8; 19 August, 7; 20 August, 7;

21 August, 7–8; 22 August, 9; 23 August 5; 25 August, 5; 26 August, 8; 27 August, 6–7; 28 August, 2.

22. Ibid., 18 June 1946, section 2.

23. Weimer interview.

24. *PM* (1946): 10 February, 2, 6; 14 February, 2–5, 23; 15 February, 2; 20 February, 4; 22 February, 2; 10 March, 9; 13 March, 2; 20 March, 7; 24 March, 10; 25 March, 8; 2 April, 2; 14 April, 11; 16 April, 2; 15 April, 2; 31 May, 2; 4 June, 1–2; 10 June, 4; 26 June, 2; 27 June, 2; 28 June, 2; 18 July, 2, 9; 11 August, 9–11; 15 August, 5; 16 August, 3; 18 August, 2, 4, 5, 12; 29 August, 2; 6 September, 2; 10 September, 3; 13 September, 1–4; 15 September, 2; 16 September, 1–3; 17 September, 3; 18 September, 1–7; 19 September, 1–2, 5; 20 September, 2; 22 September, 1–3, 5, 10–11, Picture News, 6; 23 September, 2; 24 September, 2–3; 30 September, 3–4.

25. Weimer interviews; Stewart, "The People," 123–128; *PM*, 5 November 1946, 1–2; 7 November 1946, 11.

CHAPTER EIGHT: EPILOGUE

1. *PM*, 8 November 1946, 3.

2. Ibid., 7 November 1946, 11.

3. Ibid., 19 September 1947, 5.

4. Ibid. (1947): 7 January, 3; 9 January, 3; 12 January, 5; 14 January, 3; 15 January, 3; 24 January, 2; 29 January, 4; 30 January, 2; 31 January, 2; 5 February, 2; 9 February, 6; 25 February, 2; 5 March, 1–2; 14 March, 11; 28 March, 3, 9; 8 April, 2–6, 12–13; 14 April, 4; 18 April, 5; 19 April, 2; 20 April, 6; 21 April, 2; 22 April, 2; 9 May, 3; 15 May, 2; 2 June, 2; 4 June, 1–5; 5 June, 14–15; 9 June, 5; 10 June, 2–6; 11 June, 14–18; 12 June, 13; 22 June, 4–6; 23 June, 3; 24 June, 3–4; 26 June, 2; 27 June, 3; 29 June, 3; 9 July, 2; 7 September, 8.

5. Ibid. (1947): 3 January, 5; 5 January, 2; 23 January, 5; 27 January, 3; 2 February, 2, 4–5; 9 February, 5; 11 February, 2–3; 13 February, 3; 14 February, 3; 17 February, 2–4; 18 February, 2–3; 20 February, 2–3; 6 March, 21; 12 March, 2–3; 20 March, 4; 23 March, 2–3; 30 March, 3; 8 April, 14; 11 April, 2; 4 May, 2; 27 June, 3; 2 July, 2; 3 July, 2; 10 July, 2–4; 18 July, 2; 21 July, 3; 27 August, 4; 31 August, 2, 4; 5 September, 3; 11 September, 10; 17 October, 2; 20 October, 3; 21 October, 2–3; 22 October, 1–2, 4; 23 October, 10; 24 October, 2, 3, 5, 10; 26 October, 4, 20; 27 October, 13, 24; 28 October, 1–4, 7; 29 October, 1–3, 5; 30 October, 1–3; 31 October, 1–3; 3 November, 4; 4 November, 4; 5 November, 6–7; 9 November, 40; 10 November, 4; 11 November, 22; 12 November, 6; 14 November, 2, 12; 20 November, 1, 2; 21 November, 10; 25 November, 1, 2; 26 November, 1–2, 10; 27 November, 1, 4, 14; 9 December, 10; 11 December, 10; 23 December, 11; 26 December, 10; 29 December, 6; 30 December, 2; (1948): 1 January, 10; 4 January, 13; 2 February, 3; 11 February, 4; 4 March, 10; 6 March, 16; 11 April, 2, Picture News, 15; 18 April, 13; 23 April, 12; 2 May, 16; 3 May, 10; 7 May, 10; 9 May, 2; 19 May, 10; 20 May, 10; 21 May, 10; 29 May, 5; 30 May, 12; 6 June, 16. *New York Star* (1948): 8 July, 1, 4; 21 July, 1–3; 22 July, 2, 12; 26 July, 11; 30 July, 8; 3 August, 12; 4 August, 13; 5 August, 13; 6 August, 10–11; 8 August, 17; 9 August, 11; 12 August, 11; 13 August, 10; 16 August, 11; 18 August 1–5, 14, 18, 19; 22 August, 16; 29 August, 1, 4; 30 August, 10; 5 September, 1, 6; 10 September, 10; 12 September, 10; 27 September, 10; 30 September, 13; 5 October, 10.

6. *PM* (1947): 7 January, 24; 19 January, 2; 3 February, 3; 20 July, 6; 2 November, 11, 16, Picture News, 1–24; (1948): 3 February 1, 3–4; 5 February, 3; 9 February, 1, 3–4; 17 February, 11. *New York Star*, 28 July 1948, 12.

7. *PM* (1947): 24 February, 2, 7; 25 February, 6; 26 February, 6; 27 February, 1, 7; 28 February, 6; 2 March, 5; 3 March, 7; 5 March, 7; 6 March, 7; 7 March, 3; 9 March, 4–5; 10 March, 7; 12 March, 7; 14 March, 8; 17 March, 7; 18 March, 6; 19 March, 7; 20 March, 7; 21 March, 7; 23 March, 8; 24 March, 7; 25 March, 7; 26 March, 6; 27 March, 7; 28 March, 6; 1 April, 8; 4 April, 7; 7 April, 7; 9 April, 9; 10 April, 8; 21 April, 6; 23 April, 2, 7; 24 April, 6; 25 April, 7; 28 April, 8; 5 May, 2; 12 May, 2, 3; 16 May, 2; 13 July, 4; 20 July, 8; 27 July, 2; 3 August, 2; 24 August, 2; 9 September, 10; 10 September, 10; 27 September, 2; 6 October, 10; 13 October, 8; 3 November, 12; 5 December, 12; 19 December, 10; (1948): 6 January, 10; 7 January, 10; 14 January, 1, 7; 28 January, 4; 13 February, 4, 9; 15 February, 3; 22 February, 16; 26 February, 12; 27 February, 10; 2 March, 10; 5 March, 10; 6 March, 2; 12 March, 3; 20 March, 3–4, 10; 22 March, 10; 25 March, 12; 26 March, 10, 12; 23 April, 1, 2, 12; 24 April, 10; 28 April, 10; 16 May, 4; 17 May, 3; 18 May, 4, 10; 19 May, 3; 21 May, 2; 22 May, 3; 24 May, 2; 25 May, 3, 10; 26 May, 2, 3; 27 May, 3; 28 May, 3–4; 30 May, 3; 31 May, 6; 3 June, 3; 4 June, 3; 6 June, 2; 13 June, 2; 14 June, 2; 15 June, 4; 17 June, 4.

8. Ibid. (1947): 13 January, 2; 20 January, 2; 12 February, 2; 4 March, 2; 10 March, 2; 13 March, 2–3; 14 March, 1–3; 16 March, 2; 17 March, 2, 8; 18 March, 2; 28 March, 2; 7 April, 3; 14 April, 7; 16 April, 2; 20 April, 3; 21 April, 2; 29 April, 2–3; 8 May, 2–4; 8 June, 3; 9 June, 2; 12 June, 2; 17 June, 2–3; 24 June 2–4; 1 July, 2; 6 July, 2–3; 11 July, 2; 15 July, 2; 17 July, 2; 20 July, 20; 22 July, 2; 4 August, 5; 8 August, 2; 13 August, 2; 3 September, 2–3; 4 September, 2–3; 5 September, 2; 10 September, 7; 14 September, 10; 15 September, 10; 17 September, 10; 20 September, 12; 21 September, 10; 22 September, 3, 6; 24 September, 2; 26 September, 10; 29 September, 10; 30 September, 10; 1 October, 12; 4 October, 12; 7 October, 10; 8 October, 6; 24 October, 10; 11 November, 1–2; 12 November, 4; 13 November, 14; 14 November, 12; 16 November, 17; 19 November, 3; 23 November, 17; 10 December, 10; 15 December, 2; 17 December, 10; 22 December, 10; (1948): 11 January, 16; 15 January, 10; 18 January, 16; 23 January, 3; 24 January, 3; 28 January, 10; 8 February, 3; 11 February, 10; 12 February, 10; 13 February, 12; 23 February, 10; 9 March, 2; 14 March, 3; 18 March, 3, 10–11; 28 March, 16; 1 April, 10, 11; 5 April, 10; 27 April, 10; 7 June, 10.

9. Ibid. (1947): 15 April, 2, 7; 6 May, 2–3; 24 June, 2–4; 1 July, 2; 7 July, 2–3; 15 July, 2; 30 July, 7; 22 August, 2; 2 September, 2, 7; 21 September, 10; 22 September, 6; 1 October, 12; 6 October, 8, 9; 8 October, 6, 10; 13 November, 14; 19 November, 3; 27 November, 10; 2 December, 10; 17 December, 10; (1948): 1 January, 11; 28 January, 10; 24 February, 6–7, 10; 25 February, 1–3; 27 February, 6; 1 March, 10; 3 March, 10; 8 March, 10; 11 March, 1–6, 11; 28 May, 5.

10. Ibid. (1947): 6 January, 4; 9 January, 2–3; 23 January, 2, 3; 14 March, 1, 3; 14 April, 7; 15 April, 2, 6; 16 April, 7; 23 May, 2; 28 May, 2; 15 June, 3; 20 June, 2–3; 18 August, 10; 12 September, 1, 12, 24; 9 October, 14; 31 October, 10; 11 December, 4; 18 December, 12, 15; 23 December, 11; 28 December, 3; 30 December, 3–5, 10; (1948): 1 January, 10–11; 2 January, 10; 6 January, 3; 7 January, 4, 11; 8 January, 4; 9 January, 3; 22 January, 7, 9; 1 February, 16–17, 32; 2 February, 3, 10; 8 February, 10; 9 February, 10; 12 February, 5; 22 February, 5; 15 March, 11; 18 March, 11; 23 March, 10; 24 March, 1; 25 March, 1; 26 March, 1; 28 March, 1, 10; 30 March, 1; 31 March, 2; 1 April, 2; 2 April, 2; 8 April, 10; 21 April, 10; 22 April, 11; 6 May, 10; 17 May, 10; 25 May, 9; 30 May, 10; 15 June, 10. *New York Star*, 25 August 1948, 13. Max Lerner, letters to Glen Taylor, 28 April 1947 and 29 December 1947, Lerner papers, Yale University.

11. Leipzig, Weimer interviews; Stewart, "The People," 141–160; Boyce, Hughes, and Farrell, *The Newspaper "PM,"* 30 December 1946, 28 December 1947, 30 June 1948, in *PM* papers, Harvard University; Becker, *Marshall Field*, 398–402; *PM* (1948): 15 March, 2; 16 March, 2; 18 March, 2; 19 March 2; 9 April, 2; 14 April, 2; 29 April, 1; 2 May, 1; 20 June, 1; 22 June, 1. *New York Star*, 23 June 1948, 1.

12. *New York Star* (1948): 6 July, 11; 7 July, 14, 15; 8 July, 19; 12 July, 12; 14 July, 13;

15 July, 12; 16 July, 8; 18 July, 17; 21 July, 1–3; 18; 22 July, 12, 13; 23 July, 8; 25 July, 1, 6–8, 17, 26 July, 10–13; 27 July, 13; 28 July, 12; 29 July, 13; 9 August, 10; 25 August, 13; 30 August, 11; 2 September, 11; 7 September, 10; 8 September, 10; 12 September, 11; 27 September, 11; 4 October, 10; 5 October, 11; 6 October, 13; 7 October, 1, 2, 11; 10 October, 10, 11; 12 October, 11; 15 October, 11; 17 October, 14; 18 October, 12; 22 October, 15; 27 October, 15, 17; 29 October, 11; 31 October, 15; 4 November, 14; 5 November, 13; 21 January 1949, 15.

13. *New York Star*, 19 October 1948, 11–15; 20 October 1948, 6, 7; 24 October 1948, 1; 27 October 1948, 16; 28 January 1949, 1, 2. Stewart, "The People," 164; Green interview; Jim Russell, telephone interview by author, Oakland, California, 10 May 1994.

14. *Daily Compass*, 16 May 1949, 12; 27 July 1952, 10. *New York Times*, 27 January 1952, 14; 23 May 1952, 10; 25 July 1952, 18; Kimball interview; Hoopes, *Ingersoll*, 350–363.

15. Postcard to author from an unidentified Midwestern fan of *PM*, December 1993.

16. Weimer interview.

17. Cottrell, *Izzy*, 174–294; Stone, quoted by Stewart, "The People," 165.

INDEX

ABOUT THE AUTHOR

Paul Milkman was educated in the New York City public schools, at the City College of New York, Hunter College, and Rutgers University, where he received his Ph.D. in history in 1994. A teacher since 1972, he has taught history at Rutgers, John Jay College of Criminal Justice, and Long Island University. He is currently a teacher of English at Midwood High School. Director of Camp Thoreau from 1979 to 1989, he is now a project director for the American Jewish Society for Service, which brings teenagers to work as volunteers building or improving low-income housing in cooperation with nonprofit organizations throughout the United States. Milkman lives in Brooklyn with his wife, Catherine, and his three children, Rebecca, Jesse, and Caitlyn.